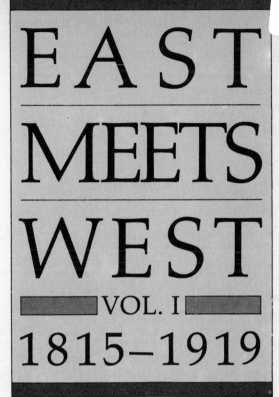

EAST MEETS WEST

VOL. I
1815–1919

A.C. Morales

Published 1986

ISBN 962 03 0254 0

Published by
MACMILLAN PUBLISHERS (HK) LTD
19/F, Warwick House
Taikoo Trading Estate
Quarry Bay
Hong Kong

Companies and representatives throughout the world

Printed in Hong Kong

Acknowledgements

The author and publishers wish to thank the following for permission to reproduce illustrations in the book:

BBC Hulton Picture Library   pp. 4, 10, 11, 29 (below), 42, 56, 68, 90, 98, 109, 125, 129, 138, 161 (above), 169, 173, 185, 186, 209, 210, 232 (below), 233, 234, 236 (below), 238, 239, 240, 244, 254

Bettmann Archive, Inc.   pp. 23, 261

Culver Pictures, Inc.   p. 237

Hong Kong Museum of Art   cover and pp. 81, 86, 87, 96

Illustrated London News   p. 177

International Communication Agency   p. 253

International Society for Educational Information, Tokyo   pp. 153, 156, 172, 194

Mansell Collection   pp. 8, 14, 16, 24, 29 (above), 31, 32, 33, 38, 53, 57, 60, 67, 70, 73, 97, 108, 112, 120, 123, 126, 127, 142, 144, 145, 167, 196 (above), 212, 229, 232 (above), 236 (above), 255, 259

Meiji Shrine, Tokyo   pp. 161 (below), 165, 168, 175, 196

Punch   pp. 15, 47, 65, 187, 188, 208, 214, 218, 219

Victoria and Albert Museum   p. 44

Every effort has been made to trace copyright but in the event of any accidental infringement, we shall be pleased to come to a suitable arrangement with the rightful owner.

Contents

Maps

Preface

This book is the first of a two-volume history of Asia and the West in the 19th and 20th centuries. It covers the period from 1815, when the Congress of Vienna resumed its work after Napoleon's defeat at Waterloo, to 1919 when the victorious powers in the First World War laid down the terms of the peace settlement.

The aim of this book is to provide students with material covering fully the first half of Section B of the new Hong Kong Certificate of Education History syllabus for senior secondary forms (Forms 4-5). It is also useful for GCE History examination candidates and as an introductory text for Forms 6-7 students sitting for the HKU Advanced Level Examination in History. However, I like to think that it is more than just an examination textbook. It could be of use to the general reader who wishes to obtain background knowledge of the times in which he lives.

The book uses a general as well as a nation-by-nation approach. At the same time, it uses an analytical rather than a narrative and descriptive approach in order to give the reader a better understanding of why the events discussed took place. In other words, the approach is one of cause and effect rather than a mere enumeration of facts.

To facilitiate the understanding of the text, there are numerous illustrations, maps, charts and sub-headings. 'Quotation boxes' provide a considerable amount of original source material without distracting the reader's attention from the main flow of events. 'Looking Back', which comes at the end of each chapter, provides a summary of the chapter and a perspective. Revision questions can also be found at the end of each chapter. There is a list of books for further reading for those who may wish to acquire more detailed information on the period covered by the book.

With the worldwide acceptance of a different system of spelling Chinese names in English, called Pinyin, to replace the traditional Wade-Giles system of romanization, this book has followed suit by using Pinyin. Readers who might be confused by the changeover should refer to the glossary at the end of the book.

In the preparation of this book, I am greatly indebted to so many previous writers on the subject and to so many of my friends and colleagues that detailed acknowledgements are impossible.

Alberto C. Morales
MA (HKU)
Hong Kong, 1985

Introduction

The 19th century has been described as a century of conflict.

In Europe in the first half of the 19th century, there was a bitter struggle in the political sphere between the reactionaries and the liberals and the nationalists. A struggle for political power also developed between the new and wealthy middle class and the old privileged classes.

In the second half of the 19th century, there was a fierce conflict in the economic sphere between capital and labour, with the socialists demanding better treatment of industrial workers. In the religious and intellectual spheres, there was a clash between the clericals and the anticlericals, with the state challenging the authority of the Catholic Church.

In Asia, the Westerners came in increasing numbers, challenging China's claim to being the cultural centre of the world and Japan's policy of isolation. China responded to the Western challenge first through the use of force, then through conciliation and finally through self-strengthening. Japan at first wanted to keep her doors closed to foreigners, but in the end she abandoned her policy of seclusion. To prevent further foreign penetration, she strengthened herself through modernization, mainly by imitating Western methods, but without sacrificing her traditional beliefs and institutions.

At the same time, the 19th century was a glorious age of democracy, social reform and scientific achievement which gave the peoples of Europe much hope for a better life. As parliamentary government developed, royal absolutism declined. Inspired by nationalist feeling, people demanded the right to govern themselves and to keep their way of life. Successful revolutions resulted in the rise of nation states in Europe.

Rapid industrialization led to an increase in material goods which improved the standard of living. The many new inventions enabled people to live more comfortably. Scientific progress brought more diseases under control. Advances in technology created new industries and new products. Growing industries made cities rich and brought wealth and luxury to the middle class. Social legislation improved the living conditions of the industrial workers. The new imperialism brought wealth and power to the colonial powers.

Thus, in spite of the disturbances, the 19th century was a golden age of progress and prosperity which led people in the West to expect an ever-rising standard of living. This optimistic feeling was shattered in the first half of the 20th century by the two most destructive wars in history, the First and Second World Wars.

In East Asia, the later years of the 19th century saw the continued weakening of China and the rise of Japan as a world power. China's weakness invited further foreign pressure, as seen in the 'scramble for concessions'. The ineffective Qing dynasty was finally overthrown in 1911. But the new Chinese Republic was no more successful in ridding the country of the foreign powers. Japan, however, succeeded in strengthening herself against the foreign threat. She achieved world power status after defeating China and Russia in war and joining the victorious powers in the First World War.

The contrast in the international status of the two East Asian countries at the end of the war is best seen at the Paris Peace Conference. Japan was treated as an equal of the Western powers and almost all her demands at the conference were granted. China failed to gain equality with the Western powers at the peace talks and all her demands were rejected.

PART I

Europe in the 19th century

With the end of the revolutionary and Napoleonic eras in Europe in 1815, the reactionary powers at the Congress of Vienna tried to restore Europe to what it had been before the French Revolution of 1789. Their task was made difficult by the Napoleonic legacy of revolutionary ideals and nationalist feeling. The Vienna settlement proved to be unsatisfactory because it ignored the twin forces of liberalism and nationalism. Discontent led to a wave of revolutions which swept through Europe between 1820 and 1848, and to the alteration of the Vienna settlement in the years that followed.

The growth of liberalism and nationalism suffered a setback with the failure of the 1848 revolutions. But after 1850, nationalist movements renewed their struggle for unity and independence. They were prepared to abandon liberalism and democratic methods to achieve their objectives.

The triumph of these nationalist struggles resulted in the rise of several nation states in Europe. Nationalism was behind the unifications of Germany and Italy, and behind the struggle of the Balkan peoples to break away from Turkish rule as well as behind the establishment of the Dual Monarchy of Austria-Hungary. It was also behind the revival of imperialism and the scramble for colonies in the last quarter of the 19th century. But extreme nationalism created dangerous movements and situations in Europe which became contributory causes of the First World War.

In the 19th century, democracy often accompanied nationalism. But until the 1870s, nationalist movements dominated the political scene in Europe, slowing down the growth of democracy — except in Britain.

It was in the last quarter of the 19th century that democratic development made tremendous progress. After 1850, too, political, economic and social reforms which promoted the welfare of the masses were introduced in many European countries. These reforms were initiated either by benevolent political leaders or by socialist parties.

Outside Europe, democracy made steady progress in the United States and in the British dominions and colonies. Its continued growth was slowed down in the early years of the 20th century by the rise of extreme nationalism — a trend that was halted by the First World War. Democracy was to flourish once again after the war.

Democracy, however, failed to take root in those European countries where there was no strong democratic tradition. Although the new Germany had a constitutional government, it was really an autocracy. Constitutional government in the Dual Monarchy did not function effectively because the ruling nationalities refused to share political control with the minority races. In the Russian and Ottoman empires, repressive measures against the subject peoples continued.

Chapter 1
Reaction and revolution, 1815–50

The history of Europe from 1799 to 1815 was the history of France. This was because Napoleon Bonaparte, the ruler of France during this period, had conquered almost all of Europe. After his downfall, the leaders who had defeated him turned against the revolutionary ideals of liberty and equality which he and his army had spread all over Europe. These reactionaries opposed change and wanted to restore absolute government. They clashed with the liberals who wanted people to have a greater voice in their government.

At the Congress of Vienna (1814-15) which was held when the revolutionary and Napoleonic eras ended, the delegates decided to return to the 'good old days' before the French Revolution of 1789. But the reactionary system they set up was not strong enough to destroy the liberal and nationalist forces directed against it. The liberals wanted people to have basic rights and more political power. They demanded an end to absolutism and the establishment of parliamentary government which would give people more participation in the political system. After 1815, those who enjoyed national liberty were determined to defend their freedom. Meanwhile the nationalists wanted people who belonged to the same race and shared common traditions to be united and independent. After 1815, those who were still under foreign rule resolved to overthrow their rulers. Revolutions broke out in many parts of Europe, reaching a climax in 1848 which is often called 'the year of the revolutions'. However, most of the revolutions were suppressed.

Reactionary rulers and diplomats at the Congress of Vienna

THE CONGRESS OF VIENNA, 1814–15

After the Napoleonic wars, the peoples of Europe had grown tired of war and wanted peace. In September 1814, during Napoleon's exile on Elba, reactionary rulers met in Vienna, the capital of Austria. The purpose of the congress was to make peace and to remake the map of Europe. Practically every state in Europe was represented at the congress. The leading delegates were Prince von Metternich of Austria, Tsar Alexander I of Russia, Talleyrand of France and Lord Castlereagh of Britain. Although they came to Vienna with different aims and ambitions, they all agreed on one objective: to make sure that the revolutionary ideals spread by France between 1792 and 1815 were destroyed. The congress was interrupted when Napoleon escaped from Elba. After Napoleon's defeat at Waterloo in 1815, the congress resumed its work.

The task the reactionaries faced at the congress was not an easy one because of the legacy of Napoleon. Should the political and territorial changes that he made be kept or should the Europe of pre-Napoleonic times be restored? Most of the changes were based on sound principles. Napoleon had abolished the hundreds of small German states and had rearranged them into larger states. He had dealt with the Italian states in a similar way. He had set up the Grand Duchy of Warsaw to satisfy the nationalist feeling of the Poles. His wars had led to the rise of nationalism in Europe. When the peoples he conquered revolted against him, they developed a feeling of national pride and unity. This feeling grew stronger after his defeat. Napoleon and his army had also spread the revolutionary ideals of liberty and equality in the lands they conquered. Wherever the French ruled, feudal practices and privileges were abolished. They made new laws to give everyone equality before the law, freedom of speech and freedom of worship.

The Congress of Vienna was faced with many problems. The most urgent one was how to remake the map of Europe. What should be done with the boundaries of France and the lands Napoleon had conquered? The countries which had fought against Napoleon also wanted some lands as a reward. Besides, what should be done with the governments he had established? Rulers who had lost their thrones wanted them back. Another problem was how to set up a new balance of power by which the great nations of Europe could work together in peace without any one of them being too strong. But the most difficult problem was what to do with the ideals of the French Revolution, which Napoleon had spread throughout Europe. The congress wanted to destroy the achievements of the French Revolution and return to the days preceding it. Nevertheless, the congress leaders knew that a complete return to the past was not possible.

Political and territorial settlements

The Congress of Vienna followed four main principles in dealing with the problem of re-establishing the political order in Europe:
- legitimacy (the restoration of previous rulers and boundaries)
- encirclement of France
- compensation (giving lands to states in place of those which they had to give up in the process of remaking the map of Europe)
- balance of power

Legitimacy It was decided that, wherever possible, the rulers who were in power before Napoleon removed them should be given back their thrones. Following this principle, almost all of the rulers set up by Napoleon were removed. Bourbon rule was restored in France, Spain and Naples while Hapsburg rule was restored in various Italian states. The House of Savoy ruled again in the Italian state of Piedmont-Sardinia while the House of Orange reigned again in Holland. The Pope regained control of the Papal States.

The restoration of the past was also the guiding principle in re-establishing the boundaries of the European countries. The congress tried to restore, as far as possible, the map of Europe to its former shape. In other words, each country should hold the same territories it held in 1789.
- France was reduced to her former size in 1789.
- The boundaries of Spain and Portugal remained unchanged.
- Italy was more or less restored to her former divisions as a result of which she was once again 'a mere geographical expression'.

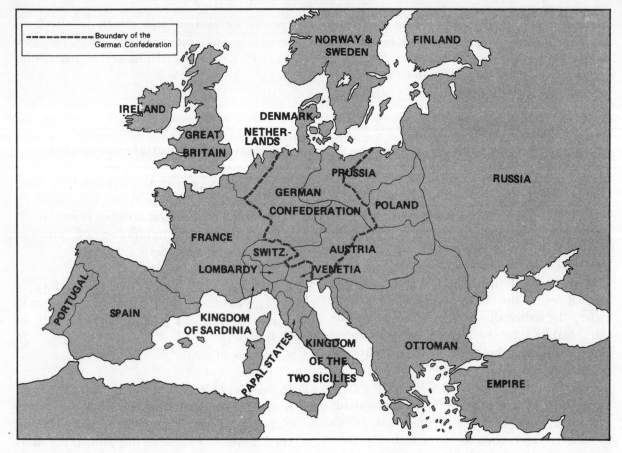

Europe after the Congress of Vienna, 1815

- Austria regained most of the territories she had lost to Napoleon.
- Piedmont-Sardinia recovered Nice and Savoy from France.
- Switzerland recovered three cantons which had been occupied by France.
- The states created by Napoleon, such as the Grand Duchy of Warsaw, the kingdom of Westphalia and the Confederation of the Rhine, were abolished.

After the restoration of all these boundaries, the map of Europe looked more or less the same as it did before the French Revolution of 1789.

However, not all of the earlier boundaries were restored.

- The Holy Roman Empire, which was composed of hundreds of small German states in pre-Napoleonic times, was not restored. In its place, the congress set up a loose German Confederation of 39 independent states under the presidency of Austria.
- Poland disappeared from the map because central Poland, which included Prussia's and Russia's share of the last partition of Poland, was given to Russia.
- Prussia received almost half of Saxony, part of Westphalia, Swedish Pomerania and some lands along the Rhine River.
- The Austrian Netherlands (Belgium) was given to Holland.
- Sweden lost Western Pomerania to Prussia and Finland to Russia.
- Genoa was awarded to Piedmont-Sardinia.

Encirclement of France As a result of the remaking of the European map at the Congress of Vienna, France was surrounded with strengthened states to prevent her from threatening the peace of Europe in future. In the north, Holland was given the Austrian Netherlands to strengthen her. To prevent any French movement in the south, the congress strengthened Piedmont-Sardinia by giving her Nice, Savoy and Genoa. To the east, extensive lands along the Rhine were given to Prussia. Switzerland was given three cantons. In addition, her independence and neutrality were guaranteed by the Great Powers.

Compensation Compensation was granted to states which had lost territories in the process of reshaping the map of Europe. To compensate Holland for the loss of a large

THE CONGRESS OF VIENNA	
Settlements	**Reasons**
Restoration of the Bourbons in France, Spain and Naples	Legitimacy
Restoration of the Hapsburgs in the Italian states	Legitimacy
Restoration of the House of Savoy in Piedmont-Sardinia	Legitimacy
Restoration of the House of Orange in Holland	Legitimacy
Restoration of the Pope in the Papal States	Legitimacy
Austria recovered Lombardy and received Venetia and the Duchy of Milan	For the loss of the Austrian Netherlands (Belgium) and some lands in southern Germany
Sweden received Norway from Denmark	For the loss of Finland and Western Pomerania and to punish Denmark
Holland received the Austrian Netherlands	For the loss of her colonies and to have a strong state to the north of France
Switzerland recovered three cantons	To have a strong state to the east of France
Prussia received Western Pomerania, parts of Saxony and Westphalia and lands on the Rhine	As reward for helping to defeat Napoleon, to punish Saxony and to have a strong barrier to the east of France
Piedmont-Sardinia recovered Nice and Savoy and received Genoa	As reward for helping to defeat Naploeon and to have a strong state to the south of France
Russia received Finland and a large part of Poland	As reward for helping to defeat Napoleon
Britain received Ceylon, South Africa, Malta, Heligoland and other lands	As reward for helping to defeat Napoleon

part of her empire, the congress gave her the Austrian Netherlands. For losing the Austrian Netherlands and some lands in southern Germany, Austria was awarded a large part of Italy, including Lombardy, Venetia and the Duchy of Milan. Members of the Hapsburg family were also placed on the thrones of the duchies of Tuscany, Parma and Modena. Austria thus gained a compact empire which gave her a dominant position in central Europe. For the loss of her Polish territory, Prussia was given parts of Saxony and Westphalia, Swedish Pomerania and territories on the Rhine. Saxony was punished for helping Napoleon. For losing Finland and Western Pomerania, Sweden received Norway, which was taken from Denmark because of the Danish alliance with Napoleon. All these territorial arrangements were made with a complete disregard for the interests of the peoples who were placed under foreign rule. These peoples later revolted against their alien rulers.

The countries which had helped to defeat Napoleon were also awarded lands. Russia received Finland and most of Prussian Poland. Britain was allowed to keep the colonies and naval bases she had captured during the Napoleonic wars. Among these were Ceylon (now Sri Lanka), South Africa, Malta, Heligoland, some islands in the West Indies and part of Guiana in South America.

Balance of power The creation of a new balance of power was made difficult by the jealousies among the victorious powers. Prussia wanted all of Saxony, but Austria feared that Prussia might become too strong. Russia wanted all of Poland, but Britain felt that an enlarged Russia might become too powerful. As a result, Prussia did not get all of Saxony and Russia did not get all of Poland. A small part of Poland was retained by Prussia. Nevertheless, all the territorial settlements strengthened and benefited the Big Four — Russia, Austria, Prussia and Britain. As for France, the defeated country, Talleyrand saw to it that French power was

Talleyrand of France

not weakened too much by the Vienna settlement. It was the smaller countries which lost the most.

Assessment of the Vienna settlement

The history of Europe during the 40 years or so after 1815 is the story of the working out of the arrangements made at the Congress of Vienna. The Vienna settlement brought peace among the Great Powers of Europe but it also created a system which led to widespread unrest because of liberal and nationalist feelings. This unrest in turn brought about changes in the Vienna settlement.

Defects of the Vienna settlement The Vienna settlement proved to be unsatisfactory in many ways.

- One of the main objectives of the Congress of Vienna was to bring about a lasting peace based on a balance of power. But the delegates of the more powerful states were eager to look after their own national interests at the expense of France and the small states. Since the peace arrangements were imposed by the Big Four upon the rest of Europe, there was bound to be discontent.
- The peacemakers ignored the growing

strength of liberal and nationalist feelings. As a result, revolutions broke out in Europe in the 1820s, 1830 and 1848.

- Although the new balance of power gave Europe a long period of peace, it had one major defect right from the start. This was Austria's desire to increase her power by exercising her influence over the German and Italian states. It caused unrest in those areas.
- The peacemakers disregarded religious, cultural and occupational differences when they transferred peoples from one ruler to another. Catholic Belgium was joined to Protestant Holland. The Belgians and the Dutch also differed in language, race and occupation. In 1830 Belgium broke away from Holland. Catholic Poland was given to Russia, whose ruler was the head of the Greek Orthodox Church. This arrangement later caused many conflicts between the Poles and the Russians. The Norwegians were also unhappy at being placed under Swedish rule.
- To satisfy both the royalists and liberals in France, the peacemakers restored the Bourbons to the French throne but with a constitution. This constitutional monarchy failed because Charles X, who became king in 1824, tried to restore absolutism. He was overthrown in 1830.
- By placing Poland under Russian rule, the congress delayed Polish independence until the end of the First World War.

Alteration of the Vienna settlement Since the Vienna settlement was unsatisfactory, the decisions made were altered in later years. After the Revolution of 1830 in France, the restored Bourbons were overthrown and replaced by the Orleanist branch of the Bourbon dynasty. Belgium, which was joined to Holland in 1815, became an independent nation after the Belgian Revolution of 1830. At first, although the kingdom of Poland was placed under Russian rule, it was not to be integrated into the Russian Empire. However, after the suppression of the Polish Revolt of 1830-31, Poland was absorbed by the Russian Empire. In the Italian states, Piedmont-Sardinia got Lombardy from Austria after the Austro-Sardinian War of 1859, and she received Venetia after the Austro-Prussian War of 1866. In 1860 France recovered Nice and Savoy from Piedmont-Sardinia. With the unification of Italy, Naples, Sicily and the Papal States became part of the new Kingdom of Italy. The German Confederation created in 1815 was abolished in 1866.

Achievements of the Congress of Vienna Although the Vienna settlement had many defects, it had its good points. It kept the peace in Europe for about 40 years. After 1815, there was no war in Europe until the outbreak of the Crimean War (1854-56). By strengthening Prussia and Piedmont-Sardinia, which led the unification movements in Germany and in Italy respectively, the congress indirectly helped to bring about the unification of both countries. By surrounding France with strong states, Europe was protected against any future French aggression. The congress also abolished the slave trade, a sign of the growing humanitarian feeling in Europe. Finally, two alliances, the Holy Alliance and the Quadruple Alliance, grew out of the Vienna settlement. They aimed at maintaining the settlement through concerted action. This led to the Concert of Europe, a new idea in international politics. The members hoped to preserve the peace through a system of international government that had the very same objective as the League of Nations and the present United Nations. As such, the Concert of Europe was the forerunner of these two peacemaking bodies.

Peace plans for Europe To keep peace in Europe through international co-operation, the Holy Alliance and the Quadruple (later Quintuple) Alliance were formed at Vienna. The Holy Alliance was proposed by Tsar Alexander I. He wanted the relations between nations to be based on the principles of

Christianity: justice, charity and peace. Most of the powers at the Vienna congress joined it but none took it seriously. The alliance was nothing more than a series of pious pledges. Castlereagh described it as 'a piece of sublime mysticism and nonsense', so Britain did not join it.

Prince von Metternich of Austria, 'conductor' of the Concert of Europe

A more effective alliance for keeping the peace was the Quadruple Alliance of Austria, Russia, Prussia and Britain. In 1818 France also joined it, and it became the Quintuple Alliance. The members agreed to hold congresses from time to time to decide what to do to keep the peace and to consult one another in solving common problems. The Concert of Europe was thus formed with Metternich as the 'conductor'.

THE CONGRESS SYSTEM

Activities of the Quintuple Alliance

Metternich was determined to suppress revolts and to uphold the Vienna settlement. He therefore organized collective action through the Quintuple Alliance to put down any revolution that might upset the peace of Europe. It was called the Congress System because the alliance worked through a series of international congresses: Aix-la-Chapelle, Troppau, Laibach and Verona. Since the Congress System was Metternich's idea, it is also referred to as the 'Metternich System'.

Aix-la-Chapelle, 1818 At the Congress of Aix-la-Chapelle, France was rewarded for her peaceable behaviour since 1815. She was treated as an equal of the other Great Powers by being admitted to the Concert of Europe. The Quadruple Alliance thus became the Quintuple Alliance. At this congress, Russia suggested sending troops to help Spain to put down the revolts of the Spanish colonies in South America. Britain objected because she did not wish to lose her trade with the colonies which had declared their independence. Thus, no joint European action was taken against the rebellious colonies. This showed that, although the powers aimed to act together, there were marked policy differences between them. These differences emerged again in the next two congresses.

Troppau, 1820 It was at the Congress of Troppau that the real purpose of the Quintuple Alliance was clearly revealed. It was not to keep the peace but to suppress people's liberties. The first attempts to alter the Vienna settlement came with the revolutions in 1820. A general uprising in Spain forced the king to accept a liberal constitution and to carry out liberal reforms. Russia proposed

THE CONGRESS SYSTEM

The principle of non-intervention is very popular in England; . . . we recognize, however, that we always have the right to answer any appeal for help addressed to us by a legitimate authority, just as we recognize that we have the right to extinguish the fire in a neighbour's house in order to prevent its spread to our own.

– Metternich, 1830

to send her troops to help the king. Britain rejected the proposal because it would violate her policy of non-intervention. France and Austria also rejected it because they were suspicious of Russia's real motives. An uprising in the Kingdom of the Two Sicilies (Naples and Sicily) in Italy also forced the king to give his people a liberal constitution. There was a revolt in Portugal with British naval support. Revolts also broke out in Piedmont-Sardinia and Greece in 1821.

THE TROPPAU PROTOCOL

States which have undergone a change of government due to revolution, the results of which threaten other states, ipso facto cease to be members of the European Alliance . . . If, owing to such alterations, immediate danger threatens other states, the powers bind themselves, by peaceful means, or if need be by arms to bring back the guilty state into the bosom of the Great Alliance.

Alarmed at the uprisings, the members of the Quintuple Alliance met at the Congress of Troppau in 1820 to deal with the revolt in Naples. Austria and Russia urged armed intervention. Britain objected, insisting that the aim of the alliance was not to interfere in the internal affairs of other states but to keep the boundaries set up in Vienna in 1815. In spite of Britain's opposition, Austria, Russia and Prussia drew up an agreement, the Troppau Protocol. This stated the intention of the Great Powers to use force to put down any revolution that might threaten the peace of Europe. Britain and France did not sign the Troppau Protocol.

Laibach, 1821 After the decision was made to intervene in the revolt in Naples, Metternich called the Congress of Laibach in 1821. In order to show her opposition to this intervention, Britain sent observers only to this congress. The congress summoned the king of

Naples before it. He was asked to support intervention. When he agreed, Austrian troops marched into Naples and restored him to his throne. The congress showed that the differences among the powers were becoming more acute. If they continued, the Congress System was bound to break down.

Verona, 1822 In 1822 the Congress of Verona was held to consider intervention in Spain. In spite of Britain's opposition, it was decided to send a French army into Spain to help the Spanish king. The French troops speedily crushed both the revolt and the reform movement there. After the Congress of Verona, Britain withdrew from the Quintuple Alliance. When Russia tried to convene the congress powers in 1824 to discuss the Greek Revolution, Britain refused to send a representative.

By the early 1820s, most of Spain's colonies in South America had already won their independence. The European powers wanted to send an army to help Spain to recover her colonies, but this intervention was prevented by Britain and the United States. Britain refused to give naval support to Spain because she wanted the colonies to break from Spain. She had developed a fast-growing trade with the former colonies. By the

President Monroe of the United States who proclaimed the Monroe Doctrine in 1823

Revolutions in Europe, 1820-21

Monroe Doctrine of 1823, the United States declared that any European interference in the affairs of the American continent would be regarded as an unfriendly act towards her. It was the support of Britain that encouraged the United States to declare such a doctrine. The Monroe Doctrine further strained the relations between Britain and the other congress powers.

The Quintuple Alliance followed Metternich's policy of suppressing not only revolutions abroad but also liberalism at home. In Austria, there was strict censorship. The Carlsbad Decrees of 1819 put liberal students and professors in the German states under close supervision by their governments. In France, Charles X (ruled 1824-30) suppressed the rights of the individual. In Britain, under George IV (ruled 1820-30), the government forbade public meetings and enforced strict censorship of the press. In Russia, Nicholas I (ruled 1825-55) abolished freedom of the press and set up a secret police force.

End of the Congress System

In spite of its successes in suppressing liberalism and nationalism in the early 1820s, the Congress System started to break up after 1823. There were three general reasons for its decline:

- the unwillingness of the congress powers to co-operate in preserving the peace when the decisions made went against their own selfish interests
- the growing strength of liberalism and nationalism
- the dissatisfaction among the small states because they were excluded from the Congress System

The direct causes of its breakdown were the withdrawal of Britain from the Quintuple Alliance, the War of Greek Independence which split the congress powers, and the outbreak of revolutions in 1830.

By 1830, the Congress System had ceased to be an instrument for the international suppression of liberalism and nationalism. But it lingered on in Austria and parts of Italy until 1848 as a means of maintaining the *status quo*. With the collapse of the system, the powers pursued their reactionary policies independently. Metternich ceased to be an influential figure in Europe although he remained in power until he was removed during the revolutions of 1848.

The withdrawal of Britain The Congress System received its first blow with the withdrawal of Britain from the Quintuple Alliance. An important cause of her withdrawal was her policy of non-intervention, along with her traditional policy of isolation and sympathy for liberal movements, which conflicted with Austria's policy of intervention. As we saw earlier, Britain refused to sign the Troppau Protocol of 1820. She opposed Austrian intervention in the uprising in Naples and French intervention in the revolt in Spain. After the Congress of Verona which authorized France to send an army into Spain, Britain withdrew from the Quintuple Alliance.

A more important cause of Britain's withdrawal was her opposition to any policy which might threaten her channels of trade. Because of the Industrial Revolution, she needed new markets for her products. She therefore refused to agree to the plan to help Spain recover her colonies in South America so that she could trade with them.

The War of Greek Independence, 1821-29
The question of Greek independence further split the congress powers and weakened the Congress System. In 1821 the Greeks revolted against Turkish rule. The Greeks were taxed heavily and brutally treated by the Turks. Nationalist ideas had also spread among the Greeks because of their frequent contacts with the West through trade and the revival of interest in the past glories of the ancient Greeks. Russia claimed the right to help the Greeks because both of them belonged to the Orthodox Church. Other reasons for supporting the Greeks were Russia's fears of a strong Turkey, and her expansionist ambitions in the Balkan Peninsula.

The other congress powers wanted to put down the revolt in order to prevent the spread of revolutionary ideas. But as Christian nations, they could not help a Muslim ruler suppress his Christian subjects. At the same time, Austria and Britain did not wish to see Turkey weakened and Russia strengthened. If Turkey lost her European territories, Russia was sure to get a large share of these lands. This disagreement among the powers was another blow to the Congress System.

Although the Greeks did not receive any support from the congress powers, they continued their struggle for independence. When they began to lose the war, Russia, Britain and France formed an alliance in 1827 whereby the three powers pledged to secure Greek independence. Austria refused to join them because Metternich was determined not to support rebels, no matter who they were. Helping the Greeks was a violation of the Troppau Protocol. Prussia followed Austria's lead.

In 1827 a combined Russian, British and French naval force destroyed the Turkish and Egyptian fleets in the Battle of Navarino. At this point, Britain withdrew from any further action. The Duke of Wellington, the new British foreign secretary, did not agree with the earlier policy of intervention. Without British support, France also withdrew, leaving Russia to deal with the problem alone.

In 1828 Russia declared war on Turkey. In a little more than a year, a Russian army had advanced to the gates of Constantinople, the Turkish capital. The sultan was forced to sign the Treaty of Adrianople in 1829, ending the Russo-Turkish War of 1828-29. By the terms of the treaty, the Turkish provinces of Moldavia and Wallachia north of the Danube became independent of Turkey and were placed under protection of Russia. Turkey recognized the independence of Greece, but the Greeks still had to pay tribute to the Turks. At the London Conference of 1832, the European powers, except Russia, demanded that Greece was to be completely independent of Turkey. When the sultan agreed, Greece became an independent monarchy.

The armed intervention of the three congress powers was yet another blow to the Congress System. By assisting the Greeks against their 'legitimate' ruler, they had violated the Troppau Protocol. From then on, Russia ceased to be a member of the Quintuple Alliance.

The Revolutions of 1830 The 1830 revolutions dealt the final blow to the Congress System. The first one was the July Revolution in France. The revolution broke out because King Charles X wanted to restore absolutism and the nobles' privileges. It resulted in the overthrow of Charles who belonged to the Bourbon dynasty which had been restored by the Congress of Vienna. Louis Philippe, who belonged to the Orleanist branch of the Bourbons, succeeded him. The July Revolution set off a wave of revolts throughout Europe.

One immediate result of the July Revolution in France was the Belgian Revolution of 1830. The root cause was that in the Vienna settlement Belgium had been joined to

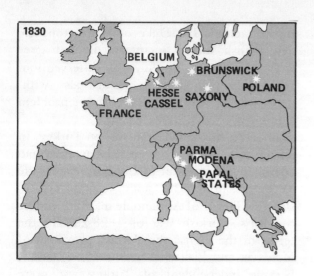

Revolutions in Europe, 1830

The July Revolution of 1830 in France

Holland without any consideration of the religious and cultural differences between the two. Belgium was Catholic whereas Holland was Protestant. The Belgians were manufacturers while the Dutch were farmers and traders. They belonged to different races and spoke different languages. The Belgians feared that they might lose their national identity under the new Kingdom of the Netherlands (Holland). Although the Belgian population was almost twice as large as the Dutch, the Belgians did not have much opportunity to serve in the government or in the army. They also felt that they were overtaxed.

These differences, combined with the tyranny of the Dutch king, aroused nationalist feeling and created discontent among the Belgians. They revolted against Dutch rule in August following the French revolt in July 1830. The Dutch were forced to withdraw from Belgium and the Belgians proclaimed their independence. The Great Powers guaranteed the independence and neutrality of Belgium by signing the Treaty of London in 1839.

The July Revolution in France encouraged revolts in other parts of Europe. Unlike the Belgian Revolution, all these revolts were unsuccessful. In central Italy, revolts broke out in Modena, Parma and the Papal States.

All were suppressed by Austria. When the news of the July Revolution reached Poland, the Poles rose against Russian rule in November 1830 and proclaimed their independence. The revolt was put down in 1831. Poland lost its independence and became a Russian province. In the German Confederation, there were uprisings in several states. Austria and Prussia saw to it that they were suppressed to prevent the spread of the revolutionary spirit.

The overall result of the revolutions of 1830 was disappointing to the liberals. Although the revolutions in France and Belgium succeeded, elsewhere in Europe the 'Metternich System' went on until 1848. Nevertheless, the overthrow of the restored Bourbons in France, the separation of Belgium from Holland, and the annexation of Poland by the Russia Empire — all violations of the Vienna settlement — finally put an end to the Congress System. Although the Congress System had collapsed, the Concert of Europe (the idea that European powers should work together in settling common problems and preserving the peace) did not die with it. Various powers still held conferences afterwards. However, each conference met to deal with a particular question, not to lay down a general policy for the whole of Europe.

THE REVOLUTIONS OF 1848

The Congress of Vienna and the Congress System tried to suppress the liberal and nationalist ideas that had swept through Europe as a result of the French Revolution of 1789 and the Napoleonic wars. The liberals and the nationalists fought back. Revolts broke out in the 1820s and in 1830, but only the French Revolution, the Belgian Revolution and the War of Greek Independence were successful. As most of these revolts failed, it seemed that absolutism was as firmly established as before and that liberalism and nationalism had been suppressed. In fact the two forces were still very much alive although they had been driven underground. The liberals and the nationalists were only waiting for another chance to fight back. It came in 1848, 'the year of the revolutions'. However, with the exception of the revolution in France, all the 1848 revolutions failed.

As in 1830, the wave of 1848 revolutions was triggered off by an uprising in France: the French Revolution of 1848, also known as

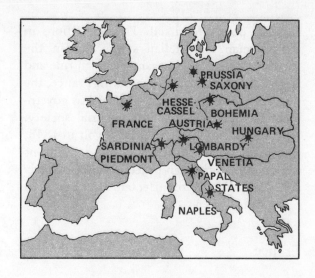

Revolutions in Europe, 1848

the February Revolution. As Metternich put it: 'When France catches cold, Europe sneezes.' The mingling of liberalism and nationalism was the driving force behind the revolutions. The two forces were really part of the same idea: the desire of the growing middle class (bourgeoisie) to overthrow the old system of absolutism and feudalism and

The 1848 revolutions: liberalism threatening the crowned heads of Europe

15

to seize power for itself. The revolutions in the German and Italian states and in the Austrian Empire were against foreign rule and against the Metternich System. In France, the disturbances were against middle-class government and the evils of the industrial society. With the exception of the Irish revolt in 1848, there was no revolution in Britain. Reforms were achieved through peaceful means. Russia and Turkey were unaffected by the 1848 revolutions.

Louis Philippe of France

France

Although Louis Philippe was the first elected king of France and his government was an improvement on that of Charles X, the people were still dissatisfied with his rule. His home policy was largely responsible for his downfall. His government favoured the bourgeoisie — the small wealthy middle class composed of rich manufacturers and businessmen — and ignored the other social classes. Business was his top priority since his main political support came from the bourgeoisie. Not surprisingly, many groups were discontented

A barricade in Paris during the 1848 French Revolution

with his rule.

The failure of Louis Philippe's foreign policy made him more unpopular. He had very few allies. Both Metternich and Tsar Nicholas I regarded him as a revolutionary because he became king after a revolution. France lost Britain as an ally because of their differences in foreign policy.

With the failure of Louis Philippe's home and foreign policies, there were frequent outbreaks of violence during his 18-year reign. His enemies finally succeeded in overthrowing him in the February Revolution of 1848. The revolutionaries (republicans and socialists) proclaimed the Second French Republic. (The First French Republic was proclaimed in 1792 and lasted until 1804 when Napoleon declared himself emperor.) Louis Napoleon, nephew of Napoleon, was elected President. As a result of the revolution, France had given herself a second Napoleon and a second republic.

The Second French Republic was short-lived. From the day he was elected, Louis Napoleon had been waiting for a chance to seize full control of the government. He wanted to be an emperor, like his famous uncle. In December 1852, he took the title of Napoleon III, Emperor of the French. The Second French Republic gave way to the Second French Empire. It seemed that France was not yet ready for republicanism.

Italy

Even before the outbreak of the February Revolution in France, there were uprisings in Italy. In January 1848, the Sicilians revolted against the king of Naples and forced him to grant them a constitution. As the revolutionary spirit of 1848 swept through Italy, more rulers, such as King Charles Albert of Piedmont-Sardinia, granted their people liberal constitutions. Absolute government almost disappeared.

When the news of the rising in Vienna and the flight of Metternich reached the Italian states, revolts broke out in the Austrian provinces of Lombardy and Venetia in March 1848. With the support of Tuscany, the Papal States and Naples, King Charles Albert assumed leadership of the whole Italian movement against the Austrians. Unfortunately, this Italian unity did not last long. By March 1849, the Austrians had succeeded in suppressing the revolts in northern Italy.

Meanwhile, the revolutionaries in Rome proclaimed the Roman Republic in February 1849 under the leadership of Mazzini. However, it lasted only for a short time. The Pope appealed to Louis Napoleon for help. Louis Napoleon saw a chance to win the support of the French Catholics for his new presidency by helping the Pope. In July, French troops captured Rome and the Roman Republic fell.

With the failure of the Italian liberal and nationalist movements in 1848-49, Italy remained weak and divided. Despotic governments were once again firmly established in almost all of the Italian states. Absolutism was restored in Naples and Tuscany. Austrian power was re-established in Lombardy and Venetia. The Pope recovered the Papal States. Only Sardinia maintained constitutional rule.

Germany

Inspired by the French Revolution of 1848, people in every German state rose in revolt the same year. By March, one German ruler after another, fearful of being overthrown, had granted constitutional reforms. Frederick William IV of Prussia was the leader of the liberalizing movement.

However, the revolutionary mood passed, and the reactionaries began to triumph. Having seen the suppression of the revolts in Austria, the German rulers, including Frederick William IV, changed their minds. They rejected the constitutions they had granted and restored absolutism. At the same time, the unification movement collapsed.

The revolutionaries were imprisoned, executed or exiled. But the parliaments established in the various German states during the revolutions were kept.

The Austrian Empire

The French Revolution of 1848 encouraged the peoples of the Austrian Empire to revolt. There were five revolutionary movements in the empire.

The first outbreak was Hungarian (Magyar). The emperor was forced to grant a constitution to Hungary. Serfdom and the special privileges of the nobility were abolished.

From Hungary, the revolutionary movement spread to Vienna, the Austrian capital, where the people were already excited by the news of the French Revolution. It was a purely German movement. Metternich was forced to flee to England. The downfall of Metternich, the symbol of tyranny for more than 30 years, stirred minority races all over the empire.

As mentioned earlier, the Italians in Lombardy and Venetia revolted against Austria in March 1848. The revolts led to a war between Austria and Piedmont-Sardinia.

The fourth rising was centred in Prague, the capital of Bohemia (now the capital of Czechoslovakia). It was anti-German rather than anti-Austrian. The Czechs were granted rights similar to those granted to the Hungarians.

The fifth rising was anti-Hungarian, not anti-Austrian. The Magyars were unwilling to grant to the other national groups in Hungary the rights granted to them by Austria. In protest, the southern Slavs revolted against Hungarian rule. Taking advantage of the situation, Austria supported the Slavs.

The success of the revolutionaries was short-lived. The revolt in Bohemia lasted for only two weeks. The imperial government recovered control of Vienna. In Hungary, fighting between the Magyars and the southern Slavs had weakened the movement.

The Hungarians succeeded in putting down the Slavic rising. However, in 1849 the Hungarians themselves were defeated by a large Russian army which marched into Hungary to help the Austrians. In the same year, the Austrians suppressed the revolts in northern Italy. Austrian rule was restored in Lombardy and Venetia and in some of the smaller Italian states.

Why the revolutions failed

There are several factors which explain the failure of the 1848 revolutions. At first, the revolutionaries united against the governments they wanted to overthrow. But when they succeeded, policy and racial differences, class rivalry and jealousies among the leaders divided the revolutionaries. This division made it easy for their enemies to defeat them.

In France, no sooner had the republicans and the socialists succeeded in overthrowing Louis Philippe's middle-class government than they began to quarrel among themselves. The split prepared the way for Louis Napoleon's seizure of power.

In Italy, troops from the Papal States, Naples and Tuscany joined the Sardinian army against Austria. But Italian unity did not last long because of the jealousies and policy differences among the leaders. Mazzini wanted a republican Italy but King Charles Albert disliked democracy.

In Germany, the revolutionaries had no political experience and wasted their time deciding whether or not to include Austria with or without her non-German parts in their unification plan. In the Austrian Empire, inter-racial disputes and the lack of collaboration among the different revolutionary movements gave the reactionaries a chance to exploit this division and regain control of the empire.

Foreign intervention was yet another reason for the failure of the 1848 revolutions. The French aided the Pope in crushing Mazzini's Roman Republic. The Russians assisted the Austrians in suppressing the Hungarian revolt.

Overall results of the 1848 revolutions

The liberal or democratic and nationalist movements suffered a setback as a result of the failure of the 1848 revolutions. A Hapsburg emperor still ruled the Austrian Empire. In France, a hereditary emperor ruled instead of an elected president. In the German states, the Prussian king survived the revolutionary storm. He introduced a constitution which in fact re-established his absolute power. Germany and Italy were still disunited. Austrian influence remained strong in Italy while the subject peoples of the Austrian Empire were forced back into their former positions. Although absolutism and reaction had triumphed over democracy and nationalism, this victory was temporary. The next 20 years saw constitutional government and nationalism make significant gains.

Nationalism continued to grow after 1848. The nationalists in Italy and Germany gave up the idea of unifying their countries through democratic methods. The Italians gave their support to the Sardinian king, Victor Emmanuel II, and his chief minister, Cavour. In Germany, the nationalists supported the Prussian king, William I, and his chancellor, Bismarck.

In spite of the overall failure of the 1848 revolutions, there were some good results. Feudal practices were not restored in the Austrian Empire. Sardinia kept her liberal constitution. All the German states had parliaments, though most of them were not democratic. After 1848, there were reforms in almost every country in Europe. Rulers, such as Louis Napoleon and Tsar Alexander II, introduced reforms to improve the living conditions of the poorer classes. Having seen that the centres of revolt were in the industrial towns and cities, the western European governments made laws to eliminate the evils of the industrial society.

QUESTIONS

1. What important problems faced the European powers at the Congress of Vienna? How did they settle these problems?
2. Show how **each** of the following principles was applied by the Congress of Vienna in restoring order in Europe:
   (a) legitimacy
   (b) encirclement of France
   (c) compensation
   (d) balance of power
3. To what extent did the Congress of Vienna restore the map of Europe to what it was before the French Revolution of 1789? Show how the territorial settlements gave rise to the discontent of some of the states.
4. Discuss the achievements and defects of the Vienna settlement of 1815.

5. Describe the efforts of European powers to keep peace by means of congresses after 1815. How far were they successful in achieving their objective?
6. 'The real purpose of the Congress System was not to keep the peace but to suppress people's liberties.' Do you agree? Give reasons.
7. To what extent did the liberal and nationalist forces in Europe succeed in achieving their aims between 1820 and 1830?
8. 'When France catches cold, Europe sneezes.' Justify this statement in connection with the revolutions of 1830 and 1848 in Europe.
9. Why did the 1848 revolutions, except the revolution in France, all fail? What were their overall results?

The main theme of the political history of Europe from 1815 to 1850 was reaction and revolution. The rulers who defeated Napoleon wanted to reverse the political and territorial changes he had made. However, this was not easy because of the Napoleonic legacy of revolutionary ideals and nationalist feeling as well as the conflicting interests of the victorious powers. In spite of these difficulties, the reactionaries in Vienna arrived at a settlement based on four principles: legitimacy, encirclement of France, compensation and balance of power. However, they ignored liberalism and nationalism. Two alliances were formed to enforce the Vienna settlement: the vague Holy Alliance and the effectual Quintuple Alliance. The Quintuple Alliance worked through the Congress System to suppress revolution and preserve peace.

Three movements led to unrest and uprisings after 1815: liberalism, which is concerned with the defence of man's natural rights; nationalism, which inspires national groups to fight for independence and freedom; and democracy, which is concerned with the enforcement of majority rule. These movements resulted in the alteration of the Vienna settlement in the next 60 years or so.

Opposition to the Vienna settlement and the Congress System can be seen in the three waves of revolution that hit Europe: in the 1820s, in 1830 and in 1848. The Congress System succeeded in suppressing the revolutions in the 1820s. But the revolutions of 1830 resulted in violations of the Vienna settlement. The Bourbons in France were overthrown again; an independent Belgium was created; and Poland was absorbed by Russia. The 1830 revolutions and the disagreement among the congress powers brought an end to the Congress System.

Revolution swept through Europe again in 1848. Only Russia and Turkey were not affected by the disturbances. Louis Philippe of France was overthrown and the Second French Republic was proclaimed. Charles Albert of Sardinia assumed control of the Italian movement and made war on Austria. In the German states, the rulers were forced to grant constitutions. In the Austrian Empire, the different nationalities were either promised or granted liberal reforms.

The popular revolutionary movements of 1848 collapsed very quickly. The February Revolution in France prepared the way for Louis Napoleon's dictatorship. Absolutism was restored in almost all of the Italian states. Austrian influence over the German states was re-established. Nationalist movements therefore failed to unify Italy and Germany. Revolutionary movements in the Austrian Empire brought about inter-racial disputes.

There were several reasons for the failure of the 1848 revolutions. One reason was the inexperience of the leaders and lack of accord between them. Another was selfish national interests which split the revolutionaries. Finally, foreign powers helped the reactionaries to regain political control.

The 1848 revolutions, however, had some important gains. Feudalism was abolished in the Austrian Empire, the liberal constitution in Sardinia was maintained, and parliaments were established in each of the German states. After 1848, many reforms were introduced in most of the European countries.

Chapter 2
Nationalism and the rise of nation states in Europe after 1850

We saw in Chapter 1 how nationalist feeling led to the creation of the nation states of Belgium and Greece. Poland, however, failed to overthrow Russian rule. Nationalist movements in the Austrian Empire, Germany and Italy, too, suffered setbacks during the 1848 revolutions. But from 1850 onwards, these movements gathered strength for a renewed struggle against foreign control. The most significant achievement of the nationalist struggle in the 19th century was the unification of Germany and Italy. The rise of these two states altered the balance of power in Europe.

Nationalism inspired the Balkan peoples to revolt against Turkish rule. Their struggle for independence led to what was called the Eastern Question.

In Austria, nationalism triumphed with the establishment of the Dual Monarchy by which the Germans of Austria recognized the equality of the Hungarians. At the same time, however, these two dominant nationalities checked the nationalist hopes of the other subject peoples.

Finally, nationalism was an important factor in the revival of imperialism after 1870. The newly unified states of Germany and Italy wanted to show how strong they were. Since having colonies was considered a sign of greatness, they wanted to have colonies like the other great nations of Europe. (The new imperialism will be dealt with in a later chapter.)

THE UNIFICATION OF GERMANY

Germany after 1815 remained disunited. The Congress of Vienna set up the German Confederation, a loose union of 39 states under the presidency of Austria. A central representative diet at Frankfurt took care of the common affairs of the confederation.

Factors working for and against German unification after 1815

Whether the German Confederation would help to bring about a unified Germany was uncertain at this point. After 1815, there were factors working for and against German unification.

Positive factors   There were three principal factors working for German unification: the formation of the Zollverein, the gradual strengthening of Prussia and the growth of nationalism.

Prussian territory was scattered across north Germany, so her trade was hindered by high tariffs imposed by the states inbetween. In 1818 she set up the Zollverein which abolished tariff barriers within her provinces. In 1834 the central and south German states joined the Zollverein because their only outlet to the sea was through Prussia. By 1854 almost all of the German States had joined the Zollverein. It placed Prussia at the head of a powerful economic union of almost all of Germany. Economic unity increased the desire for political unity. In the following years, the other German States began to look upon Prussia, not Austria, as their leader. The immediate effect of the Zollverein was the economic prosperity of Prussia.

Economic reforms after 1815 also strengthened Prussia internally. Serfdom was abolished, many feudalistic practices were eradicated and education was encouraged. These reforms speeded up the internal development of Prussia, preparing her for the task of unifying Germany later on under Bismarck.

The third factor working for the unification of Germany was the growth of nationalism. The Napoleonic wars had aroused nationalist feeling among the Germans. After the fall of Napoleon, German poets, philosophers and historians praised the idea of German unity and made the Germans feel proud of their race.

Negative factors The three principal factors working against German unification were Metternich's domination of the German Confederation, the confederation's ineffectiveness as a means of unifying Germany and Prussia's reluctance to lead the unification movement.

Metternich encouraged rivalry and jealousy among the German states to keep Germany weak and disunited. He also saw to it that Prussia, the strongest German state, followed a policy similar to that of Austria. He succeeded in suppressing liberalism by having the diet pass the Carlsbad Decrees of 1819. These decrees placed professors and students under close government supervision, forbade students' societies and imposed a censorship on the press.

The German Confederation was an ineffective means of unifying Germany. It was dominated by Austria. Member-states kept their independence. The only rule they had to observe was that they could not make war against their fellow members. The smaller states opposed the strengthening of the confederation because they feared that Austria and Prussia might use it to control them. Any effective or united action by the diet was made difficult by jealousy among the member-states and the rivalry between Austria and Prussia.

If Germany was to be unified, Austria had to be expelled from the German Confederation. The German states did not want the large non-German population in Austria to become part of a united Germany. Prussia was the only German state capable of driving out Austria. Industrial progress had made her rich and she had a strong army. However, her foreign policy was dominated by Austria and she was not yet strong enough to challenge the might of Austria. Besides, she was busy with her own internal development.

The Frankfurt Parliament, 1848-49

During the 1848 revolutions, the Frankfurt Parliament was set up by the German liberals to draw up a constitution for a united Germany. It had a great opportunity to unify Germany but failed to do so.

- The members of the parliament, who were mostly professional people, and their supporters had no political experience. Even the most experienced politicians would have found it difficult to solve the problems of unification faced by the parliament.
- If the members of the parliament were to achieve their objective, they had to act quickly. Instead, they wasted their time in fruitless discussions. The delay gave their enemies time to reorganize themselves and fight back.
- The parliament had no military force to back up its decisions.
- In March 1849, after the parliament had decided to exclude Austria from the new Germany, they offered the imperial crown to Frederick William IV of Prussia. Unfortunately, he refused to accept it

because this would mean trouble with Austria.

With the Prussian king's rejection of the parliament's offer, the last hope for a united Germany faded. In June 1849, the parliament was dissolved.

After Austria had suppressed the revolutions in her own territories, she re-established her influence over the German states and regained her dominant position in the German Confederation. Germany was again as weak and disunited as before.

The do-nothing Frankfurt Parliament of 1848-49 in session

Political conditions in Germany after the 1848 revolutions

The failure of the Frankfurt Parliament of 1848-49 ended the attempts of the German liberals to unify the German states through democratic methods. It revealed to the German people that Germany could be unified only through the leadership and strength of one state and that any unification would have to exclude Austria. The Germans would never accept the inclusion of her non-German parts. Equally, however, Austria would never agree to a unified Germany that excluded her.

Several developments had made Prussia the most likely state to drive Austria from the German Confederation and unify Germany. Prussia's wealth had been increasing since 1815 because economic reforms had stimulated her industrial development. Prussian industry and commerce were further stimulated by the formation of the Zollverein.

THE ZOLLVEREIN

The Zollverein is the first step towards . . . the Germanization of the people. It has broken down some of the strongholds of . . . hostility. By a community of interests on commercial and trading questions, it has prepared the way for a political nationality.

An English observer in the 1830s

Prussian government and administration too were modern and efficient and the Prussians were, in general, well educated. In short, by 1850 Prussia was rapidly building up the strength she would need for the task of unifying Germany.

During the 1848 revolutions, Prussia had a good chance of uniting the German states. She failed because King Frederick William IV was an inconsistent leader. One moment he favoured German unification; the next moment, he opposed it. Besides, Prussia would have had to fight not only Austria but also Russia. (The Tsar was a firm supporter of the Metternich System.) Finally, Prussia had not yet seen clearly her role as the leader of German unification. It was only after King William I and his chancellor, Bismarck, became political partners that Prussia realized her mission.

The two important leaders of German unification

King William I of Prussia (reigned 1861-88)
When Frederick William IV went insane in

1858, his younger brother William became regent. On the king's death in 1861, William I succeeded to the throne. He was more decisive than his brother and less frightened of Austria. He also had a remarkable ability to choose the right men at the right time for responsible positions. He appointed the brilliant military strategist, von Moltke, as head of the Prussian army, and von Roon as Minister of War. And he appointed Bismarck as chancellor in 1862, when he was having trouble getting funds to strengthen the Prussian army from the Prussian diet.

William opposed liberalism and believed in a strong monarchy. He thought that only Prussia, with a strong army, could unify Germany.

Otto von Bismarck (1815-98)   Bismarck belonged to the *junker* class, the landed aristocrats. He strongly opposed liberalism and democracy and was a firm supporter of the Prussian state and its king. He had no desire to see a unified Germany unless it was headed by Prussia and he believed that such a unification could only be achieved by force. He once said: 'The great questions of the day will be decided not by speeches and majority

resolutions but by blood and iron.' For this reason, he was called the Iron Chancellor.

Bismarck began his political career in 1847 as a member of the Prussian diet where he often spoke against the liberals. The Frankfurt Parliament's failure to unite Germany convinced him that Germany could only be united by force.

As Prussia's representative to the federal diet at Frankfurt, from 1851 to 1858, he learned much about German politics. He saw the possibility of unifying Germany under Prussian leadership and foresaw a struggle between Prussia and Austria. As ambassador to Russia from 1859 to 1862, he befriended Tsar Alexander II in the hope of getting his support in the event of war with Austria. He also served briefly as ambassador to France and this gave him a chance to study the character of Napoleon III, the man he would later fight.

Steps taken by Bismarck to unify Germany

Since Prussian military power was the key factor in the unification of Germany, von Moltke and von Roon proceeded to strengthen the Prussian army. To finance their military programme, the king demanded that the Prussian diet increase taxation. The liberals, who controlled the assembly, refused. They believed that the diet should control the king, not the other way round. They also feared that the strengthened army might be used to suppress liberalism. When Bismarck became chancellor, he ignored the diet and illegally collected taxes to pay for the military build-up.

There were three steps in Bismarck's plan to unify Germany: the Prussian army had to be made strong enough to defeat Austria; Austria had to be driven out of the German Confederation of which she was head; and finally, a united Germany had to be created with Prussia as leader, a move which France would strongly oppose. War was necessary for

Otto von Bismarck, the Iron Chancellor

each of these steps. Before going to war, Bismarck used all his diplomatic skill to make sure that no foreign powers would help the country he wanted to fight.

The Prusso-Danish War, 1864–65

The first of the wars that Bismarck waged to unify Germany was the Prusso-Danish War of 1864-65. The problem of Schleswig-Holstein, two duchies at the base of the Danish Peninsula, provided the immediate cause of the war. Although the king of Denmark was the duke of both states, they were not part of the Danish kingdom. The problem of Schleswig-Holstein arose from the conflicting ambitions of the Danish and German nationalists. Schleswig, which had a large Danish population, wanted Denmark to absorb both states. Holstein, whose population was mainly German, wanted it to remain as it was until it could become part of a united Germany.

In 1863, the Danish king issued a new constitution which would have separated Schleswig from Holstein and made it part of Denmark. The Germans in both duchies opposed the Danish move. Bismarck saw a chance to further his own plans and decided to make war on Denmark. His motives were:
- to arouse German nationalism by waging war on a foreign country;
- to increase Prussian influence at the expense of Austria by showing that Prussia was willing to fight for the rights of Germans everywhere;
- to try out the Prussian army and test its weapons;
- to observe the Austrian army at close quarters since he knew that Austria would be dragged into the war;
- to use the war as an excuse to start a quarrel with Austria later on;
- to prevent Denmark from taking Schleswig;
- to safeguard the security of Prussia.

But first, Bismarck carried out his policy of isolating the enemy before making war,

a policy which he used again in later wars. To secure Russia's friendship, he supported the tsar in putting down the Polish Revolt of 1863. To ensure Austrian support, he secured an alliance with her against Denmark. To encourage Denmark to risk war with Prussia, he secretly encouraged Danish hope of British military support, which he knew would never come. As for France, Napoleon III was too busy with the Mexican campaign (see p. 61) to oppose Prussian armed intervention.

After Bismarck had isolated Denmark, he proposed that the problem of Schleswig-Holstein be settled by an international conference. When Denmark refused, Prussian and Austrian armies marched into the two duchies in 1864. Denmark was quickly defeated.

In 1865 the Convention of Gastein decided the fate of the two duchies. Prussia was to administer Schleswig while Austria was to administer Holstein.

Later events showed that Bismarck purposely designed the provisions of the Gastein Convention so that he could choose his own time to start a quarrel with Austria. Austrian administration of Holstein was bound to be inefficient because it was too far away from Austria. Bismarck was soon to use the situation as an excuse for making war on Austria.

The Austro-Prussian War (Seven Weeks' War), 1866

Bismarck's diplomacy Soon after the signing of the Convention of Gastein, Bismarck began to prepare for war against Austria. His chief motive was to exclude her from German affairs by driving her out of the German Confederation. As in the Prusso-Danish War, his diplomatic strategy was to isolate the enemy first.

French neutrality was essential to the success of Bismarck's plan.

In October 1865 Bismarck met Napoleon III at Biarritz where he made use of his knowledge of Napoleon's character. Napoleon was naive and no match for Bismarck's clever diplomacy. No one knows exactly what they agreed upon, but Napoleon was led to believe that he would receive some German, not Prussian, territory for remaining neutral in the event of an Austro-Prussian war. This arrangement later led to conflicts between Prussia and France which helped to bring about the Franco-Prussian War of 1870-71.

In April 1866 Bismarck made a secret military alliance with Italy, promising her the Austrian province of Venetia if she joined in an attack against Austria. He was also confident that Russia would remain neutral because of his friendship with Tsar Alexander II.

Events leading to the war When his preparations were complete, Bismarck provoked Austria into war without difficulty. He expressed alarm at the inefficient way Austria was ruling Holstein. He then sent Prussian troops into Holstein, claiming that Prussia alone was responsible for both duchies.

Objecting to Prussian interference in Holstein, Austria appealed to the diet of the German Confederation for support against Prussia. Although the other German states had begun to turn to Prussia, not Austria, for leadership, when it came to an open conflict between the two states, almost all of them supported Austria. They felt that Prussia was too ambitious and could threaten their independence.

The war War was now only a question of time. Hostilities broke out in June 1866. Austria was confident of victory and the rest of Europe expected her to win. But they were soon astonished by the efficiency of the Prussian army. Austria's allies among the German states were quickly defeated. (Although Italy, as Prussia's ally, had also declared war on Austria, she did not make any real contribution; and on June 24 the Italians suffered a decisive defeat at the Battle of Custozza.)

Seven weeks after the start of the war Austria was defeated at the Battle of Sadowa near Koniggratz in Bohemia.

Having broken down Austria's resistance, Bismarck did not wish to humiliate her still further and turn her into a dangerous enemy in future. On 23 August 1866 the Treaty of Prague was signed, ending the war.

Treaty of Prague Knowing that war with France could not long be delayed, Bismarck wanted to obtain the goodwill of Austria in the hope that she would remain neutral in the event of a Franco-Prussian War. He therefore imposed very lenient peace terms.

- Prussia annexed Schleswig-Holstein and the small German states which had supported Austria during the war. Austria did not lose any territory of her own. She lost Venetia but it was Italian, not Austrian.
- Austria was required to pay a small indemnity to Prussia.
- Italy received Venetia from Austria as promised.
- The old German Confederation was abolished, yet another violation of the Vienna settlement of 1815.

Other results of the war By annexing territories in northern Germany, Prussia had linked together her eastern lands with the Rhine territories she had acquired in 1815. This gave her a continuous stretch of territory from East Prussia to the Rhine.

The war finally settled the question which the Frankfurt Parliament of 1848-49 had failed to resolve: whether or not Austria should become a part of a unified Germany. Prussian victory in the war meant that Austria was to be excluded.

Bismarck's greatest gain was the creation of the North German Confederation under Prussian domination, with Austria and the south German states excluded. It replaced the old German Confederation and enabled Prussia to unite more than half of Germany under her leadership, thus altering the balance of power in Europe. Since Austrian influence was at an end, the south German states would be forced eventually to accept Prussia as their leader.

Prussian control of the military forces of the new confederation played an important part in Bismarck's plan to make war on France.

The Franco-Prussian War, 1870–71

The final step in Bismarck's plan to unite Germany was the Franco-Prussian War. Bismarck wanted to use the war to arouse nationalism in the south German states so that they would join the North German Confederation. The process of unifying Germany would then be completed.

After the Austro-Prussian War, two obstacles to German unification remained.

One was the deep rivalry between Prussia and France, together with Germany's long-standing grievances against France. The French saw the rapid growth of Prussian power as a threat to their national security as well as to their international prestige. The Germans, however, had long resented the French. This resentment was based on the bitter memories left by Napoleon I's conquest of the German states and the traditional French policy of keeping Germany weak and divided.

The second obstacle was the exclusion of the south German states from the new North German Confederation. Bismarck decided to solve the two problems at the same time. He used the rivalry between Prussia and France to force the south German states to accept Prussian leadership and complete German unification.

Isolation of France Following his usual diplomatic strategy, Bismarck isolated France before he made war on her. First, Prussia had to gain the support of the south German states against France.

To check Prussia's growth, Napoleon III was pressing for the territorial compensation which he claimed Bismarck had promised him at Biarritz in 1865, in return for French neutrality in the Austro-Prussian War. He demanded that France should receive lands on the Rhine. Bismarck flatly rejected his claims and threatened to go to war. Napoleon withdrew his demands. When the people of southern Germany learned about the French demands, they became angry with France. Bismarck immediately took advantage of this opportunity to sign military alliances with the south German states.

Napoleon then asked Bismarck to help France to obtain Belgium. Again, Bismarck refused. The French claims to Belgium angered Britain, which was the protector of Belgian independence. British indignation assured Bismarck of Britain's neutrality in the event of war between Prussia and France.

Napoleon was determined to obtain lands on the eastern frontier of France despite his failures on the Rhine and in Belgium. In 1867 he decided to buy Luxembourg, a neutral state. Although her population was mainly French, Luxembourg had a close relationship with Germany. She was a member of the Zollverein and Prussian troops were stationed in her chief city. Napoleon's scheme aroused indignation all over Germany and brought the bitter rivalry between Prussia and France into the open. He was forced to give it up. A conference of European powers finally settled the Luxembourg Question. Luxembourg was to remain neutral and the Prussian troops were to be withdrawn. The Luxembourg Question worsened relations between the French and the Germans and assured Bismarck of the support of the south German states.

Bismarck isolated France from Italy without much difficulty. The Italians had acquired Venetia through Prussian help. They also resented the continued occupation of Rome by French troops.

Russian neutrality was guaranteed because of Bismarck's personal friendship with the Russian tsar. In addition, Bismarck had promised to agree to the repeal of the Black Sea clause of the Treaty of Paris (1856). Russia resented the clause because it neutralized the Black Sea and forbade her to station warships there. Napoleon III's support of the Polish Revolt of 1863 had also angered the Russians.

Austria would not help France because Napoleon III had supported Sardinia in the Austro-Sardinian War of 1859. In addition, she had not yet recovered from the Austro-Prussian War and had to watch Russia on her eastern frontiers. Besides, Austria was grateful to Prussia for not imposing harsh terms on her in the Treaty of Prague. Napoleon III's Mexican campaign had further alienated Austria because it had resulted in the death of the Austrian emperor's brother, Maximilian.

Immediate cause of the war   The immediate cause of the war was the dispute over the Spanish succession, which led to the Ems Telegram incident. After revolutionaries had overthrown Queen Isabella II of Spain in 1868, they began looking for a new ruler. They offered the crown to Prince Leopold, a Hohenzollern, who accepted it in July 1870. France protested and claimed that the move was an attempt to surround her with hostile German influence. Count Benedetti, the French ambassador to Prussia, was instructed to persuade King William I, who was at the German resort of Ems, to urge Leopold to give up the Spanish crown.

On July 12 Leopold himself withdrew without informing William I. When Benedetti met William I the following day, he had been told to obtain a promise from the king that

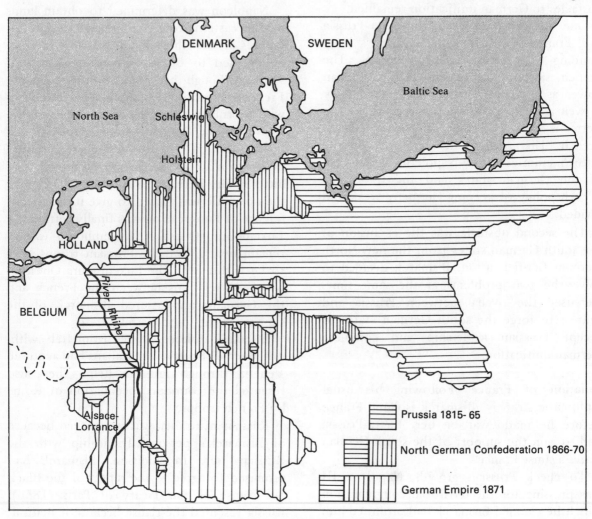

The unification of Germany, 1866-71

no Hohenzollern would ever sit on the Spanish throne. William I politely refused this unreasonable request and told Benedetti that he did not wish to continue with the interview.

Upon learning of Leopold's withdrawal, William I sent a message to inform Benedetti that, as far as he was concerned, the Spanish Succession Question was settled. He also sent a telegram to Bismarck, telling him what had happened and giving him permission to publish it.

Bismarck, von Moltke and von Roon were very disappointed by what they saw as a humiliation by France. But all was not lost. Before releasing the Ems Telegram to the press, Bismarck altered it to make it appear that the king and the ambassador had insulted each other. Both the French and the Prussians were furious. On 14 July 1870 France declared war on Prussia. Thus, by amending the telegram, Bismarck succeeded in provoking war with France. As in the wars against Denmark and Austria, he made his enemy appear to be the aggressor.

Events of the war   In August 1870 the Germans invaded France. One by one, the French generals were defeated. On September 2 the Battle of Sedan was fought. This was the greatest battle in Europe since the Battle of Waterloo. The French were defeated and surrendered the following day. The French defeat brought about the collapse of the Second French Empire. On September 4 a provisional government was established which was later to become the Third French Republic.

The Prussian victories aroused German nationalism. By November 1870, the south German states had agreed to surrender their independence and join the North German Confederation. After their victory at Sedan, the Germans laid siege to Paris. The city finally surrendered on 28 January 1871. Earlier, on January 18, the German Empire was proclaimed at Versailles with William I of

Napoleon III (left) and Bismarck the day after the Battle of Sedan

William I being proclaimed German emperor at Versailles in January 1871

Prussia as emperor. The unification of Germany was complete.

Treaty of Frankfurt   On 10 May 1871 the Treaty of Frankfurt was signed, ending the Franco-Prussian War. The terms were intended

29

to humiliate France. She was forced to surrender Alsace and eastern Lorraine to the new Germany. Franco-German relations were marred by the dispute over Alsace-Lorraine for more than 40 years. France finally recovered the territory under the Treaty of Versailles of 1919.

France was also made to pay a huge indemnity of one billion dollars and to support a German occupation army until the indemnity had been paid. Bismarck thought that it would take a long time for France to pay it. But he was wrong, for the French were able to settle it in less than three years.

The Franco-Prussian War destroyed one empire, the Second French Empire, and created another, the German Empire. In theory, the German Empire was a federation with a constitutional government and Emperor William as its president. In practice, it was a military dictatorship under Prussia. This situation continued until the fall of the Hohenzollern dynasty at the end of the First World War.

THE UNIFICATION OF ITALY

In the 19th century there was another major European country that had not yet been unified — Italy. The unification of Italy bore some resemblance to that of Germany. In both cases, the strongest state led the others under the guidance of its ministers and the protection of its army. But there were marked differences in the methods they used and in the results of their unifications.

Italy before 1830

With the break-up of the Roman Empire in the 5th and 6th centuries A.D, the Italian Peninsula was divided into many small separate states. Italy became 'a mere geographical expression'. Under Napoleon I, the old divisions were reorganized into three large states, giving the Italians a new feeling of national unity. Resentment against the rule of Napoleon strengthened this feeling. With the fall of Napoleon, the Congress of Vienna swept away the changes he had made and restored Italy to her former divisions and governments.

Although the Congress of Vienna had succeeded in abolishing Napoleon's political and territorial changes, it could not destroy liberalism completely. Instead, liberalism was strengthened by the nationalist movement of the early 19th century. The liberals were usually nationalists. There was one very serious problem which the Italians had to solve before Italy could be unified: the expulsion of Austria from Italy. Three factors made it difficult for them to expel Austria. First, the acquisition of Lombardy and Venetia by Austria gave her a base from which she could put down revolts in any part of Italy. Secondly, although the Italian states of Tuscany, Modena and Parma were not directly ruled by Austria, they were nevertheless under her influence because their rulers were Hapsburgs. Finally, not one of the Italian states at this time was strong enough to be accepted by the others as their leader against Austria.

Since the Italians could not fight for their cause in the open, they organized secret societies. Foremost among these before 1831 was the Carbonari (Charcoal-burners). As a result of the activities of these secret societies and the influence of the 1820 Spanish Revolution and the 1830 French Revolution, revolts broke out in many parts in Italy. However, they were all put down with the help of Austria.

Nationalist and revolutionary movements, 1830–48

There were three men who played an important part in the nationalist and revolutionary movements in Italy after 1830: Giuseppi Mazzini, King Charles Albert of Sardinia and Pope Pius IX.

Giuseppi Mazzini (1805-72) The idealist who first aroused a strong desire for unity among the Italians was Mazzini, a native of Genoa. He made them realize that they should be unified because they were one people. It was he who created the spirit of the Risorgimento, the movement to liberate and unify Italy.

In 1831, he founded the patriotic Association of Young Italy. With its more definite aims and inspired leadership, the Young Italy society soon displaced the Carbonari. It appealed to the youth of Italy, and before long it had about 60 000 members.

Mazzini, Italian patriot and revolutionary

In 1849 Mazzini, with the help of Garibaldi, set up the short-lived Roman Republic. Being a fanatic republican, he refused to work with the chief minister of Sardinia, Cavour. Cavour was an advocate of a unified Italy under a monarchy. Even when the Kingdom of all Italy was finally established in 1871, Mazzini refused to recognize it.

King Charles Albert (reigned 1831-49) When Charles Albert became king of Piedmont-Sardinia in 1831, the Italian patriots hoped that he would lead the unification movement. Unlike the other Italian rulers, he sincerely believed in Italian unity. He also wanted Austria to get out of northern Italy. But when Mazzini appealed to him to lead the Italian movement, he refused. Much as he wanted to see a united Italy, he disliked democracy. Later on, he realized that Italy could not be unified without the support of the liberals.

Pius IX (Pope 1846-78) Besides the Young Italians, there was a moderate group who wanted a federal republic under the presidency of the Pope. In 1846, Pius IX was elected Pope. As ruler of the Papal States, he introduced liberal reforms. The Italian patriots began to look upon him as a possible leader of the Italian movement. But when he saw that his reforms inspired uprisings in various parts of Italy, he stopped them. He then associated himself with Austria just like the Popes before him.

War against Austria, 1848-49

During the 1848 revolutions, Piedmont-Sardinia, Tuscany, the Papal States and Naples combined forces under the leadership of King Charles Albert to free Lombardy and Venetia from Austrian rule. The Austrian forces in these two provinces were forced to withdraw to northern Italy. Unfortunately, the Papal and Neapolitan troops soon withdrew from the war. The betrayal of his allies weakened Charles Albert's campaign. The Austrians launched an offensive which led to his defeat in March 1849.

The Italian unification movement suffered a setback after the Italian defeat in the war against Austria and the failure of the 1848 revolutions. Nevertheless, the liberal and nationalist movement had stimulated the desire for unity in two respects. Firstly, it strengthened national feeling so that many Italians still believed that Italy would someday be united. Secondly, for the first time, Sardinia, or Piedmont-Sardinia, was regarded by the other Italian states as the leader in the struggle for unification. (The kingdom of Sardinia included both the island of Sardinia and Piedmont on the mainland. 'Sardinia' in this book refers to the entire kingdom.) But before she could lead a successful unification movement, Sardinia had to strengthen herself.

Moreover, the Italians learned one important lesson: they could not expel Austrian influence by themselves. They needed foreign military aid.

The leaders of Italian unification after 1848

King Victor Emmanuel II (reigned 1849-78) Victor Emmanuel II became king of Sardinia after his father, Charles Albert, abdicated in 1849. After the failure of the 1848 revolutions, Austria tried to pressure him into setting up absolute rule in Sardinia, but he refused. His kingdom became a refuge for

Victor Emmanuel II of Piedmont-Sardinia, first king of a united Italy

Italian liberals who were being persecuted in other Italian states. By maintaining constitutional rule and allowing political refugees to stay in Sardinia, he made himself a possible ruler of a united Italy.

In 1852 Victor Emmanuel appointed Cavour as his prime minister and supported his measures to strengthen Sardinia and to unify Italy. During the Austro-Sardinian War of 1859, Victor Emmanuel made a wise decision in accepting the Treaty of Villafranca. Napoleon III, who had joined the war against Austria, made peace with Emperor Francis Joseph at Villafranca without consulting Sardinia. Cavour did not wish to accept the treaty, but Victor Emmanuel accepted it because he knew that he could not defeat Austria without French support.

In 1860 Victor Emmanuel made another wise move by conquering Naples and the Papal States before Garibaldi could capture Rome. If Garibaldi had attacked Rome, which was occupied by French troops, France would have intervened.

Count Camillo Cavour (1810-61) Cavour belonged to an aristocratic Piedmontese family. His political career began in 1848 when he became a member of the first Piedmontese parliament. In 1852 Victor Emmanuel II appointed him Prime Minister of Sardinia.

Since he strongly believed in constitutionalism, Cavour maintained parliamentary government and reduced the political power of the clerics, who were considered enemies of liberalism. To strengthen Sardinia, he restored financial stability, reorganized the army, promoted public works and concluded commercial treaties with foreign powers. Nevertheless, he knew that no matter how strong Sardinia became, she would still need foreign help to unify Italy.

Since foreign help was essential to Italian unification, Cavour's foreign policy had two main aims: to bring the cause of Italian unification to the attention of the great European powers and to obtain a foreign alliance against Austria. To achieve his aims,

*Prime Minister Cavour of Sardinia, builder of
Italian unification*

secretly helped Garibaldi in the latter's campaigns to conquer Sicily and Naples.

Giuseppi Garibaldi (1807-82) Garibaldi, a native of Nice, was a soldier-adventurer who engaged in irregular warfare to unite Italy. He wanted a united Italy to be a republic, not a monarchy. He was a member of Mazzini's Young Italy. During the 1848 revolutions, he fought under King Charles Albert of Sardinia in the war against Austria. After the collapse of the Roman Republic, which he and

*Garibaldi, Italian revolutionary and leader of
the Red Shirts*

Cavour resorted to propaganda. By publishing many articles calling for Italian unification, he hoped to gain the support of the two possible allies against Austria — Britain and France. Later, he concentrated on France because Britain had no quarrel with Austria.

To gain French support and sympathy, Sardinia joined France, Britain and Turkey against Russia in the Crimean War of 1854-56. As a result, she was recognized as a European power. At the Congress of Paris (1856), Cavour attacked Austria's policy in Italy, bringing the question of Italian unity to the attention of the other European powers. Most important of all, Sardinia succeeded in gaining the support of Napoleon III. Cavour's clever moves earned him the reputation of being one of the shrewdest diplomats in Europe.

In 1858 Cavour made the Pact of Plombieres by which Napoleon III promised to give armed support to Sardinia against Austria. Under the Treaty of Turin (1860), France agreed to Sardinia's annexation of the central Italian duchies and Romagna, in exchange for Nice and Savoy. Finally, Victor Emmanuel's decision to invade the Papal States was based on Cavour's sound advice. By protecting Rome, Sardinia retained the sympathy of the French. Earlier, however, Cavour had

GARIBALDI'S CALL TO ARMS

Let those who wish to continue the war against the stranger come with me. I offer neither pay, nor quarters, nor provisions; I offer hunger, thirst, forced marches, battles and death. Let him who loves his country in his heart and not with his lips only, follow me.

*Garibaldi, after the fall of
the Roman Republic*

Mazzini set up in 1849, he went into exile in America.

In 1859 Garibaldi again returned to Italy and fought in the Austro-Sardinian War. In 1860 he and his 'Thousand' volunteers (Red Shirts) conquered Sicily and part of Naples. He planned to attack Rome from Naples but was stopped by Sardinian troops. Reluctantly,

Garibaldi handed over his territorial conquests to Victor Emmanuel and refused all rewards.

Stages in the unification of Italy

Up to 1859, all attempts to unify Italy had failed for several reasons. The nationalist

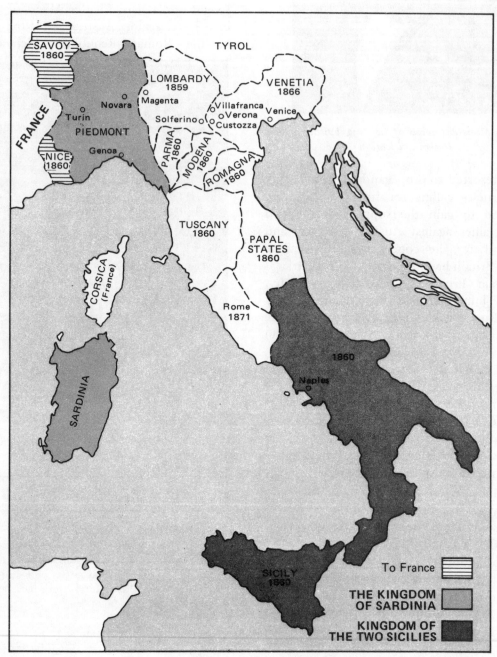

The unification of Italy, 1859-71

leaders had different objectives. One group advocated a federal republic under the presidency of the Pope. Mazzini and Garibaldi favoured a united republic. A third group wanted a united kingdom ruled by the king of Sardinia. (This last objective was the one finally achieved through the efforts of Victor Emmanuel and Cavour.)

Lack of leadership was another reason. None of the Italian states could be looked upon by the other states as their leader. Nor was there an Italian state strong enough to expel Austria or drive the French troops from Rome. Finally, the Italians had no national army. The Austrians, on the other hand, had an efficient army based in Lombardy and Venetia in northern Italy, from where they could put down revolutions in any part of the country.

From 1859, however, the Italians began to make progress in their struggle to unify Italy. The Italian unification movement can be divided into five stages.

Stage I   Austro-Sardinian War (1859)

Background: the Pact of Plombieres (1858)
After Napoleon III came to power, he promised to 'do something for Italy'. He had joined the Carbonari in his younger days because he sympathized with Italian nationalism. Besides, opposition to Austria had been a traditional part of French foreign policy.

Fulfilling his promise, however, would not be easy. The French clerical party, his main political support, opposed Italian unification because it might deprive the Pope of his lands. The country's foreign policy was also opposed to the creation of a powerful state on her southeastern frontier. Napoleon did not, in fact, want a strong unified Italy but a loose union of states. A strong Italy would upset the balance of power in Europe. Finally, his own court was pro-Austrian.

Napoleon was therefore torn between fulfilling his promise to help Italy and pleasing the French Catholics. In his efforts to please everyone, he ended up offending everyone. In 1858, an Italian exile in France named Orsini threw a bomb at Napoleon's carriage to protest at his failure to carry out his promise. The assassination attempt finally convinced him that he must do something for Italy.

In 1858 Napoleon III and Cavour met at the summer resort of Plombieres and signed a secret pact:

- France was to give armed support to Sardinia to expel the Austrians from Venetia and Lombardy — on condition that France appeared to be protecting Sardinia against Austrian aggression.
- Once Austria was expelled from Venetia and Lombardy, these two states were to join Sardinia to form the Kingdom of North Italy. The Papal States and the Kingdom of the Two Sicilies (Naples and Sicily) were to remain as they were. Tuscany was to be a separate kingdom. These four states were to form a federation under the presidency of the Pope. Napoleon obviously wanted an independent but weak Italy in which Austrian influence would be replaced by French influence.
- For helping Italy, France was to receive Nice and Savoy.
- An alliance of the royal houses of France and Sardinia was to be formed through the marriage of Napoleon III's cousin and Victor Emmanuel's daughter.

Napoleon III agreed to help Sardinia because he firmly believed in nationalism. A military victory over Austria would also increase his prestige and popularity in France. Making the Pope president of the proposed Italian Federation would enhance his popularity with the French Catholics.

Cavour was not pleased with Napoleon's proposed division of Italy, nor was Victor Emmanuel pleased to see his daughter married to Napoleon's cousin. But both men accepted the terms of the Pact of Plombieres in order to gain French support against Austria. Moreover, they hoped that the creation of the Kingdom of North Italy might lead to a Kingdom of all Italy. Cavour then proceeded to find a cause for war which would make it appear that Austria was the aggressor.

Outbreak of the Austro-Sardinian War After signing the Pact of Plombieres, France and Sardinia provoked Austria into war.

In January 1859, Napoleon III told the Austrian ambassador to France that relations between the two countries were deteriorating. Victor Emmanuel followed this up within days by telling the Sardinian parliament that Sardinia was not insensitive to the suffering in so many parts of Italy. A large French loan was then granted to Sardinia and Napoleon gave his approval to the publication of a pamphlet in Paris supporting the Italian cause. Cavour then concentrated troops on the borders of Lombardy resulting in minor clashes between Sardinian and Austrian troops. To increase provocation, he mobilized the Sardinian army.

Sensing that Europe was on the brink of war, Britain took the lead in preventing it. There was now a good chance that the differences between Sardinia and Austria would be settled.

At this point, Austria played into Cavour's hands by demanding that Sardinia demobilize her troops in three days. Cavour seized the opportunity to make Austria appear as an aggressor and refused the Austrian demand. In April 1859 Austria declared war on Sardinia. Napoleon then declared war on Austria as promised in the secret pact.

Progress of the war In May, French troops entered northern Italy and joined the Sardinian army which was placed under French command. A volunteer army under Garibaldi also joined the war. In June, the Franco-Sardinian forces defeated the Austrians in the important battles of Magenta and Solferino and the Austrians were driven out of Lombardy. The next objective was to expel Austria from Venetia. Seeing that Austrian defeat was imminent, the pro-Austrian rulers of the central duchies of Tuscany, Parma and Modena fled from their states.

With victory in sight, Napoleon suddenly made peace with Austria at Villafranca on July 11 without consulting Cavour. When Victor Emmanuel decided to accept the cease-fire, Cavour was so disappointed that he gave up his post, although he accepted it again in 1860.

Treaty of Villafranca The terms of the treaty were as follows:
- Sardinia was to receive Lombardy from Austria.
- Venetia was to be retained by Austria but was to become a member of the proposed Italian Federation under the presidency of the Pope.
- The rulers of the central Italian states who had fled were to be restored.

Several factors influenced Napoleon in suddenly making peace with Austria.
- Since he had no strong personal convictions, he was inclined to act suddenly and rashly. He was motivated by idealism one moment and by selfish interest the next.
- When the war revealed how strong and popular Sardinia was, he was alarmed. He feared that the war would unite not only northern Italy but also the whole Italian Peninsula, thereby creating a strong rival on France's southeastern frontier. A strong united Italy was not one of his objectives in helping Sardinia.
- One of his motives in supporting Sardinia was to increase the prestige of the Pope. However, a united Italy under Victor Emmanuel II would lessen the power of the Pope, thereby antagonizing the French Catholics.
- The French Catholics, moreover, did not wish Catholic Austria to suffer a humiliating defeat.
- There were signs that Prussia was ready to come to the aid of Austria. Prussia was Austria's rival for leadership among the German states and should have been glad to see Austria defeated. But a disastrous defeat for Austria would make France very

powerful and would disrupt the balance of power in Europe. Napoleon therefore decided to end the war before Prussia joined in.

- Napoleon also feared Prussian military moves on the Rhine frontier while he was busy fighting Austria.

Stage II (1860)

The Italians were angry at what they regarded as Napoleon's betrayal of their cause. The people of Tuscany, Parma, Modena and Romagna refused to take back their old rulers. Under the Treaty of Turin (1860), Napoleon agreed to plebiscites in these states to decide their fate, on condition that Nice and Savoy were ceded to France. They voted for union with Sardinia.

With Sardinia's acquisition of Lombardy (by the Treaty of Villafranca) and of the central Italian states (by plebiscite), Victor Emmanuel had become king of north-central Italy from the Alps to the Papal States, with the exception of Venetia which remained under Austrian control. The creation of the new kingdom was a big step towards Italian unification.

As a result of Napoleon's betrayal, Cavour gave up the idea of unifying Italy with the help of a foreign power. From then on, the Italians were to rely on their own efforts to achieve unification. In this struggle, Cavour was aided by Garibaldi.

Stage III (1860–61)

Garibaldi's invasion of Sicily and Naples The island of Sicily was part of the pro-Austrian Kingdom of the Two Sicilies. In 1859 the Sicilians plotted to overthrow their weak and oppressive king, Francis II. Garibaldi promised to help, provided they revolted in the name of Italy and Victor Emmanuel. They also appealed to Cavour for help. As prime minister of one state he could not openly support a revolt in another. Nevertheless, he secretly subsidized Garibaldi's plan. In April 1860 the Sicilians revolted. The following month, Garibaldi with his 'Thousand' followers (wearing red shirts) successfully invaded and conquered Sicily. Their next target was Naples.

In August 1860 Garibaldi and his Red Shirts crossed to the mainland and attacked the remaining forces of King Francis II. Except for some fortresses in the north, they easily conquered the kingdom, entering the city of Naples in September. Garibaldi proclaimed himself Dictator of Naples. Inspired by his victory, he made no secret of his plan to advance against Rome.

Victor Emmanuel's invasion of the Papal States and Naples Cavour and Victor Emmanuel were alarmed at Garibaldi's plans to attack Rome. Such an attack would provoke French as well as Austrian hostility and intervention. By allowing it, they would also antagonize the Italian Catholics. Besides, Garibaldi planned to set up an independent republic which could be an obstacle to the creation of a kingdom of all Italy. When he refused to heed appeals not to advance on Rome, Cavour intervened to prevent war and save the Italian cause.

In September 1860 Victor Emmanuel invaded the Papal States to forestall Garibaldi's threatened attack on Rome. After defeating the papal troops, he marched south to Naples. In October a plebiscite was held in which the people of Naples and Sicily voted for union with Sardinia. Realizing that he could not retain Naples by himself, Garibaldi handed over his territorial conquests to Victor Emmanuel. Soon afterwards, he retired and led the life of a simple farmer, refusing all honours and rewards for his services.

By November 1860 Sardinia had annexed Naples, Sicily, and all the papal lands except Rome and its neighbouring territory. Rome was left to the Pope in order to prevent French intervention.

In February 1861 Italy's first parliament

Meeting of Garibaldi (left) and King Victor Emmanuel II of Sardinia

met at Turin. In March Victor Emmanuel was proclaimed King of Italy. For the first time since the fall of the Roman Empire in the 5th century A.D , Italy, with the exception of Rome and Venetia, was a united country.

Cavour did not doubt that Rome and Venetia would eventually be added to the new kingdom but he did not live to see the completion of Italian unification. He died in June 1861.

Stage IV (1866)

Italy acquired Venetia through the help of Prussia. In the Austro-Prussian War of 1866, Italy joined Prussia against Austria on Bismarck's promise that she would receive Venetia if they won the war. When they did win it, Austria returned Venetia to Italy.

Stage V (1870–71)

It was through the indirect help of Prussia that Italy acquired her national historical capital, Rome. With the outbreak of the Franco-Prussian War in 1870, the French troops stationed in Rome were recalled to fight the Prussians. Following the French defeat at Sedan in September 1870, the Italians occupied Rome. In June 1871 Victor Emmanuel entered the city. At last all of Italy was unified. She was no longer 'a mere geographical expression'.

Pope Pius IX, however, refused to recognize the new Kingdom of Italy. Successive popes maintained the same policy. The question was not settled until 1929, when Pope Pius XI and Mussolini signed the Lateran Treaty. Under this treaty, the Pope was confirmed as the ruler of the Vatican City. In return, he recognized the Italian government.

COMPARISON OF THE ITALIAN AND GERMAN UNIFICATIONS

The unification of Italy bore some resemblance to that of Germany but there were also marked differences.

Similarities

- Napoleon I fostered the idea of nationalism in both the German and Italian states. He fostered it among the Germans by creating the Confederation of the Rhine and among the Italians by reorganizing the nine Italian states into three large administrative units.
- The Congress of Vienna helped both Prussia and Sardinia to assume leadership of the German and Italian states, by awarding them territories.
- The liberals in both Germany and Italy made unsuccessful attempts at unification during the 1848 revolutions: by creating the Frankfurt Parliament in Germany and by waging Sardinia's war of independence against Austria. From then on, nationalist feeling dominated the unification movements at the expense of liberal ideals.
- Germany and Italy faced a common obstacle to national unity — Austria. They had to get rid of Austrian influence before they could achieve unification.
- In both cases, the strongest state assumed leadership in the struggle for unification: Prussia in Germany and Sardinia in Italy. Both states went through a thorough economic transformation in order to strengthen themselves.
- Unification in both cases was achieved under the guidance of clever chief ministers: Bismarck in Germany and Cavour in Italy.
- In their struggle for unification, both Prussia and Sardinia tried to win friends and allies: Prussia with France, Sardinia and Russia; Sardinia with France, Britain and Prussia. In the case of France, both first befriended her and later considered her their enemy.
- Both achieved success through military victories, not democratic methods. Prussia fought three wars while Sardinia fought the Austro-Sardinian War and joined Prussia in the Austro-Prussian War.
- Both strove for national unity at about the same time and both were unified in 1870-71.
- Both the German and Italian governments clashed with the Catholic Church after unification: the struggle between Church and state in Germany known as the Kulturkampf and the refusal of the Pope to recognize the new Kingdom of Italy.

Differences

- Before Cavour could start the process of Italian unification, he had to strengthen Sardinia through internal reforms to make the other Italian states accept her as their leader. When Bismarck began the struggle for unification, Prussia was already a strong and efficient state.
- Sardinia needed foreign aid to unite Italy while Prussia relied mainly on her own strength.
- Bismarck had a definite plan to unify Germany which was formulated well in advance. Cavour had no such plan. He merely seized any opportunity that came along.
- Before Bismarck went to war, he was careful to isolate the enemy. Cavour used no such strategy.
- During the struggle for unification, Sardinia was careful not to lose the support of the predominantly Roman Catholic population of Italy. This was one of the reasons why Cavour intervened to stop Garibaldi from attacking Rome. Bismarck did not have much trouble with the German Catholics because only the south German states were predominantly Catholic.
- In the struggle for unification, Cavour had to sacrifice Italian territory: Nice and Savoy. Bismarck succeeded without losing any Prussian territory.
- After unification Germany became a federal state in which most of the local rulers kept their thrones. In contrast, Italy became a centralized state in which local rulers lost their thrones.

- Both King William I of Prussia and Bismarck were opposed to liberalism, so the government of the new German Empire was actually a military dictatorship. King Victor Emmanuel II and Cavour believed in constitutionalism, so the new Kingdom of Italy was liberal in character.
- The new German Empire had many foreign peoples within its borders, such as the Danes, the Poles and the French in Alsace-Lorraine. The population of the new Kingdom of Italy was mainly Italian.

FORMATION OF THE DUAL MONARCHY

The failure of the 1848 revolutions in the Austrian Empire was followed by harsh repression of liberal and nationalist movements. Absolute rule was imposed upon all the peoples in the empire under a new constitution in 1851. Government administration was centralized in Vienna. Germanization was carried out among the non-German people in the empire. Nonetheless, Hungarian nationalism continued to grow and finally triumphed with the formation of the Dual Monarchy in 1867.

The weakening of the Austrian Empire

Defeats in the Austro-Sardinian War of 1859 and the Austro-Prussian War of 1866 convinced the Austrians that the old political system would have to be drastically altered. If the empire was to survive, the Hungarian nationalists would have to be appeased. The German liberals and reformers in Austria were prepared to grant constitutional government to Hungary, but not independence.

The Hungarians themselves did not wish to dissolve the union with Austria. What they wanted was a federation in which both Austria and Hungary would have equal rights and equal representation.

The establishment of the Dual Monarchy

After Austria's defeat by Prussia in 1866, the Austrian emperor offered to make the Hungarians equal partners in the empire. The Hungarians accepted the offer.

The constitution which established the Dual Monarchy was adopted in 1867. It separated Austria and Hungary and gave each country its own constitution, official language, flag and parliament. But it also provided two links between the two states: the Hapsburg ruler was made Emperor of Austria and King of Hungary; finance, defence and foreign affairs were placed under ministers common to both states. These ministers were supervised by an assembly composed of 60 members from the Austrian diet and an equal number from the Hungarian diet.

Under this new arrangement the Austrian Empire became the Austro-Hungarian Empire, which lasted until the First World War.

The formation of the Dual Monarchy satisfied the Hungarian nationalists but not the minority races within the two states, such as the Czechs, Croats and Serbs. Nationalism among these subject peoples was suppressed by the two dominant nationalities. Their discontent became a source of trouble until the First World War.

Having lost her influence in the German states, Austria was overshadowed by Germany in European affairs. The Dual Monarchy then became increasingly interested in the Balkans. Its expansionist ambitions there brought it into conflict with Russia.

This Austro-Russian rivalry complicated further the already complex Eastern Question. By heightening international tension, it became a direct cause of the First World War.

THE EASTERN QUESTION

By the 19th century, the Ottoman (Turkish) Empire was decaying and declining. It was

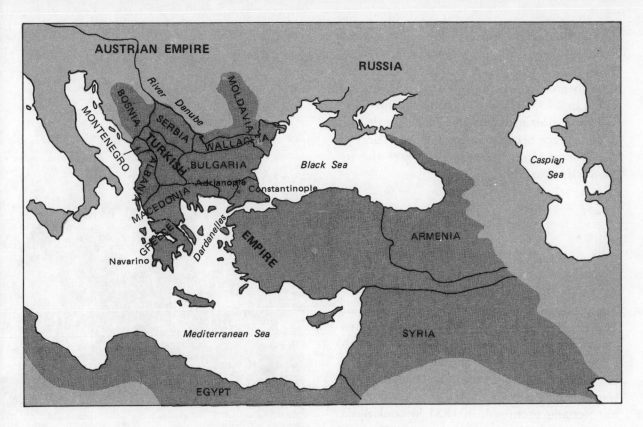

The Ottoman Empire (Turkey) in 1815

nicknamed the 'sick man of Europe' and was expected to collapse at any time.

The Eastern Question concerned the future of the Turkish possessions in the southeastern corner of Europe when the Ottoman Empire collapsed. The problem was complicated by the fact that the Turkish rulers were Muslim while most of their subject peoples in the Balkan Peninsula were Slav by race and Christian by religion. With the growth of nationalism among the Balkan peoples, there were frequent rebellions in the area.

The Eastern Question was made even more complex by the attitudes of the European powers. Russia wanted to expand into the Balkans because she needed a trade outlet into the Mediterranean. Britain, Austria and Germany wanted to preserve the Ottoman Empire in order to stop Russia from expanding. Britain regarded Russian expansion to the Mediterranean as a threat to her sea power. Austria herself wanted to expand into the Balkans. Germany did not wish to see a strong

Russia, for this might upset the balance of power in Europe. As for France, at times she opposed the Ottoman Empire; at other times, she supported it.

Rivalry among the European powers over the fate of the Ottoman Empire was one of the causes of some European alliances in the late 19th century. The Eastern Question, therefore, was a principal reason for the outbreak of the First World War.

In the 19th and early 20th centuries, the Eastern Question caused international crises on six important occasions:

- The War of Greek Independence, 1821-29 (see Chapter 1)
- Mehemet Ali and the Syrian Question, 1831-41
- The Crimean War, 1854-56
- The Congress of Berlin, 1878
- The Balkan Wars, 1912 and 1913 (see Chapter 14)
- The First World War, 1914-18 (see Chapter 14)

41

Before the Greeks won their independence, the Ottoman Empire was already losing control over its provinces in the Balkans. Montenegro gained autonomy (self-government) in 1799, and Serbia, in 1829. But both remained nominally under Turkish rule. In 1829, Greece became independent of Turkey. The War of Greek Independence gave rise to the Syrian Question.

Mehemet Ali and the Syrian Question, 1831–41

The problem of Mehemet Ali The sultan of Turkey had promised Syria and Crete to Mehemet Ali, governor of the Turkish province of Egypt, in return for his help in the War of Greek Independence. When the war ended, Mehemet Ali received Crete only, not Syria as promised. In 1831 he took Syria by force and was preparing to attack Turkey. The sultan appealed to the European powers for help.

When Russian troops began to pour into Turkey, Britain and France were alarmed, for this would give Russia the strongest influence in Turkey. The two powers intervened with the support of Austria and in 1833 they forced the sultan to give Syria to Mehemet Ali.

In 1839 the sultan invaded Syria to recover that territory. The Turks were no match for Mehemet Ali's forces, and the very existence of the Turkish Empire was soon threatened. At this point, the European powers, except France, decided to stop Mehemet Ali from gaining control of the Turkish Empire.

The settlement of the Syrian Question In 1840, the Syrian Question was finally settled by the Treaty of London which was signed by Britain, Russia, Austria and Prussia, leaving France out because she had supported Mehemet Ali. By this treaty, Mehemet Ali was to become the hereditary ruler of Egypt but

Mehemet Ali, ruler of Egypt who tried to seize Syria from the sultan of Turkey

was to give up Syria to Turkey. He refused to accept these terms until he was defeated by a joint expedition of the Great Powers. (The royal house he founded, ruled Egypt until 1952.)

In the settlement of the Syrian Question, France learned a lesson: she should co-operate with the other European powers in solving international problems. In 1841 she joined Britain, Russia, Austria and Prussia in signing the Straits Convention. The Dardanelles Straits were closed to all foreign warships in time of war.

After the signing of the Treaty of London of 1840 and the Straits Convention of 1841, the preservation of the Turkish Empire became a basic policy of the European powers, except Russia. Mehemet Ali's interference in European affairs also ended.

The Crimean War, 1854–56

The next important event arising from the Eastern Question was the Crimean War of 1854-56 which has been described as one of the most useless and costly wars ever fought. It was fought because the European powers, led by Britain, objected to Russia's policy of aggression against Turkey, and because of Napoleon III's desire to win military glory abroad.

Underlying causes The underlying causes of the war can be traced to the attitudes of Russia, France and Britain towards the Eastern Question.

For Russia, military victory over Turkey would increase her chances of securing warm-water ports in the Mediterranean and of gaining control of the Black Sea and the Dardanelles. This would give her a dominant position in the eastern Mediterranean. It would also establish her influence and control over the Turkish Empire, especially in the Balkans. As protector of the Greek Orthodox Church, Russia had to make sure that the rights and privileges of the Greek monks within the Turkish Empire were maintained. French monks in Palestine were threatening the prestige and position which had been held by the Greek monks for centuries.

In France, Napoleon III was still looking for a chance to strengthen his position at home by winning military glory abroad. To attain his objective, he made use of the rivalry between the French and Greek monks in Palestine. By protecting the French monks, he would have an excuse to make war on Russia and he also hoped to win the support of the French Catholics.

To the British, the southern advance of Russia had to be stopped at all costs. If Russia succeeded in acquiring Turkey's European possessions and became a Mediterranean power, she would upset the balance of power in Europe as well as threaten British interests in the Middle East and possibly India.

The Crimean War, 1854-56

Events leading to war When the power and influence of the Catholic Church in France declined during the 1789 French Revolution, the French monks in Palestine lost the custody of the sacred places to the Greek monks who were under the protection of Russia. In 1852 Napoleon III demanded that the sultan of Turkey return the guardianship to the French monks.

When the sultan granted the French demand in 1853, the tsar strongly objected. He demanded instead that he should be recognized as the protector of all the members of the Orthodox Church in the Turkish Empire. The sultan, encouraged by France and Britain, rejected the Russian demand whereupon Russian troops invaded the Turkish provinces of Moldavia and Wallachia in June 1853. When Russia refused Turkey's demand to withdraw her troops, Turkey declared war against her in October 1853.

The dispute over the guardianship of the holy places in Palestine thus provided the immediate cause of the Crimean War.

Progress of the war In March 1854, Britain and France entered the war on the pretext of helping Turkey to expel the Russians from Turkish soil. Sardinia joined them at the

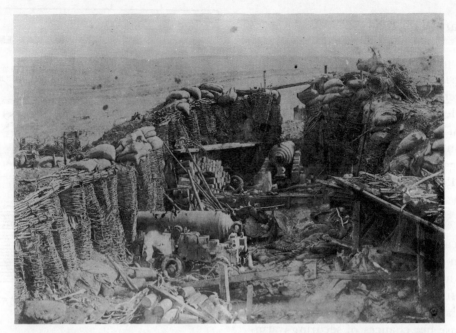

Fortifications of the Russian naval base of Sebastopol during the Crimean War

beginning of 1855. Britain's real motive was to weaken Russia while Napoleon III's was to win military glory. Sardinia entered the war to gain French support for Italian unification.

In the meantime, the Russians crossed the Danube and advanced towards Constantinople. By the summer of 1854, however, the Turks had forced the Russians to retreat back across the Danube. The war appeared to be over, but Britain and France refused to withdraw.

In the early months of 1855, Lord Palmerston, the new British prime minister, vigorously conducted the war to bring it to an end. In March, Tsar Nicholas I died. His successor, Alexander II, wanted to make peace as he was anxious to introduce reforms in Russia. Finally, in September, the allies captured the Russian naval base of Sebastopol. The fighting was over. In March 1856 the peace treaty ending the Crimean War was signed at Paris.

Treaty of Paris, 1856 The terms of the treaty were as follows:
- The allies restored their conquests to Russia but Sebastopol was not to be fortified.
- The Black Sea was neutralized. Russia and

Turkey were forbidden to maintain any military or naval bases on it. It was to be open to merchant ships but closed to warships.
- The Danube was to be an international waterway.
- Moldavia and Wallachia (modern Rumania) ceased to be Russian protectorates. They were to be self-governing but were to remain nominally under Turkish rule.
- Russia ceded Bessarabia to Moldavia.
- Russia gave up her claim as protector of the Christians in the Turkish Empire, and the sultan promised better treatment of his Christian subjects.
- The sultan promised to strengthen his rule through reforms.
- Turkey was recognized as a European power, which meant she had the right to be represented in conferences of the Great Powers in future.

The Treaty of Paris was significant in several respects:
- Russian attempts to expand into the Balkans and the Mediterranean were temporarily checked and the Turkish Empire remained intact. The treaty terms,

44

The Balkans: Treaty of Paris, 1856

therefore, satisfied Britain's policy which was anti-Russian and pro-Turkish. Nevertheless, Turkey continued to decline and Russian expansionist ambitions remained.

- As a result of the neutralization of the Black Sea, Russian naval power no longer posed a threat to British and French power in the Mediterranean.
- Napoleon III achieved his objectives of seeking military glory abroad by defeating Russia in the war and retaining French influence in the Middle East.

Later events showed that the Treaty of Paris failed to provide a lasting solution to the Eastern Question. The Great Powers made Turkey promise to reform her government, but they took no steps to see that this promise was fulfilled. The government remained inefficient. The sultan also failed to fulfil his promise to improve the conditions of the Christian minorities. Instead, he persecuted them. In 1859 Moldavia and Wallachia were united under a single government to form the state of Rumania, which was recognized by Turkey in 1862. In 1870 Russia, with the support of Bismarck, rejected the clauses neutralizing the Black Sea. She began to refortify Sebastopol and build a fleet on the Black Sea.

The non-fulfilment of the treaty terms caused more trouble which led to the Congress of Berlin of 1878.

Congress of Berlin, 1878

Revolts in the Balkans, 1875-76   The failure of the sultan to fulfil his promise to improve the conditions of his Christian subjects aroused widespread discontent among the Balkan peoples. At the same time, the Russians encouraged Pan-Slavism in the Balkans. Pan-Slavism was a movement which aimed to bring all the Slavs under the leadership of Russia, the greatest Slav power.

In 1875 the people of Bosnia and Herzegovina refused to pay taxes to the Turkish government and revolted. The disturbances spread to Serbia and Montenegro. Realizing that the revolts in the Balkans could threaten the peace of Europe, the rulers of Austria-Hungary, Germany and Russia decided to intervene. They called upon the sultan to carry out reforms as promised in the Treaty of Paris. He agreed but the rebels did not trust him and refused to end their armed rebellion.

Matters turned from bad to worse when the Bulgarians revolted in May 1876. In June and July respectively, Serbia and Montenegro declared war on Turkey. The Turks now made a determined effort to crush the rebels. They attacked Bulgaria and brutally massacred thousands, including women and children.

The Bulgarian atrocities aroused indignation all over Europe. Britain called a conference of European powers at Constantinople in December 1876 to deal with the problem. The conference failed to come up with a solution. Russia was thus left alone to act against Turkey and support the Balkan rebels.

The Second Russo-Turkish War, 1877-78 In April 1877 Russia, after securing the neutrality of Austria (by promising her a protectorate over Bosnia and Herzegovina), declared war on Turkey. Rumania, Serbia, Montenegro and Bulgaria supported her. Aided by Rumanian troops, the Russians crossed the Danube, entered Bulgaria and advanced towards Constantinople. For a while, their advance was checked by the Turks. But by December, Turkish resistance had crumbled and the Russians continued their advance towards Constantinople.

At this point, Britain and Austria-Hungary put pressure on Russia to end the war as they did not want Constantinople to fall into Russian hands. Russia yielded to this pressure and signed the Treaty of San Stefano with Turkey, ending the Second Russo-Turkish War. (The First Russo-Turkish War was fought in 1828-29.)

Treaty of San Stefano, 1878 Russia dictated the terms of the Treaty of San Stefano, which was signed in March 1878:

- Turkey was to return Bessarabia to Russia.
- Rumania was to receive part of Dobrudja from Turkey and her independence was to be recognized.
- A 'Big Bulgaria' (from the Danube to the Aegean Sea) was to be created, cutting Turkey off from her Balkan lands. It was to be self-governing but nominally under Turkish rule.
- Serbia and Montenegro were to be enlarged and their independence recognized.
- Bosnia and Herzegovina were to be self-governing but still nominally subject to Turkey.

The Treaty of San Stefano was unacceptable to the other European powers, especially Britain and Austria-Hungary, as they regarded it as too favourable to Russia. The treaty terms would put an end to Turkish power in Europe, and the Balkan states which had just

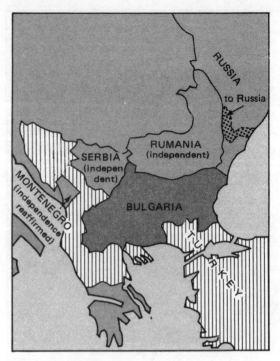

Arrangements proposed at the Treaty of San Stefano, 1878

won their independence were bound to become Russian dependencies. Such a position went against the policy of the other Great Powers. Austria-Hungary opposed the treaty because it blocked her expansionist ambitions in the Balkans. None of the other European powers wished to see Big Bulgaria become a Russian dependency, for this would increase Russian influence and upset the balance of power. Led by Britain, they demanded a revision of the Treaty of San Stefano, claiming that it violated the Treaty of Paris (1856).

Russia at first refused, but when Britain threatened war, she gave in. In July 1878 the Congress of Berlin was held to revise the Treaty of San Stefano.

The obvious choice for the chairmanship of the Congress of Berlin was Bismarck, the 'honest broker'. He was regarded as the most impartial party in that he only wanted to reconcile the two other partners of the Dreikaiserbund — Russia and Austria-Hungary. In fact, he was later secretly pleased with the

46

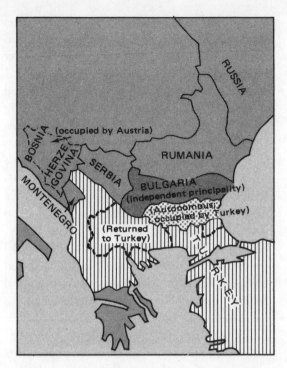

As revised by the Treaty of Berlin, 1878

Bismarck, 'honest broker' of the Congress of Berlin of 1878

Berlin settlement because it had strengthened Austro-German friendship without causing an open break between Germany and Russia. At the same time, it earned him the gratitude of Turkey which led to friendly Turko-German relations.

Provisions of the Treaty of Berlin The Congress of Berlin revised the Treaty of San Stefano as follows:

- Serbia, Rumania and Montenegro retained their independence but Montenegro was reduced in size.
- Bosnia and Herzegovina remained nominally under Turkish rule but were to be administered by Austria-Hungary.
- Russia was to retain Bessarabia.
- Big Bulgaria was to be split up into three parts: Eastern Rumelia, Macedonia and the rest of Bulgaria. Eastern Rumelia was to have a Christian governor but remain under Turkish rule. Macedonia was to remain a wholly Turkish possession. The rest of Bulgaria was to remain self-governing but still nominally under Turkish rule. After Bulgaria's victory in the Bulgo-Serbian War of 1885, she annexed Eastern Rumelia, further reducing Turkish holdings in Europe.

There were some new provisions. Britain was to receive Cyprus as compensation for Russia's retention of Bessarabia. Despite the sultan's failure to keep his promise to treat his Christian subjects well in the Treaty of Paris, he still made the same promise in the Congress of Berlin. Greece was promised Thessaly which she took in 1881.

Results of the Treaty of Berlin The Treaty of Berlin had some good results. There was no major war over the Eastern Question until the Balkan Wars of 1912 and 1913. The Turkish Empire was preserved, for it still had some control in the Balkans. Russian expansion into the Balkans had been checked. The settlement was, therefore, a diplomatic victory for Britain, Austria and Germany. Russia's diplomatic defeat forced her to give up her active policy in the Balkans for a time and she turned to Asia for expansion.

The Treaty of Berlin, however, created more problems than it solved:

- It had not settled the Eastern Question completely, so this remained a source of future conflict. It only postponed the break-up of the Turkish Empire and further complicated the Eastern Question. When the empire finally collapsed, the problems which the Berlin settlement was supposed to have solved re-emerged.

- By placing Bosnia and Herzegovina under Austrian control, the treaty smashed the nationalist hopes of the people of the two provinces. They later conspired with their fellow Slavs, especially the Serbs, to overthrow Austrian rule and create a united Slav state. The authors of the treaty had not learned anything from the disasters that followed the Congress of Vienna of 1815. They continued to ignore nationalism in their decisions. When Austria annexed Bosnia and Herzegovina in 1908, Serbia was angry because she herself wanted them. The Austro-Serbian hostility led to the Sarajevo murders which became the immediate cause of the First World War.

- Keeping the Macedonian Christians under Turkish rule showed that the authors of the treaty had not learned anything from the sultan's failure to keep his promise to give his Christian subjects better treatment. The persecution of the Christians continued, as seen in the massacre of the Armenians in 1894-96. When the Balkan League demanded better treatment of the Macedonian Christians, the sultan refused and the Balkan War of 1912 broke out.

- During the Congress of Berlin, Germany sided with her former enemy, Austria, against her former ally, Russia. This foreshadowed the division of Europe into two rival camps, which, in turn, led to the First World War.

- Bulgaria was dissatisfied with her reduced size. When she tried to expand later on, she clashed with the other Balkan states. This conflict led to the Balkan War of 1913.

- The Turks were disappointed at Britain's role in determining the treaty terms. British influence in Constantinople declined and so prepared the way for an increase in German influence over Turkey. Germany later obtained the right to build the Berlin-Baghdad Railway, an issue which created friction between Germany and Britain just before the First World War.

- In checking Russian ambitions in the Balkans, the treaty let loose another ambitious power, Austria. The congress gave her control over Bosnia and Herzegovina, which encouraged her to expand into the Balkans. This created a new problem in the balance of power in the Balkans.

- Turkey was disappointed at the action of her so-called friends, Britain and Austria. They helped to preserve the empire but they also acquired territories at her expense. Britain obtained Cyprus while Austria was given control of Bosnia and Herzegovina.

- Russia felt cheated because the treaty deprived her of her gains in the Treaty of San Stefano.

- Greece was disappointed because the congress did not take immediate action on her claims to Thessaly and Crete.

The Berlin settlement was indeed a very poor attempt and probably satisfied only Britain and Austria.

BREAK-UP OF THE TURKISH EMPIRE IN EUROPE AND THE RISE OF NATION STATES IN THE BALKANS

1799	Turkey grants autonomy (self-government) to Montenegro.
1829	Treaty of Adrianople ending First Russo-Turkish War (1828-29): • Turkey acknowledges independence of Greece but the Greeks still have to pay tribute to Turks. • Russia establishes protectorate over Turkish provinces of Wallachia and Moldavia. Turkey grants autonomy to Serbia.
1832	Greece gains complete independence.
1856	Treaty of Paris ending Crimean War (1854-56): • Great Powers of Europe guarantee self-government of Serbia, Moldavia and Wallachia. • Russia cedes Bessarabia to the Turkish province of Moldavia.
1862	Turkey recognizes existence of Rumania (combination of Moldavia and Wallachia).
1878 (March)	Treaty of San Stefano ending Second Russo-Turkish War (1877-78): • Turkey returns Bessarabia to Russia. • 'Big Bulgaria' is created, cutting off Turkey from her Balkan lands. • Serbia and Montenegro are enlarged and their independence recognized. • Bosnia and Herzegovina become self-governing but still nominally under Turkish rule. • Independence of Rumania is recognized.
1878 (June)	Congress of Berlin revises Treaty of San Stefano: • Russia keeps Bessarabia. • Big Bulgaria is split into three parts. (Turkey recovers southern section including Macedonia.) • Serbia, Rumania and Montenegro gain complete independence. • Thessaly is promised to Greece (Greece takes it in 1881.) • Austria is given the right to administer Turkish provinces of Bosnia and Herzegovina. • Britain gains Cyprus.
1885	Bulgaria annexes Eastern Rumelia.
1908	Austria annexes Bosnia and Herzegovina. Bulgaria proclaims complete independence.
1912	First Balkan War: Turkey loses Macedonia to Balkan powers.
1913	Treaty of London (May): Albania becomes independent. Treaty of Bucharest (August) ending Second Balkan War: • Macedonia is split between Serbia and Greece. • Rumania gains southern Dobrudja. • All European territories of Turkish Empire become independent, except Bosnia and Herzegovina which are still ruled by Austria-Hungary.

QUESTIONS

1. What were the principal factors working for and against the unification of Germany between 1815 and 1850?

2. Explain why the Frankfurt Parliament of 1848-49 failed to unify Germany.

3. What factors made it possible for Prussia to take the leadership of the German states from Austria and unify Germany?

4. Explain how Bismarck made use of skilful diplomacy and 'blood and iron' (use of force) to unify Germany.

5. Explain why all attempts to unify Italy before 1859 failed.

6. What part did **each** of the following play in the nationalist and revolutionary movements in Italy in 1830-50?
   (a) Giuseppi Mazzini
   (b) King Charles Albert of Piedmont-Sardinia
   (c) Pope Pius IX

7. In what ways did Austria block the unifications of Germany and Italy?

8. What did **each** of the following do for the unification of Italy?
   (a) Count Cavour
   (b) Giuseppi Garibaldi
   (c) King Victor Emmanuel II

9. What did Napoleon III do for Italian unification, and why?

10. Describe the part played by foreign powers in the unification of Italy.

11. Compare and contrast the unifications of Germany and Italy.

12. What is meant by the Eastern Question? Explain how it was made more complicated by the attitudes of the European powers.

13. How did Mehemet Ali's attempts to take Syria by force from Turkey affect international relations?

14. What were the terms of the Treaty of Paris which ended the Crimean War? Why did the treaty fail to provide a lasting settlement of the Eastern Question?

15. Trace the events which led to the Congress of Berlin of 1878. Show how the Treaty of Berlin of 1878 modified the Treaty of San Stefano.

16. 'The Treaty of Berlin of 1878 created more problems than it solved.' Do you agree? Give reasons.

Nationalism was one of the most powerful forces that shaped the history of Europe after 1850. Before 1850, it was merely an emotional loyalty to a group with a similar cultural and racial background and a desire to be free from foreign control. After 1850, however, it became an aggressive movement among people with cultural and racial ties to attain national greatness and to secure the right to decide their own fate. The triumph of nationalism resulted in the rise of several nation states in Europe.

The two most important successes of the nationalist movements in the 19th century were the unifications of Germany and Italy. They were similar in that one state led the others in the struggle for unification under the guidance of its ministers and the protection of its army. Both also had to get rid of Austrian influence before they could be unified. But they differed in the methods they used and in the results of their unification movements.

The failure of the Frankfurt Parliament of 1848-49 showed the German people that unification could only be achieved by force, not by democratic means. It could only be achieved through the leadership and strength of one state, and by the expulsion of Austria from the German Confederation. Prussia finally unified Germany through the work of Bismarck, the Prussian chancellor. He fought three wars to achieve his objectives. In each one, the use of force went hand in hand with Bismarck's brilliant diplomacy. Before going to war, he first isolated the country he was going to fight and then made it appear as the aggressor. In 1871 Germany was unified.

Unlike Prussia, Sardinia — which became the leader of the Italian unification movement — needed foreign help in its efforts to achieve unification. Napoleon III helped her to acquire Lombardy and the central Italian states. After the Austro-Prussian War of 1866, Prussia forced the Austrians to give Venetia to Italy. When Prussia waged war against France in 1870-71, the French withdrew their garrison from Rome. This made it possible for Italy to acquire her capital. Like Germany, Italy was unified in 1871. While the government of the new Germany was actually a military dictatorship under Prussia, the new Kingdom of Italy was liberal.

Nationalism, too, was behind the revolts of the Balkan peoples against Turkish rule. By the 19th century, the Turkish Empire had declined and was expected to collapse at any time. The problem of what was going to happen to its Balkan possessions, together with the Balkan peoples' struggle for independence, created the Eastern Question. This question was complicated by the Turkish government's cruel treatment of its Christian subjects in the Balkans and by the attitudes of the European powers.

To prevent disruption of the balance of power, Britain, Austria, France and Germany were determined to stop Russia from expanding into the Balkans at the expense of Turkey. Attempts by the Great Powers to settle the Eastern Question in the 19th century through war and negotiation all failed. It became one of the principal factors contributing to the outbreak of the First World War in 1914.

Chapter 3
Democracy and reform after 1850

In 19th-century Europe, democracy often coexisted with nationalism. Up to the 1870s, however, the growth of democracy, or popular government, was overshadowed by nationalist movements. Only in Britain did democracy make steady progress. The great upsurge of democracy began in the late 19th century.

Because of the substantial advances made by Britain towards complete democracy, she was regarded by many 19th-century political reformers as the model democratic nation. France, the second great democratic power, made a third attempt at republicanism with the establishment of the Third French Republic in 1870. The German Empire had a constitutional government but it was in fact a military dictatorship. In Russia, despite the reforms of Alexander II in the 1860s, there was still absolute rule. Besides Germany and Russia, two other empires failed to develop democratic institutions — the Dual Monarchy of Austria-Hungary and the Turkish Empire. Outside Europe, democracy flourished in the United States and in the British dominions and colonies.

By the early 20th century, however, extreme nationalism slowed down democratic development. It created dangerous movements which led Europe to the First World War.

THE RISE AND SPREAD OF SOCIALISM IN EUROPE

To gain a better understanding of democracy and reform in Europe after 1850, we should first look at the rise and spread of socialism. Socialism played an important part in political developments and reform movements.

Rise of socialism

The many social evils of the Industrial Revolution, which began in Britain about 1760, led to the rise of socialism in Europe. Among these evils were long hours of work, low wages, unemployment and unhealthy conditions. In the 19th century, there were thinkers who were concerned about the social injustices caused by industrialization.

The more radical of these 'socialists' condemned the capitalist system and the doctrine of laissez-faire (allow to do), which advocated non-interference by governments in industry or any other economic activity. To them, governments should not let the industrialists do as they pleased. They wanted a complete change in society which was to be brought about by revolution. Other socialists believed that there should be co-operation, not competition, in all economic activities.

A French socialist, Louis Blanc, published a pamphlet in 1839 in which he proposed that the French government should establish national workshops. These would provide employment for everyone. His socialist programme was reinforced by the work of Karl Marx, the German socialist.

The most enduring of all the socialist movements of the 19th century was Marxist socialism. Its founder was Karl Marx (1818-83), a German revolutionary leader. He later

A cartoon showing the differences in the life style of the industrial bourgeoisie and the proletariat in the 19th century

went to Paris where he became interested in socialism and met Friedrich Engels (1820-95), a German factory owner. In 1845 he was expelled from France as a troublemaker. In 1848 Marx and Engels together issued the famous *Communist Manifesto*. It called upon the workers to unite against the bourgeoisie. From 1848 until his death in 1883, Marx lived in London.

In 1864 Marx founded the International Working Men's Association, or the First International, which aimed at uniting socialist workers' movements in all countries. Although the First International was dissolved in 1876, the Marxist idea of an international brotherhood of socialism lived on. The Second International was set up in 1889 but was dissolved in 1914 on the outbreak of the First World War. The Third International or Communist International (Comintern), an international organization of communist parties, was founded in 1919 and lasted until 1943.

In 1867 Marx published the first volume of his great work, *Das Kapital (Capital)*. The last two volumes, which had been put together from the notes he left, were published after his death. *Das Kapital* has become one of the

Karl Marx, founder of Marxist socialism (communism)

THE COMMUNIST REVOLUTION

The communists...openly declare that their aims can be achieved only by the overthrow by force of all existing social conditions. Let the ruling classes tremble at a communistic revolution. The proletarians have nothing to lose but their chains. They have a world to win. Working men of all countries, unite!

— From the Communist Manifesto

most influential and important works in modern times. Many countries in the world have adopted Marxist ideas. The basic teachings of Marxist socialism, or what we call 'communism' today, are as follows:

- **The economic interpretation of history** All the great movements of history, whether political, social or intellectual, have been shaped by economic factors.
- **Dialectical materialism** Every economic system reaches a point of maximum efficiency, and then decays. Meanwhile, an opposing system starts to grow, absorbs the good points of the decaying system, and eventually replaces it. This process of the new replacing the old will go on until the perfect goal of communism is achieved.
- **The doctrine of surplus value** Only the worker creates wealth. He should therefore receive all the wealth from his work. But under the capitalist system, the worker is paid wages, and the extra wealth from his work goes to the capitalist. By taking away the money earned by the worker, the capitalist robs him of the fruits of his work.
- **Class struggle** Marx wrote, 'The history of all society is a history of class struggles.' In modern times, the struggle is between the industrial bourgeoisie (capitalist class) and the proletariat (working class). In the end, the proletariat will win and the bourgeoisie will disappear.
- **The classless society** The ultimate goal of communism is a classless society. After the workers have won the class struggle, there

will be no more social classes. However, the classless society will not come immediately. The workers will have to be prepared for it. They will be ruled by a 'dictatorship of the proletariat'. (The USSR and the People's Republic of China are now passing through this period.) Such a period will not last forever. It will lead to the 'withering away' of the state. Then there will be a truly classless society.

The Bolsheviks, who overthrew tsarist rule in the Russian Revolution of 1917, were Marxist socialists.

By the end of the 19th century, Marxist socialists were split into two groups: the revisionists and the strict Marxists. The revisionists, who comprised the majority, wanted to revise the teachings of Marx according to changing conditions. The strict Marxists believed that none of his teachings should be changed. Socialist parties in most Western countries were controlled by the revisionists. The struggle between the revisionists and the strict Marxists is still going on today.

Spread of socialism

Political parties influenced by socialist doctrines were soon formed in all major European countries. In 1875 the German Social Democratic Party was founded. In the 1880s several socialist parties appeared in France, and in 1906 the Labour Party was formed in Britain. All these parties were more inclined to achieve their objectives through peaceful means. In Russia, however, the Social Democratic Party (1895) and the Social Revolutionary Party (1902) advocated revolution to achieve their goals.

Through the efforts of the socialist parties, laws were passed to stop the ill treatment of workers and to improve their living conditions. Trade unions were allowed in Britain, France and Germany. Labour laws, which aimed to promote the welfare of workers, were also passed in many countries. In the

1880s, Bismarck introduced insurance schemes against sickness, accident and old age in Germany. In the 1890s social reforms were carried out in France, which reduced the number of working days and working hours and provided rest days for workers. A workmen's compensation act was also passed.

All these social reforms resulted in the gradual improvement of the workers' conditions in Europe, except in Russia.

BRITAIN: DEVELOPMENT OF PARLIAMENTARY GOVERNMENT

Conditions at the turn of the 19th century

During the 18th century, Britain had acquired a world empire and started the Industrial Revolution. Her political system, however, failed to remedy the evils of the industrial society.

The British government, though it appeared to be liberal because of Parliament's power, was actually very undemocratic. Representation in the House of Commons had remained unchanged since 1664 in spite of the shift of population to the industrial centres of the north. As a result, declining or non-existent villages in the south were still represented while many of the new industrial cities were practically unrepresented. At the same time, a large number of people could not vote because of property or religious restrictions. The common people and the middle class were thoroughly dissatisfied with the electoral system. Demands for democratic reform were blocked by the king as well as by his reactionary ministers and the nobility and landed gentry (owners of small estates) who controlled the government. Attempts to reform Parliament were stopped with the outbreak of the French Revolution of 1789 and the Napoleonic wars.

THE LONG HOURS OF WORK

At what age did you first go to work?
At eight.

What hours did you work?
From six in the morning to eight at night.

When trade was good, what were your hours?
From five in the morning to nine at night.

Sixteen hours?
Yes.

What happened if you were late?
I was usually beaten.

— *From the testimony of a British textile worker before a parliamentary committee in 1832*

A WORKROOM IN AN EARLY FACTORY

What I saw in the factory made me feel sick . . . The low room was full of the smells of human breath and perspiration, stale beer, the sweet sickly smell of gin, and the sour smell of new cloth. On the floor, thick with dust and dirt . . . sat about twelve untidy, shoeless men . . . The windows were closed tight to keep out the cold winter air . . .

— *From a description by a young worker in England*

Depression and reaction after 1815

Political and economic conditions did not improve after the victory over Napoleon in 1815. The government became even more reactionary and harsh measures were taken to suppress liberalism. With the end of the Napoleonic wars, the government stopped its huge purchases of war materials. Many factories were forced to close down because of the oversupply of goods. Unemployment rose rapidly and became worse because of the demobilization of about 300 000 soldiers and because the products of skilled manual labour could not compete with machine-made goods. As a result of the widespread suffering, workers resorted to violence, destroying factories and machines.

The government did not sympathize with the suffering masses. It used force to break up mass meetings calling people's attention to the economic grievances and demanding universal suffrage. Alarmed by these developments, the ruling classes passed laws restricting public meetings, repressing liberal newspapers and suspending the Habeas Corpus Act. (The right of *habeas corpus* safeguards a person against illegal detention or imprisonment.)

It was not until the late 1820s that postwar reaction ended. The liberal branch of the Tory Party (later called Conservative Party) introduced reforms which recognized labour unions, repealed the laws forbidding non-Anglican Protestants to sit in Parliament, and gave equal rights to Catholics (Catholic Emancipation Act).

The further development of parliamentary democracy was stimulated by a reform movement which started with the Reform Act of 1832. By the early 20th century, reforms had resulted in extensions of the right to vote, acceptance of the cabinet system, and the growth of the supremacy of the House of Commons.

Between 1832 and 1865, democratic development was very slow. This was mainly because the landed gentry and the middle class, which had gained power after 1832, worked together to control the government and exclude the lower classes from politics. The members of the middle class, who had earlier supported democratic reforms, felt that political reform had already gone far enough.

But after the death of the conservative leader, Lord Palmerston (1784-1865), who was prime minister during much of the period between 1855 and 1865, a new era of reform began in Britain. The new political leaders,

William Gladstone, leader of the Liberals (formerly Whigs) in Britain

William Gladstone (1809-98), a Liberal, and Benjamin Disraeli (1804-81), a Conservative, speeded up reforms. They alternated with each other as prime minister between 1867 and 1881. After the death of Disraeli in 1881, Gladstone continued to dominate British politics until he retired in 1894.

Benjamin Disraeli, leader of the Conservatives (formerly Tories) in Britain

The Reform Act of 1832

Reform Act of 1832 The passage of the famous Reform Act of 1832 marked the beginning of a series of reforms which continued into the 20th century and remedied the evils of the political and economic system. Inspired by the success of the French Revolution of 1830, the Whigs (later called Liberals), who comprised the opposition party, launched a movement to reform Parliament. By this time, there was an urgent need for electoral reform. The working class was dissatisfied with the existing system of privilege. The middle class (businessmen) wanted to break the control of the government by the aristocrats. When the Duke of Wellington, the prime minister, refused to give in on the question of political reform, there was so much public opposition that he was forced to resign. Earl Grey, the Whig leader who succeeded him, immediately set about reforming Parliament. The Reform Bill of 1832 became a law.

Although the provisions of the new law were much more moderate than the liberals expected, it was nevertheless a very significant gain. It gave most of the adult males of the middle class and almost all of the smaller landowners and tenant farmers the right to vote. However, the majority of agricultural and industrial workers were still denied the right to vote. As regards representation, villages with less than 2000 people lost their right to elect representatives to the House of Commons. Representation of slightly larger towns was cut in half. The seats that were vacated were then awarded to the industrial cities of the north. The Reform Act of 1832 did not fully democratize Britain but it led to future political reforms which were to turn her into the most democratic country in western Europe by 1900.

Since the Reform Act of 1832 had established the supremacy of the members of the middle class or capitalistic class, the two main political parties, the Liberals and the Conservatives, began to compete for their support.

A workers' demonstration in London in the 19th century

Many laws favourable to the middle class were passed. Humanitarian reforms were launched. In 1833 slavery was abolished in the British Empire. Laws were also passed to improve working conditions in the factories. In direct response to the demands of the middle class, a new law — the Municipal Corporations Act of 1835 — introduced a system of town government based on popular election. This enabled the middle class to gain control of local government.

The most significant of the reforms introduced to satisfy the middle class was the repeal of the Corn Laws in 1846. These laws restricted the import of grain and were designed to protect the landowners from foreign competition. The effect was to make the landowners wealthy and at the same time to keep the price of bread very high. Industrial capitalists had demanded the repeal of the laws for a long time because they limited foreign trade. The repeal of the Corn Laws made possible the import of low-priced wheat, thereby providing cheaper food for the people. What was more important was it marked the beginning of Britain's free-trade policy.

The Chartist Movement In the 1830s, a popular movement called Chartism, which demanded the complete democratization of the British government, had developed in Britain. Chartism got its name from the People's Charter published by its leaders in 1838. It contained six demands among which were universal manhood suffrage and no property qualifications for members of the House of Commons.

In 1848, when news of the February Revolution in France reached Britain, the Chartists decided to present a petition to Parliament accompanied by a procession of 500 000 workers. The government was alarmed and forbade the procession. However, it allowed the petition to be presented to Parliament but only with a small number of people to escort it. In fact, only about one-tenth of the number expected turned up for the Chartist procession. Although the Chartist movement ended in failure, the spirit of reform it represented did not die. All but one of the six Chartist demands later became law.

Extension of the right to vote and other reforms

The Second Reform Act of 1867 Despite the failure of the Chartist movement, agitation for universal suffrage did not die down. By 1865, both the Conservatives and the Liberals realized the urgent need for reform. In 1867, Disraeli introduced a bill to extend the right to vote in order to gain the support of the working class for the Conservative government.

The Second Reform Act of 1867 was based on household franchise: all householders in the boroughs (towns), no matter how low their rates were, should have the right to vote. The new law gave the vote to the great majority of urban workers. Only the poorest of these workers could not vote because they did not meet the minimum property requirements. About a million people got the vote, roughly doubling the electorate. Agricultural workers and miners in the countryside still could not vote because of the property qualification. Nevertheless, the passage of the bill showed that the principle of democracy had been accepted by both political parties.

The Third Reform Act of 1884 After the passage of the Second Reform Act of 1867, liberal feeling to give the agricultural workers the right to vote continued to grow. At the same time, after 1867, the majority of the voters in the towns started to come from the working class. In order to gain the support of the workers and increase the prestige of the Liberal Party, Prime Minister Gladstone proposed another reform. The Reform Act of 1884 gave the right to vote to almost all agricultural workers and those miners who had been left out before. About two million people in Britain and 700 000 people in Ireland became eligible to vote. Since women were still denied the right to vote, agitation for universal suffrage continued.

The passage of the Reform Acts of 1867 and 1884 led to other reforms. Politicians introduced social reforms to win the workers' vote. Under the ministry of Gladstone from 1868 to 1874, education was improved. Until the 1860s, Britain had no national school system. Education was largely provided by private schools and churches. The poor could not afford to send their children to school. The Education Act of 1870 made possible the building and maintenance of government and government-subsidized schools. Free and compulsory elementary education was introduced. With the provision of popular education for all young people, illiteracy dropped to a negligible percentage within 30 years. In 1870, too, the old system of employment in government service, which depended mainly on patronage and favouritism, was replaced by one based on competitive examinations.

The Disraeli ministry from 1874 to 1880 improved public health facilities, introduced housing schemes and liberalized the restrictions against trade unions. These reforms started what is now called the welfare state in Britain.

The Representation of the People Act of 1918 The 19th century thus saw the granting of the right to vote to the three important classes of British citizens: the middle class (1832), industrial workers (1867) and agricultural workers (1884). Nevertheless, universal suffrage had not yet been achieved. At the end of the First World War, women could not vote and there were still about two million disenfranchised adult males. On the other hand, about half a million rich men had the right of plural voting (the right to vote in more than one place), and some could cast as many as 20 votes each.

To remedy these remaining injustices, the Representation of the People Act of 1918 was passed. It abolished almost all property requirements for voting and granted women aged 30 or over the right to vote, thus raising the proportion of the population of Britain which could vote to almost 40 per cent. Ten years later, the age limit for women voters was reduced to 21, the same as that for men. Britain had achieved universal suffrage.

Acceptance of the cabinet system

The British cabinet is more than just a council of ministers; it is the most important part of the government. It decides general policy and initiates almost all legislation. It is responsible to the House of Commons. Once it is defeated in the lower house, it must either resign or call for a general election. After a general election, the leader of the majority party becomes the prime minister.

The development of the British cabinet system, which rests solely on custom, took a long time. It began after the Glorious Revolution of 1688-89. Earlier, Charles II (reigned 1660-85) had a so-called cabinet but it was only a council of advisers. When William and Mary came to the throne in 1689, they agreed to choose advisers who were acceptable to Parliament. This established the principle of chief ministers being responsible to Parliament, not to the rulers. William and Mary later set the precedent of choosing all chief ministers from the dominant group in Parliament.

It was during the ministry of Sir Robert Walpole in the first half of the 18th century that the cabinet became a powerful body. Walpole was the first to lead both the cabinet and the majority party in the House of Commons. As such, he was the first British prime minister as we understand the term today. Under Walpole's ministry, too, the cabinet was made responsible solely to the House of Commons.

Even after the middle of the 18th century, the cabinet system was not accepted by all. There were members of Parliament who opposed the system because they felt that it took away some of the powers of Parliament. Under George III (reigned 1760-1820), there was an unsuccessful attempt to abolish the system and go back to the days when cabinet ministers were responsible to the king. It was not until the middle of the 19th century that the cabinet system was finally accepted as a permanent part of British government.

The growth of the supremacy of the House of Commons

Until the 18th century, the House of Lords, which was composed of hereditary lords and princes of the Church, was the more powerful branch of Parliament. The growth of the supremacy of the House of Commons began during Walpole's ministry when the precedent was established that the cabinet was responsible solely to the lower house. Another precedent, established in the early 19th century, gave the House of Commons final authority to decide financial matters.

But the House of Lords remained powerful because of its power of veto, which meant that it could reject bills passed in the House of Commons. Bills had to pass through both houses before they could become laws. Since the House of Lords was controlled by the Conservatives, it often blocked the reform programmes of the Liberal government.

In 1909 a crisis developed over the veto power of the upper house. The Lords disapproved the 1909-10 budget prepared by David Lloyd George, the Chancellor of the Exchequer and backed by the Liberal government. Prime Minister Asquith dissolved Parliament and called for a general election. The Liberals won and the budget was passed. After the crisis, the Liberals and their Labour allies, who controlled the House of Commons, decided to check the powers of the Lords.

The House of Commons finally became the real law-making body in Britain with the passage of the Parliament Act of 1911 which reduced the Lords' power of veto. Money bills, which dealt with the government's power to tax and to spend money, became laws with or without the approval of the Lords, one month after the House of Commons had passed them. Any other bill passed by the Commons in three consecutive sessions became law after two years, in spite of any opposition from the Lords.

FRANCE: THE SECOND FRENCH EMPIRE (1852-70) AND THE THIRD FRENCH REPUBLIC

Democracy in France began with the French Revolution of 1789. Under Napoleon I, democratic tendencies were checked but they began to grow again from 1848, when the Second French Republic was established. In 1852, when Louis Napoleon took over the government and proclaimed himself Napoleon III, Emperor of the French, democracy in France suffered a setback. But he carried out reforms which promoted the welfare of the people.

President Louis Napoleon of the Second French Republic, who became Napoleon III, Emperor of the French, in 1852

Democratic development started to make steady progress after 1870 with the establishment of the Third French Republic. In spite of serious opposition, democracy finally triumphed in France in 1875 when the republican form of government was made permanent.

The Second French Empire

Napoleon III's home and foreign policies aimed at justifying his rule or diverting the attention of the French people from the shortcomings of his government. He did a lot for the well-being of his subjects, yet he remained unpopular because of his absolute rule and his diplomatic blunders. In his efforts to please everyone, he made more enemies than friends.

Napoleon's home policy Although his power was supposed to be based on the people's will, Napoleon III governed as an absolute ruler during his 18-year reign. His ministers were responsible to him, not to the Chamber of Deputies which represented the people. Elections were held on the basis of manhood suffrage but the government ensured that undesirable people could not vote.

Although he limited political freedom, Napoleon improved conditions for the masses. He provided the people with education, housing and insurance schemes, and promoted their welfare through better wages, hospitals and more stable employment. He encouraged trade and industry by improving banking and transport facilities. All these measures should have made him popular but they were overshadowed by his diplomatic failures.

Napoleon's foreign policy Napoleon's foreign policy was inconsistent and he made many diplomatic blunders. In 1849, he sent troops to Rome to restore Pope Pius IX to his throne in order to win the support of the Church. By placing a French garrison there to protect the Pope, he delayed Italian unification and lost the support of the French liberals. To regain their support, he helped Italy take Lombardy and Venetia from Austria. But by this move, he angered the Church and the clerics.

The disastrous failure of his Mexican Campaign (1861-67) made him even more unpopular. The expedition had two aims: to establish a great Catholic empire in Mexico in order to appease the Catholics and businessmen at home, and to win military glory abroad in imitation of Napoleon I.

The French intervened in Mexico in 1861 when the Mexican government stopped paying interest on its loans to France, Britain and Spain. Intervention was a violation of the Monroe Doctrine of 1823. Napoleon III overthrew the Mexican government, but he later withdrew his troops rather than risk a war with the United States. In 1867, the Austrian emperor's brother, Maximilian, whom he made ruler of Mexico, was put to death by the Mexicans. The Mexican Campaign therefore ended in humiliation for Napoleon and France.

Napoleon's neutrality in the Austro-Prussian War of 1866 resulted in the loss of Austria's friendship. His attempts to gain territorial compensation on the eastern frontier of France for remaining neutral in the war were all successfully blocked by Bismarck. By claiming Belgium, he angered Britain, protector of Belgian independence. By demanding lands on the Rhine and trying to buy Luxembourg, he made the south German states turn against France. By 1870 France was isolated and without friends.

End of the Second French Empire On 2 September 1870, the disastrous defeat of the French by the Germans in the Battle of Sedan brought about the end of the Second French Empire. The people of Paris, angered by Napoleon's failure to defend the nation, proclaimed a new republic on September 4. A provisional government was set up which took control of the Franco-Prussian War and made peace with the Germans in May 1871.

POLITICAL CHANGES IN FRANCE, 1792–1870

1792	First Republic	Convention 1792-95
		Directory 1795-99
1804	Napoleon	First Consul 1799-1804
	First Empire	Emperor until his defeat at Waterloo
1815	Bourbons — Louis XVIII, Charles X	Restoration of the Bourbons by the Congress of Vienna. Charles X overthrown by the Revolution of 1830
1830	House of Orleans — Louis Philippe	King after the Revolution of 1830. Overthrown by the Revolution of 1848
1848	Second Republic	
1852	Second Empire — Louis Napoleon	President and then Emperor Napoleon III. Deposed in 1870
1870	Third Republic	Established in 1870 and lasted until 1940

The Third French Republic

Following the collapse of the Second French Empire, the provisional government, which became the Third French Republic, ruled the country until a new constitution was adopted. A general election was held in February 1871 for a national assembly on the basis of manhood suffrage. A moderate republican, Thiers, was elected as 'Head of the State'.

Suppression of the Communard Revolt, March-May 1871 No sooner had the National Assembly met than the provisional government was threatened by the Communard Revolt, a socialist rising. Since the new assembly had a majority of monarchists, the people of Paris, who were strongly republican, feared that this majority might try to overthrow the new republic.

In March 1871 discontent finally erupted into violence when the government ordered its troops to seize the guns of the Parisians. The Paris mob disarmed the soldiers instead and the revolt of the Communards began. Thiers reacted by suppressing the revolt with firmness. The failure of the revolt saved the republic but serious difficulties still lay ahead.

Peace negotiations with Germany Another immediate problem facing the provisional government was to negotiate a peace treaty with Germany. Peace negotiations ended on 10 May 1871 with the signing of the Treaty of Frankfurt.

A humiliating provision of the treaty was that France had to pay a huge war indemnity to Germany and support a German occupation army until the indemnity was paid. Bismarck expected the payment of the indemnity to be a financial burden to France for years. However, it took the French less than three years to pay it off because of the amazing growth of the French economy after the war. The German occupation army was then withdrawn.

Reconstruction under Thiers, 1871-73 Yet another problem was the revival of the nation's economy after the war. Thiers appealed to the people to work hard and contribute generously to the government treasury, and he obtained loans from the wealthy middle class. As a result, French industry and trade made a remarkable recovery. Thiers proceeded to rebuild the army and strengthen frontier defences. France was once again developing into a major European power.

Putting the republic on a permanent basis The most serious problem for the provisional government was to put the republic on a permanent basis. The majority of the French people still wanted monarchical government despite its failure to provide political stability in the past. However, the monarchists were divided on the choice of a king.

At first, Thiers was in favour of a constitutional monarchy following the English model. When he saw that restoring the monarchy would divide the nation, he changed his mind. He declared his support for a republic which, he believed, would create less division. This decision cost him the presidency, as he was forced to resign by the pro-monarchist assembly in 1873.

Marshal MacMahon succeeded Thiers. As he was a confirmed monarchist, it seemed likely that the monarchy would be restored. The monarchists finally agreed on the choice of a king but failed to agree on the choice of a national flag.

The republicans benefited from the rivalry between the monarchists. In 1875 the assembly decided upon a republican form of government. There was no longer a possibility of restoring the monarchy.

It was the Constitution of 1875 which placed the Third French Republic on a permanent basis, and it remained in force until the German invasion of France in 1940.

Its provisions were as follows:
- There was to be a legislature, the National Assembly, consisting of two houses: a Senate, whose members were to serve for nine years; and a Chamber of Deputies, whose members were to be elected by universal suffrage.
- A president was to be elected by the National Assembly for a term of seven years.
- Executive powers were to be centred in the hands of ministers who were responsible to the National Assembly. The powers of the president were therefore very limited.

Soon after the declaration of the 1875 Constitution, the Third French Republic was recognized by most countries.

The republic firmly established In 1876 the National Assembly under the former government was dissolved. In the elections that followed, the republicans gained a majority in the Chamber of Deputies but the monarchists obtained a small majority in the Senate. However, the president, MacMahon, refused to accept the principle of ministerial responsibility to the assembly. In 1877 he replaced the republican ministry with a pro-monarchist one and dissolved the chamber. In the new elections, the voters returned a bigger republican majority in the chamber.

It was not until 1879 that the republicans felt secure. By that time, they had obtained a majority in both houses. MacMahon was forced to resign and the assembly elected Jules Grevy, a firm republican, as president.

France had indeed passed through critical times since her disastrous defeat in the Franco-Prussian War. Even after the declaration of the 1875 Constitution, the Third French Republic was not expected to last. Enemies of the republic exploited its difficulties, but the government succeeded in defeating all their attempts to overthrow or discredit it. By the beginning of the 20th century, the safety of the republic had been assured. France was once again recognized as a Great Power. Nevertheless, the republic remained unstable because of one serious weakness: the frequent changes of ministries. During the 40 years after the adoption of the constitution of 1875, 50 changes took place.

GERMANY: AUTOCRACY UNDER A CONSTITUTIONAL GOVERNMENT

The government of the Second German Empire

The Second German Empire (Second Reich*) was a federal union of 26 states dominated by Prussia. Although the empire had a constitution and some parliamentary features, it was in fact an autocracy. Ministers were responsible to the emperor, not to the parliament. The emperor had considerable authority over the making and execution of laws and over military and foreign affairs. As king of Prussia, he was given control of one-third of the votes in the Bundesrat, the upper house of the imperial parliament, which represented the ruling houses of the various states.

Yet the government was not completely autocratic. It had two democratic features: universal manhood suffrage and a parliament with a lower house, the Reichstag, elected by the people. The emperor could influence legislation but had no veto power. Treaties negotiated by him had to be approved by the Bundesrat. He could not use government funds without the approval of the Reichstag. The law-making powers of the Reichstag, which represented the people, were more or less the same as those of the Bundesrat.

Despite the strength of autocracy in Germany, a democratic movement led by the Social Democratic Party emerged in the 1890s and demanded electoral reforms. By 1914 the

Social Democrats had won the support of a third of the German voters. However, the development of democratic government was delayed by the lack of unity among the various opposition groups. With the outbreak of the First World War, the move towards democracy was postponed. When the German people finally achieved self-government, with the establishment of the Weimar Republic after the war, they were not sufficiently prepared to govern themselves. Not surprisingly, the republic lasted only for a short time.

William II's personal rule

When Kaiser William I died in 1888, his son Frederick succeeded him. After a reign of only a few months, Frederick died and was succeeded by his son William II. William I had been guided by Bismarck but William II was determined to dominate the German government personally. He insisted on dealing with ministers directly instead of through the chancellor. Differences of opinion soon developed between the new emperor and the old minister and, for nearly two years, the tension between them increased. It became a struggle for power between an aggressive ruler and a dictatorial chancellor.

In the election of 1890 the Bismarckian parties were defeated. Bismarck decided to restore his weakening authority by reducing the powers of the Reichstag. William II opposed the move. Seeing that no compromise was possible over their policy differences, he rudely dismissed Bismarck in the spring of 1890. (Technically, Bismarck resigned but he was actually forced out of office.) Thus ended the career of one of Germany's greatest leaders. Under him, Germany had won three wars, achieved unification and attained world power status. Embittered and humiliated, he retired to his estates in East Prussia where he died in 1898.

After dismissing Bismarck, William II began his personal rule. He launched an economic

*The First Reich was created by Otto the Great in 962, the Second Reich by Bismarck in 1871, and the Third Reich by Hitler in 1933.

Germany 'a place in the sun', he clashed with other colonial powers, Britain in particular. By making no attempt to be on good terms with Russia, he antagonized her and made her turn to those powers which opposed Germany — Britain and France. This German policy led to the division of Europe into two armed camps — another major cause of the First World War.

Germany was not, however, the only aggressive European nation. The other European powers also adopted aggressive policies because of the dangerous situations created by extreme nationalism; because of colonial and economic rivalry between all the Great Powers; and because of the failure to limit armaments, a limitation which was opposed not only by Germany but also by Britain. In Britain, there were senior government officials who wanted to attack Germany before she became too strong. The French, too, were looking for an excuse to make war on Germany to avenge their 1870 defeat and recover Alsace-Lorraine.

DROPPING THE PILOT.

The dismissal of Bismarck by Kaiser William II

programme which aimed at the rapid development of German industry and commerce. It was so successful that by 1914, Germany had become a leading industrial and commercial nation in the world, second only to Great Britain. But, as we shall see later, Germany's striking economic development became an important factor in the outbreak of the First World War.

With regard to foreign policy, while Bismarck aimed at making Germany the strongest power in Europe, William II aimed at world domination. His aggressive policy was a major cause of the First World War. By strengthening the German navy, he challenged Britain's centuries-old naval supremacy. He opposed all efforts at disarmament. By joining the scramble for colonies, in order to find

ABSOLUTISM IN RUSSIA

There was no real democratic progress in Russia before the First World War. In 1914 she was little different from what she had been a hundred years earlier.

At the turn of the 19th century, life in Russia was still based on an oppressive form of feudalism. The peasants, who comprised the majority in Russia, were tied to the soil. They had no rights and were little more than slaves. Their lords had complete control over them.

Under Alexander I (reigned 1801-25) and Nicholas I (reigned 1825-55), absolutism was firmly established in the Russian Empire. Defeat in the Crimean War, however, exposed how weak Russia really was. By the time Nicholas I died in 1855, there was a widely spreading desire for reform.

Continued reaction after 1850

Alexander II (reigned 1855-81) Though determined to maintain despotic power, Alexander was aware of the backwardness of Russia. Initially, he exercised his autocratic power in a benevolent way. He introduced some significant reforms. In the later part of his reign, however, he reverted to repressive policies.

In March 1861, despite opposition from the nobles and officials, Alexander issued the Edict of Emancipation which set the serfs free. They were no longer tied to the soil or compelled to work for the nobles. In the next few years, the government arranged to buy portions of land from the nobles which were then handed over to the peasants. The land, however, was not given to individual peasants but to village communities or *mirs*, for redistribution at intervals to their members. The *mirs* had to repay the government in instalments for their purchase of the land, collecting the amount due from their members.

Although the serfs had been freed, they were disappointed, as their new payments were often larger than those they had had to pay to their former lords. As the population increased, the share of land each peasant received whenever there was a redistribution became smaller and smaller. The peasants therefore remained as poor as before. The nobles also resented the inadequate compensation they had received from the government for the loss of their land. The people were still discontented because they wanted thorough constitutional reform. Some of them even advocated the use of force.

Nevertheless, the liberation of the serfs was significant in Russian history for it marked the beginning of the modernization of Russia. The newly freed serfs became a source of manpower for the industrial development of the country. After 1861, agricultural production gradually increased. Morever, the Edict of Emancipation stimulated demands for further reform.

In 1862 changes were made in the judicial system, including the introduction of trial by jury. In 1864 the old system of centralized bureaucracy was modified to give people some control over local affairs through the election of *zemstvos* or village councils. The *zemstvo* was composed of the chief landowners as well as delegates chosen by the townspeople and peasants. The work of the councils, however, was hampered by the lack of political experience of their members, the conflict of interests between the landowners and the peasants and the excessive use of their veto power by the imperial governors.

Alexander II also freed many political prisoners and exiles and relaxed censorship. He encouraged trade and industry by introducing protective tariffs and starting a railway system.

After suppressing the Second Polish Revolt (1863-64), Alexander II changed his policy from reform to reaction. His advisers had convinced him that the Polish Revolt was a direct result of his liberal policies, and that if these continued, there would be similar risings in Russia.

He nullified his earlier reforms by restoring arbitrary punishment, strengthening the secret police and making the acts of the *zemstvos* subject to excessive veto by the imperial governors.

Alexander III (reigned 1881-94) His rule was characterized by stern repression since he believed that opposition to the government should be dealt with by force, not through reform. Under him, complete autocracy was restored in Russia.

The only change made by Alexander III which had positive and far-reaching results was industrialization. For centuries, agriculture had been the basis of Russia's economy. Through industrialization, Alexander III hoped to make the country self-sufficient.

Industrialization in Russia brought with it the same social evils and injustices that the industrial revolution had produced in western

Europe, such as the abuses of the factory system and crowded living conditions in the cities. Industrialization, too, led to the spread of socialist and democratic ideas among the workers. Such ideas were to create serious problems for his son and successor, Nicholas II, and helped to bring about the Russian Revolution of 1905.

The Russian Revolution of 1905

Nicholas II, who succeeded to the throne in 1894, was a weak and inefficient ruler and was greatly influenced by his wife, Alexandra, a firm believer in autocracy. He refused to modify or give up autocratic rule, yet he was not strong enough to deal with the opposition. One moment, he pursued a policy of reform and the next, a policy of repression.

Nicholas II's inability to solve the many problems of Russia led to the Revolution of 1905. This revolution prepared the way for the Russian Revolution of 1917. The revolutionaries failed to overthrow the tsar but they learned a great deal from the events of 1905. The great communist leader, Trotsky, described this earlier revolution as a 'dress rehearsal' for 1917.

Nicholas II, Tsar of Russia during the Revolution of 1905

Underlying causes of the revolution

Political discontent As soon as he became tsar in 1894, Nicholas II proclaimed that he would uphold the principle of autocracy as did his late father. There would be no representative or responsible government. Nicholas tried in every way to limit the powers of the *zemstvos,* the only elected bodies in Russia.

Like the tsars before him, Nicholas II imposed many restrictions on his subjects. There was no freedom of expression. There were press censorship, close supervision of the universities and no freedom in the choice of religion. Justice was administered arbitrarily. Those accused of political crimes were usually exiled to Siberia. All these repressive measures increased political unrest.

Another source of political discontent was Russification which was used by the tsars to strengthen their control over their subject peoples. Growing nationalism meant that Russification created much unrest in such non-Russian provinces as Finland, Poland and Lithuania. It also led to the persecution of minority groups such as the Jews.

Social and economic discontent While the other European countries were making great progress, Russia remained backward. This was mainly due to her feudal type of economy. There was a wide gap between the upper and lower classes. The ruling nobles and great landowners enjoyed wealth and privilege. The common people, who formed the majority of the population, lived in extreme poverty and

67

were often without food. They were in debt to their landlords and to the government because of high taxes. They had no rights or privileges.

Before 1905, some economic and social reforms had been introduced. The Edict of Emancipation of 1861 liberated the serfs. Educational reforms made education equally available to all. Some restriction was attempted on the use of female and child labour. The effects of the reforms, however, were limited. The lower classes were still miserable and were still oppressed by the tsarist government.

The industrial revolution had been going on in Russia since 1891. Count Sergei Witte (Minister of Finance, 1892-1903 and Prime Minister, 1905-06) encouraged industrial growth. He introduced high tariffs against imported manufactured goods, issued loans to industrialists and encouraged the formation of joint-stock companies. He also attracted foreign capital to Russia. Foreign loans, particularly from France, quickened industrial growth.

However, as in western Europe, the industrial revolution produced many evils. Among them were low wages, harsh working conditions, long hours, bad housing and congestion in the towns and cities. The flow of discontented and unemployed peasants from the countryside to the urban areas only made matters worse. All these evils gave rise to a discontented working class. Popular movements demanding better working conditions were suppressed by the government, sometimes with violence.

Discontent was spread by radical parties such as the Social Revolutionaries and the Social Democrats. The Social Revolutionaries fought for the rights of the peasants. They demanded that the big estates be divided and distributed to the *mirs*. The Social Democrats were Marxists and fought for the rights of the proletariat. In 1903 this party split into two groups. The Bolsheviks, the more radical majority group, believed that Russia was already ready for a socialist revolution. The Mensheviks, the moderate minority group, disagreed. Government suppression of the radical parties only stiffened opposition.

The revolutionary movement

Growth of the movement The immediate cause of the revolution was the humiliating defeat of Russia in the Russo-Japanese War of 1904-05. It showed the Russian people how weak, inefficient and corrupt their government was.

Reports of military defeats abroad led to disorder and revolution at home. Radical groups demanded a constitution. On 22 January 1905, the factory workers of St Petersburg (then capital of Russia) marched to the tsar's palace to demand reforms. They asked for the reduction of working hours, higher wages, better working conditions and representative government. Their leader was Father Gapon. For the demonstrators, the march was meant to be a pleasant Sunday outing. But the tsar's guards fired on them. After the day's shooting was over, about 4000 people lay dead or wounded. After this massacre, which was referred to as 'Bloody Sunday', all sorts of strikes, assassinations and disturbances followed.

'Bloody Sunday' (22 Jan 1905), when Father Gapon and his followers found themselves suddenly faced with troops

68

Radical workers organized strikes and held demonstrations. Even the moderate middle class now joined in the demand for change. By the autumn of 1905 nearly all of the people in the cities staged a general strike of protest. Peasant disorders, too, broke out in the countryside.

There were two other sources of trouble. The hundreds of thousands of disillusioned Russian soldiers returning from the war with Japan were in very low spirits. Mutinies broke out. The many millions of non-Russians, who resented Russian rule, were even more hostile. There was disorder in the non-Russian provinces.

The October Manifesto By October 1905, the revolution was in full swing. It was clear, even to the slow-witted Nicholas II, that the government was in no position to suppress the revolution. On October 30 he issued his famous October Manifesto in which

- he promised to guarantee individual rights, such as freedom of speech and association;
- he promised the election of a national parliament, the duma;
- he proclaimed that all laws had to be approved by the duma.

The rights granted by the manifesto were extended to the subject peoples.

Decline of the movement The revolutionary movement was at its height when the tsar issued the October Manifesto. Afterwards, the movement declined mainly because the manifesto split the opposition. Large numbers of the middle class felt that the revolution had gone far enough. However, the radicals and the more liberal merchants and professional men wished to carry on the struggle. The split weakened the revolutionary movement and made it easy for the government to suppress the revolution.

There were other reasons for the decline of the revolutionary movement. Firstly, many of the workers lost their enthusiasm for the movement after the October Manifesto. They gave up their struggle and deserted their radical leaders. Secondly, although there were mutinies, the Russian army remained loyal to the government and fought the revolutionaries. Thirdly, the end of the Russo-Japanese War enabled the government to concentrate its efforts on crushing the revolution. Finally, Nicholas II was able to borrow money from France which he used to strengthen his government.

Results of the revolution

Dissatisfaction remained because the reforms granted were inadequate and unsatisfactory. By 1907 most of them had been withdrawn. The first two dumas were opposed to the tsar. Since Nicholas II refused to let the duma have any power, he dissolved the first one in 1906 and the second one in 1907. Peter Stolypin, who became prime minister in 1907, carried out a programme of repressing the radicals. The later dumas were therefore composed of the tsar's supporters, so the tsar had no problem with them.

The revolution, however, was not a total failure. Russia now had an elected legislative body, the duma. Although it had no power, its members could still express their views. In addition, the tsar's advisers now realized that reforms were urgently needed. Laws were passed to improve the conditions of the peasants and the workers. Stolypin introduced a land reform programme which encouraged individual ownership of farms. Finally, the failure of the revolution showed to the revolutionaries their mistakes and taught them what to do in the future.

FAILURE OF DEMOCRACY IN AUSTRIA-HUNGARY AND THE OTTOMAN EMPIRE

The failure to establish parliamentary government can be seen not only in Germany and Russia but also in Austria-Hungary and the

Ottoman Empire. The presence of different nationalities in both Austria-Hungary and the Ottoman Empire was a major factor in the failure of these two empires to develop democratic institutions. Dominant nationalities refused to share political control with the subject nationalities. Fanatical nationalism meant that some of the subject peoples were more interested in breaking away from the empire in which they lived than in developing democratic government.

Austria-Hungary

Under the Dual Monarchy established in 1867, the Austrian Empire had been split into two parts although both parts remained under the same ruler. One part, Austria, was dominated by the Austrian Germans and the other, Hungary, by the Magyars.

Austria had some democratic features, such as a liberal constitution and a two-chamber legislature elected through general manhood suffrage. Yet, truly democratic government did not develop because Austrian politics were dominated by the German landed aristocracy and rich German businessmen. They held all the important positions in the government, the legislature and the army. Hostility between the ruling Germans and the other national groups and rivalry among the different national groups hampered the functioning of the constitutional government. The emperor and his ministers took advantage of these national differences to strengthen their control through a policy of divide and rule.

The situation was even worse in Hungary where the government was dominated by the Magyars. Democracy was almost nonexistent. The subject nationalities had practically no political rights and until 1914 only a small part of the population could vote.

The Ottoman Empire

Despotism under Sultan Abdul Hamid II In a move to strengthen its rule and halt the decline of the empire, the Ottoman government issued a liberal constitution in 1876 which guaranteed parliamentary government. Unfortunately, at about the same time, a sultan came to the throne who strongly favoured absolute rule. In the more than 30 years that he was in power, Sultan Abdul Hamid II became notorious for his cruel and oppressive rule. In 1878 he withdrew the constitution and began to rule without a parliament. He imposed strict censorship and ruthlessly eliminated those who dared to oppose his tyrannical government. In spite of his repressive policy, opposition continued to grow among his Turkish subjects.

The Young Turks In 1891 some Turks who were in exile in Europe formed a secret organization, later known as the Young Turks, whose aims were both nationalistic and

Victorious Young Turks who overthrew Sultan Abdul Hamid II in 1909

democratic. They wanted to free the empire from foreign domination and to set up a constitutional government. They gained many followers in the Turkish army and this gave them the necessary military power to start a revolution. In 1908 they revolted, forcing the sultan to restore constitutional government and grant religious and personal freedom to all races in the empire. The following year, he tried to regain power through a counter-revolution, but was overthrown and replaced by his weak-willed brother, Muhammed V.

The world now expected the Young Turks to establish a liberal and democratic government in Turkey, but they did not. Like the Magyars in Hungary and the Germans in Austria during the 1848 revolutions, they refused to share political control with the subject peoples. They ensured that only a few non-Muslims were elected to the new parliament. The suppression of the subject peoples continued as before.

Discontent with the oppressive rule of the Young Turks led to the Balkan Wars of 1912 and 1913 which, in turn, influenced the outbreak of the First World War.

DEMOCRACY IN THE UNITED STATES

Outside Europe, one nation stood out in the development of democratic government: the United States. The years which followed the adoption of the Declaration of Independence on 4 July 1776 saw the establishment of a democratic system of government and the continued growth of democracy.

By 1914, the United States had the largest population and was the richest and the most powerful of the countries on the American continent. She continued to grow in wealth and strength to become one of the greatest powers in the world today.

The American Constitution

After the War of Independence, the 13 American states were not yet fully united. In 1781 they set up a new government, but it had no real authority over the affairs of each state. In 1783 the leaders of the new nation decided to have a strong central government. In 1787 the Constitutional Convention met in Philadelphia. The leaders agreed on a constitution which set up a government based on the consent of the people.

Some of the basic principles of the American Constitution are as follows:

- **Popular sovereignty** All power resides in the people.
- **Federalism** Power is divided between the national (federal) government and the state governments. (In most countries, the national or central government has all the power.)
- **Separation of powers** The American Congress, which is made up of the Senate and the House of Representatives, makes the laws (legislative power), the president carries them out (executive power), and the courts interpret them (judicial power).
- **Checks and balances** The reason for the separation of powers was to stop any one of the three branches of government from becoming too powerful.

PREAMBLE OF THE AMERICAN CONSTITUTION

We the People of the United States, in order to form a more perfect Union, establish Justice, insure domestic Tranquillity, provide for the common defence, promote the general Welfare, and secure the Blessings of Liberty to ourselves and our Posterity, do ordain and establish this Constitution for the United States of America.

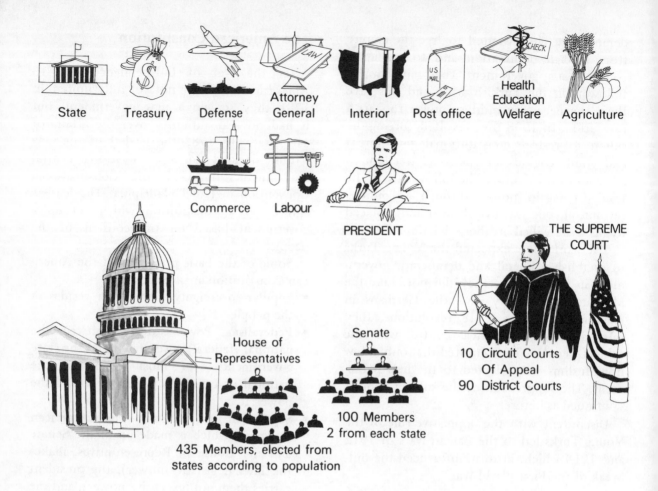

State   Treasury   Defense   Attorney General   Interior   Post office   Health Education Welfare   Agriculture

Commerce   Labour

PRESIDENT

THE SUPREME COURT

House of Representatives

Senate

10 Circuit Courts Of Appeal
90 District Courts

100 Members
2 from each state

435 Members, elected from states according to population

Constitutional government in the United States

- **Protection of the rights of the individual**
These rights were guaranteed by the first ten amendments to the constitution which are called the Bill of Rights.

The democratic system of government set up by the American Constitution set an example for other peoples all over the world.

The growth of democracy

The constitution was adopted in 1788, and went into effect from 1789 onwards. George Washington was chosen as the first President of the United States. Within five years, two political parties were formed. One, led by Thomas Jefferson, wanted states' rights rather than a strong central government. This party is called the Democratic Party today. The other, led by Alexander Hamilton, wanted a strong central government. Today it is called the Republican Party.

At this time, the American government was not yet truly democratic. Only those who owned property could vote. When Jefferson became president (1801-09), a democratic movement began which was against giving special privileges to the rich and called for equality of opportunity. Its leaders wanted education for everybody, not just for the rich. People from all social classes, not just from the rich, could then become leaders in the future. Democracy continued to grow when Andrew Jackson was president (1829-37).

The leaders of the new democratic movement strongly believed in the principle of equality. Whether a man was rich or well-educated was not important. They believed that all men were politically equal and should therefore have the right to vote. All these democratic movements put the United States on the verge of universal suffrage. Slaves and women were still denied the right to vote.

Reform movements after the Civil War

The victory of the North over the South in the American Civil War of 1861-65 ended slavery in the United States. Constitutional amendments gave former slaves citizenship and the right to vote.

After the Civil War there were many more reforms. Women wanted the same rights that men had. They fought for the right to go to public schools, to work wherever they chose, to vote and to hold government posts. Slowly, many states passed laws to give women more rights. In 1920, they were finally given the right to vote, and universal suffrage was achieved.

There were humanitarian reforms which led to free education, the building of hospitals, and laws against child labour. In addition, there were laws to reform the civil service. People had to pass examinations to get jobs in the government and those working for the government could not be dismissed without good reason. In this way, the political party in power could not give government jobs to its supporters easily.

In industry, many small companies had joined together to form big business organizations, called trusts, which often stopped free competition by fixing prices. They also had great political influence. To limit their power, the government passed the Sherman Antitrust Act in 1890.

Industrial workers also joined together to form labour unions. Through collective bargaining, they demanded shorter working hours, better working conditions, and higher wages. Today, the American labour unions have a very powerful influence on the government and economy of the United States.

Negro slaves escaping to the North during the American Civil War

1. How did the socialist movement in Europe come into being? What progress had it made in Europe by 1914?

2. Give a short biography of Karl Marx, and explain the basic teachings of Marxist socialism (communism).

3. Show how **each** of the following developments brought about the triumph of democracy in Britain by the early 20th century:
   (a) extension of the right to vote
   (b) acceptance of the cabinet system
   (c) growth of the supremacy of the House of Commons

4. Explain how **each** of the following extended the right to vote in Britain:
   (a) Reform Act of 1832
   (b) Reform Act of 1867
   (c) Reform Act of 1884
   (d) The Representation of the People Act of 1918

5. To what extent were the home and foreign policies of Napoleon III responsible for the fall of the Second French Empire (1852-70)?

6. What were the main problems which faced the Third French Republic in the period 1870-75? How did it deal with these problems?

7. Why was Bismarck dismissed by Kaiser William II in 1890? How did the kaiser's assumption of personal rule affect German policy?

8. What reforms were introduced by Tsar Alexander II? To what extent did they improve conditions in Russia?

9. What were the underlying and immediate causes of the Russian Revolution of 1905?

10. Why did the Russian Revolution of 1905 fail, and what were its results? Explain why the revolution was not a total failure.

11. Who were the Young Turks? How far did they improve conditions in the Ottoman Empire?

12. Trace the growth of democracy in the United States.

After 1850, benevolent political leaders and socialist parties initiated economic and social reforms in many European countries. Napoleon III's social reforms promoted the welfare of the masses in France. In Germany, Bismarck's insurance schemes benefited the industrial workers. Through the efforts of the socialist parties in Britain, France and Germany, laws were passed which improved the working and living conditions of the industrial workers.

After the failure of the republican movements in Rome, Hungary and France in the period 1848-52, democratic development in Europe was slowed down because nationalism prevailed. Existing national states wanted to increase their power and prestige, while new nation states struggled for survival and nationalist movements renewed their struggle for independence.

Only Britain continued to make steady progress in the development of parliamentary government. By the mid-19th century, the cabinet system had become a permanent part of the British political system. Universal manhood suffrage was achieved through the Reform Acts of 1832, 1867 and 1884 and the Representation of the People Act of 1918. The Parliament Act of 1911, which took away the House of Lords' power of veto made the House of Commons, which represented the people, the real law-making body in Britain.

Outside Europe, the triumph of democracy is best seen in the United States where a constitution set up a government based on the will of the people.

Democracy did not make real progress in Europe until the last quarter of the 19th century. The Third French Republic, set up in 1870, survived several serious threats to its existence but, by the end of the 19th century, its safety was assured.

Thus, in the closing years of the 19th century and the early years of the 20th century, political life in western Europe in general was undergoing a radical change. Mass democracy was beginning to replace the political domination by the landed aristocracy, the business classes and the Catholic Church. Limited suffrage was giving way to universal suffrage based on one vote per person regardless of property qualifications. Further growth of democracy in Europe was cut short by the First World War.

By contrast, there were some European countries where democracy did not develop because the people lacked a strong democratic tradition and were inexperienced in politics. Germany had a constitutional government, yet the government was still an autocracy. In Austria-Hungary, constitutional government could not function effectively because the dominant nationalities refused to share political control with the subject nationalities. In eastern Europe, there was continued reaction in Russia; and in the Ottoman Empire, the suppression of the subject peoples went on.

PART II

China's response to the Western challenge

Chinese civilization ranks among the oldest and richest in the history of mankind. It was shaped through the centuries by an attitude of cultural superiority in dealing with other peoples, by agriculture as the fundamental economic activity, and by Confucianism as the basis of political and ethical life.

To the Chinese, only their empire was civilized, and the peoples beyond its frontiers were 'barbarians'. China was the cultural centre — the Middle Kingdom (*Zhongguo*, 中國). Other nations therefore had to approach her as inferiors and accept vassalage or pay tribute. Such an outlook hampered the development of normal diplomatic relations with the non-Chinese world.

Agriculture was, and still is, the basis of China's economy. Over the centuries, vast areas of land were turned into cultivated fields and this made possible the growth of a large population. Under the Qing (清) or Manzhu dynasty (1644-1911), however, food production could no longer keep up with the tremendous increase in population. At the beginning of the 19th century, China had a population of roughly 350 million. Eighty per cent of the people were peasants, and most of them were suffering from lack of food as well as from the unjust actions of landlords and government officials. They were ready to accept any change, violent or otherwise, that might bring relief.

Confucianism provided the political and social foundations of life in old China. The state was one big family in which obedience, filial piety and correct behaviour, rather than strictly legal codes of conduct, governed all its members. Confucian order produced a relatively stable society dominated by the landlord-scholar-official class; China tried her best to preserve this society by adopting a policy of isolation. Not surprisingly, scholar-officials were insular in outlook and did not welcome new ideas. Under the Manzhu, emigration was forbidden.

When Western missionaries and traders started to come to China, the initial Chinese reaction was to tolerate their presence. To the imperial court, the arrival of the new-comers was no cause for alarm. As in the past, these 'barbarians' or 'foreign devils' could be driven away, if necessary, by force or persuasion; if that failed, they could be absorbed into the population eventually. But in the 18th and early 19th centuries, they came in increasing numbers by sea. They challenged China's claims to cultural superiority and to sovereignty of the civilized world, and her assertion that Confucianism was essential to civilization. It was the Guangzhou (Canton) trade, developed in the 18th century and carried on under unsatisfactory conditions, that led to the 19th century conflict between China and the West. A new China rose out of the self-awareness which was brought about by the conflict.

Chapter 4
The opening of China

The Guangzhou (Canton) trade

The British began to trade regularly at Guangzhou in 1699, and the Dutch in 1729. Other Western nations which took part, though in a minor way, in the early trade with China at Guangzhou were France (from 1698), Denmark and Sweden (from 1731), and the United States (from 1785). The foreign traders set up 'factories', which served as warehouses as well as offices and residence quarters, just outside the city wall.

In 1757 the Emperor Qianlong (乾隆, reigned 1736-95), who had become suspicious of the foreigners' intentions, issued a decree confining trade to Guangzhou. As Sino-Western contact increased at this port, the Qing court imposed the 'Eight Regulations' on foreign trade:

- Foreign warships were forbidden to enter Humen (or Bocca Tigris), the gateway to Guangzhou.
- Foreigners could not bring women to Guangzhou, nor could they bring guns and other weapons to their factories.
- River pilots and *compradores* (agents) employed by the foreigners had to be registered with the Chinese authorities in Macau.
- Foreigners could not employ Chinese servants. No Chinese, except interpreters, suppliers of food and coolies, could enter the factories. No Chinese could teach his language to the foreigners.
- Foreigners could not use sedan chairs, the most honourable form of transport in old China, nor could they row on the river.

They could not go into the city and were restricted to the factory grounds except on three specified days a month. On these days they were allowed to visit the flower gardens and monasteries of Henan Island escorted by 'interpreters'.
- Foreigners could not communicate with the interior. Communication with Chinese officials was to be done by petition through a specific group of merchants called the co-hong (*gonghang*, 公行).
- Foreigners could trade only with the co-hong. All business transactions were to be done in cash. The co-hong merchants also had the responsibility of controlling and protecting the foreign traders they dealt with.
- Foreigners could stay in their factories at Guangzhou only during the trading season, roughly from October to January. Between trading seasons, they had to withdraw to their summer residences in Macau or go home.

Since they were unable to trade freely and seek the best prices for their goods, the foreigners naturally resented these restrictions.

There were other causes of dissatisfaction with the Guangzhou (Canton) system among the foreign traders. They had to pay all sorts of charges: the usual customs duties, a weighing tax and bribes — the heaviest of all their financial burdens at Guangzhou. There were no fixed tariff rates because local customs officials increased at will the dues imposed by Beijing. However, the foreigners continued to make great profits, and as long as this con-

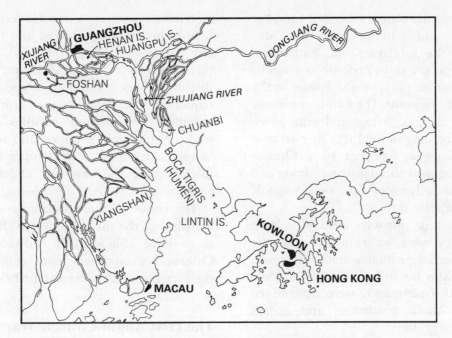

The approaches to Guangzhou

tinued, they were not likely to do anything about the unjust and unpredictable tariff system.

A further source of Sino-Western friction concerned legal jurisdiction over the foreigners at Guangzhou. A foreigner came under Chinese law only if he killed a Chinese, in which case Chinese officials demanded that the killer should be surrendered to them. When this happened, conflict was unavoidable, since Chinese and Western ideas of justice differed. Chinese law stressed collective responsibility, while Western law emphasized individual responsibility.

According to the Chinese legal concept, if a murderer could not be caught and punished, his relatives or others considered responsible for him had to be punished for his crime. The accused had to prove his innocence. In contrast, Western legal concepts presumed a man innocent until proved guilty; and there was a distinction between accidental homicide and premeditated murder. In the eyes of the foreigner, the Chinese legal procedure was unjust. There was no trial by jury and the

CHINESE LEGAL THEORY OF RESPONSIBILITY

. . . Nothing which occurs goes unpunished; if the guilty person cannot be found, convicted, and punished, then the responsible person must accept the consequences — father, family, employer, village, magistrate, or viceroy.

— *From H.B. Morse,* The International Relations of the Chinese Empire, *Vol. 1, London: 1910-18*

accused was often tortured to get a confession. The testimony of a Chinese carried more weight than that of a foreigner. Chinese courts were corrupt, and money was considered more important than evidence. In addition, foreign traders had no means of forcing Chinese merchants to observe contracts and property rights. However, many of the foreigners were rough and lawless. On several occasions, conflicts over jurisdiction threatened to disrupt the Guangzhou (Canton) trade.

China's sense of cultural superiority and her traditional treatment of foreigners were also resented by the foreigners. All 'barbarians' (夷) were expected to pay tribute as a sign of submission, and to perform the *kotow* in the presence of the emperor. The *kotow* ceremony consisted of three kneelings and nine bows. Moreover, according to the Eight Regulations, any letter from a foreigner to a Chinese official had to pass through the co-hong and be written in the form of a petition, a sign of the writer's inferior status.

Many foreign groups were inclined to leave things as they were, so as not to risk the banning of such a profitable trade. However, the British, who by this time enjoyed trade supremacy at Guangzhou, were determined to improve trade conditions and obtain diplomatic recognition.

Accordingly, the British government sent three missions to China between 1793 and 1834. The mission of Lord Macartney in 1793 was a complete failure. Emperor Qianlong regarded the mission as a tributary mission. He refused to grant the British diplomatic representation at Beijing and an extension of trade. In 1816 another mission led by Lord Amherst was sent to China. He was instructed to discuss with Emperor Jiaqing (嘉慶, reigned 1796-1820) the improvement of trade conditions at Guangzhou and diplomatic recognition. The mission failed because Lord Amherst refused to perform the *kotow* and was expelled.

Sino-British relations became worse in 1834 when the British East India Company's monopoly of the China trade was abolished and the British government took over control of affairs in China. That year, Lord Napier, who had been appointed British superintendent of trade in China, was sent to Guangzhou on a mission to settle Sino-British differences. However, he violated the established regulations on foreign trade by going straight into Guangzhou and sending a letter to the governor-general without going through the co-hong. The governor-general, who treated him merely as a *taipan* (head merchant), not as a representative of the British government, ordered him to leave the city at once. Napier stopped trade and threatened to use force. However, a group of British traders refused to support him and requested the Hoppo, the Chinese superintendent of maritime customs, to reopen trade. Napier felt betrayed and retreated to Macau where he died in October 1834. Sino-British trade was resumed under the same conditions.

The failure of these missions convinced the British that the use of force was the only way to resolve Sino-British differences. The Chinese became even more convinced that the foreigners had to be watched closely.

The First Anglo-Chinese War

The immediate cause of the war was the opium trade, which was carried on in defiance of imperial edicts. An edict in 1729 prohibited the use of opium, and another in 1796 banned its importation. Anti-opium edicts were issued repeatedly after 1800 but were usually ignored.

In 1838 the Emperor Daoguang (道光, reigned 1821-50) took drastic steps to stamp out opium smuggling, as the widespread use of the drug was undermining the nation's health and economy. Lin Zexu (林則徐, 1785-1850), a reform-minded official, was appointed imperial commissioner and sent to Guangzhou with powers to destroy existing stocks of opium and the sources of supply.

When he arrived at Guangzhou in March 1839, Lin ordered all the foreigners to surrender the opium in their possession. If they refused, all trade would be stopped. He also demanded that the foreigners should sign bonds by which they would formally agree not to bring opium to China any more. Charles Elliot, the British superintendent of trade, reluctantly ordered the British merchants to hand over their opium stocks. Lin then had the 'foreign mud' destroyed in public. However, Elliot instructed the merchants not to sign any bonds and ordered them to withdraw to Macau, where they were to await instructions from London.

In July an incident occurred which worsened the already critical situation. A band of drunken British sailors killed a Chinese villager, Lin Weixi (林維喜), at Kowloon Point. Lin Zexu demanded the surrender of the 'murderer' to the Chinese authorities, in accordance with Chinese law. When the British did not comply with his demand, he cut off all supplies to them at Macau and suspended trade. The British then left Macau and gathered in Hong Kong. Here, Lin again tried to cut off their supplies. Elliot retaliated by attempting a blockade of the Zhujiang River, but had not enough ships to enforce it. Hostilities followed.

The first major encounter was the sea battle at Chuanbi in November. Two small British warships fired upon a Chinese fleet, sinking three war junks and heavily damaging the rest. In January 1840 the emperor decreed that all trade with Britain should stop. This was in effect an official declaration of war.

In June a British fleet reached the Zhujiang River. After setting up a blockade of Guangzhou, the expeditionary force of 2000 men sailed northwards to persuade the Beijing government to come to terms. When the British reached the entrance of the Baihe River below Tianjin, the Chinese decided to negotiate. However, the Chuanbi Convention signed on 20 January 1841 was rejected by both governments, and hostilities were resumed.

The British later laid siege to Guangzhou. To save the city from destruction, the Chinese offered the equivalent of $6 million which Elliot accepted in order to free his troops for an expedition to the north. On 31 May 1841, as the British troops were leaving, they suffered slight casualties when they were attacked by a Chinese force organized by the local gentry at San-Yuan-Li. To some historians, the San-Yuan-Li Incident marked the beginning of Chinese nationalism.

The first treaty settlement

The war finally ended with the signing of the Treaty of Nanjing in 1842, the first of the 'unequal treaties' imposed by the Western powers on China. The main provisions of the treaty were as follows:
- Five ports were to be opened to British residence and trade: Guangzhou, Xiamen, Fuzhou, Ningbo and Shanghai.
- The co-hong monopoly was to be abolished.

The signing of the Treaty of Nanjing

- A fair and uniform tariff was to be introduced.
- Correspondence between British and Chinese officials was to be on the basis of diplomatic equality.
- Hong Kong was ceded to Britain permanently.
- China was to pay Britain an indemnity of 21 million dollars: $12 million for the cost of the war, $6 million for the opium destroyed by Lin, and $3 million for the settlement of co-hong debts to the British traders. (For the second half of the 19th century, unless some other kind of dollar is specially mentioned, the use of the word 'dollars' in this book refers to the Spanish and Mexican dollars that were in wide circulation in China at the time.)

The following year, the Supplementary Treaty of Humen provided for:

- A tariff rate of five per cent of the value of the goods, which could not be increased except by mutual agreement.
- Extraterritorial rights to Britain in criminal cases, i.e. British subjects who committed criminal offences in China were to be tried under British law.
- 'Most-favoured-nation' treatment, i.e. any subsequent privileges granted to other nations by China would automatically be enjoyed by Britain.

PRINCIPLE OF EXTRATERRITORIALITY

Subjects of China who may be guilty of any criminal act towards citizens of the United States shall be arrested and punished by the Chinese authorities according to the laws of China, and citizens of the United States who may commit any crime in China shall be subject to be tried and punished only by the consul or other public functionary of the United States thereto authorized according to the laws of the United States...

– *Article XXI, Treaty of Wangxia, 1844*

The privileged status of the British traders prompted the United States and France to conclude the Treaty of Wangxia and the Treaty of Huangpu respectively with China in 1844. These agreements followed the principles embodied in the British treaties, except for a few additional concessions. Both of them provided for revision after 12 years. In addition, the American treaty extended extraterritorial rights to civil cases. The French, in their role as protectors of the Catholic Church, forced Beijing to allow Catholic missionaries to live, preach and build churches at the treaty ports, and to grant religious toleration to foreign and Chinese Catholics there. These concessions, however, were not incorporated in the treaty with France.

Results of the treaty settlement

The Sino-Western treaties of the 1840s were significant in many ways. China was forced to abandon her centuries-old tribute system and submit to what came to be called the 'treaty system'. Her use of negotiation indicated that the policy of repelling the 'barbarians' was gradually giving way to a policy of conciliation. This still followed her traditional pattern of foreign relations: if China failed to expel the 'barbarians' by force, she must appease them. For the Westerners, the success of British gunboat diplomacy set a precedent for open aggression against China.

The granting of rights of trade and residence at the treaty ports to the foreigners was a sign of the partial breakdown of China's traditional policy of seclusion. Even though the Chinese tried to distance themselves from the foreigners in these ports, they could not avoid contact with them. Chinese merchants participated in foreign trade and Chinese servants worked in foreign households.

The opening of four more ports in addition to Guangzhou provided more trade opportunities for the foreigners. With the abolition of the co-hong monopoly, trade was made more direct and free, and gave the foreign traders a better chance to seek higher prices for their goods.

To some extent, China granted diplomatic equality, as she no longer insisted that foreign correspondence with Chinese officials should be in the form of a petition. She also allowed trading countries to be represented at the treaty ports by consuls, who were given the right to communicate directly with local Chinese officials.

The limitation of China's sovereignty can be seen in the provision of a moderate and uniform tariff which could not be increased except by mutual agreement. The introduction of the 'conventional tariff', a tariff fixed by convention, reduced China's freedom to impose tariffs, and led to loss of revenue since China could no longer raise customs dues whenever she wanted to.

The granting of extraterritorial rights further limited China's sovereignty. In future, the foreign powers would have jurisdiction over their respective nationals in all legal matters, protecting them from what they believed to be unjust and cruel laws. For China, it was humiliating to have people living in her territory over whom she had no control.

An important principle was introduced in Sino-Western relations. This was the toleration of Christianity at the treaty ports. As a result, missionaries came to China in increasing numbers. Their activities proved to be a source of Sino-Western friction; but China gained from the missionaries in the areas of education and medicine, if not in the salvation of souls.

The payment of a huge indemnity to Britain was a heavy drain on China's finances. Beijing was forced to raise taxes. Increased taxation only added to the misery of the peasants, causing unrest which finally broke into violence in the Taiping Rebellion.

The cession of Hong Kong to Britain gave the British a permanent base for their China trade. Loss of territory was a direct assault on China's claim to superiority.

Treaty revision after 12 years proved to be a difficult question, as the Chinese kept delaying it when the time came. The problem became one of the causes of the Second Anglo-Chinese War.

Most-favoured-nation treatment was not particularly resented by the Chinese because it was in keeping with the old principle of treating all 'barbarians' alike. This would prevent one treaty power from gaining undue advantage over the others in acquiring concessions from China.

The first treaty settlement as a whole was really a compromise, accepted by both sides but without satisfying either. It is understandable that all the concessions granted, specifically the conventional tariff and extraterritoriality, were resented by the Chinese. This was because they violated China's traditional system of foreign relations as well as her sovereign rights. China had regarded opium as the main cause of the war, and indeed the First Anglo-Chinese War is sometimes referred to as the First Opium War; yet no mention was made of the problem in the Treaty of Nanjing except in connection with the indemnity payment. This was the treaty's main defect.

The foreign powers, too, were not wholly satisfied with the settlement. They had no representation at Beijing because no provision had been made for the exchange of diplomatic officials. The vast interior of China was still closed to foreign traders and missionaries, thereby limiting their activities and giving them no protection outside the treaty ports. Some foreigners were disappointed because the opium question was not settled. They claimed that if the opium traffic continued, foreign trade interests would suffer eventually because the silver paid by the Chinese for smuggled opium could be better used to purchase foreign manufactured goods.

Although the first treaty settlement left many questions unsettled, it was a milestone in the Western penetration of China. The appearance of treaty ports, consuls, foreign concessions and settlements; the exercise of extraterritorial rights; and the enforcement of a new tariff system were signs that the wall China had built to keep out the rest of the world had been breached. However, the Western powers had to fight another war before she accepted the legal structure created by the unequal treaties.

Continued friction

As far as the Chinese were concerned, defeat in the First Anglo-Chinese War and their forced submission to the treaty system were just temporary difficulties. They had not fundamentally altered their traditional attitudes of exclusiveness and cultural superiority. Consequently, they continued to deny the foreigners diplomatic representation at Beijing and official exchanges on terms of equality.

Another treaty provision that China did not observe was the right of the foreigners to trade and reside at Guangzhou. When the British tried to exercise this right, they encountered opposition from the officials and residents of Guangzhou. Xu Guangjin, imperial commissioner at Guangzhou, and Ye Mingchen, governor of Guangdong, encouraged the people to block British entry into the city. Thus the trading activities of the foreigners remained confined as before to their factories outside the city wall.

Meanwhile, the opening of the other treaty ports, with the exception of Fuzhou, proceeded without much difficulty. No objections were raised to the arrangements for foreign trade and residence. Lands for residential purposes were leased by China to the treaty powers. In time, these foreign settlements, or 'concessions', became a familiar feature of the treaty ports. At Shanghai, the International Settlement developed into a centre of commercial activity.

The foreign powers were also partly to blame for Sino-Western friction after 1842. They did not fulfil their responsibilities with regard to extraterritorial jurisdiction. China had lost legal control over the foreigners, and yet the treaty powers did not establish consular courts and prisons at the treaty ports. Many foreign offenders went unpunished. Worse still, the foreigners at the treaty ports frequently used extraterritorial privileges to protect their Chinese employees and religious converts.

The opium problem was another source of friction. The illegal opium trade continued to flourish between unscrupulous Chinese and foreign merchants. China naturally resented its expansion, but as long as Beijing was unable to enforce its opium ban, there was very little hope that the merchants on both sides would give up the trade.

Yet another Chinese law which was often ignored was the old ban on emigration. In the late 1840s and in the 1850s, the number of emigrants rapidly increased because of the coolie trade. Countries which needed workers for their plantations, mines and railways turned to China for cheap labour. Chinese coolies were shipped mainly from Xiamen and Macau to such developing areas as the West Indies, Peru, Hawaii, the Malay States and Sumatra. When gold was discovered in California in 1848 and in Australia in 1851, coolie emigration to these areas increased.

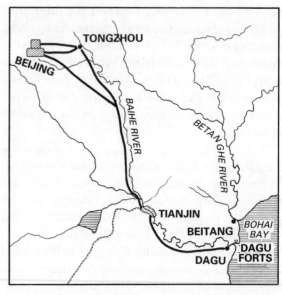

The route to Beijing from the sea, 1860-1900

The coolies received a contract which gave them a small weekly wage and food provisions. But when they reached their destinations, the terms of contract were not carried out. Worse, the conditions of travel were horrible. They were packed like animals, and thousands became sick or died on the way. When news of the maltreatment of coolies and the non-fulfilment of the contracts was received in China, coolie emigration slowed down. Foreigners and their Chinese agents then resorted to kidnapping. This inhuman coolie traffic, or 'buying of men' as the Chinese put it, increased bad feeling among the Chinese against the Westerners and led to a riot in Xiamen in 1852.

Another source of friction between Chinese and foreigners was the convoying system, a direct result of the long-standing problem of piracy on the China coast. The Chinese authorities were reluctant to take any action against piracy because the pirate junks were better armed and more numerous than government naval vessels. With the outbreak of the Taiping Rebellion in 1850, they were also too busy suppressing the rebels to be able to deal with the problem. Consequently, it became common practice for cargo or fishing fleets to seek protection from pirates by hiring well-armed foreign ships as escorts. At first, this convoying system worked to the advantage of both sides. Before long, however, Chinese shippers were forced to pay for protection even when they had no need of it. If they refused to pay, they were attacked by the very same captains who offered them protection.

Yet another source of friction was the collection of excessive inland transit dues by the Chinese government. The foreigners felt that this was an unjustified addition to the agreed tariff rate of five per cent already imposed on foreign goods at the treaty ports.

By the early 1850s the Western powers felt that the existing treaty settlement had proved inadequate and needed revision. Although the volume of trade grew after 1842, it was not expanding as quickly as they expected because the Chinese evaded their treaty obligations. The American and French treaties of 1844 had provided for treaty revision after 12 years. As a result of the most-favoured-nation clause, the Treaty of Nanjing also became due for revision. When the British pressed for revision in 1854, the Chinese authorities ignored their demand. This made Britain and the other powers realize that nothing but war would convince the Chinese to agree to treaty revision.

The Second Anglo-Chinese War

The lorcha *Arrow* affair gave Britain a convenient excuse to make war against China. (A lorcha was originally a ship designed by the Portuguese. It had a Western hull with Chinese rigging and usually had a crew of 14.)

The *Arrow* incident arose out of the custom, which began in 1855, of allowing Chinese vessels to register as British or American ships in Hong Kong. Since these ships were flying foreign flags they were not likely to be attacked by pirates or by blackmailing convoyers. The practice protected the Guangzhou-Hong Kong trade, but it soon led to abuse. Unregistered ships began flying the Union Jack. Many Chinese ships, registered or unregistered, were using British protection to supply the Taiping rebels, or to engage in opium-smuggling, piracy or the coolie trade. It therefore became difficult for the Chinese authorities to determine whether or not these ships were doing legitimate business.

On 8 October 1856 the *Arrow*, a Chinese-owned Hong Kong-registered lorcha with a Chinese crew under an Irish captain, was boarded by a Chinese river patrol as it was getting ready to leave Guangzhou to return to Hong Kong. The Chinese suspected the *Arrow* of harbouring a pirate. Twelve of her 14 crew were arrested. In the process, the Union Jack was hauled down.

The British demanded the return of the 12 men, to be accompanied by a high-ranking mandarin and an apology for the

Attack on Dagu forts (May 1858)

insult committed against the British flag. When they failed to obtain full satisfaction, they attacked and captured the forts round Guangzhou and entered the city on October 29. They quickly withdrew, however, as their forces were not sufficient to hold the city. The Second Anglo-Chinese War had begun.

Meanwhile, at the beginning of 1856, an incident occurred which gave France a good reason to join Britain later in the war against China. On February 29, a French missionary who had been peacefully preaching in Guangxi was charged with trespassing and executed after severe torture. Napoleon III saw in the 'murder' an opportunity to strengthen his position at home and to achieve prestige abroad. By making war on China, he hoped to gain the support of the French Catholics and businessmen. Association with British policy would add immensely to his international prestige.

Full-scale war did not follow immediately after the initial engagements in October. The conflict remained localized with occasional naval fighting, until an Anglo-French fleet sailed up to the mouth of the Baihe River, the gateway to Beijing, in April 1858. The invaders demanded the surrender of the Dagu forts which commanded the entrance to Tianjin. When the Chinese refused, they attacked and captured the forts, after which they moved on to Tianjin, thereby threatening Beijing which was only 90 miles away. At this stage, the Emperor Xianfeng (咸豐 , reigned 1851-61) decided to come to terms.

The second treaty settlement

On 26 June 1858, separate treaties were negotiated with Britain, France, the United States and Russia. Although there were four treaties, they may be treated as a single settlement because of the most-favoured-nation clause. The treaties of Tianjin:

- Provided for the exchange of ministers and granted foreign ministers the right of residence in Beijing, or at least the right to visit the capital; they should not be asked to perform any ceremony which was insulting to their official capacity, such as *kotow*.
- Permitted foreigners to travel in the interior under passports issued by their respective consuls and countersigned by local Chinese authorities.

- Provided for the opening of ten new ports to foreign trade.
- Allowed foreign ships to navigate and trade on the Changjiang River.
- Permitted warships to call at any Chinese port for supplies and repairs.
- Allowed missionaries to spread Christianity in any part of China and promised them the protection of the Chinese government.
- Clarified the regulations governing the exercise of extraterritorial rights. The British consul, for example, would settle disputes between British subjects while a mixed court consisting of the consul and a Chinese magistrate would settle disputes between British and Chinese subjects. In criminal cases, the accused would be tried under the laws of his own country.
- Made provisions for the extradition of criminals.
- Called for tariff revision.
- Provided for the payment of four million

taels each to Britain and France as reparation. (A tael is not a minted coin but a weight of silver roughly equivalent to one ounce. Its value varies according to the price of silver.)
- Prohibited the use of the word '夷' (barbarian) in official documents when referring to foreigners.

After the negotiations at Tianjin, a supplementary agreement was worked out in Shanghai in October, revising the tariff arrangements. The most significant change was the imposition of a tariff duty of about eight per cent on imported opium. This automatically legalized the opium trade. The collection of tariff duties was entrusted to the newly created Chinese Maritime Customs Service.

The treaties of Tianjin provided for the exchange of ratifications in Beijing. The war should have ended, but it did not. Attempts by Britain and France to carry out the

The signing of the Treaty of Tianjin

ratification arrangements led to the renewal of hostilities. The war ended when Beijing fell to the foreign invaders. In the Beijing Convention of 1860, China granted the following additional concessions:

- Tianjin became a treaty port.
- Kowloon Point and Stonecutters Island were ceded to the British permanently.
- All church property confiscated since 1724 was to be restored to the Roman Catholic Church, and Catholic missionaries were allowed to rent or buy land in any province of China and erect buildings on it.
- The recruitment of Chinese labour for work abroad was allowed. (This more or less legalized the coolie trade.)
- China consented to additional indemnities, increased from the original four million to eight million taels of silver each to Britain and France.

Again, by the principle of the most-favoured-nation treatment, all the treaty powers would enjoy the additional gains made.

The foreign power that benefited most from the Second Anglo-Chinese War was not Britain or France, but Russia. When the first treaty settlement placed her rivals in a strong position to increase their trade with China, Russia decided to strengthen her position in the Pacific area. She had in mind the Chinese territories all the way down to the border of Korea and inland to the Ussuri River. The Second Anglo-Chinese War gave her a major opportunity to achieve her ambitions. By the Russian Treaty of Tianjin, which contained the most-favoured-nation clause, she gained all the privileges which Britain and France exacted from China; by the Russian Treaty of Beijing of 1860, the region between the Ussuri and the sea (the Maritime Province) came under Russian control.

Results of the treaty settlement

The treaties of Tianjin and Beijing which ended the Second Anglo-Chinese War are known collectively as the second treaty settlement. It was a logical supplement to the first treaty settlement. By expanding the scope of the unequal treaty system, it created further difficulties for China.

With resident ministers in Beijing, the Western powers hoped that China could no longer resort to delaying tactics and lies in dealing with them. In the past, foreign governments could present their grievances only to provincial officials; now they had direct contact with the central government. Following the conclusion of the treaties, the *Lifanyuan*, (理藩院 , Colonial Affairs Office) — the central agency in charge of China's foreign relations — was replaced by the *Zongli Yamen*, (總理各國事務衙門 , Foreign Affairs Office). As the name of the new office implied, China no longer regarded the Western nations as vassal states. The settlement had thus brought about a radical change in China's traditional system of foreign relations.

Access to the interior increased the area of foreign activity in China. The right to travel inland led to a wider application of extra-territoriality, a privilege which was already strongly resented by the Chinese. At the treaty ports, the activities of the foreigners were under consular jurisdiction. But when they began to go into the interior, away from their consuls, they frequently abused their extraterritorial rights.

The opening of more treaty ports widened the scope of foreign trade. Low tariff duties facilitated the flow of Western goods to the interior from the treaty ports and on the Changjiang River. The expansion of foreign trade had the double effect of gradually taking away China's control over her own economy and of preventing the development of her own industry.

After religious toleration had been secured, the number of Christian missionaries in China rapidly increased. Besides their religious work, they were particularly active in the fields of education and medicine. Thus Christianity assisted the spread of Western ideas into many parts of China. Most Chinese, however, distrusted and disliked the missionaries. To them, Christianity was a threat to their culture and a tool of Western aggression because of its special treaty status.

The legalization of the opium trade resulted in the further spread of opium-smoking. Opium imports remained high until 1888, after which importation declined. This was not due to a decrease in opium-smoking, but rather to the cultivation of the poppy by the Chinese themselves. Nevertheless, legalization gave China much-needed revenue and stabilized the trade because it was included in treaty agreements. (It was not until the first two decades of the 20th century that China and the foreign powers, led by Britain, carried out effective measures to stamp out the cultivation and use of opium.)

The large indemnity payments almost bankrupted China. When she decided to strengthen herself after 1860, she did not have enough funds to finance the reform programmes. Lack of money was a major cause of the limited effects of the 'self-strengthening movement'.

As a consequence of the First Anglo-Chinese War, China ceded the island of Hong Kong to Britain. Her defeat in the second war saw the cession of Kowloon to Britain. The further loss of territory foreshadowed the loss of control over her dependent states before the 19th century was over.

On the whole, the second treaty settlement strengthened the position of the Western powers through their further penetration of China.

By the two treaty settlements, China was forced to accept two revolutionary changes in her foreign relations. One was a commercial change brought about by the opening of the treaty ports. The other was a diplomatic change determined by the presence of resident ministers in Beijing. The advance of foreign interests, along with the humiliating treatment of China, made her realize that she had to reform herself if she was to survive. On this assumption, the 'self-strengthening movement' was launched after 1860.

THE TAIPING REBELLION

China in the mid-19th century was troubled not only by foreign wars but also by rebellions. The most widespread and serious uprising was the Taiping Rebellion which almost succeeded in overthrowing the Qing dynasty.

A combination of economic, political and religious motives was behind the outbreak of the rebellion. At the beginning, the rebels won one military engagement after another. Their impressive reform programme was expected to win popular support. In the end, they were defeated because of poor leadership and weak military strategy in the later years of the rebellion. Their failure to carry out their reform programme and their policy of destruction lost them the support of the masses. They also failed to gain the support of the privileged classes, the anti-Manzhu secret societies and the foreigners.

ATTITUDE OF THE FOREIGNERS

I have no hope of any good ever coming of the rebel movement. . . . They do nothing but burn, murder, and destroy. . . . Trade and industry are prohibited. Their land-taxes are three times heavier than those of the Imperialists. . . . I must say, I cannot see any elements of stability about them, nor anything which can claim our sympathy.

— *From a report of Sir Frederick Bruce, British minister at Beijing, 1861*

A combination of imperial troops, regional armies, and foreign-style forces led by foreign officers finally suppressed the rebellion. Among the regional armies organized with imperial approval were the Hunan Braves of Zeng Guofan (曾國藩), the Huai

89

曾文正練水師平賊

成同間洪逆倡亂踞贛皖吳
越各省相鄰曾文正奉志計賊
以形勢多阻水欲勤賊非
水師不可乃奏請在衡州和造
戰艦南中區卒不知辦此公所
精覃恩博採衆議得之逆成大
小戰艦二百四十機募水陸萬
人訓練成軍後幸恃此以平賊

Zeng Guofan training his army for use against the Taiping

Sir Robert Hart of the Chinese Maritime Customs Service

Army of Li Hongzhang (李鴻章), and the forces of Zuo Zongtang (左宗棠) in Zhejiang. That the Qing dynasty was saved was due, to a large extent, to the loyalty of these Chinese scholar-militarists. The most famous of the foreign-style forces under foreign officers was the 'Ever-Victorious Army' financed by the merchants and businessmen of Shanghai.

Besides the tremendous loss of life and property, the rebellion had far-reaching consequences. A direct result of the rebellion was the formation of the Chinese Maritime Customs Service which became a reliable source of income for the Qing government. Much of its success in its early years was due

to the honesty and dedication of Sir Robert Hart, who served as its head from 1863 to 1911. Its officers set a good example to Chinese officials.

The formation of regional armies to fight the rebels led to decentralized government. Political power shifted from the Beijing government to the Chinese leaders of these armies. The conflict between the central and regional administrations in later years provided the immediate cause of the Chinese Revolution of 1911. The rebellion became a symbol of anti-foreign feeling and opposition to Qing rule. As such, it inspired anti-foreign and anti-Manzhu groups in later years. The effectiveness of Western weapons and Western-style forces in suppressing the rebellion convinced the Chinese leaders that China should be strengthened by borrowing Western technology. This belief helped to bring about the 'self-strengthening movement'.

QUESTIONS

1. Give a general description of the political, economic and social conditions in China before 1839.
2. What were the effects of the abolition of the monopoly of the British East India Company in 1833 on Sino-British relations?
3. Describe the conditions under which the foreigners traded with China before 1839. How did the foreign powers try to change these conditions before the outbreak of the First Anglo-Chinese War in 1839? How far were they successful?
4. Show how the Guangzhou (Canton) trade system led to war between China and Britain in 1839.
5. How far was the opium trade responsible for the outbreak of the First Anglo-Chinese War in 1839?
6. Account for the outbreak of the First Anglo-Chinese War in 1839.
7. Discuss the main terms of the Treaty of Nanjing (1842) and the Supplementary Treaty of Humen (1843). How did this first treaty settlement between China and the Western powers affect their relations?
8. To what extent did the Treaty of Nanjing settlements mark a new beginning in Sino-Western relations?
9. How did the Western powers benefit from the First Anglo-Chinese War?
10. What were the effects of **each** of the following on Sino-Western relations during the period 1842-60?
    (a) the problem of treaty revision
    (b) the activities of Christian missonaries
    (c) the suppression of piracy on the China coast
    (d) the question of diplomatic representation
11. Explain why there were still conflicts between China and the Western powers after the Second Anglo-Chinese War.
12. Explain why the Second Anglo-Chinese War broke out in 1856.
13. Outline the main terms of the treaties of Tianjin (1858) and the Beijing Convention (1860). How did this second treaty settlement between China and the Western powers affect their relations?

For centuries, China sought to preserve her way of life by adopting a policy of isolation. But a new factor was to have significant consequences for her: Western trade. During the 18th and early 19th centuries, Western traders as well as Christian missionaries came to China in increasing numbers by sea. They began to challenge her claims to cultural superiority and to sovereignty of the civilized world. She reacted by confining foreign trade to Guangzhou under conditions which the foreigners found unsatisfactory and by refusing to receive representatives of foreign powers.

While other foreign groups were prepared to leave things as they were, in order not to disrupt the very profitable China trade, the British, who had gained trade supremacy in China towards the end of the 18th century, wanted changes. They were determined to improve trade conditions at Guangzhou, expand the China trade and obtain diplomatic recognition. Three diplomatic missions were sent to China between 1793 and 1834. Their failure convinced the British that force was the only way to deal with China.

Britain waged two wars against China: the First Anglo-Chinese War of 1839-42 and the Second Anglo-Chinese War of 1856-60. The 'unequal treaties' imposed by the Western powers at the end of the two wars opened China to Western penetration. Since force and conciliation had both failed to stop the foreigners, China tried to strengthen herself against foreign aggression by reviving traditional institutions and borrowing Western technology after 1860.

While the empire was threatened from outside by foreign aggression, it was also being seriously threatened from within by the Taiping Rebellion. With the suppression of the rebellion, Qing authority was restored over most of the empire and the dynastic revival that followed delayed the fall of the Qing dynasty.

Chapter 5
China's response to foreign aggression

After 1860 some farsighted Chinese scholar-officials and Qing court officials saw the urgent need to strengthen China against foreign aggression. After her defeat by foreign powers in war and diplomacy, her traditional culture was being weakened by Western influence, especially at the treaty ports. The economic activities of the foreigners, too, threatened to upset her agrarian economy. In addition, the Taiping Rebellion had exposed the weakness of the Beijing government. Without foreign aid and the loyalty of some Chinese scholar-militarists, the Qing dynasty would have been overthrown. Even more alarming was the foreign threat to China's control over her frontier territories.

Since both force and conciliation had failed to stop foreign penetration, some other solution had to be found. Thus from 1860, China tried to strengthen herself by reviving Confucian institutions and values, by learning Western military techniques and by adopting Western technology.

THE TONGZHI RESTORATION

The attempt to preserve the Chinese state by reviving traditional institutions has been described as the Tongzhi Restoration (*zhongxing*, 中興), because the height of this restoration roughly coincides with the reign of the Emperor Tongzhi (同治, reigned 1862-75).

Both Chinese and Manzhu leaders co-operated. For a while, the Qing dynasty seemed to recover its strength. Imperial authority was re-established when the Taiping Rebellion and other disturbances were suppressed. Able men were recruited to restore civil government. They were chosen through civil service examinations, which were resumed after the Taiping Rebellion. In order to regain control of the provinces, an organized effort was made to win the support of the local population. The privileges of the gentry (landlord-scholar class) were protected and social welfare measures were introduced to relieve the suffering of the masses. Agriculture was revived through such policies as the reduction of the land tax and the opening of new areas to cultivation. Printing offices were established to help spread Confucian teachings.

Though much was achieved during the restoration period, China remained weak. The revival of traditional institutions was inadequate to meet the Western challenge.

Some of the Chinese leaders felt that Westernization was necessary but they urged that the Confucian way of life should not be abandoned. This attitude was behind the 'self-strengthening movement' which lasted from 1860 until the outbreak of the Sino-Japanese War in 1894. In the 1860s the movement was limited to borrowing Western technology; it was later broadened to include the development of Western-type institutions.

THE 'SELF-STRENGTHENING MOVEMENT'

Nature of the movement

The man who first came up with the term 'self-strengthening' (*ziqiang*, 自强) was Feng Guifen (馮桂芬 , 1809-74), a Suzhou scholar. In the 40 essays that he wrote in 1860-61 on China's modernization, he urged that Confucian ethics should continue to form the foundation of Chinese society, but that China should make use of Western science and technology. Chinese learning was to be used for fundamental principles, Western learning for practical application. Feng did not intend to make China less Chinese, or less Confucian. He also urged his countrymen to abandon their prejudices against the 'barbarians' and treat them fairly instead.

China's self-strengthening movement was not the result of any wish to create a new society; it came from a strong desire for defence against foreign pressure. Western learning was to be used only as a means to an end, not as an end in itself. Western arms were to be used; Western-style weapons were to be manufactured in China by Chinese who had studied Western science and technology in new Chinese institutions. The strengthening of the economy was to be achieved through industrialization and the improvement of transport and communications. However, it was easier to set these goals than to attain them.

The men behind the movement

If some Chinese leaders finally accepted the idea of 'self-strengthening', it was because the efficiency of Western weapons and technology had been demonstrated by foreign victory in war and during the Taiping Rebellion. Even Lin Zexu, whose strong anti-foreign measures led to the First Anglo-Chinese War, realized the need to know the West better by the time the war was over. Writing to trusted friends in 1842, he recognized the military superiority of the West and argued that China should buy and make Western-style weapons. Unfortunately for China, some 20 years passed before such ideas were fully adopted. Between 1860 and 1894, the three great administrators of the period, Zeng Guofan, Li Hongzhang and Zuo Zongtang, applied Feng's theory of self-strengthening.

Zeng Guofan (1811-72) He came from a farming family in Hunan. He obtained the *jinshi* degree and eventually became a member of the prestigious Hanlin Academy (*Hanlinyuan*, 翰林院). He spent most of the last 20 years of his life suppressing the Taiping Rebellion and Nian banditry. His success against the Taiping made him famous and influential. From 1864 until his death in 1872, he was the most important Chinese leader. Thus his active role in the Manzhu administration set a precedent for other Chinese officials and influenced the careers of such leaders as Li Hongzhang and Zuo Zongtang.

While fighting the Taiping, he employed foreigners and their weapons and saw how efficient they were. Thereafter, he was convinced of the need to use Western methods in

---

FENG'S IDEAS ON MODERNIZATION

....Western books on mathematics, mechanics, optics, light, chemistry, and other subjects contain the best principles of the natural sciences....Most of this information is beyond the reach of our people....

If today we wish to select and use Western knowledge we should establish official translation offices at Guangzhou and Shanghai....

If we let Chinese ethics and famous [Confucian] teachings serve as an original foundation, and let them be supplemented by the methods used by the various nations for the attainment of prosperity and strength, would it not be the best of all procedures?....

曾文正創設製造局

曾文正公在兩江總督兼南洋通商大臣時中外和議初成公陰懷自強雄圖之志因設內軍械所又在安慶仿造小火輪船一艘式之江可用乃設局於上海用西法製造槍砲中國機器之興自此始

to the *Zongli Yamen* in 1871, urging the need to send young men to Western countries to learn the secrets of their technology. As a direct result of this report, an educational mission was sent to the United States the following year.

Moreover, he believed in being friendly with the foreigners. He frequently received foreign visitors and officials, among whom were Sir Robert Hart of the Chinese Maritime Customs Service and Anson Burlingame, American minister at Beijing. He also favoured sending envoys abroad.

Zeng Guofan at the Shanghai arsenal (about 1870)

training soldiers, and he favoured buying as well as manufacturing Western weapons. Even before the outbreak of the Second Anglo-Chinese War, he had set up small arsenals in Jiangxi and had suggested building a navy to strengthen China's defences. In 1861 he established an arsenal and a shipyard and urged the construction of steamships. But his chief contribution to national defence was the Jiangnan arsenal at Shanghai which he established with Li Hongzhang in 1865.

The key to understanding foreign manufacturing was translation, and so Zeng argued that foreign language schools should be established. He also encouraged the translation of foreign books on mathematics and science. Quoting the old Chinese proverb 'To hear a hundred times is not as good as to see once', Zeng together with Li sent a report

ZENG'S METHODS OF SELF-STRENGTHENING

If we wish to find a method of self-strengthening, we should begin by considering the reform of government service and the securing of men of ability as urgent tasks, and then regard learning to make explosive shells and steamships and other instruments as the work of first importance. If only we could possess all their [foreigners'] superior techniques, then we would have the means to return their favours when they are obedient, and we would also have the means to avenge our grievances when they are disloyal....

— From Zeng's diary, 2 June 1862

Li Hongzhang (1823-1901) The second most important administrator during this period was Zeng's pupil and protege, Li Hongzhang, who was born into a mandarin's family in Anhui. In many ways he was like Zeng, with whom he worked closely. He was a scholar-official possessing the *jinshi* degree, and a member of the Hanlin Academy. As a scholar-militarist he fought the Taiping and Nian rebels and he supported the self-strengthening movement.

After Zeng's death, he became the most influential Chinese official of the late 19th century. He held such high posts as grand secretary, member of the *Zongli Yamen*, and viceroy of Hebei for 24 years. But it was in *yangwu* (foreign matters) that he distinguished himself, representing China in almost all the treaty negotiations with foreign powers from the 1870s until his death in 1901.

Li urged the use of Western military methods and arms to modernize China's armies. He bought Western arms, consulted foreign military experts, wrote an account of how Western arms were manufactured, and, with Zeng, set up the Jiangnan arsenal at Shanghai. He supported the idea of learning Western languages and, at his suggestion, foreign language schools were established at Shanghai and Guangzhou following the pattern of the *Tongwenguan* (同文館, Interpreters' College) at Beijing.

He advocated industrialization and sponsored many industrial projects such as cotton and paper mills and iron and coal mines. He also urged the improvement of transport and communications through the construction of telegraph lines, railways and steamships.

Li Hongzhang in England with British statesman William Ewart Gladstone (1896)

Finally, he introduced a scheme to finance modernization. Under this scheme, merchants would invest their capital in industrial projects and operate them under government supervision.

However, Li's efforts to modernize China were hampered from the beginning for several reasons. He had no overall plan; he was dependent upon corrupt and extravagant followers; and he believed that, with the exception of arms, transport and machines, China was superior to the West. In later years, his views on Westernization gradually became more conservative.

Zuo Zongtang (1812-85) The third prominent Chinese official of the period was Zuo Zongtang who was born in Hunan, the son of poor peasants. As he was poor, much of his early life was spent as a school teacher and farmer. He failed to pass the metropolitan examinations and was forced to give up the study of Confucian classics in favour of practical knowledge. The outbreak of the Taiping Rebellion gave him an opportunity to show his talent for organization and administration. As a result of his efforts in helping to suppress the rebellion, he was appointed governor-general of Fujian and Zhejiang in 1864. He then went to the northwest, where he put down the Muslim risings in Shaanxi, Gansu and Xinjiang and restored Qing authority.

Zuo's chief contribution to the self-strengthening movement was in naval affairs, and in the introduction of a modernization programme in the northwest. To him, the introduction of steamships to the Chinese navy was a matter of urgency. He also planned a shipyard, with a school for training seamen attached to it.

In the 12 years that he was in the northwest, he encouraged cotton planting and opened woollen and cotton mills; modernized the transportation system; established an arsenal, founded free schools, attempted to set up a modern bank and fought corruption and red tape.

Although he employed Western methods and foreign technicians in his attempts at modernization, Zuo still believed that the foreign powers should be expelled from China, by war if necessary.

Zhang Zhidong One other Chinese leader deserves to be mentioned, although he is better known for his work as a reformer after 1895 – Zhang Zhidong (張之洞 , 1837-1909) of Hebei. A *jinshi* degree holder, he served as governor-general of Guangdong-Guangxi and of Hunan-Hubei.

After the Sino-French War of 1884-85, which showed that Western weapons in the hands of Chinese were ineffective without proper organization and training, he was converted to the idea of modernization. The methods he proposed were similar to those of Zeng, Li and Zuo: China must industrialize and revive the teaching of the Confucian system.

Zhang's work in his early days as a reformer included the founding of academies; the establishment of the Self-Strengthening School at Wuchang; a proposal to set up a 'self-strengthening' academy, which was carried out when one was established at Nanjing in 1896; and plans to train a 'self-strengthening' army. He was also responsible for the opening of a mint, an arsenal, an iron foundry, an iron mine and cotton mills; and he encouraged railway building.

Prince Gong Some high-ranking Manzhu officials worked closely with these Chinese leaders, whereas previously they had ignored them when planning government policy. In the Manzhu court, the self-strengthening movement received strong support from Prince Gong who, with the Empress Dowager Yehonala, or Cixi, (慈禧 , 1835-1908), came into power by a *coup d'etat* after the death of the Emperor Xianfeng in 1861. He was anti-foreign at first, but after China's defeat in the Second Anglo-Chinese War, he realized how

Zhang Zhidong

Prince Gong

A painting of Cixi by a Western artist

Yamen; as the head of this special board from 1861 to 1884, he tried to improve Chinese relations with the West, to give China time to strengthen herself. He started the organization of a Westernized Manzhu army, and urged the study of foreign weapons and how they were manufactured. He sent a report to the throne, emphasizing the importance of mastering foreign languages so as to deal effectively with foreign nations; this resulted in the setting up of the *Tongwenguan*. He also stressed the need to study Western science, recommending to the emperor that a science department be attached to the *Tongwenguan*; and he provided funds to publish the Chinese translation of a book on international law, which was to be studied by officials of the *Zongli Yamen*. They would then be able to use the information against the foreign powers.

The West welcomed the change in China's foreign policy and her plans to modernize as recommended by Prince Gong. One of the aims of the 'co-operative policy' of the 1860s (see Chapter 6), by which the treaty powers agreed to take unified action in dealing with China, was to give assistance to her modernization programme.

useless it was to resist the West blindly. As regent for the Emperor Tongzhi until 1865 and head of the *Zongli Yamen*, Prince Gong sought the advice of high-ranking Chinese officials who favoured limited Westernization.

Other Manzhu supporters of the movement were the prince's two chief advisers: Guiliang, his father-in-law, and Wenxiang, a member of the *Zongli Yamen*. However, their attempts at modernization were opposed by conservatives led by Cixi and the Grand Secretary Woren, head of the Hanlin Academy and tutor of the emperor. Prince Gong's influence in official circles ended in 1884 when Cixi removed him from the *Zongli Yamen*, using as an excuse his mishandling of the French advance in Annam. (The country was called Vietnam by its own people, but China and the Western powers referred to it as Annam.)

To strengthen China, Prince Gong recommended the establishment of the *Zongli*

THE SELF-STRENGTHENING REFORMS

National defence

In imitation of Western methods, priority was given to the strengthening of China's armed forces. Arsenals and shipyards were built. Plans were made for the Western-style fortification of Dagu, and for the purchase of warships. A military school and naval schools and colleges were founded. Army officers were sent to Germany, and naval officers to England, for further training. The Beiyang fleet was organized.

Industry and trade

Various industrial enterprises were started, such as the China Merchants' Steam Navigation Company, the Kaiping coal mines, the Hanyang Iron Works and the Daye iron mine. Mints, cotton mills, a flour mill, a paper mill, a machine factory, a cement factory, and a match factory were also established.

Many of these projects were set up according to a scheme of official supervision and merchant management. A few private firms started factories and mills. Compared to government-supervised or foreign enterprises, they were small and their growth was slow. Local capitalists therefore did not benefit much from the modernization movement.

Communication and transport facilities were improved. Ports were developed and lighthouses built. A modern postal service was established, largely because of the efforts of Sir Robert Hart of the Maritime Customs, and telegraph lines were put up between Dagu and Tianjin and between Shanghai and Tianjin. However, railway building on the whole was neglected. Modern banks were created to handle financial transactions. With foreign help, the Foreign Inspectorate of Customs, which was established in 1854 during the Taiping Rebellion to collect customs dues at Shanghai, was extended to other treaty ports to facilitate trade. It became the Chinese Maritime Customs Service.

Education

In the field of education, as we have seen, schools were established along Western lines. Besides the military and naval schools, the *Tongwenguan* was started at Beijing in 1862 because the newly-created *Zongli Yamen* needed interpreters. Science and mathematics were later included in its curriculum and were taught by foreign instructors. Later on, when China decided to establish embassies abroad, most of the Chinese diplomats were chosen from among those who had studied in the *Tongwenguan*. More foreign language schools were set up in the treaty ports.

Attached to the Jiangnan arsenal at Shanghai was a school for mechanical engineering. We have already noted the Self-Strengthening School of Zhang Zhidong at Wuchang, established in 1893. There were plans to create departments in all provinces for the study of Western sciences, and to include foreign affairs as one of the subjects in the civil service examinations.

Education abroad was also encouraged. The petition sent by Zeng and Li to the *Zongli Yamen* in 1871 had stressed the need to send young Chinese to the West to acquire technical knowledge. The Western-type schools established in China were not good enough. The court finally acted on Zeng and Li's proposal and, between 1872 and 1881, 120 selected youths were sent to the United States. Thirty students from the Fuzhou shipyard went to France and England for technical training.

Chinese scholars who knew foreign languages translated books on technical subjects. A few of these works dealt with education and general subjects. Through these translations, some Chinese became aware of other nations and their achievements, and began to doubt China's claims to cultural superiority and to sovereignty over the civilized world.

Diplomatic modernization

After her defeat in the Second Anglo-Chinese War, China adopted a completely different foreign policy. The Beijing government realized the urgency of diplomatic reform to deal effectively with the treaty powers.

Prince Gong and Wenxiang started China's diplomatic modernization. On their recommendation, the *Zongli Yamen* was set up in 1861 to direct foreign affairs. Foreigners referred to it as the Foreign Office. The *Tongwenguan*, a school of foreign languages and Western studies, was established at Beijing in 1862 to provide interpreters for the newly-created *Zongli Yamen*. Similar schools were later founded at Shanghai, Guangzhou and Fuzhou. Besides the *Zongli Yamen*, two Chinese superintendents of trade, one at Shanghai and the other at Tianjin, were appointed to take charge of the foreign affairs of all the treaty ports.

During the treaty negotiations at the end of the First and Second Anglo-Chinese Wars, the Chinese negotiators conceded to the foreigners' demands on such important issues as tariff autonomy, extraterritorial rights and most-favoured-nation treatment because they knew almost nothing about international law. In 1864 Prince Gong obtained a translation of a text of international law based on Western principles which served as a guide to diplomacy for the members of the *Zongli Yamen*. Copies of it were also given out to the provincial authorities. Knowledge of how international diplomacy was to be conducted strengthened the Beijing government in negotiating with the treaty powers, as seen in the settlement of several difficult issues in the 1870s.

Although foreign missions had been established at Beijing after 1860, China had no legations abroad for some time. Then in 1868 Beijing sent its first official diplomatic mission abroad headed not by a Chinese but by the retiring American minister at Beijing, Anson Burlingame. His mission was to gain the sympathy of the treaty powers for China. The Burlingame mission prepared the way for Chinese diplomatic representation abroad. But trouble between China and the treaty powers in the 1870s delayed two-way diplomatic relations. Finally, in 1877 the first resident Chinese legation abroad was set up in London. With the establishment of legations in other Western capitals in the next two years, normal diplomatic exchanges between China and the West were established.

Diplomatic modernization led to improved Sino-Western relations. The adoption of the 'co-operative policy' by the treaty powers in the 1860s provided China with relatively peaceful conditions and time to start her self-strengthening as well as foreign help in her modernization programme.

FAILURE OF THE ATTEMPTS AT MODERNIZATION

Half-hearted Westernization

Although China had able leaders like Zeng Guofan, Li Hongzhang and Zuo Zongtang who realized the need to adopt Western methods in order to check foreign aggression, they were not prepared to revolutionize the traditional way of life and establish a new society. To them, Chinese culture was still superior, and a revival of Confucian ideas would make China strong again; Western learning would be used only within technological limits. Since modernization was mainly in the field of military defence and technology, it had very little direct effect on the lives of the majority of Chinese.

In addition, when the Westerners started to use diplomacy instead of war in dealing with China, most Chinese officials began to minimize the threat of foreign control and felt, therefore, that self-strengthening had become less urgent. Such an attitude naturally slowed down modernization.

Conservative reaction

The use of Western learning, however limited, met with a great deal of opposition and hostility. At Beijing, Prince Gong had started a modernization movement in the 1860s. This was abandoned when the Taiping Rebellion was put down and the threat to dynastic rule passed. Conservative court officials led by Woren opposed modernization projects, arguing that the strength of a nation rested not on power and science but on Confucian virtues (see box). He therefore discouraged the building of railways and telegraph lines, and criticized the *Tongwenguan* for including science and mathematics in its curriculum.

Other scholar-officials objected to schools established along Western lines because, if Western learning became popular, their knowledge of the Chinese classics and ethics would no longer gain them the respect that had always been given them. They might even lose their posts in the government. On the whole, the schools attracted few Chinese, for many young men considered studying in them a disgrace.

The conservatives were also responsible for cutting short the sending of student missions to the West. In 1881 they succeeded in having the students abroad recalled, claiming that they were spending too much time on Western learning, and neglecting Chinese studies. They argued that these students would be of no use to China if they abandoned their own culture; almost certainly they feared too that the students, particularly those in the United States, were absorbing republican ideas.

The foreign education programme was also hampered by poor administration, for the officials in charge were jealous of each other. Short-lived though the programme was, it should be noted that the few Chinese students educated abroad did in fact sow seeds of revolution that were to bear fruit in later years.

Although conservative reaction came from both Manzhu and Chinese alike, opposition was stronger among the former, because of racial differences. Manzhu officials, who had long regarded themselves as the ruling class, resented the rise to power of the Chinese leaders of the self-strengthening movement, who now received favoured treatment from the court through the influence of Prince Gong.

Conservatives found a powerful ally in Cixi, favourite concubine of Xianfeng. In the power struggle after his death, she emerged with the title of Empress Dowager when her son, Tongzhi, became emperor. Since the emperor was only five years old, a regency was created whereby she was made co-regent with the empress consort, who was senior to her but was, in fact, a mere figurehead.

In her greed for personal power, Cixi enlisted the support of Prince Gong and Prince Chun, younger brothers of Xianfeng, and

---

WESTERN LEARNING OPPOSED.

....Astronomy and mathematics are of very little use. If these subjects are going to be taught by Westerners as regular studies, the damage will be great.... Your slave has learned that the way to establish a nation is to lay emphasis on propriety and righteousness, not on power and plotting.... From ancient down to modern times, your slave has never heard of anyone who could use mathematics to raise the nation from a state of decline or to strengthen it in time of weakness....

— *From Woren's memorial to the emperor, 1867*

succeeded in seizing control of the government in 1861. Thus, though only 26 years old, she had become more or less ruler of the vast Chinese Empire. Prince Gong was appointed co-regent and head of the Grand Council. (The council was created by the Manzhu in 1729 and eventually became the top administrative body.)

To consolidate her power, Cixi turned against Prince Gong in 1865, and removed him from the regency. In 1875 Tongzhi died without an heir. To stay in power, Cixi managed to get her nephew, Guangxu (光緒 , reigned 1875-1908), named emperor. This was against all previous tradition, for Guangxu was of the same generation as Tongzhi. The emperor was only a child and the government continued to be in the hands of Cixi, this time as sole regent. When Guangxu assumed personal rule in 1889, she went into retirement; but resumed control in 1898 because the emperor carried out the Hundred Days' Reform against her wishes (see Chapter 7).

Cixi had a strong dislike of foreigners. She and her followers opposed the efforts at modernization. Li Hongzhang in 1863 and Wenxiang in 1874 had pointed out that if the Chinese did not follow the example of the Japanese, who had become strong through Westernization, China would become an easy victim of foreign aggressors. This warning was ignored by the reactionaries. Cixi's blind opposition to even limited Westernization meant that, so long as she was in power, the central government would always be conservative.

Supporters of the self-strengthening theory like Li Hongzhang were kept in provincial posts to limit their influence, while Westerners often met government opposition to their activities. With no backing from the central government, the self-strengthening movement suffered from the lack of an overall modernization plan. Projects were launched without any co-ordination.

Difficulties of industrialization

While it is true that numerous and varied industrial enterprises were established, industrialization remained slow and ineffective for various reasons.

Corruption was widespread among officials in charge of government-supervised industries. They wanted only to make money for themselves and extend their influence. Control of the financing of industry bred corruption and bribery. They misused funds for government projects; and to prevent their misdeeds from being exposed, resorted to bribery. Since the empress dowager closed her eyes to the practice of accepting 'gifts' or bribes and practised it herself, nothing much was done to punish corrupt officials. Corruption was behind the failure of the Kaiping Mining Company. After 1892, its manager had taken so much of the company's funds for himself that it had to rely on foreign loans in order to survive. Eventually, it was taken over by a British firm.

Some government enterprises failed because merchants refused to do business with them. The case of the China Merchants' Steam Navigation Company is a good example. Large shippers were reluctant to ship their goods through the company

---

LI CRITICIZES THE CONSERVATIVES

The present situation is one in which externally, it is necessary for us to be harmonious with the barbarians, and internally, it is necessary for us to reform our institutions. If we remain conservative, without making any change, the nation will be daily reduced and weakened.... Now all the foreign countries are having one reform after another, and progressing every day like the ascending of steam. Only China continues to preserve her traditional institutions so cautiously that even though she be ruined and extinguished, the conservatives will not regret it....

— Li's answer to opponents of modernization projects

because, once their names were known to corrupt officials, they would be asked for 'gifts'. Consequently, the company could not compete with British steamship lines.

Many of the industrial companies under the joint control of government and merchants failed because of mismanagement. Merchants found it difficult to work under officials who were dishonest and inexperienced in business. So, although the merchants saw an opportunity to make a profit in these business ventures, they were reluctant to accept government invitations to manage them. There were also instances when officials appointed relatives as managers of enterprises under their supervision; and these relatives, more often than not, turned out to be inefficient.

Railway construction, which was vital to industrial development, met much opposition. Prejudice against foreign methods was still strong. Among the Chinese leaders, there was the fear that railways would facilitate economic exploitation by foreigners and, in the event of a foreign invasion, help them to penetrate the interior. The uneducated masses opposed the building of railways because they were afraid of trains, and they believed that it would disturb the peace of the graveyards and upset *fengshui* (風水). It would also result in unemployment for carters and boatmen.

The success of conservative opposition to railways is best illustrated by the fact that, in the 30 years or so of modernization efforts, only about 240 miles of railway were laid. China's first railway, a short line linking Shanghai and Wu Xian, was built by a British firm in 1876 without the Chinese government's permission; but it was bought and destroyed by the Chinese authorities the following year in response to public demand.

Scholar-officials, who strongly believed in traditional values, opposed industrialization simply because it was something new.

Financing industry proved to be difficult because of Beijing's poor finances and its unwillingness to obtain foreign loans to subsidize industry. Rich merchants could have supplied much-needed capital but, by tradition, they preferred investment in land to investment in industry.

Political rivalry among the Chinese leaders of the movement, specifically between Li Hongzhang and Zhang Zhidong, was partly responsible for the slow development, if not the abandonment, of some industrial projects. Zhang, for example, tried to stop the building of the railway which was to bring coal from the Kaiping mines to the coast for the steamers of the China Merchants' Steam Navigation Company founded by Li.

Problems of military self-strengthening

Despite the introduction of military reforms, China's armed forces remained weak. It was not easy to recruit competent army officers or to provide soldiers with proper training and equipment. When war with Japan broke out in 1894, about 40 per cent of the Chinese troops were still armed with spears and swords. The condition of the navy was worse, because Cixi had used the money set aside for

GOVERNMENT-SPONSORED INDUSTRIES CRITICIZED

In recent days, although the court has ordered the governors-general and governors to develop commerce and open all kinds of manufacturing bureaus, and has authorized the inviting of merchants to manage them, the officials and merchants have habitually been unable to get along together and have distrusted each other for a long time....

Now if we wish to reorganize our commercial affairs, we must imitate the Western practice and compile a commercial code.... Thus.... the officials will not dare to squeeze the merchants and the latter will not practise fraud....

– Zheng Guanying, a comprador-scholar, c. 1892

its modernization to beautify the new Summer Palace (Yihe Yuan) instead. During the Sino-French War of 1884-85, the French took only a few minutes to destroy the Chinese fleet and the shipyard at Fuzhou. Because the army and navy were controlled mainly by provincial governors, the feeling of national loyalty in these services was not particularly strong. In view of all this, the humiliating defeat of the Chinese during the Sino-Japanese War of 1894-95 came as no surprise.

Although the limited modernization of the self-strengthening movement failed in the end to strengthen China against foreign aggression, it had one positive result. The movement marked the beginning of industrialization and modern capitalism in China. The establishment of the various Western-style institutions, such as arsenals, shipyards, schools, factories, mills and business companies, stimulated economic development in the treaty ports and other cities along the coast or on the river banks. A new working class emerged as peasants flocked to these cities and became industrial workers. At the same time, the new industries and business firms gave rise to a new professional class of managers, executives and engineers. Added to these were professional men who had been educated abroad. All of them were to play a leading role in the political, economic and social development of China in future years.

QUESTIONS

1. Explain why China tried to strengthen herself between 1860 and 1894. What were the results of this 'self-strengthening movement'?

2. Show how the Tongzhi Restoration (1862-75) tried to strengthen China. How far did it succeed in achieving its aim?

3. To what extent did China's self-strengthening movement make use of Western learning?

4. Describe China's attempts at diplomatic modernization in the 1860s and 1870s.

5. What reforms were introduced in China during her self-strengthening movement (1860-94), and how did these reforms affect her foreign policy?

6. Account for the limited effects of China's self-strengthening movement. In what ways did it promote the industrialization of China?

7. Discuss the role played by **each** of the following in China's self-strengthening movement:
   (a) Zeng Guofan
   (b) Li Hongzhang
   (c) Zhang Zhidong
   (e) Prince Gong

Since force and conciliation had failed to stop Western penetration, China decided to strengthen herself against foreign aggression between 1860 and 1894 in two ways: the revival of traditional institutions known as the Tongzhi Restoration and the 'self-strengthening movement'.

However, China remained weak because the Tongzhi Restoration proved to be inadequate in meeting the Western challenge. Since the self-strengthening movement was based on the policy of 'Chinese learning as the fundamental structure and Western learning for practical use', there was no intention to strengthen China by creating a new society through Western-style reforms.

In spite of the movement's shortcomings, the new industries and businesses greatly contributed to the development of the cities and at the same time created a new working class and a new professional class, both of which played a significant role in the overall development of China in later years.

The total effect of China's attempts at modernization was very limited. It was largely because her people were, in general, not prepared to accept reform wholeheartedly and to change their way of life. The failure of the self-strengthening movement showed that a modern state could not be built with a Confucian society as its foundation. To strengthen herself, China needed a revolution, not superficial reform. She would pay a high price for her continued weakness in the 1890s, with her defeat in the Sino-Japanese War of 1894-95 and her near-partition during the 'scramble for concessions'.

Chapter 6
China and the powers, 1860–94

During the 1860s, there were signs of improved relations between China and the West at government level. Foreign aid had been given to the dynasty to suppress the Taiping Rebellion. The foreign ministers at Beijing applied a 'co-operative policy' which aimed to maintain China's sovereignty, to preserve her territorial integrity, and to assist her in her efforts at modernization. On her part, China created the *Zongli Yamen*, which handled foreign relations with a minimum of delay. She also sent her first official diplomatic mission abroad, headed by a foreigner — Anson Burlingame.

But all these attempts to bring about peace and stability in Sino-Western relations ended in the 1870s, because of the Tianjin Massacre of 1870, the Margary affair of 1875, and the question of Chinese emigration to the United States. Friction increased when the Western powers and Japan began to challenge China's control over her border states. Behind the rising tension were the conflicting views of aggressive foreign traders, who wanted more privileges, and of anti-foreign Chinese officials, who opposed further concessions.

ATTEMPTS TO STABILIZE SINO-WESTERN RELATIONS

The 'co-operative policy'

After the Second Anglo-Chinese War, the ministers of the United States, Great Britain, France and Russia at Beijing adopted a friendly attitude towards China. The country had to become stable before they could make full use of their new trading privileges. They applied the 'co-operative policy' by which they agreed to take a common stand in upholding China's territorial integrity; together they would help her to modernize. Among the foreigners who took the lead in promoting Sino-Western co-operation were Anson Burlingame, American minister at Beijing, 1861-67; Rutherford Alcock, British minister at Beijing, 1865-69; and Sir Robert Hart of the Chinese Maritime Customs Service.

Burlingame urged his colleagues to agree on common aims in their China policy. In line with this co-operative attitude, the American, British, French and Russian ministers agreed not to limit further China's sovereign rights, not to acquire Chinese territory, and not to interfere in her internal troubles unless treaty rights were violated. The co-operative policy had two significant results. The unity of purpose among the treaty powers discouraged China from trying to evade her treaty obligations, and this strict observance of treaty terms in turn gave the powers no reason to use gunboat diplomacy. At the same time, it protected China from attempts by individual powers to take advantage of her weakness by demanding more concessions.

Alcock's part in promoting a friendly and tolerant attitude towards China is seen in his determination to protect her from the aggressive demands of British merchants. The Tianjin treaties were due for revision in 1868, and these merchants were pressing the British government to demand increased privileges such as lower customs duties, exemption from the *lika* (a tax on transit goods), and the extension of treaty rights beyond the treaty ports. Instead, Alcock signed a convention with the *Zongli Yamen* in 1869 which, in effect, protected China against further concessions that might threaten her sovereign rights.

His statesmanlike diplomacy could have placed the treaty system on a more satisfactory basis, particularly where China was concerned; but strong opposition from the merchant community in Britain forced the British government to reject the convention. The Tianjin Massacre of 1870 further justified the refusal to ratify it. This refusal was a severe blow to the co-operative policy, for it increased Chinese suspicions of Western ambitions in China. Moreover, treaty revision was postponed. When it came in 1876, it was negotiated by force, not on the basis of mutual concessions as in the Alcock Convention.

Sir Robert Hart and his Maritime Customs Service staff gave valuable assistance to the modernization of China. With their help, a modern postal service was begun and harbour facilities were improved by installing modern navigational aids. It was Hart who set aside funds from the customs dues to maintain the *Tongwenguan*. He also recommended Burlingame as leader of China's first official diplomatic mission to the West. Burlingame and Alcock both supported and encouraged modernization.

Diplomatic relations

The second treaty settlement provided for regular diplomatic exchanges between China and the West. Yet, even with the establishment of foreign legations at Beijing and the formation of the *Zongli Yamen* in 1861, diplomatic relations remained a one-way movement for some time. Although Zeng Guofan and others urged the sending of China's own envoys abroad, Beijing refused.

ON SENDING ENVOYS ABROAD

As for the item of sending envoys abroad, since China and the foreign countries have already become friendly, to have relations with them is a normal matter. Some critics fear that our envoys may bring disgrace to their mission, and others are afraid that the cost will be enormous. These are words of over-anxiety. It seems suitable to order the high ministers at the capital and elsewhere to look for men who could be envoys to distant countries and to mark their abilities for future use....

– *Zeng Guofan, 1867*

True, a semi-official diplomatic mission headed by a low-ranking elderly Manzhu official was sent to Europe in 1866 on an investigation tour; but when the mission returned it had little or no influence at all on China's foreign policy.

Then, in 1867, Beijing, in a surprise move, asked the retiring American minister Burlingame to head a mission to the West. He had won the confidence of some of the leading Chinese officials through his co-operative policy. Seeing a chance to promote his policy among the treaty powers at government level, he accepted Beijing's offer. His mission was to gain sympathy for China among the treaty powers, particularly since revision of the Tianjin treaties was due in 1868. The Burlingame mission (1868-70) visited the United States and several European capitals, but was cut short upon the death of Burlingame in St Petersburg in 1870.

Some people felt that the mission did more harm than good, because Burlingame presented a misleading picture of a China ready to accept Westernization and to embrace Christianity. This was to influence American thinking about China for many years to come.

However, the mission had beneficial effects. As China's first official diplomatic mission to the West, it prepared the way for

The Burlingame mission (1868-70)

the establishment of Chinese legations abroad; and it did arouse in the Western nations some sympathy for and interest in China. While the mission was in the United States, Burlingame and William H. Seward, US Secretary of State, concluded additional articles to the American Treaty of Tianjin. The United States agreed

AMERICAN MISCONCEPTIONS ABOUT CHINA

An impression seems to have obtained in the United States that the government of China is peculiarly friendly to our country, and that great advantages to our commerce are about to accrue from this preference....

I need scarcely say these anticipations are without foundation. The government of China may have preferences; but it has no special regard for any foreign power.

— *J. Ross Browne, Burlingame's successor as American minister at Beijing*

not to interfere in China's internal administration with reference to the building of railways, telegraphs and other material improvements. To some extent, the Seward-Burlingame Treaty of 1868 placed Sino-American relations on equal terms by granting to the Chinese reciprocal rights to trade, reside and travel in the United States. Unfortunately, soon after the signing of the treaty, agitation against Chinese workers on the Pacific Coast began.

The mission temporarily prevented moves by aggressive British traders to have the British Treaty of Tianjin revised so as to provide for the general opening of China to the foreigners. In London, Burlingame received assurances from the British government that, in future, it would not use force to threaten the independence and safety of China. But further attempts to improve Sino-British relations ended with the rejection of the Alcock Convention of 1869 by the British government and the Margary affair of 1875.

Another problem in diplomatic relations was the audience question, which involved the

A FEW CHRISTIANS OF THE YAO CHIA CHAUNG STATION

Nineteenth-century Christian converts in China

kotow. When the foreign ministers in Beijing asked for an imperial audience, the Chinese kept postponing the matter, for granting such an audience would mean recognizing Western states as the equals of China. The excuse used for the delay was that Emperor Tongzhi was still a minor. When he came of age in 1873, Chinese officials ran out of excuses. The foreign powers then put more pressure on the *Zongli Yamen* to settle the question. Finally, on June 29 the foreign ministers were granted their first official audience before the emperor. They did not *kotow*, but merely bowed three times. To the foreigners, the audience meant that China had given up her attitude of superiority. For the Chinese, however, it only strengthened the idea of superiority because the emperor received the ministers in the hall reserved for tribute-bearing missions. Nevertheless, the fact remained that for the first time, foreign ministers were able to see the emperor in person without performing the customary *kotow*.

A more satisfactory audience was eventually granted in the 1890s.

EFFORTS TO IMPROVE RELATIONS WEAKENED

The Tianjin Massacre, 1870

By the Tianjin treaties of 1858, Christian missionaries were granted the right to travel anywhere in China. In 1860, the Franco-Chinese Convention gave Catholic missionaries the right to acquire lands in any part of China and to erect buildings on them. The Chinese later refused to accept these points, claiming that the clause was inserted in the text of the treaty without their knowledge. Their claim was ignored and, before long, missionaries could be found in almost every province of China. The number of missionaries, both Catholic and Protestant, rapidly increased and missionary work expanded. While the educational and medical work of these missionaries no doubt brought benefits to the Chinese, some British and American officials in China disapproved of their activities. Most of the complaints brought before them by the Chinese were about missionaries.

In general, the Chinese attitude towards the missionaries was one of fear, suspicion and hostility. The local gentry, the landlord-scholar-official class, resented the semi-official status assumed by some of the Catholic missionaries. By claiming the right to protect their converts, these missionaries had, to some extent, taken these people away from the control of local Chinese officials. By providing relief for the poor and suffering masses, the missionaries also assumed functions which were customarily exercised by the gentry. The scholar class regarded as pure superstition such Christian doctrines as the virgin birth and the reincarnation of Christ. Missionaries claimed that Christianity was the only true religion, and this idea clashed with such traditional customs as ancestor-worship and the sacrificial offerings of the Confucian cult.

Chinese officials were suspicious because this was a religion supported by foreign governments. Moreover, the Chinese at the treaty ports saw foreign merchants, who were supposed to be Christians, violating the very same Christian principles preached by the missionaries. Finally, China had been defeated twice by foreign powers which were Christian, and her dynastic rule had been threatened by the Taiping who claimed to be Christians.

The masses showed that they shared the anti-Christian feeling of their officials, by their attacks on missionaries, converts and churches, and their readiness to believe stories about Christian hospitals and orphanages kidnapping children and mutilating them.

From this background of religious intolerance, superstition and childlike belief came the Tianjin Massacre of 1870. The immediate cause was the death of between 30 and 40 children in an orphanage run by the French Sisters of Charity at Tianjin. Although they died because of an epidemic, the local people began to believe rumours that they had been killed and that their eyes and hearts were used to make medicines. Local officials, instead of calming down the people, encouraged them to take action. Finally, on June 21

CRUELTY TO CHINESE CHILDREN DENIED

Those who slander the foreigners say that they have done all kinds of inhuman things such as gouging out the eye-pupils and hearts [of Chinese children], but who has seen it? If it is really true, why have we never heard of such things being done in their own countries?.... No intelligent person would believe this rumour.

– Tan Sitong (1865-98),
Chinese philosopher

a mob gathered. It destroyed the orphanage and the church nearby, killing the French consul, 20 other foreigners including 2 priests and 10 nuns, and about 30 Chinese servants employed by the French. It also looted or destroyed American and British chapels in the city.

The foreign powers immediately fought back. They resorted to gunboat diplomacy once again to demand satisfaction for the killings, and adequate protection against similar anti-Christian demonstrations in future. French, British and American warships gathered off Tianjin. Faced by joint foreign intervention, China yielded. Some of those responsible for the massacre were executed, others banished. France, being the treaty power directly involved, received 250 000 taels as indemnity and a note of apology from China. Her defeat in the Franco-Prussian War stopped her from presenting more severe demands. Despite the settlement, Sino-French relations continued to worsen. War eventually broke out between the two countries in 1884 over Annam.

Although the Chinese government seemed to have tried its best to protect missionaries and their converts after 1870, anti-Christian as well as anti-foreign feeling continued to grow, reaching its climax in the Boxer Rising. A more immediate result of the incident at Tianjin was that it dealt a damaging blow to the co-operative policy as well as to the self-strengthening movement.

The Margary affair, 1875

We have already seen that the British Treaty of Tianjin was due to be revised in 1868. The British government, having assured Burlingame that it would not use force in dealing with China, decided to delay the matter until the Emperor Tongzhi came of age in 1872-73. However, it soon became clear that China would negotiate only under force. The murder of a British consular official, Augustus Raymond Margary, in 1875 gave the British an excuse to use force.

For some time, the British, who had established themselves in Lower Burma, had been interested in an overland route to China's southwestern provinces (Yunnan, Guizhou and Sichuan) by way of Upper Burma. Alarmed by French penetration of Indo-China at this time, the British decided to open up trade with southwestern China. An expedition from British India had already reached Bhamo in Upper Burma in 1868. In 1874 a second expedition under Colonel Browne was organized to penetrate Yunnan from Bhamo. It was joined by Margary, who had been sent from Beijing by British Minister Thomas Wade to serve as interpreter. In 1875, when the Browne expedition left Bhamo, a party of Chinese led by Margary was sent ahead to find out whether the route was safe or not. It was attacked, most probably by Chinese, and Margary and five of his Chinese companions died.

When Wade received news of the incident, he immediately used it to force a settlement of all existing questions between the two governments. The Yantai Convention negotiated by Wade and Li Hongzhang was subsequently signed in 1876. There were three sections:
- The first section dealt mainly with the Margary case. China was to pay an indemnity of 200 000 taels, send a mission of apology to England, and allow British officers to be stationed in Yunnan for five years.
- The second section provided for the improvement of official communications, so that foreign ministers at Beijing and consuls at the treaty ports would be properly treated by Chinese authorities. New regulations were also to be made to bring about better administration of justice at the treaty ports.
- The third section dealt with trade concessions which included the opening of four more treaty ports (Yichang, Wuhu, Wenzhou and Beihai) and six ports of call on the Changjiang River.

China ratified the agreement immediately. But it was not until 1885 that Britain ratified it, for it was opposed by some British merchants, who preferred to make China observe the terms of previous settlements than to acquire new concessions.

The Yantai Convention was an important supplement to the two earlier treaty settlements and produced significant results. The Changjiang River Valley was thrown open to foreign trade and foreigners; and foreign diplomats at Beijing were given better treatment from then on.

The terms of the agreement illustrated once more how threats could be used against China to obtain new concessions. The concessions granted were out of proportion to the offence committed. This showed that Britain had not kept her promise of restraint in dealing with China. The convention also showed how difficult it was for the treaty powers to agree among themselves, for there were objections to it from France, Russia and Germany. The co-operative policy was abandoned, and the foreign powers went back to the old practice of taking separate action to further their interests in China. China was finally convinced of the necessity of having her own legations abroad. In 1877 a diplomatic legation was established in England. This was followed by the establishment of legations in Germany in 1877, the United States and

Chinese immigrants in San Francisco

France in 1878, and Russia and Spain in 1879.

The Chinese immigration question

During the 19th century, more and more Chinese were leaving to work abroad as free or contract labourers. Most of those who left on their own migrated to Australia and the American Pacific Coast; others, who were victims of the coolie trade, found themselves in Cuba and Peru. By 1867 there were some 50 000 Chinese workers in California. The Seward-Burlingame Treaty of 1868, which gave the Chinese the right to settle in the United States, increased Chinese emigration to that country. For this reason, the Chinese immigration question was more serious in the United States than in other Western nations.

At first, the Americans welcomed the Chinese because of the demand for cheap labour, especially for railway construction. As their numbers increased, so did American hostility. In 1873, there was a financial slump. This Panic of 1873 brought with it prejudice, boycotts, and violence against the Chinese. Opposition to unlimited Chinese immigration increased, led by labour groups on the Pacific coast.

As a result, the American Congress passed a bill in 1879 limiting the number of Chinese any one vessel could bring to the United States to 15 at a time. President Hayes vetoed the bill because it violated the treaty of 1868. He then sent a commission to China to obtain a revision of that treaty. In 1880 a

> ## PLEA FOR BETTER TREATMENT OF THE CHINESE
>
> The Chinese do not seek to interfere in our American political struggles; they are peaceful and law-abiding; they are always willing to bear their equal burden of taxes, and all they ask is to be treated with common humanity.
>
> — *J. Ross Browne, former American minister at Beijing*

new treaty was signed in which China agreed that the United States could regulate and even suspend Chinese immigration, though not prohibit it altogether. Congress then passed a law in 1882, suspending Chinese immigration for ten years. More restrictive measures were taken in later years. All these restrictions aroused resentment among the Chinese. They became even more angry because the ill-treatment of the Chinese already in America continued. The Chinese immigration question, therefore, increased anti-foreign feeling in China.

Foreign advance on China's border states, 1870–95

On the borders of the Chinese Empire were lesser states which had been dependencies of China for centuries because they accepted the concept of the Middle Kingdom. Among these were the Ryukyu or Liuqiu Islands, Annam (Vietnam), Burma, Sikkim, Korea and parts of Central Asia. The system of tributary states was vital to China's security, for it served as her first line of defence. Her control over these states, however, was limited to the sending of tribute-bearing missions to Beijing. So long as their rulers succeeded in maintaining peace and order, observed Confucian ideals, and accepted their vassal status, China did not interfere in their internal affairs. The relationship, therefore, was one of dependence but no control; of an elder brother watching over a younger brother in the Confucian family of nations. Such theories of foreign relations went against those of the West, which were based on the equality of nations.

Although China had lost Hong Kong and Kowloon Point to Britain, and the north bank of the Heilongjiang River and the Maritime Province to Russia, China's territorial integrity was not seriously threatened until the foreign powers began to challenge her position in the border states. Between 1870 and 1895, China lost whatever control she had

had over these states. The island kingdom of Ryukyu was the first to go.

In the mid-19th century, the Ryukyus, which lay between southern Japan and Formosa, were in fact under the control of the *daimyo* of Satsuma, though they sent tribute to China.

In 1871 some Ryukyu islanders were ship-wrecked on Formosa and massacred by aborigines. In 1873 Japan decided to make use of the Formosa incident to clarify the status of the Ryukyus. Since the Formosans were Chinese subjects, Japan, claiming the right to speak for the Ryukyuans, demanded that China punish the murderers. The *Zongli Yamen* told the Japanese that the incident did not concern them because the kingdom of Ryukyu was a tributary state of China and Formosa was part of China. The Chinese also said that they never interfered with the internal affairs of the Formosan aborigines. Japan replied that, if China did not control the aborigines, then they were not under Chinese rule. The Japanese also said that if Japan took action against them, she would not be violating Chinese jurisdiction. In 1874 they sent an expedition against Formosa. War was prevented when China agreed to pay Japan for the costs of the expedition and to compensate the families of the murdered Ryukyuans.

The settlement showed that Japan was the real ruler of the kingdom of Ryukyu. In 1879 she formally took possession of it by making it the Okinawa Prefecture. Two years later, China gave up her claim over the Ryukyus, an event which marked the beginning of the breakdown of her Confucian international system. From then on, Sino-Japanese relations became unfriendly. Moreover, the exposure of China's weakness in the Formosa incident invited further territorial aggression by foreign powers.

While Japan was strengthening her hold over the Ryukyus, Russia was moving southward to the northwestern frontiers of China. In the 1860s the Muslims there had risen in revolt against Qing authority. In 1871 Russia

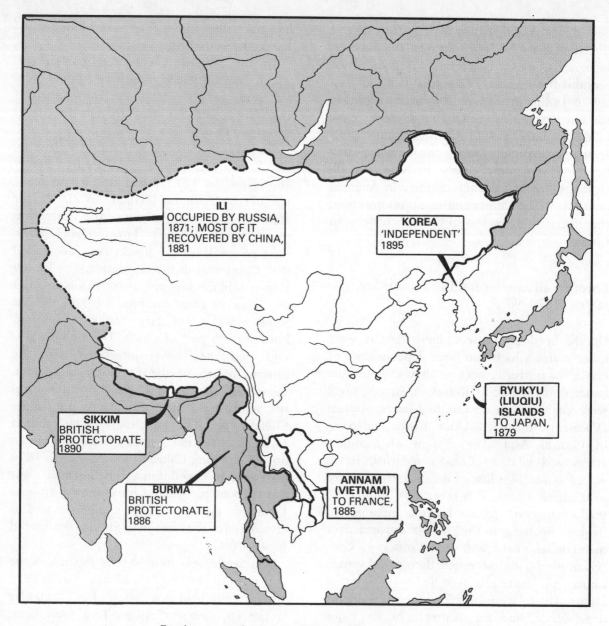

Foreign encroachment on China's border states, 1870-95

occupied the Yili region in Chinese Turkestan (Xinjiang), claiming that she had to protect her commercial interests in the area. She promised to withdraw her troops as soon as Qing authority was restored. By 1878 Zuo Zongtang had suppressed the Muslim rebellions, and yet Russia continued to hold Yili. The following year she succeeded in negotiating a treaty with a senior Manzhu official, ceding a large part of Yili to Russia. Beijing rejected the treaty.

The Yili question was finally settled by the Treaty of St Petersburg (1881), under which China recovered most of Yili (western Yili remained in Russian hands), though she had to pay the cost of the Russian military occupation. Her success in resisting Russia in the northwest encouraged her to take a stronger stand against foreign aggression.

In the south, however, China failed to stop the French and the British advance. Annam, for centuries a tributary of China, came under

The map contains the following labels:

ILI
OCCUPIED BY RUSSIA, 1871; MOST OF IT RECOVERED BY CHINA, 1881

KOREA
'INDEPENDENT' 1895

SIKKIM
BRITISH PROTECTORATE, 1890

RYUKYU (LIUQIU) ISLANDS
TO JAPAN, 1879

BURMA
BRITISH PROTECTORATE, 1886

ANNAM (VIETNAM)
TO FRANCE, 1885

French control after China's defeat in the Sino-French War of 1884-85. War broke out because of the French advance in north Annam (Tonkin). The French wanted to open up southwest China by way of Tonkin. The war ended in 1885 with the signing of a treaty between Li Hongzhang and the French minister in China, and Annam became a French protectorate. In 1886 China recognized British control of all of Burma, which Britain had occupied the year before. The country had been a tributary state of China since the 13th century. Yet another tributary state, Sikkim in northeastern India, became a British protectorate in 1890.

All these territorial settlements showed that the Confucian idea of state relations was gradually giving way to Western ideas of foreign relations. China was finally forced to give up her Confucian international theories when Korea became 'independent' as a result of the Sino-Japanese War of 1894-95.

QUESTIONS

1. Describe the attempts to improve Sino-Western relations in the period 1860-94.
2. Explain what is meant by the 'co-operative policy' of the foreign powers in China in the 1860s. Why did they abandon this policy in the 1870s?
3. Give examples to show that there was continued friction between China and the Western powers between 1870 and 1895.
4. Write a short account of **each** of the following, and show how **each** of them affected Sino-Western relations between 1860 and 1894:
   (a) the Burlingame Mission (1868-70)
   (b) the Tianjing Massacre (1870)
   (c) the Margary affair (1875)
   (d) the Chinese immigration question
5. Give an account of the foreign threat to China's border states between 1870 and 1895.
6. Explain how China lost the Ryukyus to Japan, Annam (Vietnam) to France, and Burma to Britain.

During the 1860s, Sino-Western relations improved because of China's efforts at diplomatic modernization and the 'co-operative policy' of the treaty powers. China's change of policy towards the foreign powers can be seen in the establishment of the *Zongli Yamen* and the sending of her first official diplomatic mission abroad led by a foreigner, Anson Burlingame. For their part, the treaty powers adopted the 'co-operative policy' by which they agreed that together they would preserve China's territorial integrity and help her to modernize.

In the 1870s, however, further attempts to improve relations ended because of the Tianjin Massacre of 1870, the Margary affair of 1875 and the problem of Chinese emigration to the United States. A new tide of anti-foreign feeling swept through China. At the same time, the foreign advance on China's frontier areas and tributary states in the 1870s and 1880s increased ill-feeling. So did the views of the aggressive foreign traders who wanted more concessions and the conservative officials who opposed further concessions.

The *Zongli Yamen* felt betrayed by the British government's rejection of the lenient terms of the Alcock Convention of 1869, a revision of the 1858 British Treaty of Tianjin. Chinese conservative officials condemned the British action. When the treaty was finally revised in 1876, it was negotiated by force instead of through mutual concessions. The Tianjin Massacre and the Margary affair ended the 'co-operative policy'. The treaty powers went back to gunboat diplomacy and slowed down their efforts to help China to modernize.

China's loss of her border states to foreign powers showed that the limited modernization of the 'self-strengthening movement' had failed to strengthen her against foreign aggression. It also showed that the Chinese idea of international relations based on the tribute system was giving way to Western ideas of international relations based on equality of nations. The loss of Korea after the Sino-Japanese War of 1894-95 forced China to give up her centuries-old claim to sovereignty over the civilized world.

Chapter 7
The 'scramble for concessions' and China's reaction

THE 'SCRAMBLE FOR CONCESSIONS'

The 'self-strengthening movement' had not strengthened China to a point where she could successfully resist foreign aggression. This is best seen in her defeat in the Sino-Japanese War of 1894-95 (see Chapter 11). For China, the most disastrous result of the war was the 'scramble for concessions' which was encouraged by several factors. China's weakness was exposed by the war, but this was not the only incentive; the Western powers were greedy and feared further Japanese penetration of China. Each power then determined to take its share, so that none of its rivals would have an advantage. Between 1895 and 1899, the Western powers and Japan obtained many concessions from China. These were mainly economic — for example, railway and mining rights. They also established 'spheres of influence' or 'spheres of interest', where only the privileged power could obtain concessions. In a 'sphere of influence', the privileged power had some degree of political or financial control. Before the Sino-Japanese War the powers had been interested mainly in trade; now they looked upon China as a field for investment.

France

France actually started the 'concession-grabbing', but did not immediately pursue her gains as actively as did Russia and Germany when they joined the scramble. Her interest was in southern China, because it was near French Indo-China. In June 1895 she obtained railway and mining rights in Yunnan, Guangxi and Guangdong. The next year, China permitted her to extend the Annam railway into Guangxi, and agreed not to 'alienate' (cede) the island of Hainan to any other power.

In 1898, seeing Russia and Germany obtaining concessions in the north, France asked for additional concessions. She obtained a 99-year lease of Guangzhou Bay, the right to build railways in Yunnan, and a non-alienation agreement which included the provinces of China next to the border of French Indo-China. With the exception of western Guangdong, which was within the British sphere because of Hong Kong and Kowloon, southern China became an area of French influence.

Russia

Having gained China's goodwill through the Triple Intervention (see p. 187), Russia acted immediately to make the most of this advantage. In July 1895 Russia, together with France, made a loan to China to help her pay the Shimonoseki indemnity to Japan, resulting from her defeat in the Sino-Japanese War. In December she established the Russo-Chinese Bank to obtain, among other things, economic concessions from China. By a secret treaty of alliance, the Li-Lobanov Treaty of 1896:

- Russia and China pledged to go to war if either one was attacked by Japan;
- Russian warships could use Chinese ports in the event of war;
- China consented to the building of the Chinese Eastern Railway, an extension of the Trans-Siberian Railway, across Manchuria.

It was not until 1922 that the treaty was made public.

ALLIANCE WITH RUSSIA PROPOSED

Now if we wish to make a treaty, and to have a bond of mutual assistance, naturally Russia is most convenient for us....Her behaviour is grand and generous, and cannot be compared with that of the Europeans. For example, in the church case at Tianjin in 1870, in which all the countries were busy making a clamour, Russia did not participate; and in the treaties over Yili our nation completely refused and then modified the 18 articles, and Russia generously consented. This time she has demanded the return of the territory of Liaodong for us....

— *Zhang Zhidong, August 1895*

In 1898, following Germany's acquisition of Shandong as a sphere of interest, Russia put pressure on China for more concessions. She was granted a 25-year lease of the southern tip of the Liaodong Peninsula, where the Lüshun (Port Arthur) naval base and Dalian (Dalny to the Russians) were located. She also obtained the right to construct what became the South Manchurian Railway connecting these ports with the Chinese Eastern Railway. At last Russia had an ice-free port, Dalian, which would be linked with Europe by rail. She also gained mining rights in southern Manchuria. As a result of all these concessions, Manchuria became Russia's sphere of interest.

Germany

In 1897, Germany used the murder of two German priests in Shandong as an excuse to seize Qingdao in Jiaozhou Bay. In 1898, China granted the following rights and privileges to Germany:

- a 99-year lease of the area surrounding the Jiaozhou Bay, including Qingdao as a naval base;
- the construction of forts and navigational aids in the leased territory;
- the exercise of sovereign rights in the leased territory, with China giving up authority over that area;
- the building of railways and the mining of coal in Shandong.

The province of Shandong thus came under German influence.

Britain

Britain, at first, did not take part in the scramble, because her continued economic control in China depended on a free and open market (an 'open door'). As more and more concessions were granted to the other powers, she appealed to the United States for joint action to maintain free commerce in China. Though the United States was sympathetic, because the British move coincided with her traditional policy, she was unable to help because she was involved in a dispute with Spain over Cuba. This dispute led to the Spanish-American War of 1898.

Having failed to win American support, and finding herself sandwiched between the Russian and German spheres in the north and the French sphere in the south, Britain was forced to follow the example of the other powers. In 1898, she obtained from China the following rights and privileges:

- a lease of Weihai for as long as Russia occupied Lushun, a move which was suggested by China herself to check Russian expansion;
- a 99-year lease of the New Territories;

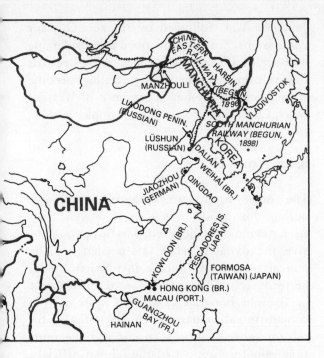

Foreign possessions and leases in China by 1899

In September 1899, Hay sent his first Open Door notes to the treaty powers, requesting each of them:

- not to interfere in the administration of any treaty port within its sphere;
- not to interfere in the collection of duties by the Chinese government in such ports;
- to impose the same harbour dues and railway charges for all foreign traders in its sphere.

Britain agreed to follow Hay's proposals if they were accepted by all other powers. Russia virtually rejected them, while the rest gave vague and evasive replies. Nevertheless, Hay announced to the American people that the powers had unanimously accepted the Open Door policy.

- nine railway concessions;
- a non-alienation agreement involving the provinces along the Changjiang River;
- a promise that, as long as Britain dominated the China trade, a British subject was to be the head of the Chinese Maritime Customs Service.

The Changjiang River Valley thus became a British sphere of interest.

The United States

The United States continued to pursue a policy of equal commercial opportunity and the preservation of China's political and territorial integrity. For a time, though, she did nothing to carry out this policy because of the dispute with Spain. When the war ended she had become a Pacific power, having acquired Hawaii, which became part of the United States by congressional action, and also the Philippines and Guam. The new Secretary of State, John Hay, decided to revive and restate America's traditional China policy.

AMERICA'S OPEN DOOR POLICY

....the policy of the government of the United States is to seek a solution which may bring about permanent safety and peace to China, preserve Chinese territorial and administrative entity, protect all rights guaranteed to friendly powers by treaty and international law, and safeguard for the world the principle of equal and impartial trade with all parts of the Chinese Empire.

— From Hay's circular note of 1900

The 1899 notes dealt with equal commercial opportunity; they did not discuss the preservation of the Chinese state. In 1900, however, foreign intervention in the Boxer Rising seemed likely to end in the partition of China. Hay issued a circular which stated again the principle of equal opportunity and, in addition, appealed to the powers to respect China's territorial integrity. None of them raised any objections to the American appeal. However, they did not take the Open Door policy seriously. They still aimed to give their citizens special treatment in their respective spheres. In the end, even the United States joined the battle for concessions, for in December 1900, Hay tried unsuccessfully to acquire a naval coaling station on the coast of Fujian. Japan opposed the American move, pointedly referring to Hay's Open Door notes.

Other powers

As for Japan, China promised her not to cede Fujian to any other power. In 1899, Italy asked for a naval station on Sanmen Bay in Zhejiang. However, her request was refused. Her unsuccessful attempt to get a concession marked the end of the 'scramble for concessions'.

With the concession-grabbing, the 'cutting up of the China melon' seemed likely to happen; the privileged powers were expected sooner or later to annex their respective spheres. The first reaction of China's leaders was to begin the Hundred Days' Reform, which attempted to carry out more radical reforms than those of the earlier self-strengthening movement. When this reform movement collapsed, chiefly because of conservative opposition, China turned to violence to drive out the foreigners. The Boxer Rising was the result.

THE HUNDRED DAYS' REFORM

In the 19th century, China was faced with many problems that threatened her very existence: foreign pressure, regional revolts, financial difficulties and over-population. Reform seemed to be the only remaining way to save both the nation and the Qing dynasty. We have seen how, after her defeat in the Second Anglo-Chinese War, China launched the self-strengthening movement, which proved to be only a poor attempt at reform. China's humiliating defeat in the Sino-

Japanese War, followed by the scramble for concessions, finally convinced a considerable number of Chinese officials and intellectuals that reform was urgent. If Japan had become strong because of her acceptance of Western ways, China must follow her example.

Kang Youwei

The most prominent advocate of reform during this period was Kang Youwei. 'Self-strengthening', he believed, was not enough to save the dynasty; what was needed was the radical reform of Chinese institutions. What he really wanted was the gradual replacement of the old imperial Confucian system by a constitutional monarchy. He knew that if his reform movement was to succeed, he must first gain the support of the scholar-officials. To win their support, he developed a reformist interpretation of Confucianism. In his work,

Kang Youwei

120

Confucius as a Reformer, he attempted to show that Confucius favoured change; in troubled times all Confucianists should be prepared to abandon traditional ideas. Other notable advocates of reform were Liang Qichao (梁啟超 , 1873-1929), Kang's chief disciple, and Zhang Zhidong, viceroy of Hunan and Hubei. Zhang's ideas on reform, however, were not very different from those of the 'self-strengtheners'. He advocated and made popular the slogan 'Chinese learning for the fundamental principles, Western learning for practical application', an idea which he borrowed from Feng Guifen. After 1895, the spirit of reform began to take root among the gentry-scholar-official class. They founded 'study societies' which held discussion meetings and issued publications supporting reform. By 1898 the problem was no longer whether or not to introduce reforms, but how radical the reforms should be.

Kang realized that he had to gain·imperial favour for his ideas. When the text of the Treaty of Shimonoseki was published in 1895, he was in Beijing to take the examinations for the *jinshi* degree. He was chosen by some 1200 examination candidates to act as their spokesman in protesting against the treaty terms and in advocating reform. In his 'Ten. Thousand Word Memorial' presented to the throne in May 1895, he outlined a reform programme for Emperor Guangxu, but the emperor did not act upon it. In 1897, when the Germans made a demand for Jiaozhou, he tried again without success; in fact, he tried seven times altogether.

Finally convinced by Kang's repeated petitions for reform, and alarmed by what seemed to be the coming break-up of the empire, the emperor decided to take action. On 11 June 1898 he issued an edict calling for reform. Five days later, he granted a personal audience to Kang, and they discussed the reforms to be introduced. In the summer of 1898, some 40 to 50 reform decrees were issued, introducing sweeping changes in the political, cultural and economic life of the country. The Hundred Days' Reform had

GUANGXU CALLS FOR REFORM

....Consider the needs of the times and the weakness of our empire! If we continue to drift with our army untrained, our revenues disorganized, our scholars ignorant, and our artisans without technical training, how can we possibly hope to hold our own among the nations, or to cross the gulf which divides the weak from the strong?...

We now issue this special decree so that all our subjects, from the imperial family downwards, may hereinafter exert themselves in the cause of reform....

– From Guangxu's first reform decree, 1898

begun. It was a comprehensive programme, unlike the self-strengthening movement which stressed only technological and military reforms.

The reforms

Reforms in education New schools were to be established where both Chinese and Western learning were to be taught. All existing schools were to be reorganized to meet the new requirements. An Imperial University was to be set up in Beijing. The 'eight-legged' essay on a classical quotation in the civil service examinations was to be replaced by essays on current affairs. The revised examination system therefore was going to test practical, not classical, knowledge. Western works on science and politics were to be translated, a task to be taken up by the newly-formed Translation Bureau. Studying abroad was to be promoted.

Reforms in government Useless posts (sinecures) were to be abolished. These included the governorships of Hubei, Guangdong and Yunnan; the director-generalship of the Huanghe River; and the posts of salt commissioner and grain intendant. Legal codes were to be simplified, so that extra-territoriality might be abolished. Provision was made for a public budget. *The Chinese Progress* edited by Liang became the official government newspaper.

Economic reforms To improve the nation's economy, it was decreed that modern banks and chambers of commerce should be established. A bureau of agriculture and commerce was to be set up to encourage the use of scientific farming methods and labour-saving machines. A transportation and mining bureau was to be created to speed up railway building and encourage mining. Postal systems were to be modernized.

Other reforms Modernization was to be extended to the army and navy, and a national militia was to be organized. High-ranking officials were to tour foreign countries. Christian missionaries were to be protected.

Collapse of the reform movement

The Hundred Days' Reform was cut short by a *coup d'etat* led by the empress dowager and Ronglu (榮祿 , d. 1903), the top Manzhu military commander. Although Cixi had been in retirement since 1889, she still controlled political and military affairs. Rumours had reached the reform leaders of a plot to depose Guangxu during an inspection of the Tianjin garrison in October, when he would be accompanied by the empress dowager. They therefore plotted with Yuan Shikai who had a modern army in Hebei, to keep the emperor in power. The plan was that Yuan should go to Tianjin as the head of an army of 7000 men to protect the emperor. He would have the empress dowager arrested and Ronglu, who would also be at Tianjin, murdered. Yuan, however, betrayed the reformers and joined forces with Ronglu. The latter then proceeded to Beijing and, on 21 September 1898, provided Cixi with the

CIXI RESUMES THE REGENCY

....WE have repeatedly besought Her Majesty to condescend once more to administer the Government. Now she has graciously honoured US by granting OUR prayer, a blessing indeed for all OUR subjects. From this day forth Her Majesty will transact the business of Government in the side hall of the Palace, and on the day after tomorrow WE ourselves at the head of OUR Princes and Ministers shall perform obeisance before Her in the Hall of Diligent Government.....

— *Imperial Decree, 1898*

military force to resume the regency, using the excuse that the emperor was ill. In the months that followed, almost all of the reforms were withdrawn.

The failure of the 1898 reform movement had other causes besides Cixi's unwillingness to give up authority, and Yuan's betrayal. The influential classes had good reasons for wishing to retain the existing social order, and they strongly resisted change.

Classical scholars who believed it was their duty to preserve Confucianism denounced Kang and his reform theories. They accused him of reinterpreting Confucianism to suit his reform programme. They called him a demon and a monster, who had brought dishonour to Confucius and his teachings.

Among the scholar-officials, there was a fear that radical reform might result in the loss of their 'rice bowls' (means of livelihood). They owed their appointments to their knowledge of the Confucian classics. The new emphasis on Western learning would lessen their importance. (Some had already lost their positions with the abolition of sinecures.) Those who were in danger of being dismissed from office, the Manzhu and Chinese alike, were greatly alarmed.

The Manzhu were further alarmed by the fact that all the reform leaders, except the emperor, were Chinese. Even those who favoured reform, such as Zhang Zhidong, found the Hundred Days' reforms too radical. They finally joined the conservatives in condemning the radical reformers. Such was the strength of the opponents of reform that only one high provincial official, the governor of Hunan, carried out the reform decrees vigorously.

The revised civil service examination system, as we have seen, proposed to test practical knowledge instead of relying on the formal 'eight-legged' essay on a classical quotation (in which the answer must be in

KANG'S REFORM THEORY CRITICIZED

Now you call the uncrowned prince [Confucius] a reformer in order to facilitate the promotion of your own reform movement. Even though the sage Confucius really had a reform intention, he only desired...to restore the ancient systems of the Sage Kings of the Three Dynasties; he had no intention of replacing Chinese institutions with barbarian systems.

— *Zhu Yixin, a classical scholar*

two halves, each divided into four 'legs' or sections). It disappointed thousands of students who had spent years studying the Confucian classics. Their hopes of passing the examinations and becoming officials were shattered.

Other officials such as Li Hongzhang opposed the movement in the belief that it was supported by the Japanese, and therefore harmful to China's interests. They favoured closer ties with Russia instead. There was opposition from Manzhu officials who were afraid that the emperor, under the influence of the Chinese reformers, might dismiss them. Plans to change monasteries into schools and hospitals angered monks, who were rather influential at court. Ordinary people did not support the movement because they did not understand why reforms were necessary.

The reformers themselves were partly to blame. The emperor himself knew very little about administration and politics. Most of his advisers too were theorists with little practical experience. Kang and Liang had no previous experience in government service. They had never been abroad before the reform movement and their knowledge of Western learning and institutions was very limited. Because of their inexperience, they introduced changes which were too radical for a country not yet ready for extensive reform.

The empress dowager

With so many forces against the reformers, it was therefore not surprising that the Hundred Days' Reform failed to achieve its goals. Nevertheless, it had some significant results.

Consequences of the Hundred Days' Reform

In the period immediately following Cixi's *coup d'etat,* many of the reform leaders were arrested, and six were executed; others were either dismissed from office or banished. Kang and Liang managed to escape to Japan.

The conservatives who had returned to power then adopted an anti-Chinese policy which further widened the gap between the Manzhu and the Chinese. Guangxu remained in forced seclusion until his death in 1908, one day before that of Cixi. He was not executed or forced to abdicate, for the supporters of Cixi feared the intervention of foreign powers, Britain and Japan in particular; they did not wish to provoke the liberals in the south; and they wanted to hide the fact that a woman was once again in control of China. Those involved in the *coup d'etat* were rewarded for their efforts. Ronglu was appointed to the Grand Council. Yuan was named governor of Shandong in late 1899, and in 1901, viceroy of Hebei and North China Trade Commissioner.

The failure of the movement convinced some reformers that reform from the top down, following the example of the Meiji reform in Japan, was not possible in China. The existing government would have to be overthrown first before changes could be made. Sun Yixian's revolutionary doctrines began to gain popular support. Kang and Liang, however, carried on their campaign for the introduction of reform among the Chinese abroad. Through his writings, Liang spread such ideas as nationalism and constitutional government. To fight reform and revolution, the empress dowager issued a decree advocating a return to conservative policies.

THE RETURN TO CONSERVATISM

....Generally speaking, there shall be no measures taken contrary to the established order of things throughout the empire. The times are critical, and it behoves us, therefore, to follow in government matters the happy mean and to avoid all extreme measures and abuses. It is our duty, without prejudice, to steer a middle course, and it is for you, our officials, to aim at permanence and stability of administration in every branch of the government.

— From a decree issued by the empress dowager in the name of the emperor, 1898

If reform was not the answer to the foreign threat, other methods would have to be found. When the conservatives regained control, the only solution they could offer was to expel the foreigners, and return to the former condition of isolation. Beijing took steps to check foreign penetration, refusing to grant further concessions until the existing ones had been fully exploited; strictly defining the limits of those already granted; and requiring that, in any business enterprise, at least half of the capital must be Chinese and the business must be controlled by the Chinese. However, since the government was weak, these regulations were ignored both by the foreigners and the local Chinese officials. In desperation, Cixi was to give her support to the Boxer Rising.

Kang's reinterpretation of Confucius aroused among the intellectual classes a critical attitude towards the Confucian classics as well as other age-old institutions. This helped to prepare the way for the revolutionary changes that took place in China in the early years of the 20th century.

The failure of the Hundred Days' Reform further discredited the Manzhu regime. In this sense, the 1898 reforms helped to hasten the collapse of the Qing dynasty.

Boxers in action

THE BOXER RISING

Background

For centuries anti-foreign feeling had existed in China and, given enough provocation, this feeling was always liable to break out into violence. The 'midsummer madness' known as the Boxer Rising, which was directed against the foreigners in general and the Christian missionaries and Chinese Christians in particular, was the most violent result of this anti-foreign attitude in the 19th century.

There was widespread resentment against the Westerners as a result of China's defeat in the First and Second Anglo-Chinese wars and her submission to the unequal treaty system. The years that followed saw the control of her trade and industry gradually passing to the foreigners, upsetting her agrarian economy and causing hardships among the peasants. Popular opposition was increased by the building of railways, a foreign invention, which frequently ran through the ancestral tombs scattered all over the countryside,

upsetting *fengshui*. In the last years of the 19th century, anti-foreign feeling increased because of China's defeat in the Sino-Japanese War of 1894-95 and the scramble for concessions. The aggressive moves of the foreign powers could lead to the partition of China.

At the same time, the Chinese resented the activities of the missionaries and their converts. By protecting Chinese Christians in legal disputes and providing relief for the poor and the sick, the missionaries aroused the hostility of many Chinese officials, who regarded such actions as interference in local government matters.

Converts, in turn, were despised by their countrymen and called 'secondary devils' and traitors, because they had abandoned some of the Chinese customs and traditions, and adopted strange Christian rites. During the celebration of festivals, which were regarded as community activities, they frequently refused to help pay for the expenses incurred, arguing that these festivals were non-Christian. As late as 1900, many people still believed that Christians killed children and made medicine from their eyes. Religious intolerance and superstition, therefore, made the Chinese look upon Christianity with fear, suspicion and hostility.

The failure of the Hundred Days' Reform meant that the anti-foreign forces were again in complete control. That same year, there was increasing peasant discontent in the north, due largely to physical disasters — poor harvests and disastrous floods. Starvation and banditry became widespread. Conservative officials, mostly the Manzhu, saw an opportunity to turn this unrest into anti-foreign feeling, blaming the foreigners for the misery of the masses. They hoped in this way to draw people's attention away from the inefficiency of the imperial government.

The rising

Against this background of political and economic discontent emerged the Boxer movement. The Boxers were so named by the Westerners because they belonged to a secret society, the *Yihequan* (Righteous and Harmonious Fists), which taught and practised a special kind of Chinese boxing. The society is believed to have started as a branch of the anti-dynastic Eight Trigrams Society, which was active in the late 18th century. Except for Manzhu attempts to suppress the *Yihequan* in the early 19th century, nothing much is known of its activities until the late 1890s.

In May 1898, an official report mentioned the Boxers for the first time, in connection with their anti-Christian activities in Shandong. Most of them were discontented peasants, and their slogan was 'Overthrow the Qing and annihilate the foreigners'. Conservatives and anti-foreign officials saw the Boxer movement as a possible weapon against the foreign powers. Yu Xian (毓賢), who was appointed governor of Shandong in March 1899, recruited Boxer bands to serve in militia forces organized in the province by imperial command to deal with German

BOXER PROCLAMATIONS, 1900

The scandalous conduct of Christians and barbarians is irritating our Gods and Geniuses, hence the many scourges from which we are now suffering. The dreadful drought afflicting vast areas this year will continue as long as one single Western devil resides between the Four Seas....

The iron roads and iron carriages are disturbing the terrestrial dragon and are destroying the earth's beneficial influences. The red liquid which keeps dripping from the iron snake is nothing but the blood of the outraged spirits of the air. Incurable diseases will strike us if these reddish drops fall near us....

The missionaries extract the eyes, marrow and heart of the dead in order to make medicaments. Whoever drinks a glass of tea at the parsonage is stricken by death: the brains burst out of the skull....

encroachments and local disorder. The *Yihequan* marked its semi-official status by changing its name to *Yihetuan* (Righteous and Harmonious Militia). By this time, too, the Boxers had become pro-Manzhu, and had changed their slogan to 'Protect the Qing and destroy the foreigners'.

The killing of Christian converts and the destruction of churches by the Boxers in Shandong, apparently with the consent of Governor Yu, drew protests from the French

A Chinese anti-foreigner cartoon of the Boxer period

The British legation in Beijing sandbagged against Boxer attacks

minister. As a result, Yu was replaced by Yuan Shikai in December 1899. Yuan immediately took action against the Boxers and succeeded in suppressing the movement in Shandong, despite the Boxers' claim that they could not be wounded by bullets. However, many of the Boxers there were able to cross to Hebei, where they continued to grow in strength.

It was in Hebei, in the early months of 1900, that Boxer bands began terrorizing the countryside. The disturbances spread to Shandong, Shanxi and southern Manchuria. Any foreign establishment they found, they destroyed: churches, mission-houses, railways, telegraph lines and post offices. They attacked missionaries and their Chinese converts. Official reaction was divided. Most of the

Chinese leaders and even the conservative Ronglu urged the court to suppress the movement. But the empress dowager allowed the Boxers to do as they pleased. Certain pro-Boxer officials, such as Prince Duan (the father-in-law of the heir-apparent), had considerable influence over her, and she feared that the Boxers might turn against the dynasty. Moreover, she was influenced by her intense dislike of foreigners, and by a childish belief that the Boxers had magic powers.

Seeing that nothing was being done to put a stop to the Boxer terror, the foreign powers decided to deal with the problem themselves. By early June 1900, some 400 troops had arrived in Beijing to reinforce the legation guards. On June 10, an international force of 2100 led by the British Admiral Seymour began to move up from Tianjin towards Beijing. Meanwhile, on June 13, the Boxers entered Beijing, attacking or destroying any sign of foreign influence. The following day, another Boxer force laid siege to the foreign concessions at Tianjin. A few days later, imperial troops attacked the foreigners for the first time, driving Seymour's expedition back to Tianjin. The foreign powers fought back by capturing the Dagu forts. On June 20, the Manzhu regime declared war on the foreign powers. On the same day, the siege of the foreign legations at Beijing began.

In July a combined force of about 20 000 British, French, American, Japanese, Russian, German, Italian and Austrian troops lifted the siege of the Tianjin settlements and proceeded to Beijing. Organized resistance by the Boxer and imperial forces collapsed on August 14, when the eight-nation expeditionary force entered Beijing and relieved the 55-day siege of the legations. By that time, some 200 missionaries and other foreigners and thousands of Chinese converts had lost their lives in northern China.

As the foreign troops occupied Beijing, many excesses were committed. Some of them looted the city, and the Germans shipped many art treasures back to their country. Early on the day following the occupation, Cixi fled to Xi'an with the emperor, leaving Li Hongzhang behind to face the demands of the foreign powers and to negotiate a settlement.

Failure of the rising

The Boxer movement had failed to achieve its aims of expelling the foreigners and destroying Christianity. The Boxers and the imperial troops were far too weak and inefficient to challenge the might of the foreign armies. In the siege of the Beijing legations, for example, the combined forces of Boxers and regular Chinese troops could not even break into the legation garrison, which was defended by only about 450 guards.

During the rising, too, the Boxers lost the support of many Chinese. They had no worthwhile programme to remedy China's ills. At the height of their power, they aroused the hatred of their countrymen by frequently committing such criminal acts as rape and looting in the areas they occupied. Many supporters were disappointed when they saw that the Boxers could be killed by bullets after all.

Most important of all, the majority of the Chinese leaders did not support the Boxers. Powerful viceroys, among them Li Hongzhang at Guangzhou and Zhang Zhidong at Wuchang, and some governors like Yuan Shikai, regarded the movement as a rebellion. Even court officials, such as Ronglu, condemned the Boxers and called for strong measures to suppress them. In general, officials in southern and central China sought to prevent the disorders from spreading and even ignored Beijing's declaration of war against the foreigners, which they believed to be suicidal. The failure of the Boxer movement to spread much beyond the north, and to develop into a truly national movement, proved to be a fatal weakness.

Europeans judging Boxers

Consequences of the rising

As matters stood at the end of the rising, there were three ways open to the foreign powers in deciding the fate of China. They could partition her; set up a new dynasty with foreign support; or keep the Qing dynasty in power and help it to strengthen the nation. In the negotiations that followed, they chose the last one. Although China had already accepted the main terms of the Boxer settlement by December 1900, negotiations continued until the summer of 1901 because of the conflicting aims and jealousies of the powers.

The Boxer Protocol was finally signed on September 7 with the following provisions:

- China was to send missions to Germany and Japan to apologize for the murder of the German ambassador and the Japanese chancellor of legation.
- Those responsible for the rising, Boxer leaders and officials alike, were to be executed or punished in other ways.
- Official examinations were to be suspended for five years in all the towns where Boxers killed or attacked foreigners.
- The importation of arms and ammunition, as well as materials for their manufacture, was banned for two years; the ban could be extended by two-year periods if the foreign powers so desired.
- China was to pay to the foreign powers in 39 annual instalments a very large indemnity of 450 million taels, or 67.5 million pounds. To help China meet these payments, customs duties were to be raised.
- The foreign powers were granted the right to maintain permanent legation guards in Beijing.
- The Dagu forts were to be destroyed, together with any obstacle that could prevent free communication between Beijing and the sea.
- The foreign powers were given the right to occupy certain strategic points to ensure

129

free communication between Beijing and the sea.

- China was to post and publish edicts designed to prevent further anti-foreign outbreaks.
- China was to create a full-scale ministry of foreign affairs to replace the *Zongli Yamen*, which had functioned as a special board under the Grand Council. (In 1901 the *Zongli Yamen* was replaced by the *Waiwubu* or Ministry of Foreign Affairs.)

Apart from the terms of the Boxer settlement, the rising had other far-reaching consequences. For China, the Boxer defeat showed the uselessness of adopting a strong anti-foreign attitude. Even Cixi seemed finally to have recognized the need for reform; the Manzhu reform programme which followed was, in many ways, similar to the Hundred Days' Reform she had suppressed. Unfortunately, the proposed changes came too late to save the dynasty.

In addition, the failure of the movement, and the harsh and humiliating terms of the protocol, showed once again the helplessness of the Manzhu when challenged by the foreign powers. The continued presence of foreign troops practically reduced China to a subject nation. The huge indemnity further weakened her already unstable financial position. The increased taxation which was necessary to meet the indemnity payments only increased popular discontent. All this convinced more Chinese that they must turn to revolutionary groups and, in this way, the rising hastened the collapse of the Qing dynasty.

Japan's role in putting down the rising strengthened her position as a world power. She would enjoy all the new rights and privileges, and would receive indemnity like all the other powers. Her rise to world power status was matched by her growing aggressiveness towards China. The rising also contributed indirectly to the outbreak of the Russo-Japanese War of 1904-05; the Russian troops which were used to suppress the rising remained in Manchuria even after the settlement. The Japanese demand that they be withdrawn, and the Russian delay in withdrawing them, provided the immediate cause of the war. Japan's victory in this war gave her a dominant position in south Manchuria and Korea.

The United States later decided to give up a large part of her share of the indemnity. It was agreed that the amount to be returned to China would be used to set up a fund for the education of the Chinese, largely in the United States. As a result, an increased number of Chinese students went abroad to study.

Finally, the rising convinced the foreign powers of the danger of further provoking China. Despite its failure, the Boxer movement showed unmistakably how much the Chinese resented foreign penetration and exploitation, and how far they would go in the face of great foreign provocation. Henceforth, the powers moderated their attitude towards China, and no longer pressed her so hard for more concessions.

WHY CHINA WAS NOT PARTITIONED

The years 1895-1901 were crowded with events that seemed to foreshadow the break-up of the empire. But the crisis passed, and China managed to preserve her territorial integrity. It is often suggested that the main reason for her survival was her clever use of a balance-of-power strategy in granting concessions by exploiting rivalries among the powers. When one power gained an advantage, she awarded a similar concession to a rival. For example, she leased Weihai to Britain for as long as Lushun was occupied by Russia, in order to offset the latter's gain.

Rivalry and jealousy among the powers themselves also helped to bring about some balance. Britain, France and Japan, which controlled a large portion of commerce with China as a whole, opposed the cession to other powers of areas where their trade was developing.

The powers felt that the 'spheres of interest' system already provided adequate advantages; they were therefore less willing to take upon themselves the administration of parts of China. In other words, they were not too eager to convert their spheres into genuine colonial possessions. An indirect method they used to further their influence was the pooling of loans to China, through an international banking group (consortium). There was, too, a growing liberal attitude towards China which coincided with the American Open Door policy. This strengthened the idea of keeping China open to free trade instead of partitioning her.

Finally, the attention of the powers was being occupied more and more by the tense situation in Europe and Africa. The partition of China might heighten rivalry, and lead to armed conflict that could easily spread to Europe. For the time being, the world powers wished to avoid war.

QUESTIONS

1. Describe the 'scramble for concessions' in China and the advantages gained by each of the foreign powers there.
2. During the 'scramble for concessions' (1895-99), how did the foreign powers try to check each other's ambitions in China? Why was China not partitioned?
3. In what ways did China react to the 'scramble for concessions'?
4. Explain what the Open Door notes were. How far did they influence the 'scramble for concessions'?
5. Trace the events which led to the Hundred Days' Reform, and discuss the reforms attempted.
6. Describe the Hundred Days' Reform and explain why it failed.
7. Why did the Hundred Days' Reform fail, and what were the consequences of its failure?
8. Discuss the part played by **each** of the following in the Hundred Days' Reform:
   (a) Kang Youwei
   (b) the Emperor Guangxu
   (c) the Empress Dowager Cixi
   (d) Yuan Shikai
9. Discuss the part played by the foreign powers in the Hundred Days' Reform.
10. Discuss the causes and results of **either** the Hundred Days' Reform **or** the Boxer Rising.
11. What factors contributed to the outbreak of the Boxer Rising? Why did the rising fail?
12. Discuss the political and social conditions in China which led to the Boxer Rising.
13. 'It was the Qing court more than the Boxers themselves that was responsible for the Boxer Rising.' To what extent do you agree with this statement?
14. How far was the Boxer Rising brought about by foreign activities in China?
15. In what ways did the Boxer Protocol of 1901 affect China's relations with the foreign powers?

China's defeat in the Sino-Japanese War of 1894-95 exposed her continued weakness in spite of the 'self-strengthening movement' while Japan's victory aroused fears among the treaty powers of Japanese penetration of China. These factors, together with the greed of the Western powers, led to the 'scramble for concessions' which, in turn, could have resulted in the partition of China. Whereas in the past the foreign powers were only interested in the China trade, now they regarded China as an area for investment. The Beijing government reacted by launching the Hundred Days' Reform movement and by supporting the Boxer Rising and declaring war on the powers.

Fearing that the 'scramble for concessions' might lead to the break-up of the empire, the emperor and his advisers started the Hundred Days' Reform. It was an attempt to strengthen China by introducing reforms even more radical than those of the 'self-strengthening movement'. However, it was cut short by the conservative Cixi who was too experienced and too powerful to be toppled by a few inexperienced reformers. Besides, the reformers attempted too much too soon. The failure of the Hundred Days' Reform convinced many Chinese officials and intellectuals that revolution, not reform, was the answer to China's problems.

When reform failed, the Beijing government resorted to violence by backing the Boxers and making war on the foreign powers. But the Boxers and the imperial forces were no match for the combined forces of the world powers. The victorious powers could have partitioned China but they chose to keep the Qing dynasty in power and help it to strengthen the country. Several factors explain why China was not partitioned. Among the most important were her clever use of a policy of playing off one power against the other, rivalry and jealousy among the powers themselves, and the unwillingness of the powers to assume the responsibility of governing parts of China.

An immediate effect of the failure of the Boxer rising and defeat in war was the Manzhu reform programme which was more or less similar to the Hundred Days' Reform. It was supported by Cixi who seemed to have been convinced at last of the urgent need for reform.

Chapter 8
The rise of the Chinese Republic

THE LATE QING REFORM PROGRAMME, 1901-11

Before the outbreak of the Chinese Revolution of 1911, and the establishment of the Chinese Republic, the Qing dynasty made one last effort to save itself by carrying out its own reform programme. After the Boxer Rising, Cixi was apparently convinced that continued opposition to change was useless. In 1901, before she returned to Beijing from Xi'an, she issued a reform decree urging that China should study carefully the strong points of the foreign powers and take the necessary steps to remedy her shortcomings. Officials both in Beijing and in the provinces were ordered to submit ideas on the reforms to be introduced. The result was the Manzhu reform movement, which was not much different from the Hundred Days' Reform. Unfortunately for the Manzhu, the reforms came too late to save the dynasty.

The reforms

Political reform   The dynasty was faced with two problems: how to centralize authority, and how to permit popular participation in government. As it was, provincial officials submitted reports directly to the emperor, while the traditional Six Boards (Civil Appointments, Revenue, Rites, War, Punishments, and Works) at Beijing had general supervision over the provincial administrations. Political reform started in 1905, when a five-man mission was sent abroad to study constitutional systems. The constitutional movement in China had received encouragement from the belief that Japan's constitutional monarchy was responsible for the Japanese victory over Russia. Upon the recommendations of the constitutional commission on its return, a programme was launched to modernize the bureaucracy and prepare for a constitutional monarchy.

In November 1906, the Six Boards were reorganized into 11 ministries. Among the new ministries were the Ministry of Foreign Affairs which replaced the *Zongli Yamen*, the Ministry of Education and the Ministry of Commerce. While creating new offices, the government abolished useless posts, such as the governorships of Hubei, Guangdong and Yunnan which the 1898 reformers had tried to abolish earlier.

MANZHU CONSTITUTIONAL REFORM

....The officials of the departments concerned in the capital and the viceroys and the governors in the provinces shall hold their subordinates to the carrying out of the plans of education and self-government among the people. The parliament will be opened as soon as the programme shall have been brought to a successful issue. In nine years, commencing from this year, the assigned work shall be completed. Then the constitution shall be promulgated and the parliament convoked....

— From the imperial decree of 1908 calling for political reform

Beijing proceeded to reduce the powers of the governors-general and the governors. Financial supervisors were sent to the provinces to have closer control over the collection of provincial revenues. Plans for the introduction of the constitutional government began to take shape. In 1908, a nine-year constitutional programme was adopted; it was planned that this should end with the calling of a national parliament in 1917. The next year, provincial assemblies were elected as part of the policy of allowing the people to take part in government. In 1910, a consultative national assembly was called as a preparatory step towards the establishment of the parliament. Pressed by members of the assembly, the regent agreed to call the parliament in 1913, instead of 1917 as originally planned. In 1911, a cabinet was formed to co-ordinate the 11 ministries.

Judicial reform Reforms were introduced with the aim of abolishing extraterritoriality. In 1910, a new criminal code reduced corporal punishment, ended torture, abolished such cruel punishments as slicing and branding, and replaced collective by individual responsibility. Steps were taken to stop corruption among magistrates.

Educational reform The general aim of the reform was to train men for government service. In 1901, Beijing called for the creation of a national school system based on Western and Japanese models. Orders were issued to the provinces to establish kindergartens, primary and middle schools, as well as colleges and universities. Besides the study of the old Confucian classics, a Westernized curriculum was introduced in these schools. It soon became clear, however, that the combination of traditional subjects and the new government school system would not work, for it would not appeal either to the conservative or to the progressive students. At the urging of Zhang Zhidong and Yuan Shikai, the imperial court decreed in 1905 that the old civil service examinations, which had

---

THE NEED FOR EDUCATIONAL REFORM

....Unless ability is trained, it is impossible to strive for national survival; unless schools are opened, it is impossible to train ability; unless the civil and military examinations are reformed, it is impossible to open schools, and unless students study abroad, it is impossible to remove our deficiencies in opening schools. An investigation of today's current situation shows that there is no alternative and no time for delay....

— *From the joint proposals of Liu Kunyi and Zhang Zhidong, 1901*

---

been held regularly since A.D. 622, would be abolished in 1906. A Ministry of Education was then set up to supervise the new school system. Through these reforms in education, many Chinese scholars were exposed for the first time to Western ideas. Ironically, the new educational system encouraged revolutionary ideas, and produced revolutionaries rather than officials loyal to the dynasty.

The provincial authorities were also ordered to send students abroad. It was hoped that on their return, they would form the basis of an efficient and capable body of government officials. At one time, there were as many as 15 000 students in Japan, and a few thousand more in the United States and Europe.

Economic reform Priority was given to railway building. An efficient national transportation system would facilitate internal trade, speed up the reforms, and give the central government greater control over the provinces. Beijing therefore decided to nationalize the railways. There were also moves to modernize the financial structure of the empire, through the introduction of a modern budgetary system and a reform of the currency system. Given encouragement by the government to set up their own business, Chinese capitalists established more than a hundred business firms, mainly in the cotton and silk industries, in the treaty ports.

Military reform Officers of the banner armies and the Chinese constabulary were no longer to be appointed on the basis of the old military examinations, which merely stressed physical abilities. They were to be recruited instead from military academies, which were established in 1901. Cadet officers were also sent to Japanese military academies. But the most urgent problem was the centralization of military authority. China had various types of military organization. In addition to the regular forces, there were the regional armies, over which Beijing had practically no control. There were also military units which had been organized in 1895 to meet Japanese aggression, such as Zhang Zhidong's Self-Strengthening Army and the imperial army under the personal leadership of Yuan Shikai.

Yuan Shikai played a major role in army reform. Between 1901 and 1907, he organized the six divisions of the Beiyang army, established military schools, and sent men to Japan to be trained as officers. With Zhang Zhidong, he urged that the army should be unified by placing all military forces under a general staff. However, this suggestion was ignored, and so China's military units continued to be developed and controlled without co-ordination.

MILITARY UNIFICATION URGED

The military system of the various provinces is not the same. The discipline is not uniform, and rations and weapons differ. The drills are so disparate that in time of peace there is no communication between various provincial army units, and in time of war there is neither co-operation nor co-ordination. It is therefore very difficult to achieve military success unless we plan a military unification.

— *From Yuan Shikai's memorial to the throne, 1903*

Social reform Some social reforms were introduced. In 1902, a campaign against foot-binding was launched and marriages between the Manzhu and the Chinese were allowed. Recognizing the harmful effects of opium-smoking, the government issued a decree prohibiting opium.

Obstacles to reform

In implementing its reform programme, the dynasty faced all sorts of difficulties and as a result, only three important reforms were actually carried out in the early stages of the reform movement: the abolition of the old civil service examinations, the setting up of modern schools and the sending of students abroad. After the Hundred Days' Reform, many dedicated reformers had been either executed or forced to leave China. Thus few of the able ones were left to carry out the proposed reforms. Many of the reformers were not sincere, and regarded reform only as a necessary evil.

Financing the programme was a serious problem. China did not have enough funds because of the heavy indemnity payments to the foreign powers.

At Beijing, the programme met opposition from the princes, who were afraid that the changes might take away their privileged positions. Meanwhile, in the provinces, officials were reluctant to carry out the proposed changes, as they looked upon the Manzhu reform as an attempt to weaken provincial autonomy.

Constitutionalists, who favoured wider popular participation in the government, were disappointed because the Manzhu constitutional reforms protected the emperor's powers. In addition, many Chinese were indifferent to the dynastic reform programme. They still considered the dynasty to be alien and, by this time, they had been attracted to the revolutionary doctrines of Sun Yixian.

The ironic result of the Manzhu-sponsored reform was that instead of strengthening dynastic rule, it created anti-dynastic forces. The students who had returned from abroad and the new intellectuals produced by the Western-type schools and universities in China were critical of the corrupt and inefficient Qing rule; so were the young officers trained in the new military schools and members of the elected provincial assemblies. All of them helped to destroy the dynasty. The outbreak of the 1911 Revolution put an end to the Manzhu reform programme.

CAUSES OF THE 1911 REVOLUTION

The Role of Cixi

Without doubt the empress dowager played a major role in hastening the collapse of the Qing dynasty. Before 1901, Cixi stubbornly resisted the modernization of China. She opposed the 'self-strengthening movement' and was chiefly responsible for cutting short the Hundred Days' Reform. The failure of these movements convinced many Chinese intellectuals that the Manzhu would have to be overthrown before reforms could be successfully introduced. She was behind various anti-foreign movements, too, particularly the Boxer Rising. When the foreigners were not expelled, the Manzhu regime lost face.

After 1901, when Cixi finally supported a reform movement for China, there were doubts as to her sincerity. The Manzhu reform programme was considered by many Chinese merely a means of preserving Manzhu rule; it seemed to them a delaying tactic used by Cixi until she could once again become strong enough to assume complete control. Even if she was sincere, the proposed changes came too late.

Cixi's greed for personal power also contributed to the dynastic decline. For most of Tongzhi's reign, the government was practically in her hands. Following the Hundred Days' Reform, she held Guangxu

captive, and controlled the Beijing government until her death in 1908. She pursued a 'divide-and-rule' policy in order to preserve her own power. She made sure that her favourites were put in high places, allowing eunuchs like Li Lianying to exert too much influence in court. When she died there was no leader strong enough to hold the Manzhu regime together.

She was corrupt, too. We have seen how she misused funds for the modernization of the navy to beautify the Summer Palace. This not only set a bad example for other officials but it also kept the Chinese navy weak, and thus contributed to the naval defeats in the Sino-Japanese War of 1894-95.

Cixi has been praised and damned for her running of the affairs of China. She has been praised for keeping the dynasty together in its declining years, but she has been strongly condemned for her short-sightedness, her greed and her lust for power. Certainly it is difficult to deny that she failed to provide China with the kind of leadership which might have checked foreign pressure. There were, however, other factors which weakened Manzhu rule.

Other background causes

There was widespread discontent because of the economic hardships. Floods and drought had become more frequent, destroying crops and causing famine. Outbreaks of plague added to the misery of the people. Huge indemnity payments resulting from defeat in foreign wars led to increased taxation. So too did the heavy expenditure on reform programmes and on the suppression of such uprisings as the Taiping Rebellion. And yet, financially bankrupt as she was, China could not raise customs dues under the conventional tariff without first consulting the foreign powers. Even the Chinese Maritime Customs Service, her most reliable source of income, was run by the foreigners. The rapid growth of population only made matters worse, as it was not accompanied by a proportionate increase in food production. Foreign trade upset China's economy. An unfavourable balance of trade lowered the value of her currency. Chinese goods, moreover, could not compete with foreign manufactured goods; industries declined and many people lost their means of livelihood.

Foreign pressure often embarrassed the Manzhu government. Repeated defeats in wars with the foreigners lowered the prestige of the dynasty, and the exposure of its military weakness encouraged rebellion and revolution. The 'scramble for concessions' provided further proof of the inability of the Manzhu to check foreign aggression. When the Boxer Rising was over, Beijing was forced to adopt a lenient attitude towards the foreign powers. Since anti-foreign feeling was still strong among the Chinese, it was felt that the Manzhu had betrayed China to the foreigners. The Manzhu government was further embarrassed by its helplessness during the Russo-Japanese War. It could not stop Russia and Japan from fighting over a Chinese province on Chinese soil, nor could it prevent the transfer of Russian rights in south Manchuria to Japan at the end of the war.

However, although anti-foreign feeling was strong, Western ideas of democracy and liberalism spread, especially among the natives of Guangdong, many of whom had been overseas. The anti-Manzhu propaganda they spread abroad through secret societies like the *Tongmenghui* (United League) increased support for the revolutionary cause.

Poor leadership led to administrative inefficiency and corruption in government. The Manzhu emperors after Qianlong were incapable of providing effective leadership. Many incompetent Manzhu occupied high positions, while more able Chinese officials were sent to remote places. The great importance given to memory in the civil service examinations produced officials with little experience and ability in solving practical problems. Corruption was widespread in government circles, from the empress dowager down to the lowliest official.

The death of the 'Old Buddha' (Lao Foye, 老佛爺), as Cixi was respectfully called, on 15 November 1908, together with that of the Emperor Guangxu the day before, left a political vacuum which further weakened dynastic leadership. Puyi (溥儀, died 1967), Cixi's three-year-old grand-nephew, succeeded to the throne as the Emperor Xuantong (1909-12). His father, Zaifeng, was appointed regent. Zaifeng, the second Prince Chun, shared with other Manzhu princes a determination to place all power in the central government, despite the growing demand for constitutionalism. They got rid of Chinese officials who might threaten their authority. For example, Yuan Shikai was dismissed in 1909 on the excuse that he was suffering from a foot disease. The hope of establishing a constitutional monarchy faded, and with it went the Qing regime's last chance of saving itself.

Nationalist-minded Chinese still regarded the Manzhu as aliens, and kept alive memories of Manzhu cruelty during their invasion of China. For two and a half centuries the Qing dynasty had ruled China, and yet it had made very few attempts to allow the Chinese to forget that they were a conquered people. There was therefore little reason for Chinese loyalty to the dynasty, once it showed signs of losing control.

SUN YIXIAN'S REVOLUTIONARY PROGRAMME

Sun Yixian was born on 12 November 1866 in the district of Xiangshan (香山) near Guangdong, of peasant parents. His original name was Sun Wen (孫文). (In Japan, he adopted the Japanese name, Nakayama, and is better known in China by the name Zhongshan, the Chinese pronunciation of the characters for Nakayama.) He was educated first in Honolulu and then in Hong Kong, where he studied at the College of Medicine.

Sun Yixian and his wife (about 1915)

He graduated first in his class. As a qualified doctor, he practised for a time in Macau and Guangzhou. From what he saw as a student abroad, he began to realize how backward China was compared to the Western nations.

As early as 1885, when China was defeated in the war with France, he had already made up his mind to overthrow the Qing dynasty which, he felt, purposely kept the people in ignorance. The development of his programme for the reconstruction of China may be divided into two periods: 1894-1900 and 1900-11.

1894-1900

The two most important developments of the first period both took place in 1894. Firstly, Sun sent a letter to Li Hongzhang in which he proposed a plan for China's economic development. His economic programme called for the full development of a man's talents, increased agricultural production, the development of natural resources, and the establishment of an efficient transportation system.

When his plan was not acted upon, Sun took his second important step. He went to Honolulu, where he founded a republican secret society, the *Xingzhonghui* ('Revive China Society'). Its manifesto (public declaration of aims) condemned the Manzhu and proclaimed that the society's main aim was to revive China against government oppression and foreign pressure. The society also aimed to find financial support for the revolutionary cause among the overseas Chinese. The society's aims, however, were vague, since at this stage Sun himself had not yet fully developed his political ideas. When he returned from Honolulu at the end of 1894, he established the society's head-quarters in Hong Kong. After an unsuccessful attempt to raise a rebellion at Guangzhou in 1895, he had to flee from China. Sun's odyssey then began.

In 1896, while he was in London, the Qing authorities almost succeeded in having him deported to China, where he would have faced certain death. He was 'kidnapped' and held for 12 days in the Chinese legation. Fortunately, he managed to smuggle a

ORIGINS OF THE SANMIN ZHUYI

After I was set free from the kidnapping in London I sojourned in Europe for a while in order to make an investigation on the spot of its politics and customs....I began to realize that to make a nation rich and strong, or to promote democracy as had been done in European nations, was not sufficient to make the people really happy....I wish to make one all-out effort and be forever at ease by adopting the principle of people's livelihood *(Min Sheng)* in order to solve the problem of nationalism and democracy simultaneously.

— Sun Yixian

message out to an old friend, Sir James Cantlie, who had been his medical professor in Hong Kong. Cantlie aroused public opinion against the Chinese action, and the British Foreign Office finally stepped in and obtained Sun's release. The world-wide publicity he received as the foremost leader of the anti-Manzhu movement encouraged him to lay down a more detailed revolutionary programme. Consequently, during his two-year stay in Europe (1896-98), he formulated the general outlines of what were to become the *Sanmin Zhuyi*, the Three Principles of the People.

In 1899, a bitter struggle for the support of overseas Chinese and the secret societies in China began between the *Xingzhonghui* and the *Baohuanghui* (Emperor Protection Society), established by Kang Youwei and Liang Qichao who had fled from China to Japan. To spread their ideas, both groups put out newspapers in Japan, Hong Kong, Honolulu and San Francisco, and formed branches among the overseas Chinese. At first, the Emperor Protection Society gained more followers, attracting many Chinese merchants in Yokohama and Honolulu, and drawing secret society leaders away from the *Xingzhonghui*. After 1905, however, the position gradually changed, as more and more of the several thousand Chinese students in Japan joined the revolutionary movement.

1900-11

The second period in the development of Sun's political ideas began in 1900. In that year he again addressed an appeal to Li Hongzhang, this time urging that he break away from the Manzhu and take steps which could lead to a democratic republic. (Republicanism had now definitely become one of Sun's political aims.) Once again, nothing came of his appeal. In the years that followed, seeing how disorganized anti-Manzhu activities were, he decided to develop a unified organization for the revolutionaries.

THE TONGMENGHUI OATH

The person writing this statement of determination by name has sworn before heaven to drive out the Manzhu barbarians, restore China to the Chinese, create a republic, distribute the land equally, and keep his good faith and maintain his loyalty from beginning to end. If he breaks this promise, he should be punished by other members as they see fit.

This came about in 1905 when the *Tongmenghui*, a combination of the *Xingzhonghui* with two other revolutionary groups, was formed in Tokyo. With the exception of Gansu, all the provinces of China were represented in the new revolutionary organization. After one year, it is estimated that it had more than 10 000 members. The Chinese revolutionary movement in Japan suffered a setback in 1907 when the Japanese government, in response to protests made by Beijing against revolutionary activities on Japanese soil, asked Sun Yixian to leave the country. From Japan, Sun went to Indo-China to carry on the struggle against the Manzhu.

In the manifesto issued by the *Tongmenghui*, Sun laid down his revolutionary programme. The new society had four aims:
- to expel the Manzhu, who were condemned for their oppressive rule;
- to restore a Chinese national state — since China was the country of the Chinese, it should be governed by the Chinese;
- to establish a republican government under which all the people enjoyed political rights and were equal;
- to equalize land ownership — to achieve this aim, a socialist state was to be created.

To attain these goals, there were to be three stages:
- The first was government by military law, with the military government taking the lead in fighting the Manzhu and eliminating abuses.
- After three years, military law was to be ended, giving way to the second stage:

government by a provisional constitution. The people would be granted the right of local self-government, while the military government would remain in control of national affairs.

- After gaining political experience for six years under the provisional constitution, the third stage — full constitutional government — was to begin. The military government was to be abolished, and a president and a parliament were to be elected, to govern China in accordance with the provisions of the constitution.

Sun's plan showed that he realized China could not be turned into a democratic republic overnight.

The four aims of the *Tongmenghui* were included in Sun Yixian's Three Principles of the People, namely:

- *Min Zu Zhuyi*, people's nationhood or nationalism, which meant overthrowing the Manzhu and expelling the foreigners — although the latter objective was not stressed to avoid displeasing the foreign powers, whose support was being sought by the revolutionaries;
- *Min Quan Zhuyi*, people's authority or democracy, which called for the establishment of a republican system, combining Western constitutional concepts and Chinese ideas of examination and control;
- *Min Sheng Zhuyi*, people's livelihood or socialism, which advocated equalizing land ownership and preventing the evils of capitalism.

The Three Principles of the People made nationalism a unifying force in China, including not only the Chinese but also the minority races. They laid the foundation of democracy in modern China. Through socialism, Sun hoped to bring about the full use of the land by equalizing land ownership. Finally, the Three Principles became the ideals of both the *Guomindang* and the Chinese Communist Party.

How important was Sun Yixian's role in the 1911 Revolution? Revolution was bound to come because the Qing dynasty had failed to remedy China's ills. Sun did not take an active part in the actual outbreak of the 1911 Revolution. Nevertheless, the revolution was, to a great extent, the result of his earlier work in outlining a revolutionary programme for the reconstruction of China. He promoted revolutionary ideas and convinced Chinese intellectuals at home and abroad that revolution was necessary to save China. In addition, he unified revolutionary activities by organizing the *Tongmenghui* and raised funds for the revolutionary cause. Most important of all, the Three Principles of the People became a guideline for the new republic in years to come. Unfortunately, these aims were not fully achieved because, as we shall see later, many new internal problems arose from the time the republic was established until the 1949 communist takeover.

CONSTITUTIONALISTS VERSUS REVOLUTIONARIES

In the meantime, the constitutionalists led by Liang Qichao continued to press for the establishment of a constitutional monarchy, as opposed to the republican aims of the *Tongmenghui*. In 1906, when the Manzhu agreed to set up a constitutional monarchy, the chances of achieving this objective seemed good. However, between 1908 and 1911, many of them were disappointed with the dynastic constitutional reforms. The changes did not really limit the powers of the emperor. He could, for example, call or dissolve the proposed parliament as he wished. The constitutionalists also considered the nine-year programme for full constitutional government, proclaimed in 1908, to be too long. Furthermore, the high property qualifications for the right to vote in the elections to the provincial assemblies of 1909 meant that the common people could not vote.

In February 1910, the constitutionalists asked for the constitutional reform programme to be speeded up, but this request was rejected by the Grand Council. In November, however, an imperial decree proclaimed the opening of a parliament in 1913, instead of 1917. The constitutionalists were to some extent satisfied, but not for long. They were greatly disappointed with the membership of the newly-formed cabinet. Of the 13 members, there were 8 Manzhu, all of whom were incompetent; 1 Mongolian bannerman; and only 4 Chinese. A petition urging the reorganization of the cabinet was presented to the throne by the provincial assembles. When this was rejected, many constitutionalists became convinced that they should give their support to the revolutionaries.

THE REVOLUTION OF 1911

Outbreak of revolution

The 1911 Revolution was sparked off by the nationalization of the railways. In the early months of 1911, anti-Manzhu feeling mounted as the result of a dispute over railways. This was part of the broader question of centralization versus provincial autonomy which arose after the Taiping Rebellion. In Beijing's view, the control of national communications through the nationalization of railways would speed up the dynastic reform programme. Provincial authorities objected to railway centralization because they themselves had built railways; control of these had brought them wealth and power, and they planned to build more. Moreover, they suspected that the central government was using the nationalization of railways as a means of limiting their freedom of action; and they realized that if the central government were to take over railway construction, it would have to borrow money from the foreign powers, a move which they strongly opposed. The Rights Recovery movement was in fact started by some of the governors to oppose foreign investment in railway building.

Despite these objections, the corrupt Sheng Xuanhuai, Minister of Communications, decided to go ahead with the railway centralization plan. In May 1911, an imperial decree was issued, calling for the nationalization of railways and placing all provincial railways under Beijing's control. Later the same month, Beijing signed a contract with a four-power banking consortium for a loan of ten million pounds to finance the proposed Guangzhou-Hankou-Chengdu Railway (Huguang project). The consortium had been formed in 1910 by British, French, German and American banks.

The foreign railway loan was strongly opposed by the provincial authorities, who claimed that the Beijing officials behind it had sold out to the foreign powers in order to enrich themselves. The opposition in Sichuan was particularly strong. Local interests there had already invested in the Huguang railway project. To the disappointment of the investors, Beijing proposed to repay them only the actual amount spent on the project, not the total amount subscribed. As a result, societies for 'railway protection' were organized in Sichuan. When their protests were ignored, workers went on strike, shops were closed, students stayed away from school, and tax payments were suspended. In September, Zhao Erfeng, military governor of Sichuan, ordered the arrest of certain troublemakers. When demonstrators demanded their release, government troops opened fire, killing about 40 people. The incident transformed the railway problem into a political issue. The people of Sichuan, including the gentry in the provincial assembly, became violently anti-Manzhu.

Another attack on Manzhu authority was the Huanghuagang (Yellow Flowers Hill) revolt, also known as the 'Guangzhou Revolution', in April 1911. It was led by Huang Xing (黃興) who ranked next to Sun Yixian in the *Tongmenghui* leadership. But, like all the other attempts at revolution organized by Sun Yixian in southern China, it was suppressed. The revolt is remembered in China's revolutionary history for having

Viceroys seeking refuge at Shanghai from provincial disturbances (1911)

produced the 'Seventy-two Martyrs'. Besides these risings, the *Tongmenghui* approved the assassination of prominent Manzhu supporters.

It was not the people of Sichuan who were responsible for the final outbreak of revolution, nor was it planned by the *Tongmenghui* since Sun Yixian was still abroad. It began in the province of Hubei, at Wuhan, which comprised the three Changjiang River towns of Wuchang, Hankou and Hanyang. In September 1911, two revolutionary study groups in Hankou — one loosely connected to the *Tongmenghui*, and the other largely composed of soldiers — made plans for a military uprising on October 6. When the Manzhu governor-general, Ruicheng, received information about the plot and took strict precautions, the uprising was postponed to October 16. However, on October 9 some of the plotters hiding in the Russian concession at Hankou accidentally set off a bomb. The explosion led to arrests and executions, and to the discovery by the authorities of a list of revolutionaries, which included the names of

SUCCESS OF WUCHANG REVOLT UNEXPECTED

The success at Wuchang was accidental and was mainly due to the flight of Ruicheng; if he had not fled, Zhang Biao undoubtedly would have stayed and kept his troops together and in order. At that time most of those in the new army at Wuchang who supported the revolutionary cause had been sent away at Sichuan. The few who remained made up only a very small part of the artillery and engineering battalions, while the other soldiers in the new Wuchang army had little appetite for the new cause. It was that small group which was prompted, by the police discovery of the revolutionary headquarters, to make the attempt without much thought for its chances of success.

— Sun Yixian

officers and men of the Wuchang garrison. To save themselves, some of the soldiers in Wuchang revolted on the night of October 10 (the 'Double Tenth'). This date is now taken

LI FORCED TO ACCEPT COMMAND

....After the revolutionary army drove Governor-General Ruicheng away from the city, soldiers surrounded my camp....I was quickly arrested and asked to become the commander of this revolutionary army. I was surrounded by guns at the time, and I might have been killed instantly if I had not complied with their request....

— Part of a letter from Li Yuanhong to Admiral Sa Zhenbing, October 1911

as the beginning of the Chinese Revolution of 1911.

At this point, the Wuchang revolt could easily have been suppressed; it was disorganized and lacked military support. Only about 3000 of a much larger total number of soldiers at Wuchang had mutinied. It succeeded mainly because of the cowardice of the governor-general and his military commander, Zhang Biao, who both fled instead of staying to fight. In the absence of a revolutionary leader, the military rebels forced a colonel, Li Yuanhong (黎元洪), to assume command of the revolutionary army. They then occupied Hankou and Hanyang. Soon after, a military government was established at Wuchang in the name of the Republic of China.

Progress of the revolution

The immediate support which was given to the Wuchang revolt from many provinces indicated that it would be something more than a serious local rebellion. It quickly became clear that this was a full-scale revolution. By November, only Hebei, Henan, Shangdong and the Three Eastern Provinces remained under Manzhu control; the rest of the provinces had established military governments and declared their independence.

Realizing the seriousness of the situation, the regent recalled Yuan Shikai in October and placed him in command of the imperial forces. The national assembly elected him premier of a new cabinet government. He was ordered to put down the revolution and carry out constitutional reform. Yuan, however, was not too eager to suppress the revolution. If it spread, the national emergency would enable him to impose his will on the Manzhu regime; at the same time he could leave open the possibility of a place in the new government if the revolution succeeded. For this double-dealing, as well as for his later betrayal of the republic, his critics in later years condemned him as an 'opportunist', an 'enemy of the people'.

Meanwhile, the need for a unified organization to direct the course of the revolutionaries threatened to weaken the revolution. As matters stood, there were various forces fighting Yuan's armies without any coordination: the Wuchang group led by Li Yuanhong and Huang Xing; a rebel government at Shanghai controlled by a group of people from Guangzhou led by Wu Tingfang, a former minister to the United States; and the provinces that had broken away from Beijing. On November 23, it was decided that the provinces should send delegates to a meeting at Wuchang to prepare for the setting up of a provisional government. However, since Wuchang was under attack, the meeting was held in the British settlement at Hankou. Here it was agreed to offer the presidency to Yuan Shikai, as soon as he changed sides from the dynasty to the republic. When Nanjing fell into rebel hands in early December, the city was made the seat of the provisional government.

The choice of leaders continued to be a source of disagreement among the provincial representatives. A few people still objected to making Yuan the provisional president. Some wanted Li Yuanhong to be appointed commander-in-chief; others preferred Huang Xing. The problem of leadership was finally resolved with the arrival of Sun Yixian in

Shanghai on Christmas Day. Four days later, the provincial representatives elected him Provisional President of China with Li Yuanhong as Provisional Vice-President. Sun accepted, but expressed his willingness to step down later in favour of Yuan Shikai, on certain conditions. On 1 January 1912, he was inaugurated at Nanjing. In his inaugural address, he said that the chief aim of the new government was to unify China.

On January 15, Sun formally declared his willingness to step down from the presidency in favour of Yuan Shikai when the monarchy was abolished, and Yuan agreed to support the republic. Several factors influenced Sun in reaching this decision.

To begin with, he did not have the military power that was so essential to the success of the revolution. Yuan, however, had a well-drilled army to support him. Another im-

SUN OFFERS TO STEP DOWN

I beg to call the attention of Premier Yuan in Beijing to the fact that....my comrades entrusted me with the responsibility of organizing a provisional government....Although I have accepted this position for the time being, it is actually waiting for you, and my offer will eventually be made clear to the world. I hope that you will soon decide to accept this offer.

— From Sun Yixian's telegram to Yuan, 29 December 1911

portant consideration was that it was likely that the northern provinces would not accept a government headed by a southerner. By giving up authority, Sun hoped to gain nation-wide support for the republic. Finally, Yuan had the support of the foreign powers. They

Sun Yixian leaving Shanghai for Beijing (1912)

regarded him as the one man who could restore peace, so vital to the continuation of their privileged position in China.

The end of the Qing dynasty

Having been assured of the presidency, Yuan proposed a voluntary abdication by the emperor to hasten the end of dynastic rule. It was no easy task; there were strong objections, particularly from the Manzhu and the Mongolian princes. Nevertheless Yuan succeeded in getting his own way. Chinese diplomats abroad were persuaded to send a joint telegram to Beijing, urging abdication. They also asked some members of the emperor's cabinet to inform him that imperial rule could not be maintained. Yuan also persuaded more than 40 military leaders to send a telegram to Beijing demanding abdication. On 12 February 1912, the Empress Dowager Longyu, widow of Guangxu, signed a decree of abdication in the name of the child-emperor, Xuantong. Qing rule was abolished,

and the centuries-old Chinese monarchical and imperial system came to an end.

The day after the emperor's abdication, Sun Yixian offered to resign, and on February 14, Yuan Shikai was elected Provisional President with Li Yuanhong keeping his post as Vice-President. However, in his letter of resignation to the Revolutionary Council at

---

THE EMPEROR ABDICATES

I [Empress Dowager Longyu] have....induced the emperor to yield to the country as a whole, determining that there should be a constitutional republic. Yuan Shikai has full powers to organize a provisional republican government to treat with the people's forces on the methods of achieving unity, so that the five races, Manzhu, Mongols, Chinese, Muslims and Tibetans may continue together in one Chinese Republic with unimpaired territory.

— From the abdication decree of 12 February 1912

Yuan Shikai (centre) as Provisional President of China (1912)

Nanjing, Sun set down three conditions: Nanjing was to remain the seat of government, Yuan was to assume the presidency at Nanjing, and the new president was to govern according to the constitution which was being prepared. Sun wanted Yuan in Nanjing, away from the corrupt and conservative elements in Beijing. Yuan was willing to accept the constitutional limitations, but had no wish to leave his headquarters at Beijing. He claimed that his presence in north China was required in order to keep the soldiers there under control.

The Nanjing Council was divided on the issue. Then on February 29, an army mutiny broke out in Beijing, followed by military riots in Tianjin and Baoding, all of which were believed to have been planned by Yuan's followers, if not by Yuan himself. There was a very real danger of foreign intervention, similar to that during the Boxer Rising. Alarmed, the council members agreed to Yuan's inauguration at Beijing, which took place on March 10. The president was to govern the country under the provisional constitution prepared by the council, until a more permanent constitutional government could be established. Sun Yixian had not previously considered his provisional presidency at an end, since not all his conditions had been met, but he formally resigned on April 1. This was followed four days later by the transfer of the government from Nanjing to Beijing.

The 1911 Revolution had established the Chinese Republic, and prepared the way for radical and far-reaching changes in China's social and economic life. However, later events proved that the revolution was a failure. Yuan Shikai, though president of the republic, tried to re-establish monarchical rule; the rise of the warlords prevented attempts to set up a truly constitutional government and to unify China; and foreign powers continued to enjoy exclusive privileges. It is important to realize that the masses remained, for the most part, indifferent to the revolutionary movement.

There had really been very little fighting, and much of that was done by professional soldiers.

Power struggle

Once Yuan Shikai became provisional president, he quickly became involved in a power struggle with the revolutionary leaders, who were beginning to realize that he was still a monarchist. The main question was whether the president of the parliament should control the cabinet. When Yuan refused to let the cabinet run the government, the premier and the four *Tongmenghui* cabinet members resigned in June 1912. From then on, the cabinet was made responsible to the president, instead of to the parliament.

In 1913, the revolutionary leaders tried to restore control of the cabinet to the parliament. The year before, Song Jiaoren (宋教仁), who shared leadership of the revolutionaries with Sun and Huang Xing, had formed a new political party, the *Guomindang* (Nationalist Party), by merging the *Tongmenghui* with four minor political parties. In the first national elections held in 1913, the *Guomindang* (KMT) won control of the parliament, and demanded control of the cabinet. Because

THE CHARACTER OF YUAN SHIKAI

....Republican by title he was, but an autocrat at heart. All the old glittering trappings of the empire he had preserved.

....His personal rule, his unscrupulous advancement to power, with the incidental corruption and cold-blooded executions that marked it, and his bitter personal feeling against all political opponents — these were not qualities that make for stable parliamentary government....

– *Paul S. Reinsch, American diplomat in Beijing, 1913*

of his criticism of official policies, Song was shot and killed by government supporters in March. Although high government officials, including Yuan himself, were suspected of being behind the murder, their involvement has never been proved.

Yuan proceeded to suppress the opposition by replacing military commanders connected to the *Guomindang* in central and southern China with his own men. Meanwhile, he arranged to borrow money from a five-power consortium comprising Britain, France, Germany, Japan and Russia without consulting parliament. Sun and Huang Xing had no choice but to lead a revolt. This second revolution began in July, but in less than two months, the uprising was suppressed; Sun and other *Guomindang* leaders were forced to leave the country for Japan. The revolutionary leaders were back where they started. The following year, Sun reorganized the *Guomindang* under the name of the Chinese Revolutionary Party, with the members of the old *Guomindang* left out.

After suppressing the second revolution, Yuan forced the parliament to elect him formally to the presidency; he then obtained recognition of his government from the major foreign powers. On 10 October 1913, he was inaugurated president of the republic and the provisional government became the regular government.

He then turned his attention to the parliament. In November, he proclaimed the *Guomindang* illegal, depriving its members of their seats in the parliament. Then, in January 1914, he dissolved the parliament and the provincial assemblies; in the following month, the cabinet was also dissolved. The provisional constitution of 1912 was then revised. Under the new constitution of May 1914, Yuan was given dictatorial powers. In December new laws governing presidential election were enacted. The presidential term was extended from five to ten years, under conditions which practically made him president for life. He then tried to get himself proclaimed emperor.

Taking advantage of a statement made by Yuan's American constitutional adviser, Dr Frank J. Goodnow, to the effect that republicanism did not suit China's political conditions, six scholars in mid-August 1915 formed the Peace Planning Society (*Chouanhui*) which started the monarchical movement. The society arranged for petitions to be sent to the Council of State, which was functioning as the central legislative body in the absence of a parliament, demanding the enthronement of Yuan. It also arranged to hold a carefully chosen 'national people's assembly' at Beijing, which unanimously voted for the establishment of a constitutional monarchy. At the same time, the assembly offered the throne to Yuan through the Council of State. After a ceremonious refusal, he agreed to accept the throne on December 12.

Dynastic rule had been restored, or so it seemed. But an anti-monarchist movement immediately sprang up. Those who hoped to see Manzhu power restored opposed Yuan's enthronement. There was dissatisfaction even among his own generals, who were not prepared to grant him unlimited powers. The attitude of the foreign powers depended largely on Japan, because the other powers were busy with the war in Europe. When the Japanese saw that the anti-monarchists were gaining ground, they decided not to support Yuan. Britain, Russia, France and Italy

THRONE OFFERED TO YUAN

Reverently representing the public opinion of the nation, we request that the president, Yuan Shikai, be made Emperor of the Chinese Empire. He will have the highest and most complete authority and sovereignty over the nation. The throne will be handed down in his royal family from generation to generation through ten thousand generations.

— *From the declaration of the 'national people's assembly', 1915*

followed the Japanese line, and Yuan's hope of obtaining foreign support vanished. But it was the opposition of the governors of a number of provinces in southern, south-western, and central China, encouraged by Liang Qichao, which dealt the strongest blow to Yuan's ambitions. The National Protection Army *(Huguojun)* was formed, and set out from the south to remove him. Yuan tried to win the rebellious provinces back by postponing his accession to the throne. When that failed, and his senior military commanders also turned against him, he gave up the throne; on 6 June 1916, he died suddenly of uremia. His death ended the monarchist movement. Vice-President Li Yuanhong assumed the presidency and restored the old constitution of 1912. Yuan's death led to the stormy era of the warlords, which made national unification more difficult than ever.

The rise of the warlords

Yuan has been called 'the father of the warlords', for among the early Beiyang officers he trained in the late 1890s, ten became military governors during his presidency because of the support Yuan gave them. All of them became leading figures during the warlord period (1916-28) in the role of *dujun*, as military governors came to be called. By his own example, Yuan showed them how to keep themselves in power by terrorism and bribery. Other lesser warlords rose from the peasantry, or were bandits who succeeded in dominating vast areas by means of violence. During the war to expel Yuan, it became common practice for generals to move from one province to another, feeding on the land and people. This set the pattern for the warlord armies.

The decade following Yuan's death was the darkest period in the history of the Chinese Republic. There was chaos and anarchy, caused by constant clashes between warlord cliques (groups) and by a power struggle between the warlords and the politicans.

Despite all this internal trouble, a series of 'governments' continued to function at Beijing and were duly recognized by the foreign powers. But real power was in the hands of the regional warlords who, in turn, delegated control of their provinces to lesser warlords. Very often, warlords allowed foreign powers to exploit China's natural resources in exchange for foreign aid.

The struggle for power between the warlords and the politicians changed character many times. In 1917, the northern warlords were against President Li Yuanhong and the parliament, a conflict which resulted in the complete domination of the parliament by the northern warlords. One of them, Zhang Xun, the 'Pigtailed General', who was military governor of Anhui, tried unsuccessfully to restore the Qing dynasty. With the Beijing government under warlord control, southern members of the parliament withdrew and organized a military government in the south headed by Sun Yixian who, by then, had returned to Guangzhou. It dominated the provinces of Guangdong, Guangxi and Yunnan.

Duan Qirui, the warlord who became premier of China after Yuan's death, needed money to destroy the break-away military government in the south. The only way he could obtain foreign loans was through China's participation in the First World War. In August 1917, Duan succeeded in convincing the parliament, which was controlled by the Anhui-Fujian (An-Fu) clique headed by him, to declare war on Germany. The following year, he borrowed a huge amount from Japan, the 'Nishihara loans', which was supposed to be used for China's war effort. Instead, he used the money to crush domestic opposition.

With the newly acquired funds, Duan moved against the southern military government. However, Feng Guozhang, who had succeeded Li Yuanhong as president, objected because he preferred using peaceful means to settle the dispute. Disagreement between the two, who were former colleagues under

Yuan's old Beiyang organization, split the Beiyang clique into two: the Anhui clique headed by Duan and the Zhili clique led by Feng. Fighting broke out between the two cliques, a struggle for power which the Zhili clique finally won with the help of another clique under Zhang Zuolin, a former bandit who was warlord of Manchuria. Disunity among the warlords can also be seen in the south where Sun's military government lost control to a Guangxi clique which, in turn, was ousted by a Guangdong clique. As the warfare among the warlords went on, new forces were arising in the south — the combined forces of the nationalists and the communists — which would put an end to warlordism in 1928 with the occupation of Beijing by the nationalist forces of Jiang Jieshi (蔣介石).

QUESTIONS

1. What reforms were introduced by the Qing dynasty to save itself during the period 1901-11? What difficulties did it encounter in carrying out its reform programme?

2. 'Instead of strengthening dynastic rule, the Late Qing Reform created anti-dynastic forces.' To what extent is this statement true?

3. Compare the Hundred Days' Reform and the Late Qing Reform with reference to their aims and results.

4. How far would you agree with the view that Cixi was primarily responsible for the decline and fall of the Qing dynasty?

5. What internal and external factors contributed to the collapse of the Qing dynasty in 1911?

6. Discuss the revolutionary programme of Sun Yixian.

7. Give an account of Sun Yixian's contribution to the revolutionary movement in China between 1895 and 1911.

8. 'The role played by Sun Yixian in the Chinese Revolution of 1911 has been exaggerated.' Do you agree with this view?

9. How far did the dispute over the control of railways between the central government in Beijing and the provincial authorities contribute to the outbreak of the 1911 Revolution in China?

10. What were the aims of the *Tongmenghui* and the Three Principles of the People? What were the three stages by which these aims were to be achieved?

11. Show how the Three Principles of the People was a programme for developing democracy in China.

12. Compare the aims of the constitutional monarchists and the revolutionaries in China from 1905.

13. Describe the political conditions in China during the Era of the Warlords.

14. Give an account of warlordism in China and the power struggle among the warlords and between the politicians.

15. Assess the role played by Sun Yixian and Yuan Shikai in the Chinese Revolution of 1911.

16. How did the foreign powers in China react to the 1911 Revolution?

17. 'The Chinese Revolution of 1911 did not create a new China.' How far do you agree with this statement?

18. Give an account of the struggle for power between Yuan Shikai and the nationalists in the period 1912-16.

After the Boxer Rising failed to stop the foreign threat in 1900-01, the Qing dynasty made an effort to strengthen itself by giving up its policy of opposing change and starting its own reform programme. But the Qing reform movement came too late to save the dynasty. It failed because of the lack of able leaders and funds to carry out the proposed reforms. Instead of strengthening the dynasty, it created anti-dynastic forces which contributed to the overthrow of Qing rule. Moreover, years of economic hardship, corrupt and inefficient government and frequent embarrassment caused by foreign pressure had convinced many Chinese officials and intellectuals that revolution was the only answer to China's problems.

Sun Yixian outlined a revolutionary programme for the reconstruction of China which gained support at home and abroad. Revolution finally broke out in 1911 and succeeded in overthrowing the Qing dynasty and establishing the Chinese Republic.

No sooner had the republic been established than its existence was threatened by new problems. A power struggle developed between Yuan Shikai, who had replaced Sun as provisional president, and the revolutionary leaders. Sun and his followers led a second revolution but they failed to overthrow Yuan.

Having gained complete control, Yuan proceeded to re-establish monarchical rule. In December 1915, he became emperor of China. However, the rise of a strong anti-monarchist movement, the opposition of the governors of several provinces and his failure to win the support of the foreign powers forced him to give up the throne. With his death in 1916, the monarchist movement ended but a new threat arose: warlordism. The rise of warlords made it very difficult for China to develop into a truly unified state with a constitutional government. As for the foreign powers, they continued to enjoy their special privileges in China.

PART III

The rise of Japan as a world power

Japan's first direct contact with the West was with Portuguese traders and missionaries, starting from 1542. Other foreign groups followed: the Spanish, the Dutch and the British. However, in 1638, the ruling Tokugawa shogun closed Japan in order to prevent the introduction of foreign ideas which might threaten his rule. (His complete title was *Sei-i-tai shogun*, which means Barbarian-Subduing Great General.)

For the next 200 years or so, Japan was almost totally isolated from foreign influence. Her only contacts with the outside world were the Dutch ships that visited the islet of Deshima in the Nagasaki harbour annually and some Chinese traders.

Under the Tokugawa shogunate, government was a feudal military dictatorship called the *Bakufu*. The '*bakufu*' was a term originally used to mean the headquarters of an army in the battlefield.

In Japan, the emperor was only a patriotic symbol. He reigned but did not rule. It was the shogun who actually ruled Japan. As military dictator, the shogun ruled directly over a quarter of the country; the rest was divided among the *daimyo* (great territorial or feudal lords). Most of the *daimyo*, in turn, left much of the administration to their retainers.

Japanese feudal society can be divided into the privileged and the non-privileged classes. Among the privileged class were the samurai; the imperial family; and the *kuge* (court nobles). The imperial family and the *kuge*

had no political power. The samurai were members of Japan's feudal ruling class; they were also the only ones allowed to wear the sword, a status symbol.

The term 'samurai' was commonly used to refer to all those of the warrior class under the shogun and the *daimyo*. These included the retainers of the shogun and the *daimyo*, the *ronin* (masterless samurai), and the samurai-peasants. The samurai class followed an unwritten code of conduct, *bushido* (way of the warrior), which, among other things, taught them not to be afraid of death and to despise money-making. Japan therefore was a feudal nation governed by the privileged military class.

The majority of the people belonged to the non-privileged class. They were the peasants, the artisans (craftsmen) and the *chonin* (townspeople), who were mainly traders and money-lenders.

Tokugawa society placed great importance on obedience to authority. The individual was controlled by the state, the community and the family. On the surface, life in Tokugawa Japan appeared peaceful and stable. But a closer look would show that internal forces were weakening the foundations of the existing feudal structure. When Commodore Matthew Calbraith Perry and his squadron arrived in 1853, Japan was ready for revolutionary changes because of widespread dissatisfaction with the *Bakufu*.

Chapter 9
Japan: collapse of isolation and Tokugawa rule

JAPAN REOPENED TO THE WEST

Unsatisfactory conditions on the eve of Perry's arrival

Each of the various social classes had grievances and wanted change. The nobles in the imperial court of Kyoto naturally wanted to see the end of the *Bakufu* and the political power of the emperor restored.

The *daimyo* of the leading western clans, Choshu, Satsuma, Hizen and Tosa, were long-time enemies of the shogun and strongly advocated change. Their part in the shogunal government was unimportant. Besides, they were closely watched.

The *daimyo* resented the system of *sankin kotai* (alternate attendance). The Tokugawa shogunate set up the system in 1635 to make sure the *daimyo* behaved themselves. They were divided into two groups. Each group alternately was forced to go to Edo, the capital of the shogun, and to stay there for a year. In the other year, when the *daimyo* returned to his feudal domain, he still had to leave behind his wife and children as hostages.

Thus the *daimyo* were kept under the close supervision of the *Bakufu* and remained poor, as they had to spend great sums in court and for the journeys to Edo. In addition to all this expenditure, they had to support their samurai with an annual rice allowance. To engage in trade might have helped them to solve their financial problems, but their social status and contempt for money-making prevented them from doing so. They were forced to borrow money from the despised merchants. Some even married into rich merchant families to seek financial relief.

The samurai were also discontented. Like the *daimyo*, their main problem was lack of money, which was beginning to replace rice as the chief medium of exchange. In the late Tokugawa period, their rice allowance from their lords was often reduced by as much as half. Moreover, the money value of rice fluctuated sharply and this reduced the buying power of their already small income. Since they spent too much but did not have the money, they often borrowed from the merchants. Some became traders, an occupation they hated; others, like their lords, married the daughters of rich merchants. They had become a useless class, for wars were unusual and they had few military duties.

The decline of the samurai class was bad for the *Bakufu*, as it formed the backbone of the entire feudal system. Discontent led to the rise of a small group of active and intelligent samurai who wanted sweeping changes. They became the nucleus of an anti-shogun movement.

The *chonin* were becoming a strong middle class, and wanted changes to improve their position. A commercial and money economy was replacing the agrarian economy. Internal trade was rapidly developing. This, together with the growth of industry, had given the *chonin* economic power and political influence. But for all their wealth, influence and power, they had no social prestige. Japanese

A Japanese feudal lord on his way to Edo

DECLINE OF THE SAMURAI

Seven or eight out of ten bannermen and retainers are effeminate. They are meanspirited, and behave like shopkeepers. Those who profess a taste for military arts do it for the sake of worldly success and to get appointments....If on taking a test they are lucky enough to hit a two-foot target and to dismount safely after bestriding a horse as tame as a cat, they are promoted for their exploits....

— *Sugita Gempaku, a Japanese scholar of the late 18th century*

society placed importance on military and scholarly activity. The *chonin* were therefore looked down upon and regarded as parasites, since they relied on the labour of others for their livelihood.

Another of the *chonin's* grievances was the abolition of mercantile and industrial guilds, which took away their monopoly of trade and manufacturing. The shogun issued decrees in 1831 and 1843 abolishing all forms of guild, because their activities were believed to be responsible for the rise in prices. Very often, too, the government cancelled the debts owed to *chonin* by the samurai to relieve the latter of financial burdens. And yet, when the government needed money, it turned to the *chonin* for loans which were frequently not paid back. So it came as no surprise that when the movement to overthrow the shogun began, the merchant class gave financial help to his enemies.

The peasants, too, were not happy, as shown by the many peasant revolts. These revolts were usually led by the *ronin*, and became more frequent in the early 19th century. The general causes of peasant discontent were corrupt officials, shortage of food, lack of arable land and sharp fluctuations in the price of rice. The Tokugawa had failed to establish a stable economy to match political stability. But what caused most suffering was heavy taxation. The peasants paid an annual land tax which was about 40 to 50 per cent of their rice yield.

Furthermore, whenever the shogunate had financial problems and tried to get money from the military and merchant classes, these classes passed on the new burden to the peasants. If the peasants had no money to pay for their taxes or daily expenses, they had to borrow from money-lenders. In time, many peasants lost their land to the money-lenders because they could not pay their debts, though there were laws forbidding the sale or lease of land. Natural disasters and epidemics added to the misery of the peasants. Discontent was not confined to the countryside. In the urban areas, there were also rice riots.

Since the central government was often short of money, it could not provide relief. Annual budget deficits kept rising, particularly when there were poor harvests and natural disasters. Increased taxation, devaluation of the currency, forced loans from merchants, and the cancellation of the debts of the military class were just temporary measures; they could not really solve the problem of the financial weakness of the government. Unless sweeping changes were made, the whole feudal structure was likely to collapse.

Growth of nationalism

Another factor which weakened Tokugawa rule was the growth of national feeling, arising from the study of Japan's past. It had two very significant political effects.

First, it created a group of scholars who began to question the legitimacy of the shogun's position. After re-examining the early history of Japan, they discovered that the emperor was the direct descendant of Jimmu Tenno, traditional founder and first earthly emperor of the Japanese Empire. He was believed to be descended from the Sun Goddess, Amaterasu. The belief in the divinity of the emperor originated from this legend. If the emperor was the rightful ruler, then the shogun was a usurper. Such an idea was not dangerous until the shogun's weakness was exposed, through his failure to check foreign penetration in the mid-19th century. There was now a growing feeling that the shogun would have to go, so that the emperor's right to rule could be restored.

The second effect was the revival of Shinto, Japan's native religion. It contributed to the growth of nationalism by stressing the worship of ancestors and ancient heroes as well as the emperor. In trying to show that Japan was not inferior to China, Shinto scholars gave much importance to the old Japanese myths and traditions; Shinto priests stressed the superiority of Shinto to Buddhism. Some of them blamed the shogunate for giving more importance to classical Chinese studies than to Japanese learning. They became potential enemies of the shogun.

By the 19th century, the Japanese had become very nationalistic. There was a general distrust of anything foreign and pride in anything Japanese. However, there were some nationalists who favoured opening the country as the first step to territorial expansion overseas. Even among the shogunate officials, there were a few who suggested resuming foreign contacts to prevent foreign invasion. There were some scholars, too, who favoured the adoption of Western learning. Through Dutch learning (*Rangaku*) at Deshima, they had become aware of Western superiority in science and technology.

Decline of shogunal rule

A strong and efficient government might have checked this increasing dissatisfaction with the shogunate. Unfortunately, the later Tokugawa shoguns were incapable and weak. With one or two exceptions, they spent too much time enjoying themselves and this attitude spread among the samurai in general. They left the government to favourites who were often corrupt and inefficient. As a result, various rival groups arose in court, trying to win the shogun's favour. They often plotted against each other. Thus when the foreigners made a serious effort to break down Japan's seclusion, the shogun could not lead his people to meet the challenge.

In short, the mid-19th century in Japan was a time of widespread discontent, caused directly or indirectly by such internal developments as the rise of a commercial and

Tokugawa Japan

money economy, the growth of industry, the rise of a strong middle class, the growth of towns and cities, the beginnings of nationalism, and a revived interest in Western learning. All this seemed to show that basic changes in Japanese society were coming. What set the forces of change in motion, and finally led to the overthrow of the shogunate, was foreign pressure following the opening of Japan by Perry.

Perry's arrival

Earlier Western attempts to reopen Japan in the first half of the 19th century had all failed. This convinced the foreigners that the use of force was the only alternative left.

Early in 1852 the Americans felt it was time to make a determined effort to resume contact. Commodore Perry was appointed to lead a naval expedition to Japan. On 8 July 1853, he and his 'black ships' (steamships) entered Edo Bay, anchoring about a mile off Uraga.

His instructions were to secure the safety of American sailors shipwrecked on Japanese shores; to seek permission for the opening of one or more ports to American ships for coal and other supplies; and to open trade relations. He was to use threats, and even force, if necessary.

When news of Perry's arrival reached Edo, the city was thrown into confusion. Panic seized the officials and the inhabitants. They knew what Perry wanted, and how powerless they were to prevent him from landing. Just as the Beijing government did when faced with a similar situation, the shogunate avoided giving an answer, and tried to gain time by ordering local officials at Uraga to tell Perry that he should withdraw to Nagasaki.

But Perry refused. To scare the Japanese, he sent out survey crews to look for an anchorage closer to Edo. Alarmed, the shogunate finally gave in and appointed two commissioners to receive Perry. On July 14, he landed with about 300 men and delivered a message from the American President Fillmore to the shogun's representatives. All along, Perry thought that he was dealing with representatives of the emperor. He did not know that the shogun, not the emperor, was the real ruler of Japan. The Japanese asked for time to consider signing a treaty with the Americans. Perry agreed. He would leave, but he expected an official reply the following spring. The expedition then left Edo Bay for the China coast.

While waiting for Perry's return, the shogunate took steps to strengthen the country. It lifted a ban on the construction of large ships, bought ships and guns from the Dutch and ordered the *daimyo* to strengthen all coastal defences. However, the *Bakufu* did not really know what to do in the event of an American invasion. Hoping to put up a

Commodore Perry — an eastern and a western impression

united stand against the Americans, Abe Masahiro, who as chief councillor was the real ruler of Japan, sent a translation of President Fillmore's letter to the *daimyo*, high-ranking officials and leading Confucian scholars, requesting their advice.

When the replies came in, they showed that many of the *daimyo* and most of the

THE CALL TO ARMS

Everyone has pointed out that we are without a navy and that our coasts are undefended. Meanwhile the Americans will be here again next year. Our policy shall be to evade any definite answer to their request, while at the same time maintaining a peaceful demeanour. It may be, however, that they will have recourse to violence. For that contingency we must be prepared lest the country suffer disgrace. Therefore every possible effort will be made to prepare means of defence.

— From a Bakufu decree, 1853

Confucian scholars favoured rejecting the American demands. The emperor and his court nobles, who were also consulted, thought the same. The Edo government accepted this view as a course of action and announced that it was the emperor's wish to have the 'barbarians' turned away.

However, the officials who had dealt with Perry, and some of the leading *daimyo*, knew that the *Bakufu* was not strong enough to fight the Americans. They felt that concessions should be granted to avoid war; and meanwhile, defences should be strengthened. Members of the shogun's Council of State, the chief ruling body, also knew that the *Bakufu* was financially weak and could not afford to make war. Furthermore, since much of Edo's food supply came in by sea, an enemy naval force could blockade the city to starve its inhabitants and throw the Edo government into confusion.

Meanwhile, Perry's squadron, anchored off Macau, was getting ready for the return trip to Japan. Perry decided to go back earlier than expected after receiving a disturbing report that the Russian Admiral Putiatin had landed in Nagasaki in August 1853. Putiatin's mission was to settle the boundaries between the two countries in the Kurils and Sakhalin, and to open trade relations. However, on learning that war was about to break out between his country and Britain and France over the Eastern Question, he decided to stop negotiations and left for China in October. He returned early in January 1854. Negotiations with the Japanese came to nothing. At one time, Putiatin suggested to Perry that they join forces, but suspicious of the Russians, Perry refused.

On 12 February 1854, Perry was back in Edo Bay with more ships than before. Alarmed by this show of force and believing that the Americans would attack if their demands were not granted, the Japanese agreed to negotiate. Perry landed at Kanagawa on March 8; and on March 31, the Treaty of Kanagawa (or Perry Treaty), a treaty of friendship, was signed.

What were the chief factors which helped the Perry expedition to end Japan's isolation? Although the majority of the *daimyo* opposed the reopening of Japan to foreign contacts, they wanted to avoid war. Foreign pressure coming at the same time from the Americans and the Russians convinced many Japanese leaders that they could not continue rejecting foreign demands. Moreover, Perry seemed

determined enough to make war if refused, and war would result in certain defeat for Japan. He also won the respect of the Japanese by his firmness in handling the negotiations; for instance, he refused to deal with minor officials.

The Treaty of Kanagawa and other treaty settlements

The Treaty of Kanagawa provided for:
- the protection and return of shipwrecked American sailors;
- the opening of the ports of Shimoda in the Izu Peninsula and Hakodate in Hokkaido to American ships in a year's time, for supplies and limited trade;
- American consular representation at Shimoda, if considered necessary (later on, a dispute arose over this provision: the *Bakufu* insisted that there would be consular representation only if the Japanese government — not either government as the Americans claimed — thought it necessary);
- most-favoured-nation treatment.

At last Japan was once again open to foreigners. But the door was only partially opened, as Shimoda and Hakodate were both far away from Edo and Kyoto, the seats of power.

The door was opened wider in October 1854, when the British obtained an agreement opening Nagasaki and Hakodate to British ships for supplies, though not for trade. In February 1855, Russia finally obtained a treaty that:
- gave Russian ships permission to call at Shimoda, Hakodate and Nagasaki for supplies;
- granted extraterritorial rights to Russia;
- settled the boundary between the two countries in the Kuril Islands, although the boundary of Sakhalin was not settled.

Holland gained a treaty settlement with Japan in November. Despite all these treaties, the

Western powers were not satisfied. The matter of fully opening Japan to trade had not been settled.

The Treaty of Kanagawa, and the other treaties which followed it, were not as aggressive as those made with China. This was because they were not the result of war. Besides, the foreigners expected there would be less material benefits from the opening of Japan than from the opening of China. Nevertheless, the treaties weakened the position of the shogunate, for they showed that it could not maintain the policy of seclusion.

The Treaty of Edo and other commercial treaties

Acting on the terms of the Perry Treaty, the American government appointed Townsend Harris, a rich New York businessman, as its first diplomatic representative to Japan. In August 1856, he arrived in Shimoda. He was very patient in dealing with the Japanese, who tried everything to get him to leave and to prevent him from gaining more concessions. This was because the earlier decision to open the country had met strong opposition. If the *Bakufu* showed a friendly attitude towards the foreigners, its enemies would criticize it. Harris refused to leave. In the end, his patience and courage were rewarded. In June 1857, a Japanese-American convention was signed:

- opening Nagasaki to American ships;
- granting to the Americans the right of permanent residence at Shimoda and Hakodate;
- fixing the rate of currency exchange.

This was followed by agreements in October which gave Holland and Russia the right to limited trade at the ports of Hakodate and Nagasaki.

Harris finally gained an audience with the shogun in December, the first granted to a foreigner since 1613. The Shogun Iesada (ruled 1853-48) agreed that 'intercourse shall be continuous for ever.'

To complete his mission, Harris had to negotiate a treaty of commerce, fully opening Japan to trade. At Edo he exploited Japanese fears by telling shogunate officials that it would be in the interest of Japan if they signed a treaty with the United States voluntarily. This would be better than signing with other powers, which were prepared to wage war against Japan and impose unreasonable treaties. The signing of the Tianjin treaties of 1858 in connection with the Second Anglo-Chinese War seems to have convinced the Japanese that he was right. On 29 July 1858, the Treaty of Edo (or Harris Treaty), a full commercial treaty, was concluded. Its main provisions were:

- the opening of four more ports, besides Shimoda and Hakodate, to trade: Kanagawa and Nagasaki to be opened immediately and Niigata and Hyogo (now Kobe) to be opened later according to specific dates;
- the opening of Edo and Osaka to foreign residents;
- the exchange of ministers and consuls;
- the imposition of import duties at very low rates;
- the granting of extraterritoriality and freedom of worship to Americans living in Japan;
- treaty revision after 4 July 1872 if either government wanted it;
- most-favoured-nation treatment.

The treaty threw the door to Japan wide open, ending once and for all her long period of isolation. In the next few months, Britain, Holland, Russia and France also obtained treaties of commerce with Japan. By the most-favoured-nation treatment, all the treaty powers enjoyed the same rights and privileges.

Although the *Bakufu* did everything within its power to obtain imperial approval of these treaties, it was not until 1865 that the emperor gave his consent. For the next 40 years or so, Japan's foreign policy aimed at the revision of these 'unequal treaties'. Still, Japan was more fortunate than China. The signing of these commercial treaties saved her from being crushed by foreign wars before she could strengthen herself against foreign aggression.

THE MEIJI RESTORATION

Internal disunity

Perry's arrival not only resulted in the breakdown of Japan's isolation; it also led to internal disunity. Between 1853 and 1868, conflicts arose between two rival political groups, chiefly over the direction of foreign policy. More important, a struggle developed between those who were loyal to the shogun and those who wanted the emperor's powers restored. The struggle ended with the abolition of the shogunate and the Meiji Restoration.

As we saw earlier, at the time Perry was pressing for a treaty, the shogunate sought the advice of the *daimyo* as well as of the imperial court. This had never happened before, as the shogunal officials had always made their own decisions on matters of state. By its action, the shogunate exposed its weakness, a situation which its enemies could readily use against it.

On the question of whether or not to give in to American pressure, the leading officials and the *daimyo* were split into two factions. One urged the immediate rejection of Perry's demands; the other group wanted to concede because they realized that Japan could not defend itself against enemy invasion and could only catch up with the West technologically and militarily by opening her doors. Whichever decision it made, the shogunate would still lose. Rejection of Perry would mean war, then defeat and humiliation; acceptance would be regarded as a sign of weakness by the foreign powers as well as by its enemies at home. When the *Bakufu* failed to stop Perry, the anti-foreign group began to turn against the shogun and to look to the emperor for leadership. The conflict became worse as anti-foreign feeling grew.

In 1858, Ii Naosuke, the pro-shogun Lord of Hikone, took over direct control of the shogunal government as Great Elder (the equivalent of chief minister). He tried to suppress the pro-emperor samurai with cruel methods. His strong leadership might have saved the shogunate. But in 1860, his enemies succeeded in killing him. His death left the shogunate without a firm leader.

Anti-foreign outbursts

Despite the signing of the Treaty of Kanagawa, many Japanese still hoped that the 'barbarians' could be driven away. However, the signing of the Treaty of Edo and all the other commercial treaties, and the arrival of foreign envoys, showed clearly that the foreigners were determined to stay.

A strong anti-foreign feeling spread throughout the country. The *Sonno Joi* (revere the emperor and expel the barbarians) movement, supported mainly by the western clans, grew in strength. From 1858 murderous attacks on foreigners became more and more frequent. Among the first victims were a Russian naval officer and two sailors who were attacked by *ronin* at Yokohama in 1859. At Edo, Harris's secretary was murdered in 1861, while the British legation was attacked twice.

To the disappointment of the treaty powers, the *Bakufu* could not protect their subjects or punish the offenders. In trying to save itself, the *Bakufu* had resorted to double-dealing, assuring the foreigners of protection while promising the anti-foreign groups it would expel the foreigners. This was another sign of its loss of authority.

In 1862 the murder of an Englishman, C. L. Richardson, finally led to British naval action. Richardson was out riding near Yokohama when he was killed by Satsuma clansmen. The British demanded an indemnity for the killing from the *Bakufu* and the Lord of Satsuma. When they did not get it, a British squadron bombarded Kagoshima, stronghold of the Satsuma clan, in August 1863. The Lord of Satsuma surrendered, and he and the shogun agreed to pay an indemnity.

An incident more serious than the Richardson affair was the bombardment of Shimonoseki. In April 1863, the emperor had summoned the shogun to the imperial court. This had never happened before; and the shogun's obedience to the imperial order was yet another blow to the power and prestige of the shogunate. At Kyoto, the emperor ordered him to drive out the foreigners by June 1863. But, upon his return to Edo, the shogun announced that he would not be able to do it. Consequently, the Choshu clan decided to carry out the imperial order. When the deadline for the expulsion of the foreigners arrived, Choshu men fired upon American, French and Dutch ships from their forts guarding the Shimonoseki Straits.

As the *Bakufu* could not control the Choshu clan, a joint naval expedition composed of British, American, French and Dutch warships bombarded Shimonoseki in 1864 and captured the Choshu forts.

The defeat of the two western clans had two important results: it broke the backbone of the anti-foreign movement; and it convinced the Choshu and Satsuma clansmen of the superiority of Western weapons. Abandoning their anti-foreign attitude, the western clans began to build up their military forces and employed foreign military advisers. Their increased military strength was an important factor in the later struggle against pro-Tokugawa forces.

In 1865 the treaty powers once again put pressure on the *Bakufu*. Nine warships carrying diplomatic representatives of Britain, the United States, France and Holland arrived in Osaka to demand imperial approval of the commercial treaties of 1858 and the immediate opening of the port of Hyogo (scheduled to be opened on 1 January 1868). The *Bakufu* referred the matter to the emperor, who reluctantly gave his approval to the treaties. He refused, however, to advance the opening date of Hyogo because it was very near to Kyoto. Satisfied that they had at least obtained the emperor's approval of the treaties, the treaty powers withdrew.

This settlement showed that the Japanese had in principle accepted diplomatic exchanges. It also showed the increasing authority of the emperor over the shogun's actions. By 1865, therefore, the immediate problem was how to abolish the shogunate and restore the imperial court to power.

The Choshu Rising

Ever since Perry's arrival, the shogunate had shown its weakness continually. But what really showed how helpless and powerless the *Bakufu* had become was the relaxation of the system of *sankin kotai* in 1862. Compulsory residence of the *daimyo* at Edo was reduced to 100 days every three years, and the system of leaving hostages was abolished.

This change of policy showed that the shogunate had given up its control over the *daimyo*. Most of the *daimyo* and their families left Edo and went to Kyoto, where they could make plans against the shogun. The balance of power was shifting from the *Bakufu* towards the imperial court.

But even at this stage, the pro-emperor clans were not united in their objectives. The extremist group led by fanatical Choshu leaders wanted to expel the foreigners and, at the same time, drive out the shogun. The moderate group, with the Satsuma clan as leader, favoured trade with the foreigners; and at the same time they wanted to unite the emperor and the *Bakufu*, a policy known as *kobu gattai*.

By mid-1863 the court was dominated by Choshu men. There were continued acts of violence against pro-foreign groups in Kyoto by *ronin* supported by the Choshu clan. This and the firing upon foreign ships in the Shimonoseki Straits made the other *daimyo* realize that the Choshu clan was going too far.

In September, Satsuma-Aizu troops drove the Choshu forces out of Kyoto. However, the following year the Choshu clansmen rose in revolt and attacked Kyoto, declaring that they would save the emperor from misguided advisers. The emperor instead ordered the *Bakufu* to suppress the rising. Before the year was over the *Bakufu*, helped by the Satsuma and other clans, defeated the rebels. The Choshu leaders agreed to a truce. But the *Bakufu* saw this as an opportunity to recover its power, and determined to wipe out the rebellious clan.

In 1865 the *Bakufu* started making preparations for a second expedition against Choshu. It marched west in July 1866. This proved to be a fatal mistake. Tokugawa troops were defeated repeatedly by superior Choshu forces. One important reason for their defeat was that the Satsuma and other powerful clans had refused to join the second expedition. Disappointed by the weakness of the shogunate, and fearing a strengthened *Bakufu*, the Satsuma leaders had decided to abandon the *kobu gattai* movement. They put aside their differences with Choshu, and in March 1866 made a secret alliance with them, aiming to restore full powers to the emperor.

The shogunate's defeat by the Choshu clan convinced other clans that the time had come to overthrow the shogunate. The Satsuma-Choshu alliance, which was later joined by three other clans, obtained the financial support of the merchants as well as of the imperial court. Even the British government gave it moral support. The combination of such powerful forces hastened the collapse of the shogunate.

Abolition of the shogunate

The death of the Shogun Iemochi (ruled 1858-66) gave Emperor Komei (reigned 1846-67) an excuse to end the war against the Choshu clan. On the death of the emperor himself, the troops of both sides were ordered to disband. Iemochi's successor, Keiki (ruled 1866-67), realized that there was nothing he could do to save the *Bakufu*.

The Meiji Emperor Mutsuhito

In November 1867, he agreed to a proposal, made by the Lord of Tosa and approved by the other western clans, to give up his powers to Emperor Komei's 15-year-old son and successor, Mutsuhito (reigned 1867-1912), who took the reign-name Meiji (enlightened government). The shogun was then to be the head of a council of the leading *daimyo* and

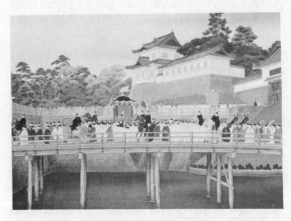

The Meiji Emperor entering Tokyo (1868)

161

to govern the nation in the name of the emperor.

However, Keiki's call for the formation of such a council was ignored. Seeing that there were still influential pro-*Bakufu* groups in the imperial court, Satsuma, Choshu and Tosa forces, helped by other clans, decided on a *coup d'etat* to overthrow the shogunate. On 3 January 1868, they seized the imperial palace, proclaiming that the shogunate had been abolished and the emperor's political power had been restored.

Nevertheless, the power struggle went on. The Tokugawa supporters were hoping that the shogun would be given an important post.

But the young samurai of the western clans who brought about the restoration not only left him out of the new government, but also took away his land. His faithful followers persuaded him to fight, and a brief civil war followed. Their crushing defeat at Fushimi-Toba on January 27 ended organized Tokugawa resistance to the new regime. In May the imperial forces occupied Edo which was renamed Tokyo (eastern capital). Shortly afterwards, the emperor moved his court to Tokyo. By March 1869 it had become the seat of the Meiji government.

Thus ended the 265-year rule of the Tokugawa shogunate.

QUESTIONS

1. Give a general description of political, economic and social conditions in Japan before the arrival of Perry in 1853.
2. Describe the attitude of the Japanese towards foreign contact before Perry arrived in 1853.
3. What factors had weakened Tokugawa rule by the time Perry arrived in Japan in 1853?
4. 'When Perry came in 1853, Japan was ready for internal change.' To what extent do you agree with this view?
5. How did the Japanese react to Perry's arrival in 1853?
6. Was the Meiji Restoration caused by pressure from outside or by changes from within Japan? Give reasons for your view.
7. Show how the various treaties signed by Japan with the Western powers after the arrival of Perry in 1853 ended the isolation of Japan.
8. Why did Japan end her policy of seclusion in 1853-54?

9. Account for the fall of the Tokugawa shogunate in 1867.
10. Discuss the role played by the Satsuma and Choshu clans in the overthrow of the Tokugawa shogunate.
11. To what extent were the Western powers responsible for the fall of the Tokugawa shogunate?
12. Trace the events which led to the abolition of the Tokugawa shogunate and the Meiji Restoration.
13. Explain how **each** of the following developments contributed to the collapse of Tokugawa rule:
    (a) the relaxation of the system of 'sankin kotai' (1862)
    (b) the Richardson affair (1862-63)
    (c) the Choshu Rising (1863-67)
    (d) the bombardment of Shimonoseki (1864)

In 1638 the Tokugawa shogunate closed Japan to the outside world in order to preserve its power. By the time Perry came in 1853, however, the country was ready for internal changes because of general dissatisfaction with the *Bakufu*. The Tokugawa shogunate had gradually declined over the long years of peace. By the mid-19th century, it had become so weak that a serious challenge to its authority was bound to have fatal consequences.

There was discontent among the *daimyo* (particularly the western *daimyo*), the samurai, merchants, peasants and scholars. They wanted changes. Some wanted to put an end to the policy of seclusion; others wanted to restore the political power of the emperor. Perry's arrival, which ended the isolation of Japan, set the forces of change in motion. The result was the overthrow of Tokugawa rule and the restoration of the emperor's political power.

Perry's determination to reopen Japan to foreign trade resulted in the signing of the Treaty of Kanagawa with the United States. This was followed by treaties with other foreign powers. But it was the Treaty of Edo which threw Japan open and laid the foundation of the unequal treaty system. The signing of the treaties led to the growth of nationalism and the rise of a strong anti-foreign feeling, as seen in the rapid spread of the *Sonno Joi* movement and the revival of Shinto.

The shogun's inability to deal with foreign pressure and anti-foreign outbursts showed how weak the shogunal government had become. When the shogun agreed to pay an indemnity to the British as a result of the Richardson affair and failed to expel the foreigners before and after the bombardment of Shimonoseki, the pro-emperor groups grew in strength. Civil war finally broke out. With the defeat of the pro-*Bakufu* forces, the shogunate was abolished and the imperial court was restored to power in 1868. This marked the beginning of the Meiji Restoration.

It was pressure from the foreign powers, the western clans and the imperial court which finally brought Tokugawa rule to an end. For the new leaders of Japan, the task of nation-building and modernization lay ahead.

Chapter 10
The beginnings of Japan's modernization

The reopening of Japan to the West in the 1850s brought with it the unequal treaty system already forced upon China, and increasing foreign pressure. Compared to China, her response to the challenge from the West was not only quicker and greater, but she was also far more successful in strengthening herself against further pressure from the Western powers. The leaders of the Meiji Restoration quickly recognized that Japan had to overcome her economic and military weakness before she could preserve her independence and gain equality with other nations. Thus, during the Meiji era, or Era of Enlightened Rule (1868-1912), they launched an intensive programme of modernization, largely through the imitation of Western methods. This changed Japan from a small and unimportant country into a strong nation and a world power within a few decades. 'A Rich Country and a Strong Army' was the slogan of this period.

THE MEIJI REFORMS

The creation of a new political system

In the early years of the Meiji era, the first task of the new leaders was to create a new political structure to replace the decentralized system of the former Tokugawa regime. This proved to be difficult, because they were not even sure what kind of government they wanted. There were also other problems which had to be solved first before a new system could be established. They had to destroy the remnants of feudal power, develop a sound economy, and strengthen their military forces. Thus the government machinery set up in the first few years of Meiji rule was temporary and experimental. The more stable constitutional government which was introduced in 1890 was, in fact, the result of trial and error methods and frequent changes.

As soon as imperial rule was restored on 3 January 1868, a simple governmental structure was set up. Authority was divided among three bodies: a Supreme Controller, a post which went to an imperial prince; a senior Council of State, consisting of court nobles and feudal lords who had supported the restoration; and a junior Council of State, which included the young samurai leaders who had planned and carried out the restoration. Shortly afterwards, a deliberative assembly and several government departments were formed.

This structure was completely revised in June when the government issued what might be called Japan's first constitution. It proclaimed new aims based on the Charter (Imperial) Oath taken by the emperor in April. The oath was made public in order to give feudal lords and government officials a general guideline and to let the people know what the government's aims were. It became the basis of Meiji policy. Its five articles were as follows:

- Deliberative assemblies shall be widely established and all government matters decided by public discussion.

Emperor Meiji listening to the five articles of the Charter Oath

sectors. Supreme authority was to be exercised by a Council of State through an assembly consisting of an upper and lower house, the president of the council and several administrative departments.

More changes were made in 1869 and 1871, but what really mattered was who exercised power. Although imperial princes, court nobles and feudal lords were appointed to the highest offices, they had no real power. Except for a few court nobles like Iwakura Tomomi and Sanjo Sanetomi, the actual running of the government was in the hands of the bright young samurai leaders of the western clans who had brought about the restoration. Among these were Ito Hirobumi and Yamagata Aritomo of Choshu, Saigo Takamori of Satsuma, Itagaki Taisuke of Tosa and Okuma Shigenobu of Hizen. At first, they served either as advisers or administrative assistants. By the 1870s, many of them had been appointed to such important posts as heads of ministries. They became the *Genro* (elder statesmen).

Besides the political effects, the Charter Oath led to modernization and to the breakdown of isolationism. It also led to state control of education for the purpose of stressing loyalty to the state and the emperor.

- All classes, high and low, shall unite in vigorously carrying out the plan of the government.
- The common people, as well as the civil and military officials, shall each be allowed to pursue his own calling so that there may be no discontent.
- Evil customs of the past shall be broken off and everything based upon the just laws of Nature.
- Knowledge shall be sought throughout the world to strengthen the empire.

It would seem that the emperor and his advisers had promised a government based on popular representative institutions. But it is highly improbable that this was their intention. Feudalism had not yet been abolished, and even the educated Japanese had little idea of how democracy worked. It is more likely that their aim was to gain favourable public opinion to forestall discontent and leave them free to deal with more urgent problems.

The new system of government imitated Western political systems and divided government into executive, legislative and judicial

The abolition of feudalism

The next step in establishing a truly centralized government and facilitating modernization was to abolish feudalism. The land and the people had to be brought under state control not only to provide a steady revenue for the government but also make sure that no political troubles arose to disturb the work of reconstruction.

To achieve this, the government had to take away the political and economic independence of the *daimyo* who, at the time of the restoration, had been asked to continue governing their lands. Fortunately, the young samurai leaders of the four most powerful western clans were able to persuade their feudal lords to surrender their lands to the emperor in 1869. These lords also offered troops to support the new regime. The rest of the *daimyo* followed their example.

By 1871, the government felt strong enough to issue an imperial decree abolishing feudalism. From then on, what was left of military and feudal rule was gradually replaced by a civil government. The former feudal lands were divided into 43 prefectures (*ken*), each under a governor appointed by the central government. Recruitment for government service was by examination. Nevertheless, the former feudal class continued to dominate Japanese life.

The abolition of feudalism had significant effects upon the status of the various social classes. The financial position of the *daimyo* was greatly improved, since they no longer had to support their samurai armies. Moreover, the government paid some of their debts and provided them with pensions. Some of them joined the merchant class, using the money they received from the government as capital.

For the samurai, the change had disastrous effects. They remained poor. Their pensions were so small that these could not make up for the loss of income from their former feudal lords. Many were forced to go into business, an occupation they hated. The establishment of a national army resulted in the loss of their privileged social status, for they lost their monopoly to carry arms.

It is not surprising therefore that from 1874 onwards there were several samurai uprisings. The most serious one was the Satsuma Rebellion of 1877 led by Saigo, who had become disillusioned with the restoration government he had helped to establish. The suppression of this rebellion by Yamagata ended all hopes of reviving feudalism in Japan.

The merchant class welcomed the abolition of feudalism, for the government paid many of the debts owed to them by the *daimyo*. As for the farmers who made up the majority of the population, their feudal lords could no

WESTERN LORDS SURRENDER FIEFS

There is no soil within the empire that does not belong to the emperor . . . and no inhabitant who is not a subject of the emperor, though, in the Middle Ages, the imperial power declined and the military classes rose, taking possession of the land and dividing it among themselves as the prize of their bow and spear. But now that the imperial power is restored, how can we retain possession of land that belongs to the emperor and govern people who are his subjects? We therefore reverently offer up all our feudal possessions . . . so that a uniform rule may prevail throughout the empire. . . .

— *From a memorial of the lords of Choshu, Satsuma, Tosa and Hizen to the emperor, 1869*

longer impose obligations on them whenever they chose. However, in many cases, they lost their status as independent farmers because they were forced by financial difficulties to become tenants of the new landlord class. Many of them later left the countryside and joined the labour force in the urban areas.

Finally, the old social classifications of warrior, peasant, craftsman and merchant were replaced. A new social system developed with the appearance of three social classes: the new nobility, *kazoku*, composed of court nobles and the former *daimyo*; *shizoku*, or gentry, comprising the former samurai; and the *heimin*, or commoners. These divisions were not as rigid as those of the former feudal society.

Demand for representative government

In the first ten years or so of the Meiji era, the government was so busy unifying and strengthening the nation that it paid little attention to the demand for representative government, which was promised in the Charter Oath. There were some representative bodies such as the Assembly of Prefectural

Governors which first met in 1875, the prefectural assemblies established in 1878, and the municipal assemblies which were first allowed in 1880. But all of them were concerned with local, not national, government.

By 1881, the demand for some sort of representative national assembly could no longer be ignored. Dissatisfied government leaders, former samurai in business, and many newspapers continually pressed for political reform, arousing public feelings in favour of representative government. Then came a scandal which increased anti-government feeling; some government officials in Hokkaido plotted with a group of Osaka merchants to buy government property in Hokkaido at a very low price. When this became known, the plan came under attack and was abandoned. Finally, on 12 October 1881, the government decreed that a national assembly would be called by 1890.

To prepare for the election campaigns, opposition groups immediately organized themselves into political parties. Itagaki, who had resigned from the government in 1876, was chosen as the first president of the Liberal Party (*Jiyuto*). Okuma, who had left government service after exposing the Hokkaido scandal, founded the Constitutional Progressive or Reform Party (*Rikken Kaishinto*). To meet this challenge, the Constitutional Imperial Rule Party (*Rikken Teiseito*) was formed to support the government.

In preparation for the promised assembly, Ito Hirobumi, who had become the most important government official, went to Europe in 1882 to study Western political systems. What he wanted was a constitution that would make the government responsible to the emperor, not to the assembly. He found the Prussian model best suited to the needs of Japan.

The drafting of the Japanese constitution began in 1884. Orders of nobility were created, following the British model. These nobles could form an upper house later if required. In 1885 the Council of State was replaced by a cabinet, whose members were appointed by the emperor. Ito was the prime minister. Three years later, a Privy Council was established to discuss the draft of the constitution and to approve it.

Ito Hirobumi, Japanese prime minister

The Constitution of 1889

On 11 February 1889, the anniversary of the traditional founding date of the Japanese state in 660 B.C, the constitution was adopted. It was handed by the emperor to the prime minister, an act which showed that it was a gift from him to the people. The Constitution of 1889 formed the base of Japan's government structure until her defeat in the Second World War. What were its main features?

Although it established three separate branches of government, the constitution gave the executive branch much more power than the legislative and judicial branches. The emperor was granted almost absolute power. His person was sacred. The Imperial House Law

167

Emperor Meiji announcing the Constitution of 1889

ensured the continuation of the imperial line. He was the supreme commander of the army and navy, and was given the power to make war or peace and to conclude treaties. He could issue ordinances which had the force of law when the diet was not in session. No one but he could introduce amendments to the constitution. Thus, the emperor also had judicial powers. He could also dissolve the diet at will. In practice, however, real power was in the hands of his advisers, the *Genro*.

The diet was to have two chambers: a House of Peers (upper house) to be composed of 'members of the imperial family, of nobles, and of deputies who have been nominated by the emperor', and an elected House of Representatives (lower house) composed of

300 members elected through a limited franchise. However, the diet had very limited powers. This was because cabinet ministers were appointed by and responsible to the emperor; and if the diet rejected the budget, the government could carry on with the budget of the previous year.

The Privy Council, the highest advisory body to the emperor, decided basic government policy. It was later controlled by the *Genro*.

By granting the ministers and the chiefs of the army and navy the right of direct access to the throne, the constitution strengthened the position of the military.

The people were granted such basic rights as freedom of speech, of association and of

The first session of the diet (1890)

worship, but all these rights had conditions attached to them so that they could not be fully enjoyed. The government could suspend these rights at will.

Quite obviously, the constitutional government was democratic only on the surface. The pattern of the government was much as before; it remained oligarchic and aristocratic. Actual power still belonged to a small ruling group, the *Genro*. They held important posts,

and were also advisers to the emperor, according to Japanese custom. Their position as advisers had no constitutional basis; they were not representatives of the people. Yet they had tremendous power and influence in government until the First World War through their control of the cabinet, the Privy Council and the House of Peers. Most of the major posts in the armed services and the bureaucracy were held by their followers.

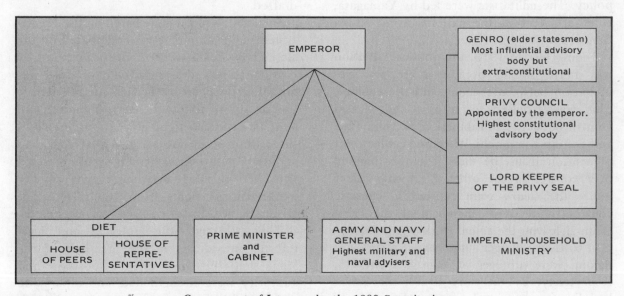

Government of Japan under the 1889 Constitution

How the constitution worked

During the early years of constitutional government, a struggle for control developed between the *Genro*-dominated cabinet and the elected House of Representatives, which was controlled by opposition parties.

The cabinet hoped to evade the decision of the diet by continuing the provisions of the previous year's budget, if no new budget was approved. This failed because the old budget could not cover the increased expenditure of the new year, which was needed for the modernization programme. Whenever the prime minister called for more money, the opposition in the diet turned down the proposals. In retaliation, he often dissolved the diet.

Eventually, prime ministers were forced to ally themselves with political parties in the diet in order to win the support of the lower house for their policies. During Ito's fourth term as prime minister in 1900-01, several party members were appointed to cabinet posts. Thus the original aim of keeping the cabinet completely free of interference from the diet was defeated. Nevertheless, party members were never able to gain control of the cabinet. Nor were they able to stop the militarists who, at times, dictated government policy. The militarists were led by Yamagata, chief architect of the national army and a *Genro*.

From 1901 to 1913, the political situation was fairly stable, because there was co-operation between the diet and the cabinet. This was achieved by alternating political control between the cabinets of Katsura Taro and Saionji Kimmochi. When one cabinet met opposition from the diet, it simply handed over control to the other. Meanwhile, after 1903, the *Genro* were content to exercise control indirectly as members of the Privy Council, leaving the actual work of administration to their younger supporters. Katsura and Saionji were proteges of Yamagata and Ito, respectively. By the early 1920s, the *Genro* had disappeared from Japanese politics.

PRIME MINISTERS, MEIJI JAPAN

1885-88	Ito Hirobumi (Choshu)
1888-89	Kuroda Kiyotaka (Satsuma)
1889-91	Yamagata Aritomo (Choshu)
1891-92	Matsukata Masayoshi (Satsuma)
1892-96	Ito Hirobumi
1896-98	Matsukata Masayoshi
Jan-June 1898	Ito Hirobumi
June-Nov 1898	Okuma Shigenobu (Hizen)
1898-1900	Yamagata Aritomo
1900-01	Ito Hirobumi
1901-06	Katsura Taro (Choshu)
1906-08	Saionji Kimmochi (former court noble)
1908-11	Katsura Taro
1911-12	Saionji Kimmochi
1912-13	Katsura Taro

Judicial reform

Judicial reform was also carried out. This arose more from a desire to abolish extra-territoriality than from any wish to administer justice efficiently. As long as Japan's legal system remained feudal, the foreign powers were unwilling to revise the treaties. With the help of foreign experts, new legal codes were drafted.

By 1890, a penal code based on the French system, and a commercial code based on the German system, were in operation. A new civil code was drafted which, at first, was heavily influenced by French ideas. Later, it was revised to follow the German pattern and so the individual's rights were subordinated to the authority of the state. After Japan had adopted these codes, Britain signed a treaty with her in 1894, agreeing to give up her extraterritorial rights from 1899. The other powers signed similar treaties soon afterwards.

Thus, through the political and legal reforms introduced in the first half of the Meiji era, the government's position and authority were strengthened, and diplomatic equality with the foreign powers was achieved.

Financial reform

A new financial system was urgently needed after the restoration to give the government a sound economic foundation. Funds were needed to modernize and strengthen the country, to compensate the *daimyo* and the samurai for the loss of their feudal privileges, to pay the debts of the shogunate and the *daimyo*, and to meet the expenses of government administration. Since the imperial treasury was empty, a uniform system of taxation had to be introduced immediately. But the government had no power to impose taxes. There was, moreover, no standard currency.

With the abolition of feudalism in 1871, the government allowed the sale of land, issued titles of land ownership, and assessed the land in order to determine a national land tax. In 1873 a new tax system was introduced. Landowners paid a money tax based on the value of their land, not their crops. Money began to flow regularly into the national treasury.

However, the government's financial obligations to the warrior class continued to drain the treasury. To win the loyalty of the *daimyo*, the new regime had granted them pensions and had taken over payment of the rice allowance of the samurai. This generous settlement was a heavy financial burden and, to relieve itself of immediate rice or cash payment, the government offered bonds instead. In 1876 the conversion of the incomes of the former warrior class into government bonds was made compulsory. Thus the government could use cash for more urgent needs.

As for currency, there were various kinds of coins in circulation: gold, silver, copper and iron. After the restoration, there were notes representing amounts of gold, silver and rice in circulation as well. This caused confusion. In 1871 the problem was solved with the adoption of the decimal system with the yen as the unit of currency. The yen was backed by gold, since this was a widely used international standard.

All these reforms strengthened the financial position of the new government. This partly explains why early Meiji Japan did not usually seek capital from abroad to finance modernization. Japan borrowed only on two occasions during this period, both from Britain: one loan was for the construction of a railway, and the other for the payment of interest on government bonds.

Industrialization

The Meiji leaders believed that the Western powers became strong because of trade and industry. They also felt that to defend Japan against the West, it was necessary to set up foreign-style industries. In pre-restoration years, Japan was already beginning to change from an agricultural to a commercial economy. Towns and cities were becoming commercial and industrial centres. Various industries were already fairly well developed. Capital which could be used for industrialization had been accumulated by rich merchant families. Now Japanese industrialization needed more capital, and also technical knowledge.

Technical knowledge was obtained by adopting successful Western educational practices, importing foreign technicians, and sending students abroad for technical studies. The merchants' capital alone was not enough, but foreign loans could have led to foreign control of Japan's economy. The government therefore chose to sponsor industry itself, using money from land taxes and merchants' loans. The government also wanted to give work to the unemployed and rebellious samurai. Industrialization might also lead to a favourable trade balance. In addition, heavy industries, such as munitions and mining, had to be developed for strategic and commercial purposes; and communications and transport had to be improved to help industrial development. All this could only be accomplished if the state led the way.

Japan's first spinning factory, opened in 1872

In the 1870s the government began to build and operate cotton and woollen mills. Spinning machinery was imported, and sold to manufacturers by instalments in order to encourage private enterprise. Western-type model factories, manufacturing such products as cement, glass, clothing, paper and beer, were set up as examples for private companies to follow. Model gold, silver, coal, iron and copper mines were operated by the state. Shipbuilding yards, powder and munitions factories, and artillery works were also established. In the 1880s the government helped private industrialists by giving them subsidies and providing them with capital and technical advice. Encouraged in this way, private corporations appeared one after another.

Having promoted and sponsored industrial enterprise, the government sold most of the industries it operated to a few large industrial and financial groups at a very low price; it retained control of the key military industries only. These financial-industrial combines, each founded and managed in most cases by single families of industrialists, were called the *zaibatsu*. The government maintained close links with them and, through them, had indirect control over industry. Though there was a wide range of industries run by small technical units, these units were often dependent on bigger companies which were controlled by the *zaibatsu*. The largest and most powerful combines were Mitsui, Mitsubishi, Yasuda and Sumitomo.

The *zaibatsu* dominated Japan's economic life and influenced government policy until the Second World War. They helped to quicken Japan's industrialization by building factories, railways and shipyards, and by providing capital for businessmen through their banks.

With the rise of this new class of bankers, Japan did not have to rely on heavy taxation or foreign loans to provide capital for her industrial revolution. Industrialization led to the expansion of domestic and foreign trade. Japanese markets extended into China and Southeast Asia. Industrialization also led to the gradual destruction of Japan's traditional agricultural economy and to the growth of industrial cities such as Tokyo and Osaka. The *zaibatsu*, too, played a leading role in developing the shipping and fishing industries.

The *zaibatsu's* close ties with the political leaders led to the development of heavy industries which were vital to national defence, and to the pursuit of a policy of military aggression. They not only helped to build up Japan's military and naval power, but they also provided financial and technical support for territorial expansion in the Ryukyus, Korea, Manchuria and China. War meant increased production and profits.

The development of Japan's industry during the early Meiji period was limited by the lack of enough capital. Rapid industrialization took place only after 1890, when it was extended to light industries as well. After Japan defeated China in 1895 and Russia in 1905, there was a tremendous growth in such old industries as mining and textiles. At the same time, new industries, mostly consumer industries, developed and expanded rapidly. Cheap labour meant lower prices, and this enabled Japanese products to compete successfully in the world market. The tremendous industrial progress was to make Japan self-sufficient.

Industrialization was accompanied by the modernization of transport and communications. In 1869 a telegraph line was put up between Tokyo and Yokohama; in 1870 construction of Japan's first railway between Tokyo and Hyogo began; and a government postal service was set up in 1871.

Various measures were carried out to facilitate trade. Among these were the development of a merchant marine with government subsidy; the establishment of banks to handle foreign trade transactions; and the provision of navigational aids such as lighthouses, buoys and beacons. However, tariff control by the foreign powers was a hindrance to rapid trade expansion. In future years, population pressure and limited natural resources were to make foreign trade the basis of Japan's economic survival.

Farming methods were improved in order to supply food for Japan's increasing population. The fishing industry developed rapidly. For a while, Japan was self-sufficient in foodstuffs. After 1890, however, food production could no longer keep up with population growth.

Strengthening military power

The creation of a strong and permanent military force was essential to Japan's modernization programme, for it would strengthen the position of the new government against domestic opposition and foreign aggression. After the restoration, the feudal lords had placed their troops under the government. But what the new leaders wanted was a national force, completely under the control of the central government.

The first important step was to pass a conscription law in 1873, which made military service universal and compulsory. Previously, the samurai had formed the major

Yamagata Aritomo, chief architect of Japan's national army

part of Japan's military system; now the peasant masses formed the base of a new national military force. The successful suppression of the Satsuma Rebellion by the peasant soldiers proved that they were superior to the samurai forces of Saigo. Japan's military tradition was glorified in the training camps, and this encouraged war-like tendencies.

LOYALTY — BASIC DUTY OF THE MILITARY

The soldier and the sailor should consider loyalty their essential duty....Remember that, as the protection of the state and the maintenance of its power depend upon the strength of its arms, the growth or decline of this strength must affect the nation's destiny for good or for evil; therefore neither be led astray by current opinions nor meddle in politics, but with single heart fulfil your essential duty of loyalty, and bear in mind that duty is weightier than a mountain, while death is lighter than a feather. Never by failing in moral principle fall into disgrace and bring dishonour upon your name.

— *From the Emperor Meiji's Imperial Rescript to Soldiers and Sailors, 4 January 1882*

In the years that followed, the army was further developed; it was modelled at first on the French, but later on the German, military system. The conscription law in 1890 gave Japan an army second only to Germany in strength. A navy was also created, following the British pattern. The man who was largely responsible for the organization of a strong and effective national army was Yamagata.

Militarism

As military strength grew, so too did Japan's reliance on it. Militarism was also fostered by other factors, which encouraged an aggressive foreign policy. The old samurai code, for example, had conditioned the Japanese to place great importance on the privilege of bearing arms.

In the process of creating a national army and navy, the military began to play a key role in the government. The 1889 Constitution gave them the right of direct access to the emperor. In other words, if they wanted war, they could disregard the cabinet and go straight to the emperor to get his approval. In 1900 a system was adopted by which only a general on active duty could be appointed Minister of War, and only an admiral on active duty could be Minister of the Navy. As ministers, they had a strong hold on the prime minister; they could resign if they did not get what they wanted, and the cabinet would then fall. To stay in power therefore the prime minister very often had to yield to the wishes of the military leaders.

Economic necessity also called for an aggressive foreign policy. Since arable land was very limited, agricultural production was insufficient to feed the increasing population. Foreign conquests could help to ease the population problem. At the same time, rapid industrialization after 1890 required raw materials and foreign markets. In addition, there was a need for investment outlets for surplus capital. It was not surprising therefore that Japan began to look to her weak neighbour, China.

Japan's desire to attain world power status was another strong reason for her militaristic policy. The unequal treaties had made her lose prestige, which might be regained by foreign aggression. This explains in part why she made war on China and Russia, joined the scramble for concessions in China, and participated in the suppression of the Boxer Rising.

In addition, the new educational system set up by the restoration government also encouraged extreme nationalism. From their earliest years, the Japanese were taught to be loyal to the state, the emperor, and their own traditions.

When Japan attained world power status, the Japanese widened the scope of nationalism, and began to regard themselves as champions of the Asian peoples against Western aggression. Also, with the presence of aggressive powers in Asia, Japan felt that she had to conquer neighbouring areas which were vital to her security. Russia, in particular, threatened her territorial ambitions in Manchuria and Korea. Japanese expansion into China was further encouraged by the ineffectiveness of Hay's 'Open Door' notes (see Chapter 7), and by China's unstable political conditions, which hindered the expansion of Japanese trade and industry there.

Developments in education

Since acquiring Western knowledge was a basic policy of the new government, as expressed in Article 5 of the Charter Oath, students were sent abroad to gain information about the West. Even before the restoration, some Japanese were already studying abroad, sent by the shogunate and the *daimyo*. More went to the West under the sponsorship of the restoration government. On their return, they became leaders in the modernization of Japan. To quicken the process of learning from the West, American and European experts were employed, and a Translation Bureau was established.

Another aim of the restoration government was to establish an organized system of education. Under the Tokugawa, there was no national school system. Education was chiefly confined to the soldier class and was the responsibility of the clans. There were a number of 'temple schools' run by Buddhist monks for the commoners. In almost all of these schools, emphasis was on Chinese studies, although in the years just before the restoration, some attention had been given to Japanese and Western studies.

With the restoration, the new leaders immediately turned their efforts to edu-

Japanese students and envoys going abroad (1871)

cation, which they considered vital to the strengthening of the nation. They introduced a plan for the national control of education. The first step was the formation of a Ministry of Education in 1871. Besides supervising schools, it aimed to eliminate illiteracy and to encourage Western learning. Then in 1872 an Education Act was issued which laid the foundations of compulsory education under state control. Its more important provisions were compulsory primary education and the division of the country into districts in which universities, middle schools, primary schools, and technical schools were to be established and organized on Western lines.

The attitude towards education was utilitarian. That is, education had to serve a particular purpose. Japan needed young people with the knowledge and skills to establish her as a world power. Great importance was therefore placed on scientific and technical knowledge. Such an ambitious plan for education could not be accomplished in a short time. Problems connected with school building, teacher training, new curricula, and textbooks had to be solved. A great deal of money was required.

Even more serious was the problem of getting the idea of compulsory education accepted. Some feared that the new scheme would lead to heavy taxation. The local governments were suspicious of centralization, as it might lead to their loss of control. With this in mind, the government granted some degree of local autonomy in educational matters in 1879. However, there was still a lack of interest in education among the local governments, and this made the government resume complete control in 1880.

In the 1880s the compulsory primary education scheme was carried out vigorously. In addition, the original idea of education to meet the needs of the individual gave way to education to serve the state. The Education Act of 1886 stressed the role of education as an instrument of the state. Nationalism and absolute obedience to the emperor were emphasized. As a result, the educational policy was a combination of nationalistic principles and utilitarian aims. It was designed to produce citizens who were literate, technically skilled and patriotic, not informed citizens free to think for themselves.

By 1890, it was feared that the enthusiasm for Western education might lead to the abandonment of the Japanese way of life and the loss of national identity. To prevent this from happening, an Imperial Rescript on Education was issued in 1890. It urged the people not to give up their native traditions such as ancestor-worship, filial piety, and loyalty to superiors and to the state. Students were told to carry on with their studies of Western science and technology, but that they should not adopt Western moral and political philosophy. This was against the fifth article of the Charter Oath, which urged the seeking of knowledge from all over the world.

The development of a national system of education produced two significant results. It brought about a high degree of literacy which helped to provide the technical knowledge which is so essential to industrialization. At the same time, the emphasis on loyalty to the state and to the emperor encouraged an extreme form of nationalism, which led to a policy of imperialist expansion.

THE NATURE OF JAPAN'S MODERNIZATION

Results of modernization

Japan's efforts at modernization were highly successful. She emerged as a strong national state with a centralized bureaucratic government. The rapid growth of industry and commerce brought about a stable economy. In a few decades, Japan was transformed from a developing country into a highly industrialized one, a process which took a much longer time even among the Western powers. Business boomed in the 1880s and in the years following the Japanese victories in the wars with China and Russia. In foreign trade, the value of her exports exceeded that of her imports by 1883. After 1894, however, the trend was reversed, because she needed

The craze for Western-style clothes

machinery and raw materials for her industries. Economic expansion would have been more spectacular if there had not been a rapid growth of population, which rose from 35 million in 1873 to 46 million in 1903.

The improvement of transport and communications, mainly through railways and telegraph lines, transformed Japan into a compact geographical unit which made it easier to defend the country against domestic uprisings and foreign invasion.

Reform in education produced a high degree of literacy. However, the ultra-nationalistic feeling developed by the educational system was to have disastrous consequences in the years ahead.

By 1899, all the Western powers had given up extraterritorial rights in Japan. The Anglo-Japanese Alliance of 1902, which was concluded on equal terms, showed further that she had achieved equality with the Western powers. She recovered tariff autonomy with the signing of a treaty with the United States in 1911. The unequal treaty system in Japan thus came to an end.

Furthermore, the success of her military strengthening resulted in an aggressive foreign policy. After her victory in the Sino-Japanese War of 1894-95, her intervention in the Boxer Rising of 1900, and her victory in the Russo-Japanese War of 1904-05, she was fully recognized as a world power.

Westernization, a surface reform

At first it seemed that the Japanese, during the Meiji era, had given up their traditional beliefs and institutions one after another in favour of Western models. There were many examples of Westernization: railways, shipping lines, telegraph lines, a postal service, foreign-style factories, improved agricultural methods, a central bank, currency reform, legal reforms, translations of Western books, the adoption of the Western calendar, an abundance of newspapers, gas lights, electric lights, the wearing of Western-style suits, Western-style haircuts, Victorian-style buildings — the list seems almost endless. Nevertheless, the Japanese remained essentially Japanese. Whatever changes were introduced were largely shaped by the past. This was understandable, because the leaders of the early Meiji era were men brought up in the feudal atmosphere of pre-restoration days.

Although feudalism was abolished and replaced by a civil administration based on Western models, the former feudal class still dominated Japanese politics. The emperor's advisers, for example, who exercised real authority, were former samurai from the western clans.

As for the system of government, the Constitution of 1889 would seem to show that the Western idea of representative government had gained wide acceptance. The Charter Oath did promise, though in very general terms, a government based on public opinion. However, this 'opinion' turned out to be the opinion of a small group of permanent advisers to the throne — the *Genro*. This was government by a few, in other words, an oligarchy. It was not very different from the aristocratic shogunate rule. In fact, traditional Japanese political principles formed the basis of the constitution. There is much evidence to support this statement.

Firstly, Japan had a strong tradition of unquestioning obedience to authority, and such a country could not turn into a liberal democracy within a few years. The new educational system fostered this idea of submission by emphasizing loyalty to the state and the emperor. Hence nationalism, rather than liberalism, determined political

development in Japan. So, when Ito went abroad to study Western constitutional systems, he was not looking for one that would change Japan's entire political structure, but one that would suit Japanese nationalistic feeling. The Prussian constitution, with its emphasis on a strong monarchy and militarism, proved to be the most suitable for Japan.

As the oligarchs were determined to keep their power and position, many of the provisions in the constitution limited representative government. The emperor was given broad executive powers. There was no universal suffrage. Only adult males paying 15 yen or more in taxes could vote. The powers of the diet were limited, as it had no absolute control over the cabinet or the budget. Above all, the constitution could not be criticized, for it was the emperor's gift to the people. It was not drawn up by the people's representatives.

Political parties were formed, but they never really gained the power and influence that such parties had in the West. They could not function effectively because of the limited powers of the House of Representatives, the only elected body in the national government.

In education, the Japanese established a school system organized on Western lines. They also introduced compulsory primary education and education for women. But the aims of education remained basically Japanese; as we have seen, the Imperial Rescript on Education of 1890 urged the people to be loyal to the state and not to give up their native traditions.

Religion, too, was made a tool of the state. In the early years of the restoration, the Bureau of Shinto Religion was the most important of all the government departments. Shintoism, which stressed the divine nature of the emperor and patriotism, became the state religion. Owing to the opposition of Shinto supporters, Christianity never had much influence in Japan, though it was tolerated from 1873 onwards.

In industry, the Japanese did not follow the doctrine of *laissez faire*, which was popular in the West. The government's sponsorship of industrialization and its alliance with the *zaibatsu* made it difficult for the individual capitalist to start his own business.

In strengthening her defences, Japan developed a Western-style national army and navy. However, the powerful position of military leaders in the government was not characteristic of most of the Western nations.

Thus the society that arose during the Meiji era cannot be described as truly Western. As one recent book has put it, 'It was a peculiarly Japanese product coloured by Western influence, shaped in some respects by Western forms, and occasionally partaking of the Western spirit; but its intellectual and philosophic foundations were, in the main, Japanese, derived principally from Japanese historic ideals, political and social institutions, and from prevailing conditions within Japan.'

QUESTIONS

1. What were the objectives of Meiji Japan's modernization programme? What were the results of these efforts at modernization?
2. Discuss the steps taken by the Meiji leaders to establish a strong centralized government in Japan.
3. Write a short account of **each** of the following, and explain their importance in the modernization of Japan:
   (a) the Charter Oath
   (b) the abolition of feudalism
   (c) the *zaibatsu*
4. In what ways did the abolition of feudalism in Japan affect Japanese political, social and economic life?
5. What were the post-restoration grievances of the samurai which brought about rebellions after 1874 and culminated in the Satsuma Rebellion of 1877?
6. Trace the events which led to the introduction of the Meiji Constitution of 1889.
7. What were the main features of the Meiji Constitution? To what extent was the constitutional government truly democratic?
8. Give an account of the Meiji economic and social reforms and how they contributed to the modernization of Japan.

9. What industrial and educational developments took place in Japan during the Meiji era? What were their effects on Japan?
10. Give an account of the *zaibatsu*, explaining what they were and why they developed in Meiji Japan. Discuss their influence on Japan's economic life and expansionist policy after 1890.
11. How far did the Constitution of 1889 (Meiji Constitution) contribute to the rise of militarism in Japan?
12. Explain why Japan pursued an aggressive foreign policy from 1890 onwards.
13. 'The Westernization of Japan in the second half of the 19th century was only a surface reform.' Do you agree with this statement?
14. Compare and contrast the efforts of China and Japan to strengthen themselves in the second half of the 19th century by imitating Western methods.
15. Why did Japan succeed in strengthening herself in the second half of the 19th century while China remained weak?

The chief aim of China and Japan in imitating Western methods was to strengthen themselves against foreign aggression. Japan succeeded in establishing a strong national state and became a world power, but China remained weak. There is no simple explanation for this, but the following factors may help to explain it.

Over the long years of the seclusion period, internal developments were already preparing Japan for the rapid modernization that took place during the Meiji era. Among these were the revival of interest in Western learning; the growth of national consciousness; and the tremendous expansion of commerce and industry, which was accompanied by the rise of a commercial and money economy, the growth of towns and cities, and the rise of a rich capitalist class. In contrast, the political, economic and social conditions in China during the same period remained more or less the same, because of the traditional fear of change.

The Middle Kingdom idea had given the Chinese a strong sense of cultural superiority, which encouraged a strong anti-foreign attitude. The Chinese therefore found it difficult to accept the idea of learning from the 'barbarian' West. In contrast, the Japanese had been cultural borrowers for centuries. Much of their early culture was derived from the Chinese. Because of this respect for foreign learning, they saw nothing wrong in absorbing Western ideas and methods. Since the Japanese leaders were better informed about Western science and technology because of Dutch learning at Deshima, they immediately saw the advantages of employing Western arms and military experts. The Chinese leaders, however, were slow to recognize this fact.

Moreover, Chinese scholar-officials looked upon Westernization as a threat to their prestige and privileged position. They had gained power and influence because of their knowledge of the Confucian classics. Many of Japan's high-ranking officials, on the other hand, rose to power because of their familiarity with Western learning.

China's failure to drive out the foreigners convinced the Japanese that reform was a more effective weapon than war.

After the suppression of the Taiping Rebellion, the Beijing government found it difficult to regain control of the provinces, because of the rise and growth of provincial and regional armies. Decentralization set in. There was therefore no strong central government to carry out modernization. Japan had a strong national and centralized government which was committed to modernization. Japan was also much smaller in area than China, so communication between the central and local authorities was not as great a problem. This made the task of nationwide modernization easier for her than for China.

Moreover, the strong tradition of obedience to authority, an effect of Shintoism and the worship of the emperor, made it easier for the Japanese leaders to carry out their plan for modernization.

Japan's geographical isolation fostered a strong sense of national identity. She was therefore in a better position than China to develop as a modern nation state. This national consciousness gave the Japanese a more compelling reason to advocate and accept reform, in order to make them strong enough to resist further foreign pressure.

Chapter 11
The First Sino-Japanese War, 1894-95

SINO-JAPANESE RIVALRY IN KOREA

The Korean problem

Since the time of the Tang dynasty, Korea had been China's most important tributary state, though the relationship, as China herself described it, was one of dependence but no control. Over the centuries, Korean tribute missions were sent regularly to Beijing. For some time, too, before and after the Japanese invasion of Korea in the late 16th century, tribute missions were sent to Edo. In 1636 the Manzhu conquered Korea, but kept the ruling Yi dynasty (1392-1910) in power and seldom interfered in her internal affairs. China did not take an active interest in Korea until the second half of the 19th century, when her 'Confucian' control there was threatened by the attempts of the Western powers and Japan to penetrate the country.

In 1866, France, using as an excuse the murder of some French missionaries and their converts, tried without success to establish relations with Korea. Two years later, a similar attempt by the United States also failed. The Americans made a more determined effort in 1871 by sending an expedition to Korea, just as they sent Perry to Japan. Nothing was achieved.

Japan was the first nation to succeed in penetrating the 'Hermit Kingdom'. For Japan, the development of relations with Korea was not the only important aim. She had always considered the kingdom vital to her security because of its geographical position; it was 'a dagger pointed at the heart of Japan' if controlled by a hostile power. It could also provide her with a bridge to the continent, from which she could attack China or check Russian ambitions in Manchuria. Moreover, acquiring Korea would make up for the loss of prestige Japan suffered when she was forced to resume contact with the West.

The constant unrest in Korea which was caused by rivalry among political groups was also a nuisance to the Japanese government, particularly because Japan was then trying to stabilize herself. Japan's constitutional government was not functioning as smoothly as expected, because of the opposition of the political parties in the diet. It was felt that foreign expansion, such as the invasion of Korea, would gain support for the government and unify the country. At the same time, the unstable political conditions in Korea invited foreign intervention, which might endanger Japan's security. Economically, Korea could provide Japan with raw materials for her developing industries, a ready market for her surplus products, and land and food for her rapidly growing population.

Japan's policy in Korea was naturally opposed by China, as she claimed that the kingdom was her vassal state. A peaceful solution to the problem was unlikely, because

Japanese ultra-nationalists were determined to conquer territory on the Asian mainland. For a time, their attempts at territorial expansion were checked by moderates of the ruling oligarchy, who wanted to establish internal order and unity. The ultra-nationalists eventually won in 1894 because of the steady growth of nationalism and the rapid progress of modernization. China was unwilling to go out of her way to arrive at a peaceful settlement. In the 1880s there was a very conservative and anti-foreign group at Beijing which believed that China was strong enough to defeat Japan if there was war. Continued interference in Korean affairs by both countries eventually led to war.

Events leading to war

Under the restoration government, in 1868, 1869 and 1872, Japanese envoys were sent to Korea to negotiate a treaty establishing relations with that country. Not only was their request refused, but they were also insulted by the Koreans. The more aggressive Japanese leaders like Saigo and Itagaki, who favoured immediate expansion to the mainland, demanded war to avenge the insult. In 1873 they obtained the emperor's approval to send a military expedition to Korea. Through this foreign venture, they also hoped to appease the discontented samurai by employing them in the war. However, the invasion plan was abandoned because of

opposition from the returning members of the Iwakura mission, which had gone abroad in 1871 to study the West and to try to obtain treaty revision. Internal improvements, they pointed out, should come first.

An incident in 1875 gave Japan an excuse to force Korea to negotiate. A Japanese warship which was surveying the Korean coast was fired upon by the Koreans. Japan immediately sent a mission to Beijing, and another one accompanied by a strong naval force to Korea, to demand satisfaction. China denied responsibility for the incident, and allowed Japan to deal directly with Korea. This was a mistake which would later make it difficult for China to reassert her authority over Korea.

In 1876 Korea signed the Treaty of Kanghwa with Japan, agreeing to establish diplomatic relations with Japan and to open two ports to Japanese trade in addition to Pusan, where Japanese were already allowed to reside. But the most significant clause was Japan's recognition of Korea's independence which implied that Korea was no longer tributary to China.

Realizing the implication of this clause but unable to correct it, China decided to limit Japanese influence at Seoul by opening Korea to the Western powers. With Chinese assistance, the United States, Britain, Germany, Italy and France signed similar treaties with Korea between 1882 and 1886. In all these treaties, the independence of Korea was recognized despite the claim of Li Hongzhang, who had been put in charge of Korean affairs, that she was a dependency of China. So, instead of protecting the country from the Japanese, the treaties helped them to gain control later, for they strengthened the Japanese claim that Korea was independent.

Factional struggles in the Korean court were an important cause of further friction between China and Japan. At the time the Western powers and Japan were trying to penetrate Korea, a bitter struggle for power was going on in Korea. The main contestants were the queen's faction (*Min*) which favoured opening up the country and was friendly to Japan, and the conservative and anti-foreign faction (*Yi*) of the regent, Taewongun (Grand Prince), father of the boy-king Kojong (1864-1907). When the king came of age, he fell more and more under the influence of the *Min* faction.

Treaty of Chemulpo

In 1882 the conservatives led by Taewongun arranged an anti-foreign uprising. Riots broke out in Seoul, during which the Japanese legation was burned and the Japanese were driven away. Both China and Japan sent troops to Korea to restore order. When Chinese and Japanese troops came face to face, war seemed imminent. But China could not afford to go to war at this time, because of her trouble with France over Vietnam (see Chapter 6). To show the Japanese that she did not want war, she punished Taewongun by taking him away to Tianjin. This move also had the advantage of keeping Taewongun safe until China could make use of him. (Three years later, China sent him back to Korea to oppose the pro-Russian faction in the Korean court.)

Japan then demanded reparation for the attack from Korea. The crisis was settled when Japan and Korea signed the Treaty of Chemulpo (now Inchon) in 1882. The Japanese obtained from Korea a promise to punish those who had attacked them; an apology and an indemnity; and the right to have legation guards at Seoul and to travel inland. These concessions increased Japan's influence in Korea. Not to be outdone, Li Hongzhang ignored the independence clause of the Treaty of Kanghwa. He stationed six Chinese battalions in Korea and sent Yuan Shikai to Seoul to train the Korean army. Yuan was later appointed Chinese Resident in Korea in 1885, a post he held until 1894. Li also arranged for the appointment of a German as Inspector-General of Korean Customs. A Chinese official was appointed to supervise trade.

All this was confusing to the Westerners. China claimed she was the overlord of Korea, and yet Japan negotiated directly with the Korean government. Korea, too, admitted she was dependent on China, and yet she seemed to be running her affairs independently.

The Li-Ito Convention

After 1882, the character of the factional struggle in Korea changed. The *Min* faction became conservative and pro-Chinese; while a group of reformers, the Progressives, looked to Japan for help and advice. In 1884, when China was busy in the war with France over Vietnam, the Progressives led by Kim Ok-kyun took advantage of the situation, and seized the king with the help of Japanese troops. Chinese troops led by Yuan came to his rescue and succeeded in driving away the Japanese. Kim fled to Japan. Again, the Japanese legation was burned. By a convention signed in 1885, Korea apologized to Japan, paid an indemnity, and agreed to rebuild the Japanese legation quarters.

The events of 1884 convinced China and Japan that they had to come to an agreement over their conflicting interests in Korea. Neither was as yet prepared to go to war over the Korean issue. In Japan, modernization was more important than foreign wars. China was confident she could tighten her control over Korea in time.

The Treaty of Tianjin (Li-Ito Convention) of 1885 temporarily settled the issue. Both countries were to withdraw their troops from Korea within four months, leaving the Koreans free to reorganize their army without Chinese or Japanese assistance. If further disturbances took place, neither country would send troops to Korea without notifying the other in writing. Japan gained a partial diplomatic victory with this treaty, since it limited the freedom of China to intervene in

Korean affairs, and therefore strengthened the Japanese argument that Korea was independent. In spite of the treaty, both countries strengthened their hold on Korea. Such rivalry could only lead to war.

So long as the struggle for control was with China only, Japan could still afford to wait. In the 1880s, however, a series of Russian moves alarmed the Japanese. To them, Russia, not China, was the real obstacle to their ambitions in Korea. As early as 1861, Russian marines had occupied Tsushima, an island between Korea and Japan, but they had been forced to leave because of British opposition. In 1884 Russia made an agreement with Korea, allowing her to use an ice-free port on the Korean east coast in exchange for training the Korean army. The Chinese, supported by the British, put pressure on the Korean king not to carry out the plan, and the agreement was rejected. In 1888, Russia obtained a commercial treaty

with Korea. In 1891, when Russia announced her plan to build the Trans-Siberian Railway, Japan realized she had to act quickly to bring about a crisis with China over the Korean question. Korea had to be brought under her control or, at least, recognized as an independent state. Only this could stop Russia's eastward expansion. Since China was unwilling to give up her domination of Korea, war was the only solution left.

THE WAR

Outbreak of hostilities

The immediate cause of the war was the rebellion of the *Tonghak* (eastern learning), an anti-foreign and anti-government religious group, in March 1894. When the Koreans requested aid to suppress the rebellion, China sent a small force (1500 men) to Korea in June after notifying Japan in accordance with the Li-Ito Convention. Japan's reaction was to send a larger force (7000 men), claiming that her subjects there needed protection. What she really feared was that China might gain complete control in Korea.

Events later proved that foreign troops were not needed, as the Korean government itself managed to suppress the uprising. Consequently, China proposed a simultaneous withdrawal of Chinese and Japanese troops. Li and Yuan expected Japan to accept the proposal; they believed that she would not make war because of political disunity at home. Japan refused, for she now felt strong enough to go to war and was determined to use the situation to make war. Anti-Chinese feelings had already been aroused in Japan by the murder in early 1894 of Kim, who had led the *coup d'etat* of 1884. He had been persuaded to go to Shanghai, where he was killed by a pro-Chinese Korean. The Chinese authorities then sent his body back to Seoul, where it was quartered and exhibited in public.

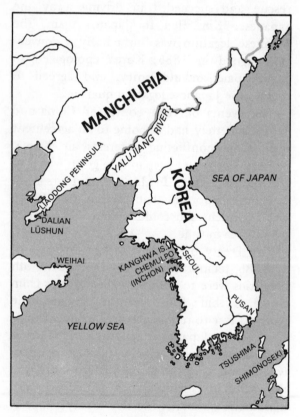

Korea in 1894-95

The sinking of the Gaosheng

Japan, determined to gain control in Korea, proposed to China that they jointly carry out reforms. China refused, saying that Korea should be given freedom of action to start her own reforms. Japan then presented the Korean king with a programme of reforms, and asked him to carry them out. When she did not receive a satisfactory answer to her demand, Japanese troops seized the royal palace on July 23, and Japan set up a new Korean government. This government then asked the Japanese to expel the Chinese troops. Two days later, the Japanese sank the *Gaosheng*, a Chinese troop-ship under British registration which was carrying reinforcements to Korea. Anti-Japanese feeling in China was aroused by the Japanese action, particularly since war had not yet been officially declared. War had now become inevitable. On 1 August 1894, Japan declared war on China.

The course of the war

To neutral observers, Japan's defeat seemed certain, but they were wrong. Although Japan's army and navy were much smaller than China's, they were far superior. Many Chinese soldiers were still armed with spears or swords.

The Japanese Imperial Army easily drove the Chinese troops out of Korea across the Yalujiang River. However, the decisive battles were fought at sea, not on land. Without railways, China could only reinforce her troops in the battle zones by sea. Japan's strategy therefore was to control the North China waters to prevent the shipment of Chinese reinforcements. This was achieved in September, when the Japanese Imperial Navy inflicted a crushing blow on the Beiyang fleet in the Battle of the Yellow Sea. Japanese gunfire was faster and more accurate. The

A 19th-century Chinese soldier

A Japanese force then crossed the Yalu into Manchuria. A second force which landed on the Liaodong Peninsula (Guandong), captured Lushun in November and swept across south Manchuria. In early 1895, Weihai, where the Beiyang fleet was confined, surrendered to the Japanese. The two Japanese armies in Manchuria joined up and were soon moving towards Beijing. Japan's spectacular military victories surprised the world.

Peace negotiations

When it appeared that nothing could stop the Japanese from advancing to Beijing, the Chinese asked for peace. As a price for an armistice, Japan asked for the cession of three cities in northern China, the payment of a huge indemnity, and the granting of special privileges to Japanese subjects in the interior of China. Li Hongzhang found the conditions too harsh and rejected them. He nevertheless went to Shimonoseki to seek less severe terms. An unsuccessful attempt on Li's life by a Japanese fanatic persuaded the Japanese government to moderate its demands; such an attack on an official peace negotiator was a serious violation of international law. It could bring Western intervention, which might deprive Japan of the benefits of her victory.

Although the modified version of the Japanese demands was still severe, Li could not obtain any further changes. On 17 April 1895, Li and Ito signed the Treaty of Shimonoseki, officially ending the First Sino-Japanese War.

China's defeat showed the limited effect of her self-strengthening movement. Despite her efforts to modernize her army and navy, these remained weak and disorganized. In contrast, Japan's military and naval forces, though smaller, were well equipped and efficiently organized — proof of how successful Japan's modernization programme was.

Chinese also ran out of ammunition. If Cixi had not misused the funds for strengthening the Chinese navy, they might have had a better chance against the Japanese.

CHINA'S NUMERICAL SUPERIORITY

The army of Japan upon a war footing is only 120 000 men, while the Viceroy Li alone has 50 000 foreign drilled troops armed with modern arms, and of fine discipline and efficiency. Besides these there are many thousand foreign-drilled troops in other parts of the empire, and a practically inexhaustible supply of the old fashioned native soldiery.

— *Charles Denby, American minister at Beijing, 1894*

JAP THE GIANT-KILLER.

How the British viewed Japan's victory in 1895

RESULTS OF THE WAR

The Treaty of Shimonoseki

By the Treaty of Shimonoseki, Japan gained many advantages. China recognized the full independence of Korea, ending its tributary status; Japan could now strengthen her influence in Korea. She immediately put pressure on the Korean government to carry out a reform programme, in the hope that Korea would become a stable buffer state. The Koreans, however, opposed modernization. With the support of Russia, the king cancelled all the reforms. From then on, the struggle for the control of Korea would be between Japan and Russia.

China opened several new treaty ports on the Changjiang River and on the Grand Canal. Most-favoured-nation treatment and extra-

territorial rights were granted to Japan. China had to pay an indemnity of 200 million taels of silver, which was of great economic benefit to Japan. Japan was to occupy Weihai until the indemnity was paid, and until a Sino-Japanese treaty of commerce was signed.

Formosa, the Pescadores, and the Liaodong Peninsula were ceded to Japan permanently. The first two gave Japan control over a chain of islands stretching from southern Japan to the waters of southern China; the third gave Japan her first piece of territory on the continent. However, not long after the conclusion of the treaty, Russia, France and Germany presented a joint note to Japan, demanding the restoration of the Liaodong to China. Russia, who led this Triple Intervention, claimed that Japan's possession of the territory threatened Beijing, the independence of Korea, and the peace of East Asia.

187

THE COREAN COCK-FIGHT.

Bruin. "HA!—WHICHEVER WINS, I SEE MY WAY TO A DINNER!"

How Russia saw the Sino-Japanese War

Russia did this partly because she was afraid that Japan's establishment on the mainland would block her own expansion to the south, and partly because she hoped China would grant her more privileges as a reward for her help. The three powers threatened military action if Japan did not do as they demanded. Exhausted financially and militarily, Japan could not afford another war so soon. Reluctantly, she gave in, but on one condition: China was to pay her an additional indemnity of 30 million taels. (China later obtained a loan from Russia to pay off the indemnity.)

Other results of the war

The revelation of Japan's strength and China's weakness upset the international balance of power. Thereafter, any foreign power which wanted to put pressure on China would have to take Japan into consideration.

The Sino-Japanese commercial treaty of 1896 made Japan equal with the Western powers in China; she gained the same privileges. In addition, she gained the right to engage in manufacture and industry in the treaty ports, a right not previously granted to the Westerners. Japanese products manufactured in the interior of China were to be exempt from tax. This concession was also granted to the other treaty powers, and it proved disastrous for China's economy. She would not have a chance to develop her own industry.

The Triple Intervention made the Japanese bitter against the Russians, and this bitterness was increased in 1898 when Russia herself obtained a 25-year lease of the Liaodong Peninsula. Thus Japan and Russia were brought nearer to armed conflict over Manchuria as well as Korea. However, Britain's policy of non-intervention during and after the war pleased Japan; this resulted in closer ties which led to the Anglo-Japanese Alliance of 1902.

In Japan, victory justified the arguments of those who favoured militarism and expansionism. The prestige of the army and navy increased. An armaments programme was launched to make Japan a leading military power. This stimulated economic, industrial and financial activities. The value of foreign trade increased; merchant shipping, shipbuilding and navigation made rapid progress. Victory and the territorial gains also stimulated Japan's national pride. However, when Japan was forced to return the Liaodong Peninsula, public opinion turned against the government. The pre-war conflict between the cabinet and the diet was resumed.

As for China, her loss of control over Korea meant that the old Confucian theory of foreign relations was finally destroyed. Since she no longer possessed tributary states, the Middle Kingdom concept was abandoned and replaced by Western ideas on treaties and international law.

Her defeat showed how weak and corrupt the Manzhu government had become, and how limited the effect of the self-strengthening movement was. After the war, China lost her superior position in East Asia to Japan. Many Chinese leaders were now convinced that the strengthening of their country could not be achieved merely by imitating Western military and industrial methods. Kang Youwei advocated reforms (Hundred Days' Reform) more thorough than those attempted before the war. The Manzhu also launched their own reform programme, but the reforms came too late and the Manzhu government was overthrown by the 1911 Revolution. Some, like Sun Yixian, felt that the Manzhu regime had become useless, and so they advocated revolution.

But the most disastrous result of the war for China was the 'scramble for concessions' (see Chapter 7). This came as a result of the exposure of China's weakness, and fear among the Western powers of Japan's ambitions in China. Before the war the interests of the powers, except Russia, were mainly commercial; after the war their interests also became territorial and financial. The 'slicing of the China melon' began. Between 1895 and 1899, the treaty powers each obtained exclusive economic concessions from China.

The Sino-Japanese War of 1894-95, therefore, had very important results for Japan and China. On the one hand, it put Japan on the road to world power status; on the other hand, the 'scramble for concessions' that followed it led to the near-partition of China and the Boxer Rising. She managed to save herself mainly because she played off one power against the other.

QUESTIONS

1. How did Sino-Japanese rivalry in Korea lead to war in 1894?
2. Account for the outbreak of the Sino-Japanese War of 1894-95. What were the effects of Japan's victory in the war on Sino-Western relations up to 1898?
3. Trace the events which led to the outbreak of the Sino-Japanese War of 1894-95, and examine the consequences of the war.
4. How far were economic and strategic factors responsible for the outbreak of the Sino-Japanese War of 1894-95?
5. Write a short account of **each** of the following with reference to the Sino-Japanese War of 1894-95:
   (a) the Treaty of Chemulpo (1882)
   (b) the Li-Ito Convention (1885)
   (c) the Treaty of Shimonoseki (1895)
   (d) the Triple Intervention (1895)
6. How do you explain Japan's victory in the Sino-Japanese War of 1894-95?
7. To what extent was the Sino-Japanese War of 1894-95 responsible for the 'scramble for concessions' in China?

The cause of the Sino-Japanese War of 1894-95 (also called the First Sino-Japanese War) was rivalry between China and Japan in Korea. Both claimed Korea as their vassal state; both regarded her as vital to their security. Their continued interference in the affairs of Korea finally resulted in war. Japanese victory in the war startled the world, for it was generally believed that China was much stronger than Japan. It also showed how successful Japan's modernization programme was and how limited were the effects of China's 'self-strengthening movement'.

The war had far-reaching consequences for Japan, China and the foreign powers. For Japan, it was the first step in her expansionist ambitions in China, and victory marked her rise as a world power. Fear of Japan's penetration of China after her victory was one of the main reasons why the Western powers started the 'scramble for concessions'. Since the Japanese were determined to increase their influence in Korea, they were bound to clash with the Russians who also had ambitions in Korea and Manchuria. The Triple Intervention led by Russia also angered Japan. War finally broke out between them in 1904.

For China, her defeat and the exposure of her weakness led to the 'scramble for concessions' and her near-partition. China's response to the foreign threat can be seen in the Hundred Days' Reform, the Boxer Rising and the Qing reform programme, all of which failed. This chain reaction of events, together with the growth of Sun Yixian's revolutionary movement, finally culminated in the 1911 Revolution.

Chapter 12
The Russo-Japanese War and its aftermath

After her victory in the Sino-Japanese War of 1894-95, Japan increased her efforts to achieve world power status.

In 1898, as we have seen, Japan asked for and received assurances from China that Fujian would not be ceded to another power. By 1899, the Western powers were satisfied with the progress of Japan's judicial reforms and gave up their extraterritorial rights. Japanese intervention in the Boxer Rising helped to establish her claim to equality with the other nations, for Japan enjoyed all the rights and privileges granted by China to the foreign powers in the Boxer settlement. The Anglo-Japanese Alliance of 1902 raised her prestige in international politics, for it was the first treaty in modern times signed by a Western power with an Asian country on equal terms.

Her victory in the Russo-Japanese War of 1904-05 established beyond doubt that Japan had achieved world power status. The war was a direct result of the rivalry between Russia and Japan for the control of Korea and Manchuria.

RUSSO-JAPANESE RIVALRY

Conflicting interests in Korea and Manchuria

With her expansion in Europe delayed by military and diplomatic defeats in 1856

(Crimean War) and in 1878 (Treaty of Berlin), Russia had steadily pushed her frontiers eastward at the expense of China. Earlier, Russia had established posts on the north bank of the Heilongjiang River (Amur River). In 1858, she acquired the Heilongjiang River frontier, and in 1860, the Maritime Province, where she later established the naval base of Vladivostok. In 1861, serfdom was abolished in Russia. Many of the freed peasants migrated to Siberia. In 1875 the island of Sakhalin, which had been jointly occupied by Russia and Japan, was taken over completely by Russia. In 1884 Korea agreed to let Russian warships use a port on her east coast in exchange for Russian help in training her army. But owing to Chinese and British objections, the plan was not carried out. In 1888 Russia signed a commercial treaty with Korea. In 1891 she started building the Trans-Siberian Railway, which was completed in 1903. Because of the strategic and economic importance of this railway, the tsarist government encouraged Russian settlements along the railway lines. All these moves made Japan suspicious of Russian territorial ambitions in Korea and Manchuria.

There were several reasons for Russia's interest in Korea and Manchuria. One very important factor was her long search for a warm-water port. Her earlier efforts to obtain such a port in the Mediterranean had been blocked consistently by Britain, and she was therefore determined to obtain one in north-east Asia. As Vladivostok was ice-bound in winter, she looked towards the ice-free ports of Lüshun (Port Arthur) and Dalian (Dairen), which she later obtained from China.

Russia also realized that to complete the Trans-Siberian Railway on her own soil would be expensive and inconvenient. If the railway could cut across Manchuria to the sea, construction costs could be kept down. Manchuria's rich natural resources, too, were very attractive.

In addition, when Russia acquired control of the Liaodong Peninsula, she wished to extend her influence in Korea. This was to prevent any hostile power from building fortifications that might threaten Russian communication by sea from Lüshun and Dalian to Vladivostok. Russian control of Korea and Manchuria, therefore, was vital to her interests in Asia.

Japan, too, was determined to expand her control in Korea and Manchuria, since both areas were vital to her economy and security. Moreover, the growth of Japanese militarism was accompanied by a strong desire for expansion. Korea and Manchuria were the two most likely targets for Japanese territorial ambitions, because of their nearness to Japan. Colonial expansion would also raise Japanese hopes of obtaining recognition as a world power. Japan therefore feared Russian penetration of Korea and Manchuria.

The contest for Korea

Japan hoped to strengthen her influence in Korea by introducing reforms similar to those of her own modernization programme. When the Japanese occupied Seoul in July 1894, they restored Taewongun to power, hoping that he would take the lead in carrying out reforms under Japanese supervision. But they soon discovered that he was interested only in taking power for himself. Immediately after the war, reforms were introduced by the Japanese minister to Korea, with the help of pro-Japanese Korean reformers. However, their efforts at reform were blocked by the conservatives, led by the Korean queen. In desperation, the Japanese hatched a plot with Taewongun in October 1895, which resulted in the murder of 'Queen Min' and the seizure of the Korean king. The Koreans were angry at Japan's part in the plot.

In February 1896, the king managed to escape, and fled for safety to the Russian legation. For a year or two, Japanese influence in Korea was overshadowed by that of Russia, for the king turned to the Russians for advice, and granted them timber and mining concessions. All this increased Japanese hostility towards Russia. Japan had succeeded in ending Chinese influence in Korea, only to see it replaced by Russian, not Japanese, influence.

Two attempts were made through negotiation to put an end to Russo-Japanese rivalry in Korea. Under the Yamagata-Lobanov Protocol of 5 June 1896, both powers agreed that they would enjoy equal rights and privileges in Korea, withdraw their troops from the country, and press the Korean government to carry out financial reform.

As soon as the protocol was signed, however, Russia began to violate its terms. She sent advisers to help reorganize the Korean army; at the same time, the Japanese-trained forces were disbanded. Russia also obtained the agreement of the Korean government to a proposal that a Russian should be appointed to take charge of Korean finances.

When the Koreans saw that their country was in danger of being dominated by Russia, they began to resist Russian influence. In view of Korean as well as Japanese opposition, Russia decided to negotiate another agreement with Japan. On 28 April 1898, the two powers signed the Nishi-Rosen Convention, recognizing the independence of Korea and agreeing not to assist Korea in reorganizing her army and her finances. Russia also promised not to oppose the development of Japanese commercial and industrial interests in Korea.

Despite these two agreements, Russo-Japanese rivalry in Korea continued. Japan vigorously promoted her economic interests in the country, while Russia tried to check Japanese influence. After the Boxer Rising, Japan proposed the division of Korea into Japanese and Russian spheres of influence, with the 38th parallel as the dividing line, but Russia rejected the proposal. The struggle for Korea ended only after Japan had defeated Russia in war.

Russian penetration of Manchuria

After 1895, Russia strengthened her position in Manchuria in several ways. The Russo-Chinese Bank was established. The Trans-Siberian Railway was extended by building the Chinese Eastern Railway across Manchuria through Harbin to the Maritime Province, and by the South Manchurian Railway linking it with Lüshun and Dalian. A 25-year lease of the tip of the Liaodong Peninsula was acquired in 1898, and this in particular embittered the Japanese against Russia. This was because Japan had acquired this very same territory after her victory in the Sino-Japanese War, but had been forced to return it to China as a result of the Triple Intervention led by Russia.

The outbreak of the Boxer Rising gave Russia a perfect opportunity to tighten her hold on Manchuria. While the other powers were busy dealing with the rising, Russia poured troops into Manchuria, supposedly to keep the peace and protect her rights in the area. She promised to withdraw them as soon as order was restored. In fact, she had no intention of keeping her promise, as later events showed.

In November 1900, the Russian governor-general of the Liaodong Peninsula forced the viceroy of Shenyang (Mukden) to sign a draft agreement which, if ratified, would make Manchuria a Russian protectorate. When the agreement was made public, the United States raised strong objections, as it was against the Open Door policy. The Chinese government itself refused to ratify the agreement, so it was dropped. In February 1901, Russia again tried to negotiate an agreement with China which would make Manchuria a Russian protectorate. Once again the idea was dropped after protests from Britain, the United States and Germany, whose commercial interests in China would be threatened by a Russian occupation of Manchuria. France did not protest because she had been an ally of Russia since 1893 (the Dual Alliance).

The Anglo-Japanese Alliance, 1902

To oppose Russian ambitions in Manchuria and Korea, Japan and Britain entered into an alliance on 30 January 1902. It is understandable that Japan should be keen to form such an alliance, but Britain's choice of Japan as an ally needs some explanation.

At the turn of the century, Britain had realized that her traditional policy of 'splendid isolation' had become unrealistic. The Boer War of 1899-1902 had taught her a lesson, for no power had supported her. Faced with the problem of dealing single-handed with Russian and French hostility, and with a German challenge to her naval superiority, she badly needed an ally. Having no real friend in Europe, she turned to Japan. Britain was also clever enough to see that modernization had transformed Japan into a strong nation.

The Japanese prime minister announcing the text of the Anglo-Japanese Alliance to the House of Peers

Although Britain and Japan announced that the aim of their alliance was to preserve the *status quo* in East Asia, their real motive was to isolate Russia by preventing France from coming to her assistance in the event of war. The provisions of the Anglo-Japanese alliance were as follows:

- Both powers agreed to respect the independence and integrity of China and Korea but recognized Britain's special interests in central China and Japan's special interests in Korea.
- In the event of disturbances in China or Korea, each would take action to protect its interests.
- Each promised to maintain strict neutrality if the other was at war, and to come to the assistance of the party at war if another power joined its enemy.
- The alliance was to remain in force for five years in the first instance.

The Anglo-Japanese Alliance was significant in many ways. It slowed down, at least temporarily, the Russian penetration of Manchuria. The Open Door policy suffered a setback, for the recognition of special interests in China and Korea by both parties meant recognizing that spheres of influence actually existed.

The alliance marked Britain's abandonment of her 'splendid isolation'. The alliance set a precedent for Britain, and she was soon drawn into the system of alliances in Europe, an involvement which led to her participation in the First World War. With Japan as an ally, Britain could now move some of her warships from East Asia to Europe to meet the challenge of the fast-growing German navy.

For the Japanese, this alliance with a Western power on equal terms restored national pride. It helped them to forget the shame of their submission to the unequal treaty system and the humiliating terms imposed by the Triple Intervention. It increased Japan's international prestige and enhanced her position as a world power.

A point of more immediate significance was that the alliance gave Japan the confidence to challenge Russia, and to wage war, if necessary, without fear of intervention from a third power such as France. If war broke out and Japan won, the alliance guaranteed that Japan would not be deprived of the benefits of victory, as she was by the Triple Intervention.

The last stages of negotiations

Faced by increasing opposition to her occupation of Manchuria, Russia finally signed the Manchurian Convention with China in April 1902. She agreed to withdraw her troops within 18 months in three stages, so that the withdrawal would be completed by October 1903.

The first stage of the evacuation took place as promised but, instead of carrying out the second stage, Russia pressed for further concessions in Manchuria from China. In 1903, a Russian viceroy of the Far East was appointed, with Lüshun as his base. All these moves showed that Russia was determined to stay in Manchuria. The completion of the Chinese Eastern Railway linking St Petersburg with Dalian and Vladivostok in 1903 strengthened the Russian position.

Ultra-nationalist groups in Japan began to press for war against Russia. The Black Dragon Society, for example, was formed in 1901 and aimed to expel the Russians from Manchuria. (In later years, it promoted the idea of 'Asia for the Asians'.) Despite this pressure, the Japanese government still hoped that war could be avoided, if Russia could be persuaded to recognize Korea as a Japanese sphere of influence. In return, Japan would recognize Manchuria as a Russian sphere of influence.

Japan proposed such an arrangement to Russia in August 1903. Russia, however, wanted both Manchuria and Korea. The following month, she presented a counter-proposal which would give her a free hand in dealing with China while offering Japan the right to promote her economic, but not her political, interests in Korea. In January 1904, Japan strongly urged Russia to accept a revised Japanese proposal.

This was practically an ultimatum. The opening of negotiations was purposely delayed by the Russian leaders, who believed that the decision to make war or not lay with them. The Japanese eventually lost their patience. On February 6, Japan broke off diplomatic relations with Russia. That same day, Russian troops crossed the Yalujiang River into Korea.

THE WAR

Outbreak of hostilities

On February 8, two days after diplomatic relations were broken off, the Japanese Imperial Navy made a suprise attack on Lüshun, and the war began. The attack crippled Russia's Pacific Squadron at very little cost to the Japanese fleet. In addition, the rest of the Russian fleet was confined to Lüshun. Japanese troops also landed in Chemulpo, proceeded to Seoul and occupied the city.

On February 10, two days after the first shots were fired, Japan officially declared war on Russia. The effects of the Anglo-Japanese Alliance immediately became clear. Britain granted loans to Japan to help her in her war effort. The other Western powers proclaimed neutrality. China ignored her 1896 alliance with Russia, and also declared her neutrality.

So began the Russo-Japanese War, the first major war of the 20th century. As in the First Sino-Japanese War, neutral observers gave Japan very little chance of defeating mighty Russia. They had overlooked Japan's military preparations and her determination to win; the decaying empire of tsarist Russia provided a sharp contrast. Nevertheless, Russia had the manpower and materials to win, if she could mobilize her resources in time. The Japanese were fully aware of this fact and decided to aim for a quick victory and a quick peace settlement. When the war started, their chances of achieving this objective were good.

Progress of the war

Japan's victory in a bloody battle on the Yalujiang River in May gave her control of all Korea. Even more important, a European power had been defeated in battle by an Asian country. The morale of the Japanese troops rose, for the 'little yellow monkeys' had proved that they could win against the 'invincible White Man'. The Japanese then pushed on towards southern Manchuria. Liaoyang, where Russian forces were concentrated, was captured in September.

Meanwhile, another Japanese army laid siege to Lüshun. Russia feared that what was left of her Pacific Squadron might be captured if the fortress fell. The ships were ordered to break through the Japanese naval

A Russian ship under attack off Lüshun, August 1904 (contemporary picture)

blockade in an attempt to reach Vladivostok. This was the Russian move which the Japanese had been waiting for. In the battle that followed, they defeated the Russian fleet, although the main body slipped through their hands and succeeded in returning to Lüshun. The ships nevertheless fell into Japanese hands when Lüshun surrendered in January 1905 after a seven-month siege.

The last land battle, which turned out to be the largest single action of the war, was fought at Shenyang from February to March. The Japanese defeated the Russian armies.

Defeat at Shenyang seriously affected Russia's hopes of winning the war on land. Two months later, she lost the chance of winning at sea. In June 1904, Nicholas II, realizing that the war was going badly for the Russians, decided to send a fleet to the East; this, he hoped, would destroy Japan's naval superiority and avoid defeat.

The Japanese Army entering Shenyang during the Russo-Japanese War (March 1905)

196

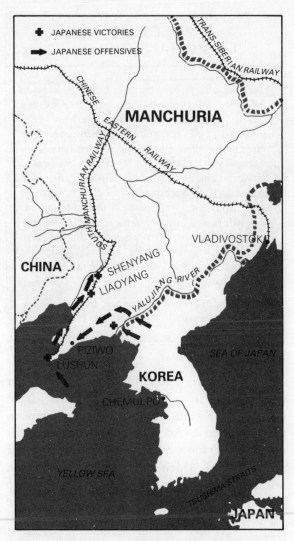

Major engagements of the Russo-Japanese War on land

The Second Pacific Squadron, as it came to be called, consisted of 42 warships. It left the Baltic for the East by way of the Cape of Good Hope, but its 18 000-mile voyage ended only in defeat in the Battle of Tsushima Straits (also known as the Battle of the Sea of Japan) on 27-28 May 1905. Only one cruiser and two small destroyers managed to reach Vladivostok, while a few escaped to neutral Asian cities. The Japanese lost only three torpedo boats.

The Russian armada was much larger than the Japanese fleet, but only four of the Russian warships were new; the rest were out-of-date. Tactical errors and inferior firepower contributed to the Russian defeat. The battle has been described as the greatest sea battle since Trafalgar, and the Japanese victory as the most complete naval victory in history.

Negotiations to end the war

At this stage of the war, the netural powers no longer wished to see the conflict continue. France wanted Russia to be able to fulfil her obligations to the Dual Alliance in Europe. Earlier, Germany had wanted a weak Russia; now she felt that Russia had been weakened enough. Moreover, general discontent was sweeping Russia partly as a result of her disastrous defeats, and revolution was imminent. If Nicholas II was overthrown, the idea of revolution might spread to Germany and threaten Kaiser William's rule. Britain had no wish to see Russia totally weakened. The United States wanted the war to end for humanitarian reasons, and because she desired a continuing Russian presence in East Asia to maintain the balance of power.

Japan and Russia themselves desired peace. True, Japan had gained one victory after another, but large Russian armies still had to be destroyed. The country was already financially exhausted, her resources of manpower and war materials were running low, and her communication and supply lines were already greatly extended. Russia, like Japan, was feeling the financial burden of the war. Moreover, she was having serious political troubles at home, which were heightened by the disastrous war with Japan. Liberals were demanding a share in the government; workers were demanding better working conditions. The country was on the brink of revolution.

At the end of May 1905, Japan requested American mediation in bringing about peace. President Theodore Roosevelt had been waiting for such a request, and agreed to act as mediator. On instructions from Roosevelt, the American ambassador in St Petersburg

197

brought up the matter with the Russian government. The tsar responded favourably. On August 10, peace negotiations began in Portsmouth, New Hampshire.

RESULTS OF THE WAR

The Treaty of Portsmouth

On September 5, the Treaty of Portsmouth was signed. The peace terms included the following:

- Russia agreed to recognize Japan's 'paramount political, military, and economic interests' in Korea.
- Japan acquired control of the Liaodong leasehold, the South Manchurian Railway, and some coal mines operated by the Russians in southern Manchuria. Since Manchuria was Chinese territory, the transfer of all these Russian rights to Japan required the consent of China.
- Russia ceded Karafuto, the southern half of Sakhalin below the 50th parallel, to Japan. (In 1875, Japan had given up claims to Sakhalin, in exchange for full Japanese control of the Kuril Islands.)
- Both countries agreed to withdraw their troops from Manchuria, with the exception of the railway guards.
- Both further agreed not to interfere in the commercial and industrial development of Manchuria by China.
- Railways in Manchuria, with the exception of those in the Liaodong Peninsula, were to be used for commercial and industrial, not political, purposes.

To the disappointment of Japan, Russia refused to pay any indemnity. Japan did not press the matter because she knew that if she did, Russia was prepared to renew the war. This did not stop the Japanese, however, from blaming the United States for what happened.

The Japanese government obtained China's consent to the transfer of Russian rights to Japan in the Sino-Japanese Treaty of Beijing

of 22 December 1905. Japan received further concessions in southern Manchuria from China in an additional agreement signed on the same day. According to the Japanese, secret agreements were also signed, the most significant of which was a promise by China not to allow the building of any railway in Manchuria which might compete with the Japanese-controlled South Manchurian Railway.

On the whole, the Treaty of Portsmouth stopped the Russian penetration of Manchuria and Korea. Japan inherited Russia's special position in southern Manchuria which, together with Korea, became a Japanese sphere of influence. Most of the Western powers were pleased by Japan's victory, but at the same time, they began to fear the rise of a strong Japan, and its possible effects on the balance of power in Asia.

Other results of the war

Quite apart from the terms of the Treaty of Portsmouth, the war had other far-reaching results.

By her victory, Japan had definitely become a world power. In June 1907, France and Japan agreed to support each other in preserving their spheres of influence in China. The following month, Russia and Japan made a similar agreement concerning their respective spheres in Manchuria. Now that Japan had proved how strong she was, the Anglo-Japanese Alliance of 1902 was revised and renewed in 1905 and again in 1911.

In Europe, Russia's defeat prepared the way for the formation of the Triple Entente of Britain, France and Russia in 1907. Britain had nothing more to fear from Russian aggression in East Asia. Japan by herself had shown she could stop Russian expansion in that part of the world.

Japan's acquisition of exclusive privileges in Manchuria and Korea through the Treaty of Portsmouth went against the Open Door policy of the United States. From then on, the friendly relations between the two countries, which had been maintained for 50 years, gradually gave way to friction. Tension was increased by American fear of Japanese ambitions in the Philippines, and by Japanese resentment of racial discrimination on the American West Coast.

Attempts were made to ease the tension. Already in 1905 both powers had signed the Taft-Katsura Agreement: the United States would not interfere with Japanese political control in Korea, once established, and in return, Japan denied any aggressive policies towards the Philippines. In the Root-Takahira Agreement of 1908, both nations pledged to maintain the *status quo* in the Pacific; this again implied that the United States would respect the Japanese position in Korea, and Japan would not interfere with the American position in the Philippines.

When Japan tried to strengthen her new position in southern Manchuria by establishing a monopoly of railway development, the battle for railways in the area began.

In 1907 a British firm obtained China's consent to extend a British-Chinese railway, which had been built in 1902. Japan protested that this railway concession was a violation of one of the secret Sino-Japanese agreements signed in 1905. China, however, did not agree with Japan's interpretation of this secret agreement. Since the Anglo-Japanese Alliance was still in effect, the British government persuaded the British firm to give up the project.

In 1909 the Americans obtained from China the right to build a railway across Manchuria from Jinzhou to Aihui. They followed this up with a suggestion that the entire Manchurian railway system be neutralized; however this 'Knox Neutralization Plan for Manchuria' was rejected by the other powers. The effect of the Knox Plan was to draw Japan and Russia closer together; in 1909, 1911 and 1916, they signed treaties to protect their respective spheres in Manchuria from outside interference.

Not long after the signing of the Treaty of Portsmouth, Japan took steps to tighten her hold on Korea. She had already laid the basis for a protectorate during the war. On 23 February 1904, barely two weeks after the outbreak of war, Korea signed an agreement accepting Japanese advice in matters of government administration.

By the terms of another agreement in August of that year, a Japanese subject was to be appointed financial adviser to the Korean government, and Korea was to consult Japan before signing agreements with any other power. On 18 November 1905, Prince Ito Hirobumi, president of the Privy Council, signed an agreement with the Korean king which made Korea a Japanese protectorate. Japan was to direct Korea's foreign relations; Ito was appointed Resident-General at Seoul.

In 1907, when the Korean king appealed to an international conference at The Hague to put an end to Japanese control, the Japanese forced him to abdicate in favour of his son, Crown Prince Yi. Japan took over the internal administration of Korea.

In 1909, Ito was assassinated at Harbin by a Korean patriot. Unable to tolerate continued Korean opposition, Japan annexed

Korea on 22 August 1910 and renamed it Chosen ('land of the morning calm'). The annexation of Korea was made easier by the Anglo-Japanese Alliance. So long as Britain was on Japan's side, the other powers were less likely to make a determined effort to stop Japanese territorial expansion.

Control of both Korea and the Liaodong Peninsula gave Japan a foothold on the Asian mainland which, in the years ahead, served as a base for new aggression against China.

At home, Japan's victory was followed by an industrial boom. Consumer industries, in particular, enjoyed great prosperity. Victory also strengthened the position of the Japanese militarists, and thus contributed to the growth of militarism.

Although northern Manchuria remained a Russian sphere of influence, Russia's influence in East Asia as a whole suffered a temporary decline. At home, the disastrous war with Japan brought discontent with the autocratic rule of the tsar. There were strikes and uprisings.

Since her plans for expansion in Manchuria and Korea had suffered a setback, Russia began to strengthen her position in Mongolia, which had been a Chinese possession since 1697. Now that Russia was not involved, southern Manchuria became a cause of trouble between Japan and China. Continued friction finally erupted into violence in the Shenyang Incident of 1931.

The war illustrated yet again how weak China was. It was fought not only over the control of a Chinese province, but also on Chinese soil. When the war ended, China stood helplessly by, unable to do anything about the transfer of rights from one power to another in her own territory. The war therefore increased discontent with the Manzhu regime and contributed to the collapse of the dynasty.

Japan's victory further convinced the Chinese of the urgent need for political reform. Since there was a widespread belief that constitutional government had made Japan strong, people thought that a constitutional monarchy would do the same for China. The constitutional movement grew in strength, and Cixi was forced to include representative government in the Manzhu reform programme (see Chapter 8).

Now that China no longer belittled Japan's efforts at modernization, Chinese students poured into Japan to learn from the Japanese. By 1906, there were some 13 000 of them in Japan. While there, they were exposed to Sun Yixian's republican ideas; many of them, including Jiang Jieshi, then a young military cadet from Zhejiang, joined the *Tongmenghui*, Sun's revolutionary organization.

Finally, the revelation that an Asian country could defeat a world power like Russia helped to develop nationalist feeling in other Asian countries, and encouraged opposition to colonial rule. Japan began to consider herself the champion of Asian peoples against Western imperialism. Asian nationalistic hopes, however, would be realized only after the Second World War.

1. Show how Russo-Japanese rivalry in Korea and Manchuria led to the Russo-Japanese War of 1904-05, and examine the consequences of the war.

2. Explain how Russian expansion in East Asia in the second half of the 19th century led to the Russo-Japanese War of 1904-05. How did Japan's victory in the war affect the Western powers in East Asia?

3. Explain why the Anglo-Japanese Alliance of 1902 was signed. What did the two sides gain by signing it?

4. Give an account of **each** of the following agreements with reference to Russo-Japanese relations:
   (a) Yamagata-Lobanov Protocol (1896)
   (b) Nishi-Rosen Convention (1898)
   (c) Anglo-Japanese Alliance (1902)
   (d) Treaty of Portsmouth (1905)

The main cause of the Russo-Japanese War of 1904-05 was rivalry between Japan and Russia over Manchuria and Korea. Japan had ambitions in these two areas because they were vital to her security and her economy. Since Russia's expansionist ambitions in Europe were checked by military and diplomatic defeats, she was determined to expand eastwards. Her success during the last two decades of the 19th century alarmed the Japanese and made them suspicious of Russian ambitions in Manchuria and Korea. Russia, in fact, wanted to gain control of these two areas, for they were vital to her interests in East Asia.

In the 1890s, both Japan and Russia increased their influence in Korea. To put an end to their rivalry, they concluded the Yamagata-Lobanov Protocol and the Nishi-Rosen Convention. But these two agreements failed to settle their differences. War finally broke out in 1904 because of Russia's refusal to withdraw her troops from Manchuria, which she had occupied during the Boxer Rising.

The Anglo-Japanese Alliance of 1902 had given Japan the confidence to make war on Russia without fear of intervention by a third party. As in the Sino-Japanese War of 1894-95, neutral observers gave Japan no chance of winning the war. But again the Japanese startled the world by defeating the Russians on land and at sea. Through the mediation of the United States, the war ended in 1905.

Besides the provisions of the Treaty of Portsmouth, the war had other far-reaching results. Japan's victory definitely established her as a world power. It also ended Russian expansion in East Asia, particularly in southern Manchuria and Korea. Japan's dominant position in these two areas was recognized. She annexed Korea in 1910. Her control of Korea and southern Manchuria gave her a base on the Asian continent from which she could carry out her expansionist policy against China. But her violation of the Open Door policy of the United States led to growing friction between the two countries. Russia's humiliating defeat was the immediate cause of the Russian Revolution of 1905. As for China, Japan's victory convinced her that she should carry out Western-style reforms. Finally, the defeat of a world power like Russia by an Asian country aroused nationalism and opposition to colonial rule among the Asian countries.

PART IV

The First World War

Europe in modern times has always been faced with the problem of war. Throughout the 17th and 18th centuries, Europe had been shaken by long and bloody wars. The defeat of Napoleon in 1815 was followed by a comparatively peaceful period. But in the two decades before 1871, Europe was once again torn by war. Five major wars were fought: the Crimean War of 1854-56, the Austro-Sardinian War of 1859, the Prusso-Danish War of 1864-65, the Austro-Prussian War of 1866 and the Franco-Prussian War of 1870-71. All these wars broke out mainly because of nationalist feeling.

In 1871 the unification of Italy was completed when King Victor Emmanuel II occupied Rome. The unification of Germany was also completed. After 1871 a period of peace followed which lasted for over 40 years. But it was an uneasy peace. During those years, forces were already at work which would lead to the First World War.

Chapter 13
Underlying causes of the war

The causes of the First World War can be traced back to the history of Europe for over a century. But most of them date from the 1870s. Like any great historical event or movement, the war was the result of various interlinking causes. Among the underlying causes of the war were nationalism, imperialism and economic rivalry, the system of European alliances and militarism.

NATIONALISM

Nationalism is the desire of the people of one nation to govern themselves and to keep their way of life. This desire comes from patriotism (love of one's country). Nationalism began to grow in Europe after the French Revolution of 1789. The Napoleonic Wars in the early 19th century led to the rise of nationalism

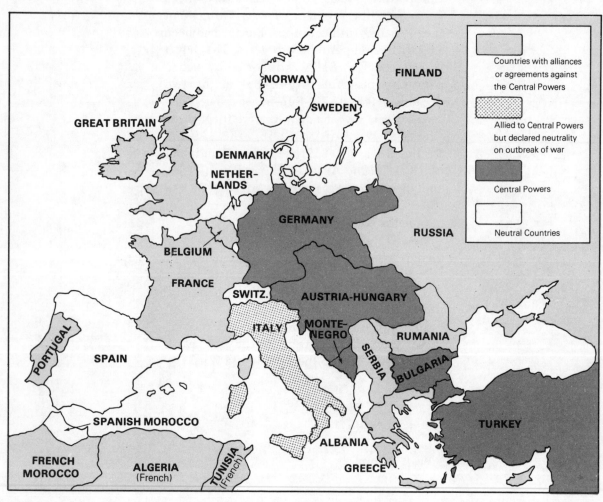

Europe on the eve of the First World War, 1914

in other parts of Europe. When the subject peoples under Napoleon revolted against him, they developed a feeling of national pride and unity. Nationalism led to the unifications of Italy and Germany and inspired the peoples in the Balkan Peninsula to revolt against Turkish rule.

As the nationalist spirit grew stronger and stronger, it developed into a feeling of extreme patriotism. Extreme nationalists believed that their country was always right, making it difficult for the European nations to agree on anything peacefully. Also, because of this extreme feeling, nations which had been defeated earlier often tried to seek revenge or regain the lands they had lost.

Nationalism, too, became a divisive rather than a unifying force. On the one hand, subject peoples wanted to break away from foreign control by creating their own national states or by joining their fellow nationals in other states. On the other hand, some states wanted to annex those areas in other states where the people were similar to their own in race and culture.

By the early 20th century, nationalism had created dangerous movements which were to lead Europe to war. Among these were the Greater Serbia movement, the Pan-Slav movement, the Pan-German movement and the revenge movement in France.

The Greater Serbia movement

The Eastern Question The Greater Serbia movement was a direct result of the Eastern Question, which we discussed in detail in Chapter 2. It had to do with what was going to happen to the European possessions of the Ottoman Empire (Turkey), which had been declining gradually since the 17th century. By the 19th century, it was expected to collapse at any time. The Eastern Question

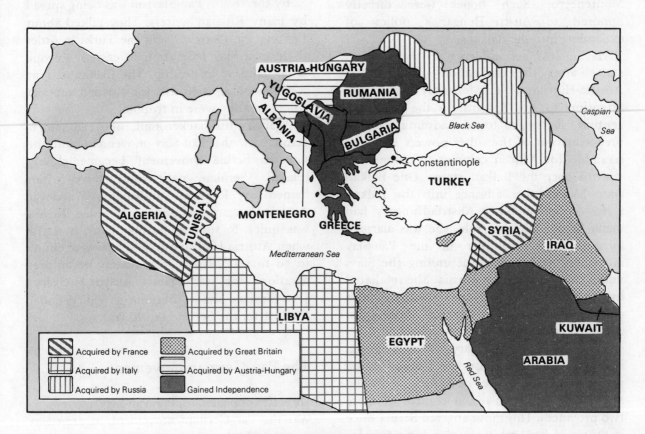

The break-up of the Turkish Empire

was further complicated by the rise of nationalism among the Turkish subject nationalities in the Balkans and by the increasing interest in the fate of the Balkans among the European powers. By 1913 the Ottoman Empire had lost all of its lands in the Balkans, except a small area north of Istanbul (Constantinople) (see p. 205).

The Greater Serbia movement and Austria-Hungary Serbia had gained complete independence from Turkey at the Congress of Berlin of 1878. At the turn of the century, little Serbia started thinking of extending her control over neighbouring areas inhabited by peoples whose race and culture were similar to those of the Serbians. The Greater Serbia movement began. Serbia hoped to create a Yugo-slav state by uniting the Turkish provinces of Bosnia and Herzegovina, which were administered by Austria-Hungary, the Turkish province of Albania and the state of Montenegro. Such hopes were directly opposed to Austria-Hungary's policy of expanding into the Balkans.

Having lost her influence in the German states after the unification of Germany, Austria-Hungary (Dual Monarchy) turned her attention to the Balkans. In the late 19th century, she hoped to take advantage of the preoccupation of the other powers with the scramble for African colonies to extend her control over the Balkan states. One Balkan state blocked her advance into the Balkan states — Serbia. Since Austria-Hungary had many Slavs under her rule, she was alarmed by Serbia's leading role in the Pan-Slav movement which aimed at uniting the Slavs under the leadership of Russia. She retaliated by closing her markets to Serbian products and encouraging anti-Serbian feeling in Albania and Bulgaria.

In 1908 Austria-Hungary annexed Bosnia and Herzegovina because the Young Turks, who had risen to power in Turkey, indicated that they wanted to regain control of these two provinces. This move angered Serbia since it thwarted her ambitious plan for a Greater

Serbia and led to the Bosnian Crisis of 1908. From then on, she encouraged the 25 million Slav subjects of the Dual Monarchy to overthrow Austrian rule. There were many plots to disturb the peace of the Dual Monarchy. The assassination of Archduke Francis Ferdinand, heir to the Austrian throne, by a Bosnian student on 28 June 1914 resulted in war between Austria-Hungary and Serbia. When the other powers joined the war, the First World War began.

The Pan-Slav movement

Pan-Slavism was a movement to bring all Slavic nations under Russian leadership. It was based on the idea that all Slavs belonged to one great family and that Russia, being the greatest Slav power, should be their guide and protector. The movement began with the Pan-Slavic Congress which met in Prague in 1848.

By the 1870s, Pan-Slavism was being spread by many Russian writers. They talked about fighting the Germans and the Turks in order to form a Slav federation in eastern Europe under Russian leadership. The Balkan nations were encouraged to ask for Russian support whenever they were in trouble.

Against this background, one can understand why the Pan-Slav movement and the Greater Serbia movement became closely related. Serbian nationalists were often helped by Russian Pan-Slavists. Whenever Austria-Hungary and Serbia quarrelled, Russia was quick to support Serbia. Thus, in 1914 when Austria-Hungary and Serbia were about to go to war, Russia immediately began preparations for war against Austria-Hungary. (Pan-Slavism almost became a reality under Stalin after the Second World War.)

The Pan-German movement

Directly opposed to the Pan-Slav movement was the Pan-German movement. It aimed at uniting all the Germans of central Europe under one great German state. A few of its leaders proclaimed that this state was going to rule not only central Europe but the whole world.

In the 1890s the idea of Pan-Germanism was spread by the Pan-German League. The league, though it did not have a large membership, influenced the thinking of many middle-class and upper-class Germans. They began to believe in the racial superiority of the Germans and the right of Germany to annex her weaker neighbours. At the same time, Pan-Germanism opposed Pan-Slavism and created friction between Germany and Russia. Thus, when Russia backed Serbia in her quarrel with Austria in 1914, Germany proclaimed her support for Austria, a German nation. (Pan-Germanism almost became a reality under Hitler.)

The revenge movement in France

Yet another dangerous form of nationalism after 1870 was the French desire for revenge. The French people could not forget their humiliating defeat in the Franco-Prussian War of 1870-71 and the loss of the French provinces of Alsace and Lorraine to the new Germany. Extreme nationalists wanted to take revenge on Germany for the defeat of France and to recover the lost provinces. French newspapers kept alive this idea of revenge. School children were taught to hate Germany. The events of 1914 gave France the long-awaited chance to fight a war of revenge.

IMPERIALISM AND ECONOMIC RIVALRY

Two other causes of international tension after 1871 were imperialism and economic rivalry. Imperialism is the policy of gaining political and economic control over other countries, especially those that are backward. Control may take the form of concessions, protec-

IMPERIALISM

Imperialism is the endeavour of the great controllers of industry to broaden the channel for the flow of their surplus wealth by seeking foreign markets and foreign investments to take off the goods and capital they cannot sell or use at home.

— *J.A. Hobson, 1902*

torates or annexations. To grant concessions means to give economic rights and privileges to foreign powers. In a protectorate, a native ruler is allowed to govern his country under the guidance of the 'protecting' nation. When a foreign power annexes a territory, it has complete control over it.

Between 1871 and 1914, colonial rivalry, which was linked with economic rivalry, caused considerable tension among the European powers. This rivalry was an important cause of the formation of European alliances and the armament race during this period. On many occasions, large-scale war almost broke out because of the competition for raw materials and markets and rival territorial claims.

The revival of imperialism

Imperialism as a national policy of the European powers started during the Age of Geographical Discoveries and Expansion (1450-1650). By the early 19th century, imperialism had declined. But after 1870, imperialism was revived mainly because of the industrial revolution. The European nations needed new sources of raw materials for their industries as well as new markets for their surplus products. They needed new lands for their increasing populations. They turned to Africa, Asia and the Pacific. By the early 20th century, one-fifth of the world and one-tenth of the world population were under the control of the European powers.

There were other reasons behind the new imperialism. One was nationalism. The new states of Germany and Italy wanted to show that they were just as strong as the other European powers, or even stronger. They felt that having colonies like the other Great Powers was a sign of greatness. Colonial rivalry developed between these new powers and the old colonial powers. There was also a religious reason. Large numbers of Christian missionaries went to Africa and Asia to convert the natives to Christianity. Finally, there was a humanitarian reason. The colonial powers believed that it was their duty to 'civilize' the peoples of backward countries.

The European scramble for African colonies

Before the 19th century, Africa was called the Dark Continent because very little was known about it. But by the end of the 19th century, European explorers had travelled into its interior.

The exploration of Africa showed that the continent was very rich in natural resources. The need for sources of raw materials, together with national pride, led to the scramble for Africa. The man who started the scramble was King Leopold II of Belgium. In 1876 he took the rich Congo area in central Africa. The old colonial powers and the new states of Germany and Italy joined the scramble. By 1912 almost all of Africa had been colonized by the European powers.

Imperialism in Asia

In the late 19th century, the European powers hoped to divide the whole of Asia among themselves. China, with her 400 million people, was their chief target. In the 'scramble for concessions' in 1895-99 in China, it seemed that China was going to be partitioned by the Great Powers. But she was saved from partition mainly because she made

IN THE RUBBER COILS.

The cruel exploitation of the Congo Free State

use of the rivalry and jealousy among the powers to divide them. Japan saved herself from foreign aggression by starting a programme of modernization. By the early 20th century, she had become a strong nation and a world power. However, by 1914, all of Southeast Asia, except Siam (Thailand), was colonized by the Great Powers.

Colonial rivalry

The scramble for colonies in Africa and Asia caused rivalry among the European powers. Much friction developed, which created ill feeling among them and increased the risk of a general war.

France and Italy Before the scramble for Africa, France had already taken Algeria in North Africa. Her next target was Tunisia. In 1881 she established a protectorate over Tunisia. Italy was angered by the French move because she wanted Tunisia for herself. The following year, she joined the Dual Alliance (between Germany and Austria-Hungary) which then became the Triple Alliance. This alliance was directed against France in particular.

Franco-Italian rivalry in North Africa ended in 1900 when they signed a secret agreement to settle their differences. Italy recognized French interests in Morocco, while France recognized Italian interests in Tripoli. In 1912 Italy annexed Tripoli which became part of Libya.

Britain and France The desire of France to gain territories in North Africa also clashed with Britain's territorial ambitions. Colonial rivalry between them started over Egypt. The country had become important to British trade after the opening of the Suez Canal in 1869. In 1879, when Egypt was faced with bankruptcy, Britain and France jointly seized control of her financial affairs. Later France withdrew because the Egyptians resented foreign control. But Britain stayed on and established military control over Egypt in 1882. France was not pleased because the British move frustrated her ambitions in Egypt.

The next subject of disagreement was the Egyptian Sudan. In 1898 France and Britain almost went to war because of the Fashoda Incident. Two years before, Anglo-Egyptian forces under Lord Kitchener invaded Sudan which had revolted against Egyptian rule. No sooner had Lord Kitchener defeated the Sudanese in the Battle of Omdurman in 1898 than he heard that the French had occupied Fashoda in the Egyptian Sudan. Fashoda is in the White Nile region. The control of the waters of the Nile was extremely important to British interests in Egypt. There was great tension as the British and the French forces faced each other for several weeks. War seemed likely but was avoided when the French withdrew.

Following the Fashoda Incident, Anglo-French relations improved. The Entente Cordiale of 1904 between France and Britain ended Anglo-French rivalry in North Africa.

The Battle of Omdurman, 1898

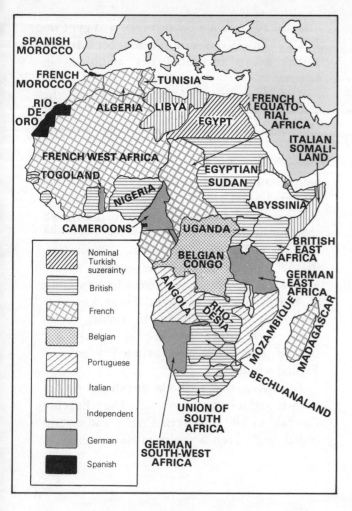

The colonization of Africa up to 1914

Map legend:
- Nominal Turkish suzerainty
- British
- French
- Belgian
- Portuguese
- Italian
- Independent
- German
- Spanish

Britain and Germany As German industry and commerce grew, Kaiser William II decided to find Germany 'a place in the sun' and join the scramble for colonies. However, most of the desirable territories had already been taken by other powers. Whenever the Germans tried to acquire a colony, they faced opposition from other imperialist powers, usually Britain.

In 1884-85 Germany acquired Togoland and the Cameroons and obtained a territory farther south which became German Southwest Africa. They also proclaimed a protectorate over German East Africa.

The German annexations threatened British territorial ambitions in Africa. Nevertheless, Britain concluded an agreement with Germany in 1890, recognizing the new German possessions. In return, Germany recognized British claims to Uganda, Nyasaland and Zanzibar.

Another source of Anglo-German friction was German sympathy for the republics of the Transvaal and the Orange Free State of the Boers, who were Dutch farmers in South Africa. Britain recognized their independence in the 1850s. Later, the discovery of diamonds and gold in Boer territory caused the British to take a new interest in the two republics. When a British raid on Transvaal territory failed in 1896, Kaiser William II sent a telegram to the Boer President Kruger. He congratulated him on his success in driving back the raiders without foreign help. The Kruger Telegram angered the British.

German sympathy for the Boers in the Boer War (1899-1902) between Britain and the two Boer republics further angered Britain. Nevertheless, Germany did not intervene in the war and remained friendly with Britain.

In other areas, Britain was not pleased with German control of the Pacific islands of Samoa and New Guinea. She regarded this as a threat to the security of Australia, a British colony. She was also displeased with the German plan to build the Berlin-Baghdad

Men who fought the British during the Boer War (1899-1902)

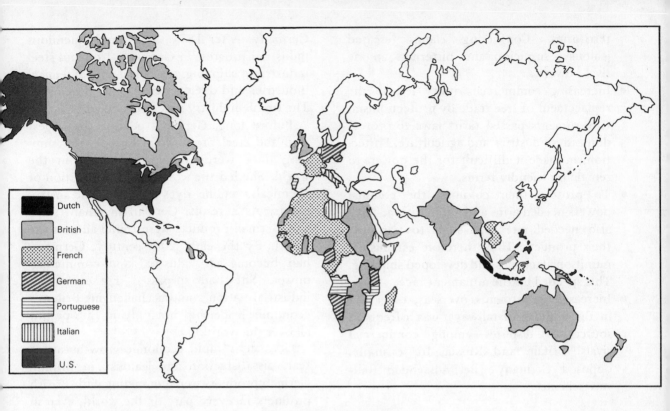

Colonial empires by 1914

Legend:
- Dutch
- British
- French
- German
- Portuguese
- Italian
- U.S.

Railway. Kaiser William II discussed the plan with the government of Turkey when he visited Constantinople in 1898. Britain regarded the railway scheme as a threat to her position in India and to her economic interests in Persia and Mesopotamia.

Russia and Germany Germany's Berlin-Baghdad Railway scheme and her friendship with Turkey aroused Russian jealousy and suspicion. Russia feared that such a railway might strengthen the Ottoman Empire and postpone its break-up. Her expansion into the European lands of the empire would then be delayed.

France and Germany The desire of France to possess Morocco, which was rich in mineral resources, brought her into conflict with Germany. Germany wanted the sultan of Morocco to remain independent. The conflicting attitudes of the two powers led to the Moroccan Crises of 1905, 1908 and 1911, which nearly started war in Europe.

The dispute was really a test of prestige between the Triple Alliance and the Dual Entente, later Triple Entente. War was prevented by means of compromises. The Moroccan affair drew France and Britain closer together but increased ill feeling between France and Germany.

Economic rivalry

The struggle for empire was very often caused by the needs of industrial development. For this reason, colonial rivalry was closely linked with industrial and commercial rivalry. Economic rivalry contributed to the outbreak of the First World War in several ways.

- With rapid industrial progress, the European powers competed for the control of markets and sources of raw materials. In the process, they demanded concessions, established protectorates and annexed territories. Conflicting claims created jealousy, suspicion and bitterness among rival powers.

- Increasing commercial rivalry led to the replacement of free trade by protectionism. Governments passed tariff laws to protect domestic industries and agriculture. Protectionism made it difficult for the powers to remain on friendly terms.
- To protect their colonies, the colonial powers needed arms and ammunition. They also needed merchant ships to transport their products. They therefore established munitions factories and developed shipping. This speeded up the armament race.
- Increased investments overseas, especially in the building of railways, was a frequent source of disputes among commercial rivals. Britain and Russia, for example, opposed Germany's Berlin-Baghdad Railway scheme.

Economic warfare between Britain and Germany Economic rivalry at this time was particularly bitter between Britain and Germany. After 1871 there was tremendous industrial progress in Germany. Iron and steel industries, shipping, electrical and chemical industries and dyeing were rapidly developed. The textile industry was mechanized.

Before long, Germany became the largest iron and steel producer in Europe. Her shipping lines were among the largest in the world. She led the world in the production of chemicals, aniline dyes and scientific instruments. As a result, German merchant ships and German products were found all over the world. By the early 20th century, Germany had become an industrial and commercial power. She had surpassed France as an industrial nation and was challenging Britain's economic leadership not only in Europe but all over the world.

Germany's rapid economic growth caused fear, dissatisfaction and jealousy in Britain. German products were competing with British products in every part of the world, even in Britain itself. German merchant ships were competing strongly against British ships for orders. The British thought that the Germans

The Krupp Works, the huge armaments plant at Essen, Germany

were deliberately waging economic warfare upon them. They therefore felt justified in taking every precaution to defend their interests against German competition.

Economic rivalry among other nations
France also felt threatened by German industrial and commercial expansion. Germany had already acquired the rich mineral deposits of Lorraine in 1871. These deposits became important to her economic development. France now feared that Germany might grab more of her mineral deposits in the north. A bitter rivalry also developed between them as they both wanted to exploit commercial opportunities and mineral resources in Morocco.

Russian plans to acquire the Ottoman Empire's lands in Europe aroused the jealousy of Germany and Austria. Both countries wanted to obtain trading privileges in the Ottoman Empire. For this reason, Germany wanted to build the Berlin-Baghdad Railway. Russia opposed the railway scheme because it conflicted with her territorial ambitions. There was also commercial rivalry between Russia and Austria in the Balkans. This was one of the reasons why Austria opposed the spread of Russian influence in the Balkan states.

However, one must not exaggerate the importance of imperialism and economic rivalry as underlying causes of the First World War. No doubt colonial and economic rivalry were influential factors, but they were not so important as is commonly believed. Other causes such as nationalism, rival alliances and militarism were more important.

By 1914 the rival powers were already able to settle most of their conflicting territorial claims peacefully. As regards the industrial rivalry between Britain and Germany, Britain was in no real danger of losing her economic leadership. Her foreign trade was still expanding, though not as rapidly as that of Germany. Likewise, the economic rivalry between Germany and Russia was not really serious. Russia at this time was not yet an industrial

nation and so she had no surplus products to sell abroad.

Nevertheless, we must remember that economic rivalry often leads to political rivalry. Political rivalry, in turn, often leads to war. For example, the British suspected that Germany might annex Belgium and the Netherlands in order to obtain more resources for her rapid economic development. German annexation of these two countries would threaten Britain's security.

Moreover, in a capitalist nation, there are always powerful industrialists who want to protect their own selfish interests even at the risk of war. Armament manufacturers at this time tried to increase their sales by creating war scares and by encouraging competition among rival buyers. They also urged their governments to take aggressive action against their competitors. Before 1914 such big armament firms as Krupp in Germany, Schneider in France, and Armstrong-Whitworth in Britain were very influential in government.

THE SYSTEM OF EUROPEAN ALLIANCES

Extreme nationalism combined with colonial and economic rivalry and the armament race would have been enough to make many of the European nations go to war. But there was another factor which made a general war in Europe inevitable. This was the existing system of European alliances which made it difficult to prevent a local quarrel from becoming a general war. The secrecy surrounding the formation of most of these alliances gave rise to a feeling of fear, suspicion and jealousy among the European powers.

By 1907 Europe was divided into two armed camps: the Triple Alliance (Germany, Austria-Hungary and Italy) and the Triple Entente (Britain, France and Russia). If one power went to war, the others were bound to be involved.

Why the alliances were formed

- Between 1871 and 1914, the new Germany had become the most powerful state on the continent. She had the largest population in central Europe. She had a strong army and an increasingly powerful navy. She had made tremendous industrial progress, especially in heavy industry. All this aroused jealousy and fear among the other European powers.
- Austria-Hungary was weak and wanted to find a powerful ally against Russia, her rival for the control of the Balkans. She turned to her strong neighbour, Germany.
- France had been weakened by her defeat in the Franco-Prussian War of 1870-71. Determined to take revenge on Germany for her defeat, she was looking for an ally against Germany. She turned to Russia, hoping to get the military support of Russia's huge manpower.
- Russia needed money to prevent revolution and to develop industry and communications. France could provide this through loans. Besides, both countries feared German power. In addition, Russia needed allies if she was to gain control of the Balkans. After her defeat in the Russo-Japanese War of 1904-05, she had revived her policy of expansion into the Balkans.
- Britain was alarmed at the growing naval and industrial power of Germany. This was a threat to her naval supremacy and her control over her vast empire.

The Triple Alliance

The alliance system in Europe can be traced back to the 1870s. The man who started it was Bismarck, the great German chancellor. With this system, he hoped to preserve peace in order to build up the newly created German Empire through internal development. To stop France from starting a war of revenge, Bismarck decided to isolate that country by making friends with her potential

THE GAME OF THE DAY.

Bismarck. "COME, ANDRASSY, WE KNOW EACH OTHER'S 'FORM.' YOU AND I TOGETHER AGAINST THE LOT!!"
Russia (to France). "I THINK, MADAME, *WE MIGHT BE A MATCH FOR THEM*!"
France. "THANKS! I PREFER TO SIT OUT AT PRESENT!" England (to Italy). "NOBODY ASKS *US*!!"

A cartoon illustrating Bismarck's system of diplomacy

allies. However, the alliance system increased international tensions.

The Three Emperors' League In 1872 Bismarck succeeded in bringing Germany, Austria-Hungary and Russia together with the formation of the League of the Three Emperors (Dreikaiserbund). Its aim was to preserve peace and maintain the *status quo* (existing state of affairs). After the Congress of Berlin (1878), however, the league collapsed. Russia blamed Germany and Austria-Hungary for the loss of her gains by the Treaty of San Stefano. She then began to draw closer to France.

Dual Alliance of 1879 When the Three Emperors' League was not renewed in 1878, Germany and Austria-Hungary took steps to safeguard themselves from Russia. In 1879 they signed a secret treaty to form the Dual Alliance. Each agreed to help the other in case of a Russian attack. If one were attacked by a power other than Russia, the other would remain neutral. This alliance became the basis of Austro-German relations until the First World War.

Formation of the Triple Alliance As a result of the French seizure of Tunisia in North Africa in 1881, Italy drew closer to Germany and Austria-Hungary. She had hoped to get Tunisia for herself. Besides, the Italian government, which was not on good terms with the Vatican, feared French intervention to defend the Pope.

Both Germany and Austria-Hungary were only too happy to gain Italian support. For Germany, it would mean another ally against France; for Austria-Hungary, another ally against Russia. Austria-Hungary also wanted to stop Italian opposition to her rule over the Italians in the South Tyrol, a region just north of Italy.

In 1882 Italy made a secret agreement with Germany. She joined the Dual Alliance which thus became the Triple Alliance. Should one of these Central Powers be attacked by two powers, the other two powers would come to its aid. However, because of her good relations with Britain, Italy made Germany and Austria-Hungary agree not to regard the alliance as directed against Britain.

With the Triple Alliance, the area controlled by the Central Powers cut through central Europe from the Baltic Sea to the Mediterranean. This upset the balance of power in Europe and alarmed the other European powers. In 1883 Rumania allied herself with the Central Powers.

Isolation of France With the renewal of the Three Emperors' League in 1881 and the formation of the Triple Alliance, Bismarck had successfully isolated France. Only one country might be able to help her — Britain. But at this time, the British were still following their traditional policy of 'splendid isolation' in foreign affairs. Besides, Bismarck was careful to keep friendly relations with Britain by repeatedly offering an alliance.

The Three Emperors' League broke up again in 1887 because of continuing Austro-Russian rivalry in the Balkans. Nevertheless, Germany managed to remain friendly with Russia until 1890. By the Reinsurance Treaty of 1887, Germany promised to support Russia in the Balkans. In return, Russia promised not to join France if France waged war on Germany.

Breakdown of Bismarck's alliance system Between 1890 and 1907, all the efforts of Bismarck to preserve peace through alliances failed. There were several reasons for the breakdown of Bismarck's alliance system.

- Bismarck was dismissed in 1890 because of disagreements with William II, the new kaiser. His successor refused to renew the Reinsurance Treaty with Russia. Russia then drew closer to France.
- France and Russia had become friendlier because of the flow of French money into Russia for the development of industry and communications. This prepared the way for a military alliance between the two countries.
- The Pan-Slav movement increased Austro-Russian rivalry in the Balkans.
- Britain ended her policy of 'splendid isolation' in foreign affairs because of the growing power of Germany.
- Italy had lost interest in the Triple Alliance. She did not want Tunisia any more and wanted instead to recover territories from Austria. She also needed French support for the conquest of Tripoli in North Africa. Finally, with the republicans in power in France, there was no more danger of French intervention to defend the Pope.

The Triple Entente

An important result of the breakdown of the Bismarckian system of alliances was the formation of the Triple Entente in 1907. It came into being by stages.

Franco-Russian Alliance of 1893 Franco-Russian relations had improved in the early 1890s because of the large French investments in Russia. For example, France had arranged large loans to build the Trans-Siberian Railway in 1892. Both countries were also threatened by the aggressive policy of Kaiser William II and were each looking for an ally. After the renewal of the Triple Alliance in 1891, Italy repeatedly stressed her good relations with Britain. This convinced France and Russia that Britain was about to join the Triple Alliance.

France and Russia finally signed a secret military agreement in 1893. Each promised to help the other in case of a German attack, or an Austrian or Italian attack supported by Germany. The Franco-Russian Alliance (Dual Alliance) was followed by the Anglo-French Entente Cordiale.

THE FRANCO-RUSSIAN ALLIANCE, 1893

France and Russia, being animated by an equal desire to preserve peace, and having no other object than to meet the necessities of a defensive war, provoked by an attack of the forces of the Triple Alliance against the one or the other of them, have agreed upon the following provisions:

(1) If France is attacked by Germany, or by Italy supported by Germany, Russia shall employ all her available forces to attack Germany. If Russia is attacked by Germany, or by Austria supported by Germany, France shall employ all her available forces to fight Germany.

(2) In case the forces of the Triple Alliance, or of one of the powers composing it, should mobilize, France and Russia . . . shall mobilize immediately . . . .

Entente Cordiale (Anglo-French Entente) Before 1904 France and Britain had often quarrelled over colonies and trade. In 1898 they almost went to war at Fashoda in the Egyptian Sudan. When France gave up her claims there, Anglo-French relations improved.

Two other factors drew France and Britain together. One was the growth of German naval and industrial power, which posed a threat to Britain's security and to her overseas empire. The other was Britain's decision to give up her old policy of isolation, as shown by the signing of the Anglo-Japanese Alliance of 1902. In Europe, the Triple Alliance and the Franco-Russian Alliance had left Britain diplomatically isolated. She now had to choose which alliance she was going to join in order to protect her own interests.

In 1904 Britain concluded the Entente Cordiale (Dual Entente) with France. This was a friendly agreement, not a military alliance. It settled outstanding disputes in North Africa. France agreed not to interfere in Egypt. In exchange, Britain agreed not to interfere in Morocco. The Anglo-French Entente prepared the way for a military alliance between the two countries.

The Anglo-Russian Entente The last step in the formation of the Triple Entente was the Anglo-Russian Entente of 1907. In the 19th century, Britain had opposed Russian ambitions in the Balkans. In the early years of the 20th century, however, Anglo-Russian relations improved. France, an ally of Russia, encouraged Anglo-Russian friendship. In addition, Britain's fear of Russian expansion in East Asia was removed with the signing of the Anglo-Japanese Alliance of 1902 and Russian defeat in the Russo-Japanese War of 1904-05. Moreover, at this time, she had more reason to fear Germany than Russia.

In 1907 the Anglo-Russian Entente was formed. Like the Anglo-French Entente it was not a formal alliance but a mutual understanding between the two countries. They simply settled their differences in central Asia. The Dual Entente had now become the Triple Entente. Japan was not a member of the Triple Entente, but she was allied to Britain by the Anglo-Japanese Alliance of 1902.

The Triple Entente provided a counterbalance to the Triple Alliance, splitting

TRIPLE ENTENTE

Britain France Russia

1907

TRIPLE ALLIANCE

Germany Austria Italy

The Triple Entente and the Triple Alliance, 1907

Europe into two armed camps. The system of alliances became a source of suspicion and fear. Rivalry speeded up the arms race and produced several international crises. The two hostile camps could not exist side by side forever. The only solution was war, and it came with the First World War.

Weakness of the alliances

Before we leave the problem of alliances, the weakness of the Triple Alliance and the Triple Entente must be pointed out. The members did not keep to the agreements of these alliances whenever these were against their own interests. In fact, Italy and Britain did not act according to the agreements of their respective alliances.

Italy later ignored her obligations under the Triple Alliance. In 1900 she signed a secret treaty with France in which she agreed not to interfere with French ambitions in

Morocco. In return, France agreed not to interfere in Tripoli. In 1902 they signed another secret agreement. Both agreed to remain neutral if one of them were attacked by a third power. Italy also signed a friendly agreement with Russia in 1909. She would not interfere with Russia's plans to control the Dardanelles and Constantinople. In exchange, Russia promised support for the Italian conquest of Tripoli.

The Triple Entente was just as unstable as the Triple Alliance. Britain and France refused to support Russia in her quarrel with Austria over the Austrian annexation of Bosnia and Herzegovina in 1908. In 1913 Britain co-operated with Germany and Austria in stopping Serbia, an ally of Russia, from annexing Albania. In fact, until the outbreak of the First World War, none of the other powers knew exactly what Britain was going to do if a general war broke out in Europe.

MILITARISM

Militarism was yet another underlying cause of the First World War. Militarism is the belief in being always militarily prepared for war and the use of force to gain advantages. Between 1871 and 1914, the European powers adopted a policy of militarism. Extreme nationalism, the competition for colonies and markets and rival alliances drove them to develop large armies and navies. At the same time, production of military and naval equipment increased.

Germany led the other powers in following a policy of militarism in the late 19th century. At the turn of the century, an armament race began, which became a constant threat to peace. The formation of rival alliances speeded up the race. The leader of an alliance had to be well armed to gain the confidence of its partners. An unarmed power was useless as an ally. None of the powers dared to withdraw from the armament race for fear of being overcome by the others.

The armament race

Military conscription After 1871 all the European powers, except Britain, carried out military conscription, or compulsory military training for able-bodied men. Germany soon had the strongest army in Europe. All the big European states, except Britain, enlarged their armies, reorganizing them on the German model. Russia soon had a huge army. Even small nations, such as Norway and the Netherlands, enforced military conscription.

As a result of compulsory military training, people began to regard war as a part of life. They were prepared to pay higher taxes to support armament programmes. Large sums of money were spent on military and naval equipment. New industrial processes resulted in the production of deadlier weapons, such as torpedoes, mines, high-explosive shells and machine guns. Bigger battleships, the invention of the aeroplane and the submarine made it possible for men to destroy each other not only on land and sea but beneath the sea and in the sky.

The failure of the Hague conferences to limit or reduce armaments speeded up the enlargement of armies. In 1912 when Austria-Hungary expanded her army, Russia did the same. The following year, France also enlarged her army. Alarmed at the military build-up of Russia and France, Germany increased her army to about 800 000 men. By the time the First World War broke out, Germany and France had approximately the same number of armed men. With two armed camps facing each other, the risk of a general war was greatly increased.

Anglo-German naval rivalry There was also the naval competition between Britain and Germany. Kaiser William II wanted not only a strong army but also a large navy to protect Germany's colonies and sea-borne trade. Plans were outlined in the Naval Laws of 1898 and 1900 for a great expansion of the German navy. The naval building programmes of 1900 and 1907 alarmed the British. They

COPYRIGHT EXPIRES.

A cartoon illustrating Anglo-German naval rivalry

were convinced that the Germans wanted to take over from them the control of the sea.

The British were not prepared to give up their centuries-old naval supremacy. It was vital to their trade and to the control of their vast colonial empire. In 1903 they started

218

their own naval programme. In 1906 they began to produce the first of several *Dreadnoughts*. This armour-plated battleship, which had a speed of 21 knots and ten 12-inch guns, was more powerful than all previous battleships. By 1911 Britain was far ahead of Germany in the naval race.

H. M. S. 'Dreadnought', the most powerful battleship in the First World War

The Hague conferences

The widespread belief that the armament race could only end in war with its disastrous consequences caused many anxious people to organize peace societies. They called for the limitation of armaments and the settlement of international disputes through arbitration. The desire for peace led to the holding of two international peace conferences at The Hague, the political capital of the Netherlands.

The First Hague Conference In 1898 Tsar Nicholas II of Russia issued an appeal to all powers to hold a conference on disarmament. It was ignored by the large states. A second appeal was more successful. It resulted in the First Hague Conference of 1899 which was attended by representatives from 26 nations.

At the conference, no serious attempt was made to limit armaments. When disarmament was proposed, Germany strongly objected to it. Britain also refused to give up her naval supremacy. The conference was saved from complete failure when the representatives agreed to the creation of a permanent court of international arbitration. Disputes between nations might be submitted to this body.

The Second Hague Conference The Second Hague Conference met in 1907 at the suggestion of President Theodore Roosevelt of the United States. Representatives from 42 nations attended the conference. It was no more successful in limiting armaments than the first conference mainly because of German opposition. The Permanent Court of Arbitration was strengthened but it was found to be ineffective. It had no power to force nations to refer grievances to it for arbitration. It also had no means of enforcing its decisions.

All the efforts of the Hague conferences failed because the powers were not willing to limit or reduce armaments. Besides, the powers felt that the Permanent Court of Arbitration was powerless to prevent war. With the failure of the Hague conferences, the European powers continued their policy of militarism. The armament race went on. The Great Powers' possession of large armies and navies made a general conflict almost inevitable.

1. Briefly explain how **each** of the following helped to bring about the First World War:
   (a) nationalism
   (b) imperialism and economic rivalry
   (c) the system of European alliances
   (d) militarism

2. Define nationalism. Explain how **each** of the following nationalist movements contributed to the outbreak of the First World War:
   (a) the Greater Serbia movement
   (b) the Pan-Slav movement
   (c) the Pan-German movement
   (d) the revenge movement in France

3. Show how colonial rivalry in Africa affected relations among the European powers before 1914 and increased the risk of a general war.

5. How did economic rivalry among the European powers during the period 1870-1914 contribute to the outbreak of the First World War?

5. 'Colonial and economic rivalry among the European powers were important causes of the First World War, but they were not so important as is commonly believed.' How far is this statement true?

6. Give a short account of **each** of the following, showing how they increased international tensions before the First World War:
   (a) the Eastern Question
   (b) the Fashoda Incident (1898)
   (c) the Boer War (1899-1902)
   (d) the Berlin-Baghdad Railway scheme

7. Give reasons for the formation of the European alliances during the period 1870-1914. What were the weaknesses of the Triple Alliance and the Triple Entente?

8. Trace the steps which led to the formation of the Triple Alliance and the Triple Entente. Show how the existence of these two rival alliances in Europe contributed to the outbreak of the First World War.

9. Define militarism. How did militarism and its consequences help to bring about the First World War?

10. Describe the attempts of the European powers to prevent war by holding the Hague conferences of 1899 and 1907. Why did these conferences fail to achieve their objectives?

Europe made tremendous progress during the 19th century. In the early 1900s the advances which had been made gave the peoples of Europe the feeling that the world was constantly growing better. And yet, why did a general war break out in 1914 which shattered this feeling of optimism? The answer is that these European countries failed to develop ways of settling their differences and living together in peace. Instead, they were driven apart by aggressive nationalism and colonial and economic rivalry which, in turn, led to the formation of rival alliances and the adoption of a policy of militarism.

Nationalism was behind the conflict between Serbia and Austria-Hungary, the clash between Pan-Slavism and Pan-Germanism, and the desire of France to take revenge on Germany for her defeat in the Franco-Prussian War and to recover Alsace-Lorraine. Colonial rivalry in Africa and Asia, along with economic rivalry inside and outside Europe, increased international tensions. It is true that most of the colonial disputes had been settled by 1914, and industrial and commercial rivalry was not so serious a problem as it seemed. Yet, the ill feeling created by the colonial and economic rivalries remained.

Jealousy, suspicion and fear combined to make the rival powers look for possible allies. Foreign rivalries in the Balkans and in the remaining European lands of the Ottoman Empire drew Germany and Austria-Hungary together but drove Germany and Russia farther apart. Colonial rivalry between France and Italy in North Africa drew Italy closer to Germany and Austria-Hungary. Fear of Germany's growing power brought France and Russia together. Anglo-German naval and industrial rivalry drew Britain closer to France and Russia. The result was the formation of two rival alliances: the Triple Alliance and the Triple Entente. The original aim of the alliance system was peace, not war; defence, not offence. However, the system increased the risk of a general conflict.

With two hostile camps facing each other, the rival powers pursued a policy of militarism. The desire to be always militarily prepared for war led to an armament race. If one power enlarged its armies or increased military expenditure, its rivals matched the increase.

At this point, it was obvious that Europe was heading straight for the disaster of a general war. Attempts were made to prevent it. Peace societies were organized and two international peace conferences were held in The Hague. All these efforts failed mainly because Germany opposed disarmament and Britain refused to give up her naval supremacy. What followed was one crisis after another which finally led to the outbreak of the First World War.

Chapter 14
Events leading to the war and course of the war

In the last decade before 1914, increasing tension between the Triple Alliance and the Triple Entente gave rise to a series of international crises which pushed Europe to the brink of war. Three crises arose over the French penetration of Morocco and another two concerned disputes in the Balkans. After each of these crises, the European powers were left with either a feeling of dissatisfaction and a wish for further gains, or a feeling of bitterness and a desire for revenge. These crises therefore hastened the outbreak of a general war. The First World War eventually broke out on 28 July 1914. The war lasted for more than four years. It ended with the signing of the armistice on 11 November 1918.

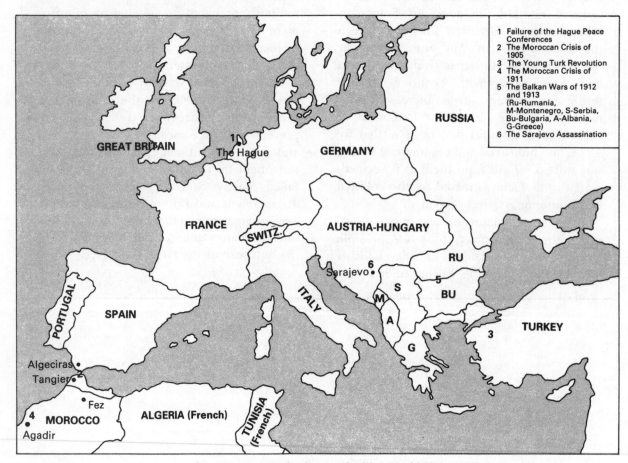

1 Failure of the Hague Peace Conferences
2 The Moroccan Crisis of 1905
3 The Young Turk Revolution
4 The Moroccan Crisis of 1911
5 The Balkan Wars of 1912 and 1913
(Ru-Rumania, M-Montenegro, S-Serbia, Bu-Bulgaria, A-Albania, G-Greece)
6 The Sarajevo Assassination

Important events leading to the First World War

CRISES OVER MOROCCO

At the turn of the century, Morocco was an independent country ruled by a sultan. The European powers, France and Germany in particular, had long wanted to make use of Morocco's mineral and agricultural wealth. The country also had excellent trading opportunities. In 1880 the Great Powers signed the Madrid Convention in which they agreed that all nations would have equal economic privileges in Morocco.

France was not happy with the decision. She wanted to add Morocco to her North African empire, which already included Algeria and Tunisia. She hoped to recruit men in Morocco for her armies. The country could also be used as a base for the defence of Algeria. Attempts to expand her power in Morocco brought her into conflict with Germany in 1905, 1908 and 1911. Germany had long been envious of French expansion in North Africa.

The Moroccan Crisis of 1905

To prevent any opposition to her ambitions in Morocco, France obtained the consent of Italy (1900) and Spain (1904) to her control of Morocco. She also gained the support of Britain in the Anglo-French Entente of 1904. Both powers proclaimed their determination to preserve Moroccan independence. The secret terms of the agreement, however, provided for just the opposite. That part of Morocco facing Gibraltar was to go to Spain. The rest of the country was to go to France. The Anglo-French Entente led to the Moroccan Crisis of 1905.

How much the German government knew about the secret arrangement to partition Morocco is difficult to tell. (The secret terms were not revealed until 1911.) Somehow, the Germans suspected that France and Britain were up to something. Fearing that their commercial and political influence would be excluded from Morocco, they decided to intervene in Moroccan affairs in 1905. It was a favourable moment to oppose France because Russia, her ally, had just been defeated in the Russo-Japanese War of 1904-05. France would not dare go to war until Russia had recovered from her defeat.

The crisis In March 1905, Kaiser William II visited Tangier, Morocco's chief port. The visit was meant to show how important Morocco was to Germany. The kaiser then made a speech which was directed against France. He pointedly said that the German government recognized the independence of Morocco. He also expressed the hope that 'Morocco will remain open to the peaceful competition of all nations'. In April, Germany demanded the holding of an international conference on Morocco. Germany also hinted that the French foreign minister, Delcasse, architect of the Anglo-French Entente, should resign in order to ease the situation.

German interference in Morocco challenged both the French position in that country and the newly formed Anglo-French Entente. The immediate effect was the Moroccan Crisis of 1905. Would France yield to the German demand for a conference? Delcasse opposed it, but the French cabinet did not support him. In June 1905, he resigned. The French gave in and agreed to the German proposal for a conference. In 1906 an international conference of 12 states met at Algeciras, Spain, to settle the status of Morocco.

Results of the crisis At the Algeciras Conference, a compromise was reached to settle the Moroccan question. The delegates affirmed the sovereignty and independence of Morocco. It seemed that Germany had won a great diplomatic victory. The truth, however, was that France gained more from the conference. She was supported by Britain, Russia and Spain and even by Italy, a German ally. Only Austria-Hungary supported Germany. The conference authorized France and Spain to keep order in Morocco. It also gave France a major role in running the country and some control of its finances. French control of Morocco was therefore strengthened.

Britain's support of France in the crisis strengthened the ties between the two powers. The Anglo-French Entente of 1904 was just a diplomatic understanding to settle their colonial difficulties. Now, they moved towards a military understanding. After the crisis, military talks between France and Britain began.

For a long time, Britain had been suspicious of Russia's territorial ambitions in Asia. The Moroccan Crisis of 1905 brought the two powers together. Since both of them opposed Germany at the Algeciras Conference, they drew closer together. Friendly feelings led to the Anglo-Russian Entente of 1907. The entente introduced a new balance of power in Europe.

The Moroccan Crisis of 1908

In spite of the settlement at Algeciras, rivalry between France and Germany over Morocco continued. In 1908 another crisis developed, though not a serious one. Three German deserters from the French Foreign Legion in Morocco had taken refuge in the German consulate at Casablanca. When the French attacked the consulate to arrest them, the Casablanca Incident developed. In 1909 the crisis was settled. Germany recognized French political supremacy in Morocco. In return, France promised to respect Germany's economic rights in Morocco.

The Moroccan Crisis of 1911

In 1911 friction between France and Germany broke out once more. By this time, there were frequent disturbances in Morocco. The sultan, unable to control his subjects, appealed to France for help. In 1911 French troops occupied Fez, the capital of Morocco, to restore order.

The crisis Germany regarded the French action as a step towards full French control of Morocco. It violated the decisions of the Algeciras Conference. The German government then sent the gunboat *Panther* to the Moroccan port of Agadir as a sign of protest. This action caused the Moroccan Crisis of 1911. It was the most serious of the Moroccan crises. Both sides prepared for war. This time the French were determined not to concede to the Germans. Britain showed her firm intention to support France by preparing her fleet for action. It was Germany's turn to back down, and she agreed to a compromise.

Results of the crisis In November, 1911, a Franco-German agreement was signed. Germany agreed to give up all her privileges in Morocco. France was finally allowed to establish a protectorate over that country. In return, she ceded a part of the French Congo to Germany.

Although the Moroccan question had been settled, bitterness between France and Germany remained. The French claimed that the Germans had forced them to give up valuable territory. The Germans, however, claimed that the French territory they received was not enough compensation for the loss of their privileges in Morocco.

The crisis strengthened the Triple Entente. Britain had shown that she would fight to help France, her ally. Another result was the speeding up of the armament race. Germany decided to expand both her naval building programme and her already powerful army. The other powers immediately did the same. The crisis increased tensions between the Triple Entente and the Triple Alliance. The two camps became more clearly opposed to each other. Finally, the feelings of uncertainty, fear and hate produced by the crisis set the stage for war.

CRISES IN THE BALKANS

The Balkan settlement which was made at the Congress of Berlin (1878) did not ease the basic tensions underlying the Eastern Question. The Balkans continued to give Europe a great deal of trouble. There was much jealousy among the Balkan nations. By the early 1900s, Serbia, Bulgaria and Montenegro were all pro-Russian while Rumania was more in favour of Austria-Hungary and Germany. With all the Great Powers ready to make use of local disputes to further their own interests, one can easily understand why the Balkan area was often described as 'the powder keg of Europe'. An accidental spark could easily set off an explosion which would bring about a general war.

Between 1908 and 1914, two crises in the Balkans increased European rivalries. They were more serious than the Moroccan crises. One was the Bosnian Crisis of 1908; the other was the Balkan Wars of 1912 and 1913.

The Bosnian Crisis of 1908

In the early 1900s, rivalry between Austria and Serbia in the Balkans was fast developing into open hostility. Austria was worried about Serbia's plan to expand into neighbouring areas (Greater Serbia movement), in particular Bosnia and Herzegovina. The Congress of Berlin had given Austria the right to administer these two Turkish provinces.

Serbia wanted Bosnia and Herzegovina because their inhabitants were mostly Slavs. About a miliion of them were Serbs. Annexation of the territory would also double her size and give her a valuable outlet to the

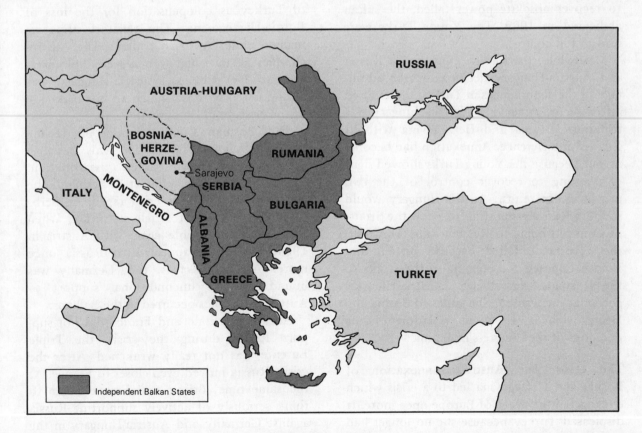

The Balkans, 1914

Adriatic Sea. To stop her, Austria planned to annex the territory herself when the opportunity came. It came with the outbreak of the Young Turk revolution in Turkey.

The Young Turk revolution Nationalism, which had stirred the Balkan peoples to revolt against Turkish rule, also spread to Turkey. Many Turkish patriots were disgusted with the weakness of their rulers. In less than a century, the Ottoman Empire had lost most of its lands in Europe as well as in North Africa. In 1876 reformers forced Sultan Abdul Hamid II to introduce a constitutional government. But he soon ignored the constitution and re-established absolute rule.

In the 1890s, a group of young reformers set up the Committee of Union and Progress. They became known as the Young Turks. In 1908 they revolted against the tyranny of Sultan Abdul Hamid II and forced him to restore constitutional rule. When his attempt to recover absolute power failed, the sultan abdicated in 1909. The Young Turks were now in full control.

Meanwhile, the foreign ministers of Russia and Austria-Hungary decided to take advantage of the disturbances in Turkey and entered into a secret agreement. Austria-Hungary was to annex Bosnia and Herzegovina without Russian interference. Annexation had become urgent because the Young Turks showed signs of wanting to recover control of the two provinces. In return, Austria-Hungary would support Russia's ambition to open the Straits of Constantinople to Russian ships. However, the agreement failed because Britain and France opposed the opening of the straits to the Russians. Nevertheless, Austria-Hungary got what she wanted. She annexed Bosnia and Herzegovina in 1908, in violation of the decisions of the Congress of Berlin.

The crisis The Austrian annexation of Bosnia and Herzegovina led to a crisis which endangered the peace of Europe once more. It displeased Turkey because she no longer had a chance of recovering the two provinces.

It angered Serbia because the Austrian action crushed her hopes of annexing the provinces herself.

The Serbs quickly prepared for war and appealed to Russia for help. Russia threatened to go to war to support them. Germany then stepped in and warned Russia that Germany would support Austria. Europe was now on the verge of war.

Russia backed down. She had not yet fully recovered from her defeat in the Russo-Japanese War and from the Russian Revolution of 1905. Besides, she could not depend on the active support of Britain and France. These two powers did not support Serbia's territorial ambitions. Russia therefore advised the Serbs to avoid war and wait for a more favourable time. The Serbs reluctantly agreed, and the crisis ended.

Results of the crisis Austria-Hungary paid two and a half million pounds to the sultan of Turkey as compensation for the loss of Bosnia-Herzegovina. The territory thus remained under Austrian control. The Austro-German alliance had won a great diplomatic victory. Nevertheless, Austria-Hungary was disappointed because she could not make use of the crisis to crush Serbia.

The Bosnian Crisis increased ill feeling between Austria and Serbia. This hostility eventually led to the Sarajevo assassination. In addition, Russian support of Serbia at the beginning of the crisis encouraged the Serbs to look to Russia for help in future. When Serbia was in trouble again with Austria in 1914, the Serbs appealed to Russia once more. After the crisis, too, Germany was bound to give unconditional support to Austria if troubles occurred in the Balkans.

Although Britain and France did not support Russia during the crisis, the Triple Entente was not really weakened. After the crisis, Russia moved even closer to France. At the same time, Britain and France began to think seriously of actively supporting Russia against Germany and Austria-Hungary in the future. Finally, the rivalries stimulated by the crisis led to another crisis in the Balkans: the Balkan Wars of 1912 and 1913.

THE BALKAN WARS

The results of the Moroccan crises and the Bosnian Crisis did not seriously disturb the balance of power in Europe. But the overthrow of the Ottoman Empire would certainly affect the balance of power and heighten European rivalries. The Balkan Wars of 1912 and 1913 completed the break-up of the Ottoman Empire in Europe and increased tensions between the Triple Alliance and the Triple Entente.

The Balkan War of 1912

A chain reaction followed the establishment of the French protectorate over Morocco in 1911. To counterbalance French gains, Italy decided to take over Turkish territories in North Africa. In 1911-12, she made war on the Ottoman Empire. After her victory, she annexed Tripoli. The Italian success encouraged the Balkan nations to fight against the Turks and drive them out of the Balkans. At this time, Albania, Macedonia and Thrace were still under Turkish rule.

The war After the Young Turks came to power, they began to strengthen Turkey. The Turkish attempt to tighten control over the Macedonians aroused the sympathy of their fellow Slavs throughout the Balkans. It gave the Balkan nations an excuse to make war on Turkey.

In 1912 Serbia, Montenegro, Bulgaria and Greece formed the Balkan League, an alliance for the conquest of Macedonia. The war against Turkey began in October. In less than two months, Turkey was completely defeated. She had to give up whatever was left of her European possessions, except for a small area north of Constantinople.

Treaty of London A conference of the Great Powers in London confirmed the results of the war. The distribution of the conquered Turkish territories was decided in the Treaty of London (May 1913). Serbia had expected to get the Turkish province of Albania. At the London Conference, however, Austria-Hungary, which feared the expansion of Serbian power, obtained the support of Germany and Britain in making Albania an independent nation. Thus Serbia again lost a possible outlet to the Adriatic Sea.

The Treaty of London gave North and Central Macedonia to Serbia. Greece received South Macedonia and the island of Crete. Bulgaria was given Thrace and the Aegean coast.

The Balkan War of 1913

Not long after the signing of the Treaty of London, the Balkan League broke up. Bulgaria, dissatisfied with her share of the conquered Turkish territories, declared war on her former allies in June 1913. Turkey joined the war against Bulgaria and regained Adrianople. Rumania also entered the war against Bulgaria in the hope of obtaining new territories.

Treaty of Bucharest With so many countries fighting against her, Bulgaria was quickly defeated. In August 1913, she signed the Treaty of Bucharest. She was forced to cede southern Dobrudja to Rumania. Serbia retained North Macedonia while Greece kept South Macedonia. Turkey recovered Adrianople while Bulgaria managed to keep Western Thrace. Although the Treaty of Bucharest violated the territorial settlements of the Treaty of London, the Great Powers dared not intervene. Intervention might lead to a general conflict because it would put Germany and Austria-Hungary on one side and Russia, France and possibly Britain on the other.

Results of the Balkan Wars

The settlement in the Balkans following the Balkan Wars was unsatisfactory and the potential for future conflict remained. None of the Balkan nations believed that the territorial changes would last. They expected a new war very soon. Serbia thought that she would have to fight Austria-Hungary to preserve her gains. Defeated Bulgaria would be only too happy to have another war in order to recover her losses in Macedonia. The Turks' recovery of Adrianople aroused patriotism. They decided to strengthen their army and hoped to use it to recover their lost territories.

The Balkan settlement, too, changed the balance of power in Europe. Turkey had been weakened by the Balkan Wars. It seemed that she was in great danger of being absorbed by Russia. To meet the Russian threat, she turned to Germany. She arranged for a German military mission to reorganize her army. Germany was only too glad to help Turkey because Turko-German co-operation would give her a great opportunity for economic expansion and railway penetration into the Middle East. German ambitions were sure to increase hostility between Russia and Germany. Russia did not wish to see a foreign power, especially Germany, establish control in Turkey.

The balance of power was further changed when Rumania moved away from the Austro-German combination. She was not happy with the oppression of about three million Rumanians in Hungary by the Hungarian government. Bulgaria began moving towards Austria-Hungary and Turkey. She needed foreign support in order to take revenge on her former allies in the Balkan League. Austria-Hungary herself wanted a diplomatic alliance with Bulgaria. This would isolate Serbia and put pressure on Rumania to rejoin the Austro-German combination.

The Balkan Wars also led to a further military build-up among the Great Powers. The wars convinced Germany that a general war was inevitable. If it came, she was not sure that Italy, though a member of the Triple Alliance, would support the Austro-German combination. But she was fairly certain that Britain would join France and Russia. She therefore began to increase the strength of her army. At the same time, France, Russia and Britain speeded up their military expansion.

This constant military build-up created a danger because it tempted military leaders to go to war. Moreover, these leaders noted the speed with which the Balkan League defeated Turkey and the rapid defeat of Bulgaria. If a general war came, they thought of following the example of a similar lightning war and began to make preparations for it.

Yet another result of the Balkan Wars was to sharpen the conflict between Pan-Slavism and Pan-Germanism in the Balkans and in Turkey. Pan-Slavism was spread by Serbia supported by Russia. Austria, supported by Germany, was behind the Pan-German movement in the Balkans. This rivalry was quite dangerous at this time because Germany was committed to unconditional support for Austria-Hungary. At the same time, France was becoming stronger and was prepared to give Russia active support.

The most dangerous result of the Balkan Wars was to worsen the conflict between Austria and Serbia. The Balkan settlement had made Serbia much larger and stronger. Fearful of Serbian power, Austria was determined to stop further Serbian expansion. Although her size and population had increased, Serbia was still dissatisfied because she could not get an outlet to the Adriatic Sea. This was the second territorial disappointment she had suffered in less than five years because of Austrian intervention. The increasing violence of anti-Austrian plots and propaganda finally ended in the Sarajevo assassination.

OUTBREAK OF THE FIRST WORLD WAR

In the Bosnian Crisis of 1908, Austria-Hungary had not been able to make use of the chance to crush Serbia. Since then, she had been waiting for another chance. It came in 1914 with the Sarajevo assassination. This time, she was not going to let the opportunity slip by. With the full support of Germany, she was determined to make war on Serbia. The Sarajevo assassination provided the immediate cause of the First World War.

Archduke Francis Ferdinand and his wife, a few minutes before they were assassinated

The Sarajevo assassination

Since the Austrian annexation of Bosnia-Herzegovina in 1908, anti-Austrian secret societies in Serbia had plotted acts of violence and spread anti-Austrian propaganda in Bosnia. As Slavs, the Bosnians themselves were pro-Serbian and hated Austrian control. In 1914, in spite of warnings, the Archduke Francis Ferdinand, heir to the Austrian throne, and his wife visited Sarajevo, the capital of rebellious Bosnia. On June 28, Gavrilo Princip, a Bosnian student who belonged to a Serbian anti-Austrian secret society, shot the archduke and his wife. They were riding through the streets of the city when they were murdered.

The assassination infuriated Austria because of the archduke's position. He was soon to become emperor. The reigning emperor, Francis Joseph, was already 84 years old and was expected to die at any moment. Although at that time Austro-Hungarian investigators found no clear evidence that Serbia was behind the assassination, Austria held the Serbian government responsible for it. (In recent years, considerable evidence has been found which shows that the Serbian government knew of the plot to assassinate the archduke.)

For three weeks, Austria took no action against Serbia. She first wanted to make sure that Germany would stand by her. Germany knew that support for Austria would mean war with Serbia as well as Russia. She nevertheless promised to give Austria a 'blank cheque' (unconditional support) to act against Serbia probably because she was convinced of Serbia's guilt by Austria. Assured of German support, Austria sent a harsh ultimatum to Serbia on July 23, giving her 48 hours to reply. The ultimatum included three demands:

- Serbia was to suppress all anti-Austrian societies;
- Serbia was to dismiss all officials whom Austria objected to;
- Austrian officials were to enter Serbia to make sure that the first two demands were carried out.

Austria knew that Serbia would not accept the ultimatum, for it would mean the end of Serbian independence. Austria, therefore, intended to provoke war with Serbia. She had already mobilized her troops even before Serbia had replied.

Serbia gave a mild reply to the ultimatum. She agreed to meet the first two Austrian demands but not the third one. If Austria found the reply unsatisfactory, Serbia offered to submit the whole problem to an international body for arbitration. Serbia expected Austria to reject her reply. Just before she sent it, she ordered the mobilization of her troops.

All the European powers, except Austria-Hungary, believed that Serbia's reply was satisfactory. Even Germany urged Austria to make a peaceful settlement. But Austria's determination to make war on Serbia and the war-readiness of Europe made a general war inevitable.

Outbreak of the war

As expected, Austria rejected the Serbian reply to her ultimatum. On 28 July 1914, exactly one month after the Sarajevo assassination, Austria-Hungary declared war on Serbia. This local war quickly became a general war, and the First World War began. Within a week, all of the European powers were at war.

Russia supported Serbia and ordered a general mobilization of her army on July 30. Germany, Austria-Hungary's ally, reacted by sending an ultimatum to Russia, demanding that her mobilization should stop. Another ultimatum was sent to France, Russia's ally. This demanded that France declare her intentions should a Russo-German war break out. Russia did not reply while France replied that she would act according to her interests. Germany then declared war on Russia on August 1 and on France, on August 3.

What would Britain do now that the two other members of the Triple Entente were at war? She was worried about the fate of Belgium. The independence and neutrality of this small country had been guaranteed by all the European powers in 1839. Britain's traditional policy had been to prevent the Low Countries, which included Belgium, from falling into unfriendly hands. Domination by a strong hostile power, like Germany, would threaten the security of Britain because the Low Countries lie directly across the English Channel.

To avoid a costly attack on the strong French defence line along the Franco-German border, the Germans demanded free passage through Belgium in their march to Paris.

STATEMENTS MADE AT THE OUTBREAK OF THE FIRST WORLD WAR

German Statement

The present situation is the result of an ill will which has been active for many years against the power and prosperity of the German Empire.

No lust of conquest drives us on ... In a defensive war that has been forced upon us, with a clear conscience and a clean hand, we take up the sword. ...

— *Emperor William II*
4 August 1914

French Statement

... France has become the object of a brutal and premeditated aggression which is an insolent defiance of international law. Before a declaration of war was addressed to us, before even the German ambassador had asked for his passport, our territory was invaded. ...

— *President Poincare*
4 August 1914

Russian Statement

... We have now to intercede not only for a related country [Serbia], unjustly attacked, but also to safeguard the honour, dignity, and integrity of Russia, and her position among the Great Powers. ...

At this hour of threatening danger, let domestic strife be forgotten. ...

— *Tsar Nicholas II*
2 August 1914

British Statement

If I am asked what we are fighting for I reply in two sentences. In the first place, to fulfil a solemn international obligation [to protect Belgium]. ... I say, secondly, we are fighting to vindicate the principle ... that small nationalities are not to be crushed, in defiance of international good faith, by the arbitrary will of a strong and overmastering power. ...

— *Prime Minister Asquith*
6 August 1914

When the Belgians refused, Germany invaded Belgium on August 4. Britain condemned the violation of Belgian neutrality and declared war on Germany on the same day. Even if Belgian neutrality had not been violated, Britain was bound to be dragged into the war. She had already promised to help France if the German fleet attacked the French coasts.

The Great Powers of Europe were now drawn up for battle: the Allies (Triple Entente) on one side and the Central Powers (Germany and Austria-Hungary) on the other. Though a member of the Triple Alliance, Italy declared herself neutral. She claimed that Germany was not fighting a defensive war and she was therefore under no obligation to help her. In fact, she had made a secret agreement with France in 1902 in which both powers agreed to remain neutral if one was attacked by a third power. After being promised Austrian and Turkish territories, Italy joined the Allies in 1915.

BRITAIN'S DETERMINATION TO DEFEND BELGIAN NEUTRALITY

He [German chancellor] said that the step taken by His Majesty's Government [demanding German withdrawal from Belgium] was terrible to a degree; just for a word — 'neutrality', a word which in war-time had so often been disregarded — just for a scrap of paper [1839 treaty guaranteeing Belgian neutrality] Great Britain was going to make war ... I ... said that ... it was, so to speak, a matter of 'life and death' for the honour of Great Britain that she should keep her solemn engagement to do her utmost to defend Belgium's neutrality if attacked. That solemn compact simply had to be kept, or what confidence could anyone have in engagements given by Great Britain to the future?

— British ambassador in Berlin, writing to Sir Edward Grey, British foreign secretary, just before Britain declared war on Germany on 4 August 1914

Spread of the war

Other nations were quickly drawn into the war, especially those bound by alliances. Japan joined the Allies partly because of the Anglo-Japanese Alliance. But her main purpose was to take over German interests in China and seize Germany's island colonies in the Pacific. Having signed an alliance with Germany on August 1, Turkey joined the Central Powers in October. Bulgaria also entered the war on the side of the Central Powers. She had not yet forgotten her defeat in the Balkan War of 1913. All the other Balkan nations went over to the side of the Allies.

As the war went on, more nations joined the Allies. Altogether 28 nations, with their colonies, participated in the war — 24 Allies and 4 Central Powers (see box on p. 232).

COURSE OF THE WAR

The war was truly a world war as fighting took place on 4 continents and involved about 65 million men. Much of the fighting, however, took place in Europe — on the Western Front from the North Sea to Switzerland, and on the Eastern Front from the Baltic Sea to the Carpathian Mountains in southeastern Europe. New weapons of war were used with deadly effect by both sides. The armoured tank, the submarine, the aeroplane and giant airships (Zeppelins) used for bombing brought new terrors to the fighting. Poison gas, high-powered explosives, the machine gun and heavy guns added new horrors to the fighting on land.

The strength of both sides

When the war broke out, each side enjoyed certain advantages. On land, the Central Powers had the advantage. Although the

NATIONS THAT TOOK PART IN THE FIRST WORLD WAR

Nation	Year Entered the War
The Allies (24)	
Serbia	1914
Russia	1914
France	1914
Belgium	1914
Great Britain	1914
Montenegro	1914
Japan	1914
Italy	1915
San Marino	1915
Portugal	1916
Rumania	1916
United States	1917
Panama	1917
Cuba	1917
Greece	1917
Siam	1917
Liberia	1917
China	1917
Brazil	1917
Guatemala	1918
Nicaragua	1918
Costa Rica	1918
Haiti	1918
Honduras	1918
The Central Powers	
Austria-Hungary	1914
Germany	1914
Turkey	1914
Bulgaria	1915

During the First World War, tanks were used for the first time.

est in the world. Naval supremacy enabled the Allies to recruit men and obtain supplies from their colonies. It also enabled them to buy food and arms from neutral countries. The Allies, too, had more abundant natural resources and greater economic and financial power.

While it is true that the Allies were stronger, the Central Powers held the military advantage when the war began. Their geographical location made it easier for them to move their armies from one front to another. Their armies also had complete unity of command under German leadership. (The Allies did not have a unified command on the Western Front until April 1918.) Besides, the German army was the most efficient striking force in the world.

Allies had more soldiers and larger reserves of manpower, the German army was the best-trained and best-equipped military force in the world. At sea, the advantage was with the Allies. The German navy was the second largest in the world, but it was no match for the combined navies of Britain, France and Russia. The British navy alone was the strong-

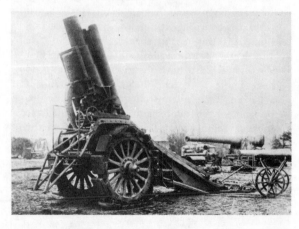

'Big Bertha', a German heavy gun

Kaiser William II of Germany with his generals

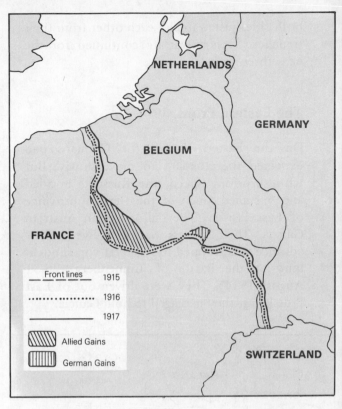

The Western Front: stalemate for 3 years, 1915-17

The Western Front, 1914–16

German invasion of Belgium At the outbreak of the war, the Germans already had a military plan — the Schlieffen plan. They planned to conquer France quickly through Belgium, then turn east to attack Russia and later Britain. On 4 August 1914, they invaded Belgium. The violation of Belgian neutrality brought Britain into the war. Unexpectedly, the Belgians put up a strong resistance and delayed the German advance. The delay upset the German timetable. It gave the Allies time to move their armies into position.

First Battle of the Marne From Belgium, the Germans pressed forward to Paris. When they were only a few miles from the city, the French forces under General Joffre stood firm. They stopped the German drive in the First Battle of the Marne (September 6-12). The French then took the initiative and drove the Germans back to the Aisne River. Here the Germans dug in. The failure of the Schlieffen plan ended Germany's hopes of a quick victory over France.

Trench warfare After the failure of the first German offensive, the war on the Western Front became a slow war of entrenched positions (trench warfare) instead of a fast war of movement. Both sides built lines of trenches extending along a battle front almost 700 miles long, from the Belgian coast to the Swiss border. Fighting continued by means of 'over the top' raids and artillery fire. Once in a while, a general offensive was launched. For most of the time, the men on

Allied soldiers in their trenches, 1916

both sides just watched each other from their trenches. Trench warfare continued for the next three years.

The Eastern Front, 1914–16

On the Eastern Front, the Germans had expected the Russians to move slowly. But with surprising speed, the Russians invaded and occupied much of the German province of East Prussia. They also overran Austrian Galicia. Their success was short-lived. Their advance was stopped by General von Hindenburg at the Battle of Tannenberg (26-31 August 1914). They were driven out of East Prussia but they managed to hold Galicia.

In 1915 an Austro-German army pushed the Russians back to their own frontier. Before long, Russian Poland, Serbia, Montenegro and Albania were occupied by the Central Powers. In 1916 Rumania, encouraged by a few Russian victories, joined the Allies. Her entry into the war was not of much help to the Allies.

At the end of 1916, all of the Balkan states, except Rumania and Greece, were under the control of the Central Powers. Russian defence was collapsing. Nevertheless, the Russians made a valuable contribution to the Allied war effort by engaging large numbers of German soldiers who otherwise could have been sent to the Western Front.

Other fronts

The Southern Front In 1915 war began on the Southern Front when Italy joined the Allies. She had been bribed to enter the war by promises of Austrian and Turkish territories in the secret Treaty of London of 1915. That year, she declared war on Austria, and about a year later, on Germany. The Italians

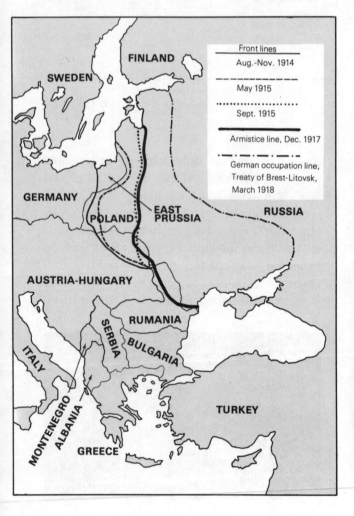

The Eastern Front

British soldiers going 'over the top'

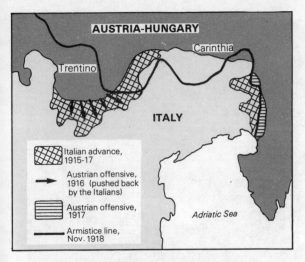

The Southern (Italian) Front

The Dardanelles, 1915

immediately attacked the Austrians, but neither side made significant gains until 1917. The Italians did, however, divert Austrian troops from the Eastern Front and helped to stop supplies from reaching the Central Powers by way of the Mediterranean.

The war against Turkey   Hoping to break the deadlock on the Western Front, the young Winston Churchill, then First Lord of the Admiralty of Britain, proposed a naval attack on Turkey. He wanted to knock Turkey out of the war, to open a supply line to Russia and to prevent Bulgaria, which was still neutral, from joining the Central Powers.

In February 1915, a combined Franco-British fleet tried unsuccessfully to force its way through the Dardanelles (the straits leading from the Black Sea to the Mediterranean). The British then landed troops on the hilly Gallipoli Peninsula overlooking the straits. However, the Turks drove them back. The British suffered heavy losses and finally gave up the Gallipoli campaign. One result of the Allied failure was the entry of Bulgaria into the war on the side of the Central Powers in October 1915.

In the Middle East, however, the British campaign against the Turks was successful. During the war, Turkey lost many territories. The British occupied Egypt early in the war.

By 1917, they had occupied Palestine, Syria and nearly all of Mesopotamia.

The war in the colonies   At the very start of the war, the Japanese occupied the German base at Jiaozhou in Shandong province in China. They then took over all other German interests in that province. They also helped Britain in seizing the German-owned islands in the Pacific. As for the German colonies in Africa, they were occupied by British and French forces during the war.

The war at sea

While the French did most of the fighting on land in the west, the British played the most important part in the war at sea. Naval supremacy enabled them to blockade Germany's ports. As the war went on, Germany suffered shortages of food and raw materials. In addition, the British navy succeeded in keeping the German fleet under control in the North Sea. There were several minor naval engagements in 1914 and 1915. The main forces of the British and German navies finally confronted each other at Jutland off the coast of Norway in 1916.

The Battle of Jutland, 1916: a German battle cruiser burning

Though the British lost more ships than the Germans, they still remained in control of the seas.

Allied merchant ships, however, were constantly under attack. Germany's most powerful naval weapon was the submarine or U-boat (U for untersee). In February 1915, the Germans announced that the waters around the British Isles were a 'war zone'. Their submarines would destroy any merchant ship found in this zone. The United States strongly protested against unrestricted submarine warfare, which ignored the rights of neutral countries at sea.

In May 1915, a German U-boat torpedoed the British liner *Lusitania* off the coast of Ireland. One hundred and twenty-four

Hungry German children, victims of the Allied blockade of Germany

The sinking of the Lusitania

236

Americans lost their lives. President Woodrow Wilson of the United States protested vigorously to the German government. As a result, the Germans promised not to sink liners without warning and without ensuring the safety of the civilians on board.

The final years, 1917–18

The war had been going on for more than two years, yet neither side could win a decisive victory. At this point, the Central Powers had the advantage. But two events in 1917 dramatically changed the course of the war. One was the entry of the United States on the side of the Allies and the other was the withdrawal of Russia from the war.

AMERICAN WAR AIMS

The world must be made safe for democracy. Its peace must be planted on the tested foundations of political liberty. We have no selfish ends to serve. We desire no conquest, no domination. We seek no indemnities, no material compensation for the sacrifices we shall freely make. We are but one of the champions of mankind. We shall be satisfied when those rights have been made as secure as the faith and freedom of nations can make them.

— *President Wilson*
April 1917

The United States enters the war Although the Americans favoured the Allies, they had hoped to stay out of the war. In 1917, however, they joined the Allies. There were three main reasons why they entered the war. First, Germany had resumed unrestricted submarine warfare. Second, a German attempt to involve the United States in a war against Mexico was revealed. Third, there was sabotage by German agents in the United States. There were also many Americans who believed that the United

States could not afford to let the Allies lose the war. The Allied nations had borrowed large sums of money from American financiers which they used to buy war materials and food from the United States. If Germany won the war, these nations would find it difficult to repay the loans.

At the beginning of 1917, the Germans determined to end the war quickly. In January, they declared their intention to resume unrestricted submarine warfare. President Wilson immediately broke off diplomatic relations with Germany. He also warned Germany that the United States might go to war if American ships were attacked by German U-boats. The Germans ignored the warning because they hoped to win the war before effective American help reached Europe.

In February, America's anger was further aroused with the publication of the Zimmermann Telegram. The month before, the German foreign minister, Zimmermann, had sent a telegram to the German minister in Mexico instructing him to propose a military alliance with Mexico against the United States. This telegram was intercepted by British intelligence and delivered to President Wilson.

American soldiers arriving at a French port

237

Reports of the sinking of several American ships by U-boats in March pushed the United States to the brink of war. On 6 April 1917, she declared war against Germany to 'make the world safe for democracy', as President Wilson put it. She later declared war against Austria-Hungary, but not against Turkey and Bulgaria. The Allies immediately received badly needed supplies from the United States. By the end of 1917, about 200 000 American soldiers under the command of General Pershing had reached France.

Russia withdraws from the war The Russian people had long been discontented with tsarist rule. This long-standing discontent, together with Russian military defeats and famine during the First World War, brought about the Revolution of 1917.

The 'February Revolution' forced Nicholas II to abdicate. A provisional government was set up which promised to carry on the war vigorously. The 'October Revolution' of the Bolsheviks overthrew the Provisional Government. One of the first things that the Bolsheviks did after taking over Russia was to sign an armistice with Germany in December 1917. In March 1918, Russia officially left the war by concluding the Treaty of Brest-Litovsk with Germany. By signing this treaty, Russia lost the right to take part in the Paris Peace Conference after the defeat of Germany. (For more on the Russian Revolution of 1917, see Volume Two, Chapter 1.)

The withdrawal of Russia from the war completely cut off Rumania from Allied aid. She surrendered and signed the Treaty of Bucharest in May 1918. Thus during 1917-18, Germany had eliminated her enemies on the Eastern Front. She was now free to devote all her time to winning the war on the Western Front.

The last German offensive As their manpower was dwindling, the Germans decided

The all-Russian Congress of Soviets which proclaimed the end of the war with Germany.

to launch a great offensive against the Allied forces in France before more American troops reached Europe. This was their last offensive. Late in March 1918, they began their drive into France. By the end of May, they were back on the Marne. Paris was again threatened and the Germans were again on the verge of victory as in 1914. But with the help of fresh American troops, the French under Marshal Foch, who had been appointed Allied commander-in-chief, stopped the German drive. In July, the Allied armies defeated the Germans in the Second Battle of the Marne.

What really turned the tide of battle on the Western Front was the arrival of large numbers of American soldiers in France. After stopping Germany's last mighty offensive, the Allies, strengthened by fresh American troops, took the initiative. By the end of October, they had driven the battered and weakened German forces almost completely out of France and Belgium. Germany was left with the choice of asking for peace or being invaded.

End of the war While the Germans were in retreat along the entire Western Front, the other Central Powers were being driven out of the war. Bulgaria surrendered in September

The last German offensive on the Western Front, 1918

and Turkey, at the end of October. As for Austria-Hungary, she was winning the war against Italy in 1917. By 1918, however, her people were in revolt and her army was being pushed back by the Italians. She surrendered at the beginning of November.

Germany was left to fight alone. By this time, the German people were disillusioned, hungry and miserable. The German soldiers and sailors were demoralized. Mutinies broke out in the German navy. A spirit of revolution began to sweep Germany. On November 9, Kaiser William II abdicated. A temporary government under the control of socialists was set up. It was this government which signed the armistice on 11 November 1918. After 4 years and 15 weeks of fighting, the First World War finally came to an end. To humiliate Germany further, the Allies forced her to agree to the continuation of the Allied blockade until a final settlement was made.

WHY THE ALLIES WON THE WAR

Superior manpower of the Allies In the final stages of the war, Germany's manpower was dwindling. Britain and France, too, were faced with the same problem. But then the United States entered the war. The arrival of fresh American troops in Europe was a tremendous help to the Allies.

Extensive resources of the Allies The Central Powers had taken on too much. There were only 4 of them against 24 Allies, with their colonies. The resources of the Central Powers, therefore, could not match the combined resources of the Allies.

Allied control of the seas The naval superiority of the Allies enabled them to recruit men and obtain supplies from their colonies and to buy war supplies from neutral countries. The Allied blockade of German ports greatly reduced Germany's material power. Germany fought back by using unrestricted

Armistice Day celebration in Paris

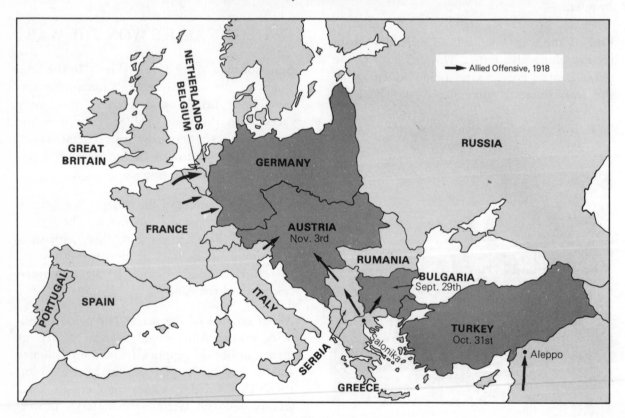

The surrender of the Axis Powers

submarine warfare. This submarine campaign failed to destroy Allied naval power and led to America's entry into the war instead.

Failure of the last German offensive Determined to end the war quickly, Germany launched a great offensive on the Western Front in 1918. It failed because of the lack of German reserves and the arrival of fresh American troops in Europe.

Surrender of Germany's allies With Germany losing the war in 1918, Bulgaria, Turkey and Austria-Hungary surrendered. Left alone to fight the Allies, Germany was forced to surrender.

Discontent among the German people Shortage of food and war supplies together with military defeats in the last stages of the war destroyed the fighting spirit of the Germans. There were mutinies in the German navy and signs of indiscipline among the German troops. At the same time, the German people were in revolt. Faced with these problems at home, there was nothing left for Germany but to surrender.

QUESTIONS

1. What brought about the Moroccan crises of 1905 and 1911? What were the effects of these crises on international relations?
2. Give an account of the Bosnian Crisis of 1908 and the Balkan Wars of 1912 and 1913, and show how they affected international relations.
3. Trace the growth of conflict between Austria and Serbia which led to the Sarajevo assassination.
4. Give a short account of **each** of the following, showing how they increased international tensions before the First World War:
   (a) the Young Turk Revolution (1908)
   (b) the *Panther* gunboat incident (1911)
   (c) the Treaty of London (1913)
5. 'The assassination of the Archduke Francis Ferdinand at Sarajevo in 1914 was a major cause of the First World War.' How far do you agree with this statement?
6. Explain how the Sarajevo assassination led to the First World War. How far would you consider Austria to be responsible for the outbreak of the war?
7. Compare the strength of the Central Powers and the Allies at the beginning of the First World War. Why did the Allies win the war?
8. Write a short account of **each** of the following events, and explain how they affected the course of the First World War:
   (a) the entry of the United States into the war (1917)
   (b) the withdrawal of Russia from the war (1917)
   (c) the great German offensive on the Western Front (1918)

LOOKING BACK

Between 1905 and 1914 the rival alliances in Europe were involved in a series of international crises — three arose out of the Moroccan question and two out of disputes in the Balkan Peninsula. Each crisis pushed the Great Powers of Europe to the brink of war. Each time some sort of compromise was arrived at and the crisis passed. A general war did not occur mainly because one or more of the powers involved were not prepared to go to war. However, these international disputes created tensions, anger and distrust which finally led to the Sarajevo assassination. This last dispute provided the immediate cause of the First World War.

At the beginning of the war, the Central Powers had the advantage on land and the Allies, at sea. As the war went on, the Central Powers seemed to be heading towards victory. The turning point of the war came with the entry of the United States on the side of the Allies.

With the failure of Germany's last great offensive, the Central Powers collapsed in quick succession. Discontent at home contributed to the collapse of Germany. The surrender of Germany brought the First World War to an end.

Chapter 15
China and Japan in the war

PARTICIPATION IN THE WAR

China's entry into the war

When the First World War broke out in 1914, Beijing proclaimed China's neutrality. At first, President Yuan Shikai thought of joining the war, more through fear of Japanese aggression than through any particular hostility towards Germany. He hinted to the Allied Powers that he was prepared to occupy the German leased territory of Jiaozhou. However, not one of them showed any sign of supporting Chinese entry into the war. Japan opposed China's participation as this would go against her plans to acquire the German interests in Shandong province. As we shall see, Yuan's fears were realized when Japanese troops violated China's neutrality by moving into Qingdao. China could have declared war on her own, but dared not move unless the Allied Powers agreed. The Beijing government was in financial difficulties, and was dependent on foreign loans for its survival.

By 1915 Britain, France and Russia wanted China in the war; they had plans to take over German ships detained in Chinese ports. First, however, Japan had to agree to China's entry into the war. She refused, and the plan was abandoned. The situation had changed by 1917: by this time there was a new Japanese government which was friendly to China. Urged by the Americans who had joined the war in April 1917, China finally declared war on Germany on August 14.

Duan Qirui, the warlord who became premier of China after Yuan's death, also played an important part in China's decision to enter the war. At that time, he needed money to destroy Sun Yixian's military government at Guangzhou in order to increase his personal power and influence. After convincing the Chinese parliament to declare war on Germany, he found an excuse to borrow a huge sum of money from Japan, the 'Nishihara loans', amounting to 145 million yen (US$240 000) the following year. The money was supposed to be used for China's war effort, but he used it in his military campaign against the southern military government.

China's aim in joining the war was not so much to contribute to the war effort as to gain equality with the Western powers and Japan at the peace conference in the event of Allied victory. Once given international recognition, she would be in a better position to get rid of the 'unequal treaties'. Through representation at the peace conference, she also hoped to undo the results of Japanese political moves during the war, such as the Twenty-one Demands.

China's major contribution to the war was the provision of paid Chinese labourers. By the end of the war, there were 175 000 Chinese working behind the Allied lines in Europe.

Japan's entry into the war

Legally, Japan had to support Britain in the war against the Central Powers under the

Japanese gun at Qingdao (1914)

renewed Anglo-Japanese Alliance of 1911, but in fact Britain was not particularly anxious to enforce the alliance. However, the alliance gave Japan an excuse to enter the war on the side of the Allied Powers. Japan also joined in because of her hostility towards Germany. She had not forgotten Germany's part in the Triple Intervention of 1895. But the main reason for her entry was her desire to place herself in a dominant position in China at the expense of Germany. On 15 August 1914, she sent an ultimatum to Germany, demanding the unconditional surrender of Jiaozhou. This was ignored and Japan eventually declared war on Germany on August 23.

Japan then violated China's neutrality by attacking the Germans at Jiaozhou. China had earlier set up a war zone round Jiaozhou Bay in order to limit the area of hostilities. Japanese troops, however, assisted by a small British force, went beyond the borders of this zone. By November, they occupied

Jiaozhou, including the port of Qingdao. Japan took over the German leasehold as well as all other German interests in Shandong, such as the Qingdao-Jinan Railway. She then went on to occupy the Marshalls, Carolines and Marianas, German island colonies in the Pacific.

Taking advantage of the preoccupation of the other powers with the war in Europe, Japan proceeded to improve her position on the Asian continent by forcing China to accept the notorious Twenty-one Demands. These demands aimed at complete Japanese control of China.

THE TWENTY-ONE DEMANDS

Presentation of the demands

After Japan had taken over the German interests in Shandong, Beijing attempted to get rid of the Japanese troops by abolishing the war zone round Jiaozhou on 7 January 1915. Japan protested against what she described as an unfriendly act and used the Chinese action as an excuse for forwarding to Beijing the Twenty-one Demands. On January 18, the Japanese minister in Beijing presented the demands to Yuan Shikai. He requested Yuan to keep the negotiations secret, for Japan hoped to obtain China's acceptance quietly and inform the Western powers later. The demands were divided into five groups.

Group 1 dealt with Shandong. China was required:

- to accept any agreement reached between Japan and Germany concerning German rights in that province;
- to agree to the building of the Yantai-Wei Xian Railway by Japanese capitalists if Germany gave up her plan to finance it;
- to agree to the opening of additional areas in the province to foreign trade and residence;
- to agree not to cede or lease any part of the province to any other foreign power.

These demands aimed at preventing the restoration of German rights in Shandong at the end of the war.

Group 2 covered south Manchuria and eastern Inner Mongolia. Among other things, the demands provided for:

- the extension of the Guandong leasehold and the Andong-Shenyang Railway agreements from 25 to 99 years;
- the right of Japanese subjects to lease or own land for commercial, industrial and agricultural purposes in south Manchuria and eastern Inner Mongolia;
- the seeking of Japan's consent before China granted railway concessions to any other power, or extended industrial credits in these areas;
- consultation with Japan before China used foreign advisers in the same areas.

These demands, if granted, would confirm Japan's dominant position in south Manchuria and eastern Inner Mongolia.

Group 3 resulted from Japan's attempts to make sure that she had enough supplies of iron ore. She wanted the Hanyeping Company, a Chinese firm which owned some of the richest coal and iron properties in central China, to be converted into a Sino-Japanese firm and to be given a mining monopoly in parts of the Changjiang River Valley.

Under Group 4, Japan asked China not to alienate to any other power any part of her coastal territory. Here, her objectives were to prevent the return of Germany when the war ended as well as the granting of territorial concessions to other powers, in particular the United States.

Group 5 was regarded by China as the most hateful. It included 'wishes' that China should:

- declare Fujian a Japanese sphere of interest;
- use Japanese advisers;
- grant Japanese schools, hospitals and temples in the interior the right to own land;
- put her police under Sino-Japanese control in places where there was trouble between the two countries;
- grant to Japan a railway concession in southern China;
- obtain arms from Japan or share the administration of her arsenals with Japan.

If China had accepted all these demands, she would have become a Japanese protectorate.

In the hope of arousing foreign opinion against the demands, and obtaining foreign support, Yuan revealed them 'unofficially' to the world. The news angered the Chinese and caused great concern among the Western powers. The unfavourable reaction influenced Japan to modify her proposals.

The settlement of 1915

On May 7, Japan finally gave China an ultimatum, calling for her acceptance of all the demands under Groups 1-4. (Japan omitted the fifth group because of strong Chinese opposition, and the possibility of Western intervention.) Yuan realized that no Western power was likely to use armed intervention on China's behalf, and so he conceded. Besides, he was preparing for the restoration of the monarchy and he wanted financial aid from Japan. On May 25, Sino-Japanese treaties and notes covering the main features of Groups 1-4 were concluded. Negotiations on Group 5 were postponed.

The settlement of the Twenty-one Demands produced significant results. While Japan did not get everything she demanded, she nevertheless obtained a dominant economic position in China. From then on, her policy on the continent was motivated by a combination of territorial and economic aims. In addition, Japan's acquisition of special privileges of a type previously only granted at the treaty ports established a dangerous precedent, particularly since these privileges involved extraterritorial rights.

Although the Japanese demands were mainly economic, they had political effects all over China. Nationalism was aroused among the Chinese; anti-Japanese demonstrations and strikes were staged, and there were boycotts of Japanese goods. The demands showed clearly to the Chinese that Japan was their chief enemy, for there was no longer any doubt that her aim was to gain complete control of China.

Abroad, the demands aroused suspicion and hostility among the Western powers, particularly the United States. The Americans no longer looked upon Japan as a friend; she had become a potential threat to American interests in East Asia.

Reaction of the Western powers

The Western powers knew very well that Japan's objective in imposing the Twenty-one Demands was to make China a Japanese protectorate. They were all jealous of Japan's growing influence in China, yet none of them was prepared to challenge Japan openly. They were too occupied with the war elsewhere to interfere in the matter. Besides, they did not wish to anger Japan, whose naval support they needed in the war against the Central Powers. Britain's response was restrained because of her alliance with Japan. She was willing to let Japan have her way, provided British rights in the Changjiang River region were not affected.

Only the United States voiced public objections to the Japanese demands. She proclaimed what came to be known as the 'non-recognition doctrine', which notified both Japan and China that she would not recognize any agreement that would interfere with her treaty rights in China, or violate China's integrity and the Open Door. It is likely that American objections did to some extent stop Japan from imposing some of her more extreme demands. Nevertheless, the United States was not prepared to use force to stop her.

To protect and strengthen her new position, Japan entered into secret agreements with those Allied Powers which might oppose her claims when the war was over. In 1916, she obtained Russian recognition of the settlement of the Twenty-one Demands in exchange for Japanese recognition of Russian claims to Outer Mongolia.

Meanwhile, the war in Europe was not going well for the Allies. By 1916, there were doubts as to whether Japan would continue fighting for the Allied cause. In order to keep her in the war, Britain, France and Italy signed separate secret treaties with Japan in the early months of 1917 in which they agreed to support her claims in Shandong and the German North Pacific islands at the peace conference. These treaties coincided with their plans to deprive Germany of her colonies.

Only the United States now opposed Japan. In the Lansing-Ishii Agreement of November 1917, the American government acknowledged, though in vague terms, that because of Japan's 'territorial propinquity' (nearness), she had 'special rights' in China. This agreement was clearly against America's Open Door policy. The United States therefore declared that she was relying on Japanese assurances to maintain the Open Door. Finally, even the warlord government at Beijing itself recognized Japan's position in Shandong in a secret exchange of notes with the Japanese government in 1918. As we saw earlier, Japan had granted China a huge loan, so Premier Duan Qirui could not afford to displease the Japanese. Supported by these agreements with her allies, Japan was confident that all her claims would be confirmed at the peace talks.

CHINA AND JAPAN AT THE PARIS PEACE CONFERENCE

The demands of China and Japan

The First World War ended with the signing of the armistice on 11 November 1918. On 18 January 1919, the peace conference officially opened in Paris. The Chinese delegates were determined to press for the cancellation of all existing agreements that violated China's sovereign rights. Their aim opposed the demands of the Japanese delegates, who were even more determined to hold on to Japan's wartime gains.

In Paris, the Chinese delegates, representing both the Beijing and Guangzhou governments, presented to the conference the following demands:

- All rights and privileges formerly enjoyed by Germany and Austria by virtue of the 'unequal treaties' should be restored to China. (This called for the cancellation of the Sino-Japanese agreements of 1915 and 1918 relating to Shandong.)
- The Sino-Japanese agreements signed in May 1915 in connection with the Twenty-one Demands should be cancelled, since China had accepted the settlement against her will and the agreements had not been ratified by the Chinese parliament.

- On a broader scale, the foreign powers should give up all the rights and privileges they had acquired from China since 1842 under the 'unequal treaties'.

The Japanese delegation pressed for:

- the confirmation of the Japanese claims to the former German holdings and rights in Shandong;
- Japanese control of Germany's North Pacific island colonies which Japan had occupied in the early stages of the war;
- the acceptance of racial equality as one of the basic principles of the proposed League of Nations, a demand specifically aimed at the United States and certain British dominions which had established immigration restrictions for Asian peoples.

JAPAN DEMANDS RACIAL EQUALITY

The equality of nations being a basic principle of the League of Nations, the high contracting parties agree to accord as soon as possible, to all alien nations of states, members of the league, equal and just treatment in every respect, making no distinction, either in law or fact, on account of their race or nationality.

— From Baron Makino's proposal to the League of Nations Commission, February 1919

Settlement of the demands

The Chinese demands relating to the Twenty-one Demands and the 'unequal treaties' were rejected by the conference, which declared them to be beyond its terms of reference. A more genuine reason was that the treaty powers represented at the conference were unwilling to give up their special privileges in

China. China's case over the Shandong Question was weakened from the start by Japan's revelation of the secret agreements of 1917 by which Britain, France and Italy had agreed to support the Japanese claims in Shandong.

China's last hope lay with the United States. At the Council of Foreign Ministers, the American delegation proposed that the former German rights in Shandong should be taken over by the Big Five, which included Japan but not China, with the aim of restoring them eventually to China. Japan naturally vetoed the suggestion. When she hinted that she might withdraw from the peace conference if her claims in Shandong were not confirmed, American President Woodrow Wilson gave in on the Shandong issue to save the conference.

All the major demands of China were thus rejected. Nevertheless, by the terms of the Treaty of Versailles (June 1919), she was granted the following:

- relief from her obligations to Germany under the Boxer Protocol;
- the abrogation of the 'unequal treaties' with Germany and Austria;
- the return of the German concessions at Tianjin and Hankou;
- membership of the League of Nations.

In the end, the Chinese delegates refused to sign the Treaty of Versailles, because their request to sign the treaty with reservations, because of the Shandong clauses, was not granted. But China's gains under the treaty were not sacrificed, for they were included in the treaties she later signed with Germany and Austria.

The war between China and Germany officially ended on 15 September 1919 by proclamation of the Chinese president. Under the Sino-German treaty of May 1921, Germany gave up all her special rights and privileges in China. The terms of the agreement were reciprocal, not 'unequal' as before. This was to be the pattern of the treaties signed by China with the new states that emerged from the First World War.

Among the Japanese demands, the declaration of racial equality was rejected. President Wilson refused to accept it because it involved the problem of immigration, which was a matter of internal policy. The Australians opposed it in order to preserve their White Australia policy.

However, Japan secured what she really wanted most: succession to the German rights in Shandong, although she promised to restore China's political, but not economic, rights in that province eventually. As a result, Japanese troops continued to occupy Shandong. She was also awarded control of Germany's North Pacific islands but was to administer them as 'mandated territories'. (Under the mandate scheme, the proposed League of Nations was to be responsible for the administration of such territories, but could delegate its administrative powers to a particular member state.) Except for a prohibition against fortifying the islands, Japan was completely free to do as she pleased with them. They proved to be of great strategic value to her during the Second World War.

THE MAY FOURTH MOVEMENT

Chinese dissatisfaction with the Paris decisions

The Paris decisions on the Shandong Question aroused great dissatisfaction among the intellectual classes in China. Patriotic feeling had been growing ever since Japan's occupation of Jiaozhou in 1914, and her imposition of the Twenty-one Demands in 1915. In 1919, the decision of the Council of Foreign Ministers to confirm Japanese claims in Shandong further angered the Chinese; and the revelation of the Beijing government's secret agreement with Japan in 1918 made matters worse. Everything was ready for a violent explosion of nationalistic sentiment, which rocked China in May and June 1919, and came to be known as the May Fourth Movement.

In its broader sense, the term 'May Fourth' refers to the whole intellectual movement in China in the years 1917-21. During these years, freedom of thought flourished because of the weakness of the Beijing government. In 1917 Chinese intellectuals, who had studied abroad, started a literary revival which condemned Chinese traditional society. Articles appeared in journals blaming Confucianism for China's ills. They supported such ideas as individualism, utilitarianism, liberalism and socialism which were then popular in the West and Japan. The new literature of protest was written in coloquial style to go with modern thinking as well as to reach the masses. This literary revolution influenced the student organizations responsible for the 'May Fourth' incident and led to the New Culture Movement in the years following the incident.

On 1 May 1919, student organizations in Beijing held a meeting. They decided that a mass demonstration should be held on May 7, which they named 'National Humiliation Day' to commemorate China's forced acceptance of the Twenty-one Demands. When news of the Paris decision on the Shandong issue reached China, they brought forward the date of the demonstration to May 4. On the afternoon of that day, some 3000 students from 13 colleges and universities assembled and marched to the Legation Quarter. Unable to get past the legation guards, they attacked Chinese officials, whom they regarded as pro-Japanese and therefore 'traitors'.

This violent demonstration in Beijing gained the support of students, merchants, educators and workers all over the country; political leaders such as Sun Yixian; and warlords of the An-fu clique. There began a nationwide movement of protest marked by demonstrations, strikes, anti-Japanese boycotts, and the closure of schools. They protested not only against China's failure to obtain an answer to her grievances at the peace talks but also against the warlords' policy of self-interest which was blocking attempts at national unity. What started as a student demonstration had become a truly national movement.

Significance of the movement

The May Fourth Movement is considered a milestone in the history of modern China: it marked the emergence of nationalism as the most powerful force in Chinese politics. Among the most immediate effects of the movement were the dismissal of leading pro-Japanese officials and the refusal of the Chinese delegates at the peace conference to sign the Treaty of Versailles.

Chinese students became active in politics, forming student unions for political action which were later mobilized by the Guomindang and the Chinese Communist Party in their struggle for power. The literary revival which had begun earlier was further stimulated, and gave rise to the 'New Culture Movement'. This movement was characterized by the spread of intellectual revolution through the publication of many newspapers, periodicals and books in colloquial rather than literary style; by increased interest in Western social and political theories; and by unfavourable criticism of Chinese traditional learning and thought. The net effect of all this was that more and more Chinese intellectuals turned to communism which they felt was the answer to China's problems.

THE SIBERIAN QUESTION

Background

Besides the Shandong Question, another East Asian problem which arose from the events of the First World War was the Siberian Question. The final collapse of the tsarist regime, brought about by the Bolshevik Revolution late in 1917, created confusion in Siberia. A struggle for control of the vast territory followed, fought mainly between the Bolsheviks and the anti-revolutionary White Russian armies. By November 1918, the White Russians had succeeded in establishing a government which claimed control of Siberia.

The situation in Siberia was complicated by a large Czecho-Slovak force, which had been part of the Russian army. When Russian military resistance against the Central Powers collapsed, the Czechs were granted permission by the Bolshevik government to leave Russia for France by way of Siberia and the Pacific so that they could fight for the Allied cause on the Western Front. However, following the signing of the Treaty of Brest-Litovsk in March 1918 between Russia and Germany, the Bolsheviks tried to disarm the Czechs in May. The latter resisted.

Inter-Allied intervention

At this point, the Allies led by the United States and Japan decided to intervene.

Although they claimed to be giving help to the Czech forces, their real purpose was to check the spread of communism by preventing Bolshevik control of Siberia.

About 9000 American troops and a smaller force from Britain and France were sent to Vladivostok; Japan, however, sent 70 000 men. Moreover, while the other foreign troops stayed in Vladivostok, the Japanese troops penetrated the Siberian interior in large numbers.

THE UNITED STATES AND JAPAN INTERVENE

The United States and Japan are the only powers which are just now in a position to act in Siberia in sufficient force....The government of the United States has therefore proposed to the government of Japan that each of the two governments send a force of a few thousand men to Vladivostok, with the purpose of cooperating as a single force in the occupation of Vladivostok and in safeguarding, so far as it may, the country to the rear of the western-moving Czechoslovaks; and the Japanese government has consented.

— *From the statement issued by the American government, 3 August 1918*

By 1920, it was obvious that inter-Allied intervention had failed to check the spread of Bolshevism to Siberia. The White Russian government had fallen by the end of 1919. Besides, there was no longer any point in trying to help the Czechs since the war had ended. The Western forces therefore withdrew from Siberia. Despite the end of the intervention, the Japanese troops stayed on. They also occupied North Sakhalin in 1920. All these Japanese moves were dictated by a desire to annex the Maritime Province and North Sakhalin and to gain control of the Manchurian railways.

QUESTIONS

1. Why did China and Japan join the First World War? In what ways were their relations affected by the war up to 1923?
2. What were the Twenty-one Demands, and how were they settled? What were the consequences of the settlement?
3. How did the Shandong Question develop, and how did it affect Sino-Japanese relations up to 1922?
4. What did China and Japan gain by joining the First World War?
5. Discuss Sino-Japanese relations during the First World War. Show how the terms of the Treaty of Versailles (1919) affected these relations.
6. What demands were made by China and Japan at the Paris Peace Conference (1919)? To what extent did the conference grant their demands?
7. In what ways did the First World War strengthen Japan as a world power?
8. 'Nationalism in China began with the May Fourth Movement.' Discuss.

China and Japan entered the First World War with conflicting motives. China wanted to be recognized as an equal of the world powers at the peace conference in the event of an Allied victory and to rid herself of the unequal treaty system. Japan wished to strengthen her position in China by taking over the German leasehold and all the other German interests in China. She took advantage of the European powers' pre-occupation with their war effort to impose the Twenty-one Demands on China.

When the war ended, the Chinese delegates to the Paris Peace Conference demanded the cancellation of the agreements connected with the Twenty-one Demands and all of the unequal treaties. The Japanese demanded the confirmation of their claims to Germany's former rights and privileges in China, Japanese control of Germany's Pacific island colonies, and the acceptance of racial equality.

When all of China's major demands were rejected, the Chinese refused to sign the Treaty of Versailles. As a result, Chinese nationalism was aroused against foreign pressure and reached its climax in the May Fourth Movement. This movement marked the beginning of nationalism as the most powerful force in Chinese politics.

Japan succeeded in obtaining what she wanted most: the German rights in Shandong. She was also given control of the German colonies in the Pacific, though she was to govern them as mandated territories. However, her demand for a declaration of racial equality was rejected.

Two East Asian problems remained unsettled at the end of the First World War. These were the Shandong Question and the Siberian Question. China still objected to Japan's acquisition of the German rights in Shandong. Despite the failure of the inter-Allied intervention which aimed at preventing Bolshevik control of Siberia, Japan refused to withdraw her troops from the area. The Shandong Question and the Siberian Question were finally settled at the Washington Conference of 1921-22.

Chapter 16
Results of the war

The armistice of 11 November 1918 ended the First World War, but it could not end the suffering and misery in Europe. Now both the victors and the defeated were faced with the huge problem of restoring normal life and securing a just and lasting peace. If the victors succeeded in creating a world in which all peoples could live together in peace, the war would not have been fought in vain. As it turned out, they failed.

THE PEACE SETTLEMENT

Wilson's Fourteen Points

The terms of the peace settlement were to a great extent influenced by the peace programme outlined by President Wilson in January 1918. This programme aimed at a just and lasting peace and included the Fourteen Points. Nine of the points dealt with the rearrangement of territories and frontiers in Europe. Five of them aimed at removing the causes of war.

Wilson's Fourteen Points are summarized as follows:

1. No secret agreements among nations.
2. Freedom of the seas.
3. Removal of all economic barriers to trade among all nations.
4. Reduction of armaments.
5. Readjustment of all colonial claims, taking into consideration the interests of the subject peoples.
6. Evacuation of Russian territory occupied by the Central Powers.

President Wilson of the United States put down the Fourteen Points as a basis for the peace settlement.

7. Evacuation of Belgium and the restoration of her independence.
8. Evacuation of French territory occupied by Germany and the return of Alsace-Lorraine to France.
9. Readjustment of Italian frontiers according to the principles of nationality.
10. Recognition of the right of the peoples of Austria-Hungary to decide what kind of government they want.
11. Restoration of Serbia, Rumania and Montenegro, and access to the sea for Serbia.
12. Self-government for the subject peoples of Turkey, with the Dardanelles to be permanently opened.

13. Establishment of a free and independent Poland, with access to the Baltic Sea.
14. Formation of a League of Nations to guarantee 'political independence and territorial integrity to great and small states alike'.

People in the defeated countries looked with hope at Wilson's Fourteen Points, for they promised a peace without bitterness. As we shall see, however, the peace treaties in many respects disregarded them. Only points 7, 8, 10 and 14 were accepted without changes. The rest were either neglected or changed.

The Paris Conference

In January 1919, 70 delegates from 32 nations met in Paris. Their purpose was to draw up the peace treaties and to form an international organization (League of Nations) which would preserve world peace. The defeated nations were not represented which meant that the victors wanted to dictate the peace terms. Russia was also not represented. She had lost the right to take part in the peace talks by withdrawing from the war. Nevertheless, she regained most of her former territory.

The Paris Conference was dominated by the five principal powers: Britain, France, the United States, Italy and Japan. Later, Japan dropped out from this decision-making group. Premier Orlando of Italy withdrew from the conference when he could not get what he wanted for his country. The main decisions therefore were made by the Big Three: the French premier, Clemenceau; the British premier, Lloyd George; and the American president, Wilson.

Of the Big Three, Clemenceau was the most forceful figure and was nicknamed 'the Tiger'. He had an intense hatred for anything German and strongly believed in upholding French power and prestige. His only concern at the Paris Conference was to safeguard the security of France. He was determined to protect his country against another German attack by inflicting heavy punishment on Germany which would destroy her military and economic potential. To him, Wilson's aim of establishing a just peace was too idealistic. Lloyd George stood between the two men. He took upon himself the task of arriving at a compromise between their conflicting views. At times, he sided with Clemenceau and at other times, with Wilson. In the end, Wilson agreed to give up or modify most of his Fourteen Points in order to gain support for the establishment of a League of Nations.

The Big Four. From left to right: Lloyd George, Orlando, Clemenceau and Wilson

The peace treaties

Five treaties were drawn up at the Paris Conference and were collectively known as the Peace of Paris. They were based in general on two programmes: Wilson's Fourteen Points and the various secret agreements made by the Allies during the war. The Covenant (constitution) of the League of Nations was made a part of each treaty. Each of the treaties takes its name from the place where it was signed.

The Treaty of Versailles (1919) The most important of the peace treaties was the Treaty of Versailles, which mainly concerned Germany. The terms of the treaty are outlined briefly below:

- Germany had to return Alsace-Lorraine to France.
- The coal mines of the Saar Basin were given to France to be exploited by her for 15 years; at the end of this period, Germany would have the opportunity to buy them back; the Saar territory itself was placed under the control of the League of Nations until 1935 when its inhabitants would vote to decide whether the territory should remain under the league's control, be returned to Germany, or be given to France.
- Germany lost some territories to Belgium, Denmark, Czechoslovakia and Lithuania.
- The German province of East Prussia was cut off from the rest of Germany by the 'Polish Corridor' to give Poland a passage to the Baltic Sea.
- The German port of Danzig was made a free city under the control of the League of Nations.
- To make sure that Germany would not attack France or Belgium in future, the Rhineland was demilitarized; in other words, Germany was not allowed to have soldiers or fortifications in the Rhineland, the German area closest to France and Belgium.
- Germany had to give up all her colonial possessions; her colonies were to be administered by Allied nations as mandated territories under the League of Nations. (The mandate was a new type of government. The idea behind this mandate system was that certain countries were too backward or too weak to become independent. They were therefore placed under the control of other countries which were responsible to the league for the way they governed these dependencies.)
- Germany was disarmed: her army was limited to 100 000 men with no conscrip-

The signing of the Treaty of Versailles, 28 June 1919

tion, and she was forbidden to make tanks, heavy artillery or planes; her navy was limited to a small number of surface ships, and she was forbidden to have submarines.
- For all the loss and damage suffered by the Allies, Germany had to pay heavy war reparations. (In 1921, it was decided that this should be £6600 million or US$33 000 million.)
- Germany was forced to accept the 'war-guilt' clause, that is, she had to accept full responsibility for the war.
- Germany was forbidden to unite with Austria (*Anschluss*).

The treaty terms were very harsh and Germany accepted them only under pressure. From 1919 to about 1925, she tried to have them modified. When her attempts failed, she decided to accept them as final and co-operate with the Allies. But then the Great Depression (1929-31) came. Germany's economy collapsed, causing great discontent among the German people. The Nazi leader, Adolf Hitler, made use of this discontent to arouse hatred of the Treaty of Versailles. When he came to power in the 1930s, he repudiated the treaty terms.

The Treaty of St Germaine (1919) The Treaty of St Germaine decided the fate of Austria. She was reduced to a small state. Not only was she forced to recognize the independence of Poland, Hungary, Czechoslovakia and Yugoslavia but she was also made to give up large parts of her territory to these countries. She also gave up territory to Italy. The Austrian portion of the Dual Monarchy (Austria-Hungary) lost three-fourths of its old territory and previous population. Like Germany, Austria had to reduce her military forces and pay reparations.

The Treaty of Neuilly (1919)   The Treaty of Neuilly was signed with Bulgaria. Since she had little to do with causing the war, the Allies treated her leniently. Nevertheless, she had to give up territory to Rumania, Yugoslavia and Greece.

The Treaty of Trianon (1920)   When the Dual Monarchy collapsed at the end of the war, Hungary became an independent state. The Allies therefore made a separate treaty with her. Under the Treaty of Trianon, Hungary was to give up territory to Czechoslovakia, Rumania and Yugoslavia. Hungary thus became a small state with a small population. Like Austria, she had to reduce her armed forces and pay reparations.

The Treaty of Sevres (1920) and the Treaty of Lausanne (1923)   Two treaties were made with Turkey. Under the Treaty of Sevres, only the city of Constantinople and the northern and central parts of Asia Minor remained Turkish. Although the terms were harsh, the sultan had to sign the treaty. However, the treaty was rejected by a revolu-

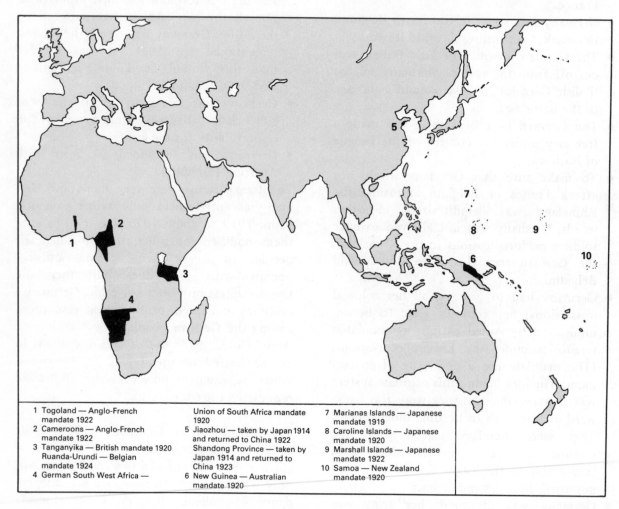

1 Togoland — Anglo-French mandate 1922
2 Cameroons — Anglo-French mandate 1922
3 Tanganyika — British mandate 1920 Ruanda-Urundi — Belgian mandate 1924
4 German South West Africa —
 Union of South Africa mandate 1920
5 Jiaozhou — taken by Japan 1914 and returned to China 1922 Shandong Province — taken by Japan 1914 and returned to China 1923
6 New Guinea — Australian mandate 1920
7 Marianas Islands — Japanese mandate 1919
8 Caroline Islands — Japanese mandate 1920
9 Marshall Islands — Japanese mandate 1922
10 Samoa — New Zealand mandate 1920

Germany loses overseas possessions.

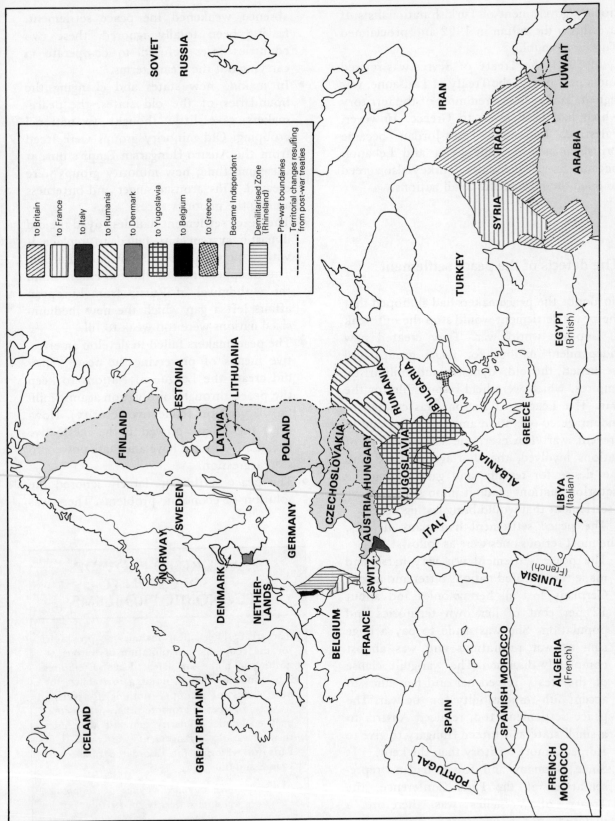

Territorial changes in Europe and the Middle East resulting from the First World War

tionary government of Turkish nationalists. It overthrew the sultan in 1922 and proclaimed Turkey a republic.

In 1923, the Treaty of Sevres was revised and a new treaty, the Treaty of Lausanne, was signed. Turkey recovered most of the territory which had been given to Greece. However, Palestine, Iraq and Trans-Jordan became British mandates while Syria and Lebanon became French mandates. Turkey also agreed to open the Dardanelles to all nations.

The defects of the peace settlement

No doubt the peacemakers had all hoped that the peace settlement would stop the outbreak of another world war. They created new independent nations for racial groups and weakened the old, dynastic and militaristic empires, which were held responsible for the war. The League of Nations was created to encourage co-operation among nations and to prevent war. However, the large number of nations involved, the shortage of time, and the desire for revenge and gain among the victorious nations made it impossible to have a settlement that would bring lasting peace.

The peace settlement had many defects. The most serious ones were as follows:

- The peace settlement was very harsh and made the defeated nations bitter and angry. Germany lost all her colonies and about 12 per cent of her own territories and population. She was made to pay a huge sum as war reparations and was almost completely disarmed. The 'war-guilt' clause of the treaty forced her and her allies to accept full responsibility for the war. The peace settlement, too, reduced Austria to a small state and forced Hungary to give to Rumania more territory than she kept.
- Since Germany and Russia had no representatives at the Paris Conference, the Treaty of Versailles was therefore a dictated, not a negotiated, peace. Their

absence weakened the peace settlement. Having been totally ignored, these two countries later refused to co-operate in carrying out the treaty terms.

- In making new states and changing the boundaries of the old states, the peacemakers gave little thought to national grouping. Old minority groups were freed from the Austro-Hungarian Empire but, at the same time, new minority groups were created. This aroused anger and bitterness among the minority races.
- The peace settlement had destroyed the old dynastic system but failed to replace it with a new balance of power in Europe. The disappearance of the old empires and the withdrawal of Russia from European affairs left a gap which the new medium-sized nations were too weak to fill.
- The peacemakers failed to develop an effective means of preserving the peace. They did create the League of Nations to keep the peace through joint action against military aggression (collective security). However, the league proved to be ineffective because it did not have adequate powers to stop aggression.
- The peace settlement largely ignored the solution of economic problems. There was

FAILURE TO PROVIDE A SOLUTION TO ECONOMIC PROBLEMS

The treaty [Versailles] includes no provisions for the economic rehabilitation of Europe, — nothing to make the defeated central empires into good neighbours, nothing to stabilize the new states of Europe, nothing to reclaim Russia; nor does it promote in any way a compact economic solidarity amongst the Allies themselves; no arrangement was reached at Paris for restoring the disordered finances of France and Italy . . . .

— *John Maynard Keynes, world-famous economist, writing in 1919*

no programme for unified action to deal with economic problems and this later resulted in wide-scale economic rivalry.

With all these defects, it is not surprising that, 21 years after the peace settlement, the world was thrown into another war even more destructive than the First World War. (For more details of the defects of the peace settlement, see Volume Two, Chapter 7.)

THE LEAGUE OF NATIONS

Before the formation of the League of Nations, there had been earlier attempts at international co-operation to preserve peace. In the early 19th century, the European powers had co-operated in the Quadruple (later Quintuple) Alliance and the Concert of Europe. Another attempt was made in the Hague peace conferences of 1899 and 1907. Although all these efforts failed to prevent war, they served as examples.

After the First World War, there was a widespread demand for some way of keeping international peace. People were shocked by the suffering caused by the war. The victorious nations were determined to prevent Germany from disturbing the peace again and

THE PREAMBLE OF THE COVENANT OF THE LEAGUE OF NATIONS

The high contracting parties,
In order to promote international co-operation and to achieve international peace and security;
    By the acceptance of obligations not to resort to war;
    By the prescription of open, just, and honourable relations between nations;
    By the firm establishment of the understandings of international law as the actual rule of conduct among governments;
    And by the maintenance of justice and a scrupulous respect for all treaty obligations in the dealings of organized peoples with one another;
Agree to this Covenant of the League of Nations.

to stop Soviet Russia from achieving its aim of world revolution. They hoped to preserve peace by establishing collective security. This idea was behind the adoption of Point 14 of President Wilson's peace plan which called for a League of Nations. The Covenant of the League of Nations became a part of every treaty drawn up at the Paris Conference.

The Assembly of the League of Nations in session

Aims

The chief aims of the league were to prevent war and to promote international co-operation. To achieve these aims, its tasks were:

- to require members to respect and preserve the territorial integrity and political independence of all states, big or small;
- to require members to submit all their disputes to arbitration;
- to take various economic and military measures (sanctions) against an aggressor nation; these sanctions could take the form of a refusal to ship essential materials to this nation or to cut off all trade relations with it;
- to persuade nations to limit armaments;
- to forbid secret treaties, all treaties to be published and registered with the league's secretariat;
- to settle problems which might lead to war, such as colonial disputes, refugee problems, and conflicts over points of international law.

Organization

The permanent headquarters of the league was set up at Geneva, Switzerland. The league came into operation in January 1920. Its organization was based on three bodies:

- an assembly, in which each member nation had one vote; it discussed international disputes referred to it, and a unanimous vote was required for any important decision;
- a council, which advised the assembly on what action to take and was therefore the most powerful organ of the league; it consisted of four permanent members (Britain, France, Italy and Japan) and four temporary members (increased to six in 1922 and to nine in 1926) chosen by the assembly for a three-year term;
- a secretariat headed by a secretary-general; it consisted of various officials who recorded and administered the work and decisions of the league.

The league's membership was world-wide. When the assembly first met in November 1920, almost all of the Allied nations had joined the league. Some of the new European nations and a number of nations which had remained neutral during the war also joined it, bringing the total to 41 (see box). By 1935 the league had 62 member nations.

THE ORIGINAL MEMBERS OF THE LEAGUE OF NATIONS

Argentina	Japan (withdrew 1933)
Australia	
Belgium	Liberia
Bolivia	Netherlands (Holland)
Brazil (withdrew 1926)	
Canada	New Zealand
Chile (withdrew 1938)	Nicaragua (withdrew 1936)
China	Norway
Colombia	Panama
Cuba	Paraguay (withdrew 1935)
Czechoslovakia	
Denmark	Persia (Iran)
El Salvador (withdrew 1937)	Peru (withdrew 1939)
France	Poland
Great Britain	Portugal
Greece	Siam (Thailand)
Guatemala (withdrew 1936)	South Africa
	Spain (withdrew 1939)
Haiti (withdrew 1942)	Sweden
Honduras (withdrew 1936)	Switzerland
	Uruguay
India	Venezuela (withdrew 1938)
Italy (withdrew 1937)	Yugoslavia

(Germany entered the league in 1926 but withdrew in 1933; Russia entered in 1934 but was expelled in 1939.)

The work of the league

The league was never a brilliant success in achieving its aim of preventing war. It was successful in settling disputes only when the parties involved were small nations. It failed in every dispute involving one or more major power. It did its best work in the ten years following the end of the war. In the next ten years it declined rapidly until it became a useless organization for preserving the peace. This decline was due to the Great Depression, which began in 1929, and the rise of dictatorships.

Achievements In the 1920s the league settled several disputes involving small nations. In 1920 it settled a quarrel between Sweden and Finland over the Aaland Islands. In 1921 Serbian troops withdrew from Albania when the league threatened to impose economic sanctions. In 1925 the league stopped Greece from attacking Bulgaria by threatening to carry out an economic boycott. It also found solutions to frontier disputes in other parts of eastern Europe.

Besides settling international disputes, the league helped to solve the following social and economic problems:

- It helped to find homes for refugees, for example, the Greek refugees from Asia Minor and Eastern Thrace were sent back to Greece.
- It supervised the administration of mandated territories, the Free City of Danzig and the Saar, and conducted plebiscites (decision made upon a political question by the votes of all citizens) in disputed areas.
- It arranged for international loans for needy nations.
- It set up technical organizations which provided experts to deal with problems concerning health, drugs, refugees, communications and transport, labour conditions and finance. Such organizations helped to check the drug traffic and the slave trade and helped poor and backward countries to improve their health conditions.
- In 1919 the International Labour Organization (ILO) was set up in Geneva as a self-

The peace palace at The Hague, seat of the International Court of Justice

governing body affiliated to the league. It is now an agency associated with the United Nations. The ILO collects and distributes information on labour conditions and encourages governments to pass laws to raise the standard of living of workers.

- In 1921 the league set up the Permanent Court of International Justice at The Hague. It began its sessions in 1922. Its function was to deal with legal disputes between nations. Such disputes might be caused by violations of treaty terms or by different interpretations of points of international law. It had one weak point: it could not force nations to attend its court or to carry out its decisions. The present International Court of Justice under the United Nations is its successor.

Failures Despite its success in settling disputes between small nations and providing solutions to social and economic problems, the league failed to preserve peace among major powers. For this reason, it failed to prevent the outbreak of the Second World War.

In 1923 an Italian general with an allied mission went to investigate where the boundary between Greece and Albania should lie. Four Italians, including the Italian general, and one Albanian were murdered on Greek territory. It was believed that they were murdered by Greek assassins. Italy therefore bombarded and occupied the Greek island of Corfu. When the league stepped in, Italy refused to submit to its authority. The dispute was finally settled not through the league but through the mediation of Britain and France.

From then on, in every great crisis involving a major power, the league was either defied or ignored. Japan seized Manchuria in 1931 and Italy conquered Abyssinia in 1936. Both times, the league intervened but the aggressor nations disregarded its authority. In 1938, when Hitler threatened to take over part of Czechoslovakia, the league had become so weak that member nations saw no point in asking it to intervene.

Why the league failed

The league failed to achieve its aims because it had four serious weaknesses.

- The league was just a loose association of nations. Its success therefore depended on the goodwill of its members. However, the members ignored it whenever their own interests were affected. Its work was further hindered by the requirement that important decisions had to be made unanimously.
- The league did not have the necessary power to stop or punish aggressor nations. It had no independent armed force and it did not have enough funds to enforce its decisions.
- The members, including the Great Powers, were not willing to work together and use force to stop aggressors. Even economic sanctions were imposed without much enthusiasm. Britain and France could not agree on how to uphold the principles of the league. Britain was determined to maintain peace but France adopted an aggressive policy towards Germany. France wanted to keep Germany weak. Britain, however, wanted to see Germany recover from the war in order to revive world trade.
- The league found it difficult to act because it did not possess the membership of all the Great Powers at the same time. The formation of the league was the original idea of President Wilson. Yet, the United States did not join it. The American Congress rejected the Treaty of Versailles mainly because ratification would mean American membership of the league. There was a strong feeling of isolationism among the Americans after the war. They did not wish to be involved again in European affairs. The United States then signed a separate treaty with Germany in 1921.

One result of the American withdrawal was that the league council hesitated to impose economic sanctions. What was the use of imposing such sanctions if the United States carried on trade with the offending nation?

Another result was that the United States did not join the Permanent Court of International Justice. But, in many ways, she co-operated with the work of the league. In 1924 she joined the International Labour Organization.

Russia did not join the league from the start because of the confusion and political instability which followed the Revolution of 1917. Besides, she distrusted the Western powers because of their intervention in the Russian Civil War (1918-21). She therefore refused to co-operate with them and condemned the league as a capitalist organization. The Western powers were not eager to have Soviet Russia as a member of the league because Russia was committed to world revolution.

Why did Russia finally join the league in 1934? By this time, political stability in Russia had been restored. In addition, her relations with the Western powers had improved. By 1933 all of them had recognized the Soviet government. Russia had also relaxed her policy of world communism. Finally, with the rise of Hitler and the strong anti-communist propaganda launched by the Nazis, Russia wanted protection from the German threat. She hoped to obtain allies by joining the league.

Importance of the league

Although the league proved to be an ineffective organization for preserving the peace, it was the first sincere attempt to prevent war by means of international co-operation. Previously there had been no permanent international organizations, such as the three organs of the league. Nor had there ever been an international body which had members from all over the world.

The league prepared the way for the present United Nations and provided it with valuable lessons. There was also the good work of the various international bodies, technical organizations and commissions set up by the league.

OTHER ATTEMPTS AT INTERNATIONAL CO-OPERATION

Since there were still many nations which were not members of the league, other attempts at international co-operation to keep the peace had to be made outside the league. Several conferences were held to limit armaments: the Washington Conference (1921-22) and the London Conference (1930) which tried to limit naval armaments, and the Geneva Conference (1932-34) which tried to limit not only naval armaments but also all kinds of weapons. (For more details of these conferences, see Volume Two, Chapter 7.)

Another attempt at international co-operation was the signing of the Locarno treaties (1925) by seven European nations. By safeguarding the Rhine frontiers (Franco-German and Belgo-German frontiers), these treaties tried to eliminate the danger of war in Europe.

The increased prosperity and optimism in Europe at this time made it easier for European nations to act on more friendly terms. The Germans were more co-operative. This was partly due to the acceptance of the Dawes Plan of 1924 and the withdrawal of French troops from the Ruhr that same year. The plan was proposed by an American, General Dawes, and it suggested much lower reparations payments for Germany. It also helped German economic recovery as its proposal that the United States should grant loans to Germany was carried out. In 1926, Germany joined the League of Nations. In 1929, the Young Plan reduced German reparations payments still further.

The height of international co-operation in the 1920s was reached with the signing of the Kellogg-Briand Pact or Pact of Paris (1928). Sixty-five nations renounced war as a means of settling international disputes.

Like the efforts of the league, all these attempts at international co-operation failed to save the peace. The countries which signed the various agreements were not willing to use force to stop aggression. Instead they tried to appease the aggressor nations. They were also unwilling to carry out the agreements when their own interests were threatened or when faced with economic difficulties.

OTHER RESULTS OF THE WAR

Political results

End of absolutism in Europe Towards the end of the war, the three great European dynasties of Romanov, Hapsburg and Hohenzollern collapsed. Royal absolutism finally ended in Europe.

In Russia, the 'February Revolution' of 1917 resulted in the abdication of Tsar Nicholas II. The long reign of the Romanov dynasty came to an end. A provisional government was set up by liberals and moderate socialists. Kerensky, a moderate socialist, became premier in July. In the 'October Revolution' of 1917, radical socialists or Bolsheviks (communists) led by Lenin and Trotsky overthrew the Kerensky government. Civil war (1918-21) followed. The communists finally defeated the counter-revolutionaries and their foreign allies in 1921 and gained complete control of Russia.

On 3 November 1918, the day Austria surrendered, the Hungarian prime minister, Karolyi, announced the complete independence of Hungary. The Dual Monarchy (Austria-Hungary), which was established in 1867, ended. The long reign of the Hapsburg dynasty came to an end with the collapse of the Dual Monarchy. The Emperor Charles, last of the Hapsburg rulers, went into exile in Switzerland. Both Austria and Hungary became republics. However, the republican government in Hungary did not last long.

On 9 November 1918, seeing that the military situation was hopeless, Kaiser William II of Germany abdicated. The reign of the Hohenzollern dynasty was brought to an end. The following day, the kaiser agreed to go into exile in Holland. A provisional government was set up under the socialist leader, Ebert. Early in 1919, a national assembly met at Weimar and adopted a republican constitution. The Weimar Republic lasted until 1933.

The new nations of Europe With the collapse of the Hapsburg Empire, new nations emerged in eastern Europe. Hungary became independent. Czechoslovakia was created and developed into a liberal democracy. An enlarged Serb-Croat-Slovene state was created which became the Kingdom of Yugoslavia. Poland, which had been partitioned in the 18th century, was reborn and became a republic.

New states also emerged around the Baltic Sea at the end of the war. These were Finland, Estonia, Latvia and Lithuania. When revolution broke out in Russia in 1917, Finland declared itself independent. Soviet attempts to reconquer the country failed, and in 1919 the Finnish Republic was set up. Soviet republics were established in Estonia and Latvia and were recognized by Russia in 1918. British intervention brought these communist regimes to an end, and new non-communist governments replaced them in 1919. As for Lithuania, the Great Powers recognized her independence in 1922. Estonia, Latvia and Lithuania all had democratic forms of government.

It would seem that liberalism and democracy had triumphed after the war. Almost all of the new nations as well as Germany, Austria and Turkey had become republics. Even Russia appeared to have adopted a liberal government. Popular rule (democratic rule), however, proved to be ineffective. It was not long before many of the democracies turned to strong government and strong men to solve the problems left by the war.

Economic results

The First World War was the most costly and the most destructive war up to that time.

Material costs amounted to over 300 billion American dollars or 75 000 million pounds. There was tremendous destruction of property. Agriculture and industry broke down. Inflation, high prices, unemployment and high taxes came after the war. Most of the victorious nations had to pay huge war debts. The defeated nations were made to pay heavy war reparations. All of these shattered the economies of the European nations. Europe became a very poor continent.

For Europe's economy to recover, the European nations had to regain their former position in world trade and industrial production. During the war, they had lost their markets to the United States, Japan and the South American countries. In the ten years after the war, Europe's economy steadily improved. However, hopes of further improvement were smashed by the Great Depression in 1929. Europe was never able to regain her pre-war position in world trade and industry.

Social results

Estimates of the number of lives lost during the war vary considerably. But the number was definitely very large. From nine to ten million men were killed in action or reported 'missing'. About 21 million men were wounded. The number of civilians killed was estimated to be almost the same as the number of soldiers who died. Rough estimates put the total number of war dead at 17 million.

At the end of the war, Europe was also faced with many social problems such as disease, broken homes and a decline in morals. (The results of the war in Asia have already been dealt with in Chapter 15.)

QUESTIONS

1. Summarize the Fourteen Points of President Wilson. How far did the peacemakers at the Paris Conference of 1919 incorporate these points in the peace treaties?

2. What terms were imposed on Germany, Austria, Bulgaria, Hungary and Turkey in the peace treaties ending the First World War?

3. Explain the aims and organization of the League of Nations. How did it propose to achieve its aims, and why did it fail?

4. Discuss the achievements and failures of the League of Nations. Although it failed to preserve the peace in the end, why is the work of the league still considered to be important?

5. Explain why the United States did not join the League of Nations, and why Russia did not join it until 1934. Why did Russia finally join the league in 1934?

6. Explain how the First World War resulted in the end of absolutism and the emergence of new republican states in Europe.

The peace settlement of Paris appeared to have solved the problems which caused the First World War. However, few permanent gains were made. The peacemakers created more problems than they solved and sowed the seeds of a new and more destructive conflict in the future.

Royal absolutism was destroyed and republics were set up in many parts of Europe. However, popular government proved to be ineffective. Before long, strong governments arose which were even more despotic than the old dynastic empires.

Militarism was destroyed in the defeated countries, but it was soon revived. Twenty years after the fighting ended, there were almost twice as many men under arms as in 1913, just before the outbreak of the First World War. In addition, little was done about nationalism. National rivalries and racial hatreds increased, creating suspicion and fear as before.

The greatest disappointment was the League of Nations. It failed to cut down or eliminate the danger of war. It was finally dissolved on 18 April 1946 and another international organization, the United Nations, replaced it.

The Allies had indeed won the war but they lost the peace. As one historian put it, the history of the period between the First World War and the Second World War was essentially the history of the breakdown of the peace settlement of Paris.

Time-chart: major events, 1815–1919

1815

Congress of Vienna	1814-15
Holland receives Austrian Netherlands (Belgium); German Confederation formed	1815
Amherst mission to China	1816
Congress of Aix-la-Chapelle; setting up of Zollverein in Prussia	1818
Carlsbad Decrees (German Confederation)	1819

1820

Congress of Troppau	1820
Congress of Laibach	1821
War of Greek Independence	1821-29
Congress of Verona	1822
Monroe Doctrine	1823
Charles X becomes king of France	1824

1825

Nicholas I becomes Russian tsar	1825
Battle of Navarino	1827
First Russo-Turkish War	1828-29
Treaty of Adrianople ending first Russo-Turkish War; Catholic Emancipation Act (Britain)	1829

1830

July Revolution in France; Louis Philippe becomes king of France; Belgian Revolution	1830
First Polish Revolt	1830-31
Founding of the Association of Young Italy	1831
Reform Act of 1832 (Britain)	1832
Treaty of Unkiar-Skelessi (Russia-Turkey)	1833
Abolition of British East India Company's monopoly of the China trade; Napier mission to China	1834

1835

Treaty of London (Belgian independence and neutrality)	1839
First Anglo-Chinese War	1839-42

1840

Frederick William IV becomes king of Prussia; Treaty of London (Syrian Question)	1840
Straits Convention (Dardanelles Straits); Chuanbi Convention (Britain-China)	1841
Treaty of Nanjing ending First Anglo-Chinese War	1842
Supplementary Treaty of Humen (Britain-China)	1843
Treaty of Wangxia (US-China); Treaty of Huangpu (France-China)	1844

1845

Repeal of Corn Laws (Britain)	1846
Outbreak of revolution in France, Italian and German states, Austrian Empire and Ireland; downfall of Louis Philippe and Metternich; Marx and Engels issue *Communist Manifesto*	1848
Frankfurt Parliament	1848-49
Second French Republic with Louis Napoleon as president	1848-52
Roman Republic; Victor Emmanuel II becomes king of Piedmont-Sardinia	1849

1850

Taiping Rebellion	1850-64
Xianfeng becomes emperor of China	1851
Second French Empire with Napoleon III as emperor	1852-70
Commodore Perry arrives in Edo Bay	1853
Treaty of Kanagawa (US-Japan); Foreign Inspectorate of Customs (later the Chinese Maritime Customs Service) set up in Shanghai	1854
Crimean War	1854-56

1855

Alexander II becomes Russian tsar	1855
Treaty of Paris ending Crimean War	1856

Second Anglo-Chinese War   1856-60
Treaties of Tianjin; Treaty of Edo (US-
    Japan); Pact of Plombieres (France-
    Sardinia)   1858
Austro-Sardinian War; Treaty of Villafranca
    ending Austro-Sardinian War   1859

1860

Beijing Convention ending Second Anglo-
    Chinese War; Treaty of Turin (central
    Italian states)   1860
China's 'self-strengthening movement'   1860-94
Edict of Emancipation (Russia); William I
    becomes king of Prussia; *Zongli Yamen*
    formed; Emperor Xianfeng dies: Empress
    dowagers Ci'an and Cixi assume regency   1861
American Civil War   1861-65
Napoleon III's Mexican Adventure   1861-67
'Co-operative policy' of the Western powers
    in China   1861-76
Richardson affair (Japan)   1862-63
Tongzhi Restoration   1862-75
British squadron bombards Kagoshima   1863
Second Polish Revolt   1863-64
Choshu Rising   1863-67
Bombardment of Shimonoseki by Western
    warships   1864
Prusso-Danish War   1864-65

1865

Convention of Gastein ending Prusso-Danish
    War; Biarritz interview (Bismarck and
    Napoleon III)   1865
Austro-Prussian War; Battle of Sadowa;
    Treaty of Prague ending Austro-Prussian
    War; German Confederation abolished
    and replaced by North German
    Confederation; Italy acquires Venetia   1866
Mutsuhito becomes emperor of Japan;
    establishment of Dual Monarchy of
    Austria-Hungary (*Ausgleich*); Reform
    Act of 1867 (Britain)   1867
Meiji Restoration: Tokugawa rule ends;
    Imperial (Charter) Oath proclaimed
    (Japan); Seward-Burlingame Treaty (US-
    China)   1868
Burlingame mission (sent by China to the
    West)   1868-70
Meiji era   1868-1912
Alcock Convention (Britain-China)   1869

1870

Ems Telegram incident; outbreak of Franco-
    Prussian War; Battle of Sedan; end of
    Second French Empire; Tianjin Massacre   1870
William I of Prussia becomes emperor of the
    new Germany; Treaty of Frankfurt
    ending Franco-Prussian War; Communard
    Revolt in Paris; unification of Germany
    and Italy completed; imperial edict
    abolishing feudalism in Japan   1871
Iwakura mission to the West   1871-73
League of the Three Emperors
    (Dreikaiserbund)   1872
Kulturkampf   1872-79

1875

Constitution of 1875: Third French
    Republic firmly established; Margary
    affair (China); Guangxu becomes
    emperor of China: second regency of Cixi   1875
European scramble for African colonies
    begins; Yantai (Li-Wade) Convention
    (China-Britain); Treaty of Kanghwa
    (Japan-Korea)   1876
Satsuma Rebellion; first Chinese legation
    established (in London)   1877
Second Russo-Turkish War   1877-78
Treaty of San Stefano ending second Russo-
    Turkish War; Congress of Berlin   1878
Dual Alliance (Germany and Austria-
    Hungary); Japan acquires the Ryukyus
    from China   1879

1880

Zaibatsu system begins   1880s
Alexander III becomes Russian tsar; Treaty
    of St Petersburg (Russia-China); Hokkaido
    Scandal   1881
Triple Alliance formed; Treaty of Chemulpo
    (Japan-Korea)   1882
Reform Act of 1884 (Britain); Kim Ok-
    kyun's *coup* in Korea   1884
Sino-French War   1884-85

1885

Treaty of Tianjin or Li-Ito Convention
    (China-Japan)   1885
Reinsurance Treaty (Germany-Russia)   1887
William II becomes emperor of Germany   1888
Meiji Constitution proclaimed; Empress
    Dowager Cixi retires from the regency   1889

1890

William II dismisses Bismarck	1890
Dual Alliance (France-Russia)	1893
Nicholas II becomes Russian tsar; *Xingzhonghui* founded by Sun Yixian; Tonghak Rising in Korea	1894
Sino-Japanese War	1894-95

1895

Treaty of Shimonoseki ending Sino-Japanese War; Triple Intervention	1895
'Scramble for concessions' in China	1895-99
Li-Lobanov Treaty (China-Russia); Yamagata-Lobanov Protocol (Japan-Russia); Sun Yixian detained in the Chinese Legation in London; Italy fails to conquer Abyssinia (Ethiopia)	1896
Hundred Days' Reform in China; Empress Dowager Cixi's *coup d'etat;* Nishi-Rosen Convention (Japan-Russia); Fashoda Incident (Egyptian Sudan)	1898
First Hague Conference; Boxers attack Christian converts in Shandong; Hay's first Open Door notes	1899
Boer War	1899-1902

1900

Boxer Rising; Hay's second Open Door notes	1900
Boxer Protocol	1901
Qing reform programme	1901-11
Anglo-Japanese Alliance	1902
Entente Cordiale (Britain and France)	1904
Russo-Japanese War	1904-05

1905

Revolution in Russia; Moroccan Crisis; Second Hague Conference; *Tongmenghui* founded; Sun Yixian proclaims Three Principles of the People; Treaty of Portsmouth ending Russo-Japanese War; Anglo-Japanese Alliance renewed; Taft-Katsura Agreement (US-Japan)	1905
Algeciras Conference	1906
Anglo-Russian Entente: Triple Entente formed	1907
Young Turk Revolution; Moroccan Crisis; Austria-Hungary annexes Bosnia and Herzegovina (Bosnian Crisis); death of Emperor Guangxu and Empress Dowager Cixi; Gentlemen's Agreement on Japanese immigration to America; Root-Takahira Agreement (US-Japan)	1908
Xuantong becomes emperor of China	1909

1910

Japan annexes Korea	1910
Moroccan Crisis; Huanghuagang revolt; Chinese Revolution: fall of the Qing dynasty; Anglo-Japanese Alliance renewed	1911
Sun Yixian inaugurated Provisional President of China (January); Emperor Xuantung abdicates; Yuan Shikai inaugurated Provisional President of China (March); Emperor Meiji dies: succeeded by Emperor Taisho (Yoshihito)	1912
Balkan League	1912-13
Balkan Wars	1912, 1913
Yuan Shikai inaugurated first President of China	1913
Assassination of Archduke Francis Ferdinand; outbreak of First World War; Japan declares war on Germany	1914

1915

Italy joins Allies; Sino-Japanese agreements in connection with Twenty-one Demands	1915
Yuan Shikai's monarchical scheme	1915-16
Yuan Shikai dies: Li Yuanhong becomes President of China	1916
Warlord Era in China	1916-28
Revolution in Russia; US and China enter First World War; Lansing-Ishii Agreement (US-Japan)	1917
Treaty of Brest-Litovsk (Germany-Russia); 'Nishihara loans' to China; Dual Monarchy of Austria-Hungary ends; signing of the armistice ending First World War; Representation of the People Act (Britain)	1918
Civil war in Russia	1918-21
German Republic established (constitution adopted at Weimar in 1919)	1918-33
Paris Peace Conference; Treaty of Versailles (with Germany); Treaty of St Germain (with Austria); Treaty of Neuilly (with Bulgaria); establishment of the League of Nations; establishment of the Communist International (Comintern); May Fourth Movement in China; inter-Allied intervention in Siberia (Siberian Question)	1919

Further reading

THE WEST

Beacroft, B.W, *The Making of America: from Wilderness to World Power*. Longman, 1982

Brett, S. Reed, *European History 1900-1960*. Murray, 1978

Breet, S. Reed, *Modern Europe 1789-1939*. Murray, 1966

Burns, M.B, *Western Civilization*. W.W. Norton and Company, Inc, 1963

Clement, H.A, *The Story of Modern Europe, 1870 to Present*. Harrap, 1974

Derry, T.K. and T.L. Jarman, *The European World 1870-1975*. Bell, 1977

Dorpalen, A, *Europe in the 20th Century*. Collier-Macmillan, 1968

Duffy, M.N, *The 20th Century*. Basil Blackwell Publisher, 1983

Ecclestone, A.E, *Modern Europe 1789-1960*. Bell, 1967

Ergang, R, *Europe since Waterloo*. Heath, 1966

Grant, A.J. and H. Temperley, *Europe in the Nineteenth and Twentieth Centuries*.
    Longman, 1952

Hill, C.P, *A History of the United States*. Arnold, 1968

Isaac, M.L.R, *A History of Europe since 1870*. Arnold, 1977

Knapton, E.J. and T.K. Derry, *Europe and the World since 1914*. Murray, 1967

Larkin, P.J, *Europe and World Affairs*. Hulton, 1969

Lipson, E, *Europe 1914-1939*. Black, 1962

Shaw, A.G.L, *Modern World History, 1780-1955*. Cheshire, 1972

Smith, W.H.C, *Twentieth Century Europe*. Weidenfeld and Nicolson, 1968

Southgate, G.W, *A Text Book of Modern European History 1789-1960*. Dent, 1966

Taylor, A.J.P, *The Origins of the Second World War*. Hamilton, 1961

Thomson, D, *Europe since Napoleon*. Penguin, 1966

Wallbank, T.W. and A.M. Taylor, *Civilization Past and Present*, 2 vols.
    Scott and Foresman, 1960

Wood, A, *Europe 1815-1960*. Longman, 1984

THE EAST

Allen, G.C, *A Short Economic History of Modern Japan.* Macmillan, 1981

Beasley, W.G, *The Modern History of Japan.* Weidenfeld and Nicolson, 1969

Buss, C.A, *Asia in the Modern World.* Collier-Macmillan, 1968

Cameron, M.E, T.H.D. Mahoney and G.E. McReynolds, *China, Japan and the Powers.* Ronald Press, 1960

Clubb, O.E, *Twentieth Century China.* Columbia University Press, 1978

Clyde, P.H. and B.F. Beers, *The Far East.* Prentice-Hall, 1975

De Bary, W.T. and others, *Sources of the Chinese Tradition.* Columbia University Press, 1960

Hsu, Immanuel C.Y, *The Rise of Modern China.* OUP, 1983

Kennedy, M, *A Short History of Japan.* New American Library, 1965

Latourette, K.S, *A Short History of the Far East.* Collier-Macmillan, 1967

Li Chien-nung (trans. by S.Y. Teng and J. Ingalls), *The Political History of China 1840-1928.* D. Van Nostrand, 1956

McAleavy, H, *The Modern History of China.* Weidenfeld & Nicolson, 1967

Michael, F.H. and G.E. Taylor, *The Far East in the Modern World.* Holt, Rinehart and Winston, 1964

Reischauer, E.O, J.K. Fairbank and A.M. Craig, *East Asia, the Modern Transformation.* George Allen and Unwin, 1967

Reischauer, E.O, *Japan Past and Present.* Charles E. Tuttle, 1970

Reischauer, E.O, *The Japanese.* Harvard University Press, 1981

Sansom, G.B, *The Western World and Japan.* Cresset Press, 1965

Storry, R, *A History of Modern Japan.* Penguin, 1983

Teng, S.Y. and J.K. Fairbank, *China's Response to the West, A Documentary Survey 1839-1923.* Atheneum, 1967

Tsunoda Ryusaku and others, *Sources of the Japanese Tradition.* Columbia University Press, 1958

Vinacke, H.M, *A History of the Far East in Modern Times.* George Allen and Unwin, 1967

Yanaga, G, *Japan since Perry.* Archon Books, 1966

Glossary (China)

Readers should note the following peculiarities in the pronunciation of Pinyin:

c is pronounced *ts* (as in *ts*etse fly)
eng is pronounced *ung* (as in s*ung*)
o is pronounced *aw* (as in l*aw*)
ou is pronounced as *o* (as in s*o*)
q is pronounced *ch* (as in *ch*eat)
x is pronounced *sh* (as in s*h*eep)
zh is pronounced *j* (as in *j*ust)

Pinyin	Wade-Giles
Andong-Shenyang Railway （安東瀋陽鐵路）	Antung-Mukden Railway
Anhui （安徽）	Anhwei
Baihe River （白河）	Peiho
Baoding （保定）	Paoting
Baohuanghui （保皇會）	*Pao-huang hui*
Beihai （北海）	Pakhoi
Beijing （北京）	Peking
Beitang （北塘）	Peitang
Beiyang （北洋）	Peiyang
Betanghe River （北戴河）	Pehtang Ho
Bohai Bay （渤海灣）	Gulf of Chihli
Changjiang River （長江）	Yangtze River
Chengdu （成都）	Chengtu
Chouanhui （籌安會）	*Ch'ou-an hui*
Chuanbi （穿鼻）	Chuenpi
Chun, Prince （醇親王）	Ch'un, Prince
Cixi （慈禧）	Tz'u-hsi
Dagu （大沽）	Taku
Dalian （大連）	Dairen
Daoguang （道光）	Tao-kuang
Duan, Prince （端郡王）	Tuan, Prince
Duan Qirui （段祺瑞）	Tuan Ch'i-jui
Dujun （督軍）	*Tu-chün*
Feng Guifen （馮桂芬）	Feng Kuei-fen
Feng Guozhang （馮國璋）	Feng Kuo-chang
Foshan （佛山）	Fatshan
Fujian （福建）	Fukien
Fuzhou （福州）	Foochow

Pinyin	Wade-Giles
Gansu （甘肅）	Kansu
Gaosheng （高陞）	*Kowshing*
Gong, Prince （恭親王）	Kung, Prince
Gonghang （公行）	*Kung-hang* (Co-hong)
Guandong （關東）	Kwantung
Guangdong （廣東）	Kwangtung
Guangxi （廣西）	Kwangsi
Guangxu （光緒）	Kuang-hsü
Guangzhou （廣州）	Canton
Guangzhou Bay （廣州灣）	Kwangchow Bay
Guomindang （國民黨）	*Kuomintang*
Hankou （漢口）	Hankow
Hanlinyuan （翰林院）	*Han Lin Yüan*
Hanyeping （漢治平）	Han-Yeh-P'ing
Hebei （河北）	Chihli, Hopei
Heilongjiang River （黑龍江）	Amur Rver
Henan （河南）	Honan
Huang Xing （黃興）	Huang Hsing
Huanghe River （黃河）	Yellow River
Huanghuagang （黃花崗）	Huang Hua Kang
Huangpu （黃埔）	Whampoa
Hubei （湖北）	Hupei
Huguang Railway （湖廣鐵路）	Hukuang Railway
Huguojun （護國軍）	*Hu-kuo chün*
Humen （虎門）	Bogue, The
Jiang Jieshi （蔣介石）	Chiang Kai-shek
Jiangnan （江南）	Kiangnan
Jiangxi （江西）	Kiangsi
Jiaozhou Bay （膠州灣）	Kiaochow Bay
Jiaqing （嘉慶）	Chia-ch'ing
Jinan （濟南）	Tsinan
Jinshi （進士）	*Chin-shih*

Pinyin	Wade-Giles
Kang Youwei （康有爲）	K'ang Yu-wei
Lao Foye （老佛爺）	Lao Fo-yeh
Li Hongzhang （李鴻章）	Li Hung-chang
Li Lianying （李連英）	Li Lien-ying
Li Yuanhong （黎元洪）	Li Yüan-hung
Liang Qichao （梁啓超）	Liang Ch'i-ch'ao
Liaodong （遼東）	Liaotung
Lifanyuan （理藩院）	*Li-fan-yuan*
Lika （釐金）	Likin
Lin Weixi （林維喜）	Lin Wei-hsi
Lin Zexu （林則徐）	Lin Tse-hsü
Liu Kunyi （劉坤一）	Liu K'un-i
Liuqiu （琉球）	Liu-ch'iu
Longyu （隆裕）	Lung Yü
Lüshun （旅順）	Port Arthur
Manzhu （滿清）	Manchu
Min Sheng Zhuyi （民生主義）	*Min-sheng chu-i*
Min Quan Zhuyi （民權主義）	*Min-ch'uan chu-i*
Min Zu Zhuyi （民族主義）	*Min-tsu chu-i*
Nanjing （南京）	Nanking
Nian （捻）	Nien
Ningbo （寧波）	Ningpo
Qianlong （乾隆）	Ch'ien-lung
Qing dynasty （清朝）	Ch'ing dynasty
Qingdao （清島）	Tsingtao
Ronglu （榮祿）	Jung-lu
Ruicheng （瑞澂）	Jui-ch'eng
Sanmin Zhuyi （三民主義）	*San-min chu-i*
Shaanxi （陝西）	Shensi
Shandong （山東）	Shantung
Shanxi （山西）	Shansi
Sheng Xuanhuai （盛宣懷）	Sheng Hsüan-huai
Shenyang （瀋陽）	Mukden
Sichuan （四川）	Szechwan
Song Jiaoren （宋教仁）	Sung Chiao-jen
Sun Yixian （孫逸仙）	Sun Yat-sen
Suzhou （蘇州）	Soochow
Taiping （太平）	*T'ai-p'ing*
Tan Sitong （譚嗣同）	T'an Ssu-t'ung
Tianjin （天津）	Tientsin

Pinyin	Wade-Giles
Tongmenghui （同盟會）	*T'ung-meng hui*
Tongwenguan （同文館）	*T'ung-wen Kuan*
Tongzhi （同治）	T'ung-chih
Tongzhou （通州）	Tungchow
Waiwubu （外務部）	*Wai-wu Pu*
Wangxia （望廈）	Wanghsia
Wei Xian （濰縣）	Weihsien
Weihai （威海市）	Weihaiwei
Wenxiang （文祥）	Wen-hsiang
Wenzhou （溫州）	Wenchow
Woren （倭仁）	Wo-jen
Wu Tingfang （伍廷芳）	Wu T'ing-fang
Wu Xian （吳淞）	Wusang
Xiamen （厦門）	Amoy
Xi'an （西安）	Sian
Xianfeng （咸豐）	Hsien-feng
Xiangshan （香山）	Hsiang-shan
Xingzhonghui （興中會）	*Hsing-Chung hui*
Xinjiang （新疆）	Sinkiang
Xu Guangjin （徐廣縉）	Hsu Kuang-chin
Xuantong （宣統）	Hsuan-t'ung
Yalujiang River （鴨綠江）	Yalu River
Yangwu （洋務）	*Yang-wu*
Yantai （烟台）	Chefoo
Ye Mingchen （葉名琛）	Yeh Ming-ch'en
Yichang （宜昌）	Ichang
Yihe Yuan （頤和園）	I Ho Yüan
Yihequan （義和拳）	*I-ho ch'uan*
Yihetuan （義和團）	*I-ho t'uan*
Yu Xian （毓賢）	Yü-hsien
Yuan Shikai （袁世凱）	Yüan Shih-k'ai
Zaifeng （載灃）	Tsai-feng
Zeng Guofan （曾國藩）	Tseng Kuo-fan
Zhang Biao （張彪）	Chang Piao
Zhang Xun （張勳）	Chang Hsün
Zhang Zhidong （張之洞）	Chang Chih-tung
Zhang Zuolin （張作霖）	Chang Tso-lin
Zhejiang （浙江）	Chekiang
Zhili （直隸）	Chihli
Zhongguo （中國）	*Chung-kuo*
Zhongshan （中山）	Chung-shan
Zhu Yixin （朱一新）	Chu I-hsin
Zhujiang River （珠江）	Pearl River
Zongli Yamen （總理衙門）	Tsungli Yamen
Zuo Zongtang （左宗棠）	Tso Tsung-t'ang

Index